E-Commerce Developer's Guide to Building Community and Using Promotional Tools

E-Commerce Developer's Guide to Building Community and Using Promotional Tools

Noel Jerke

SYBEX®

San Francisco • Paris • Düsseldorf • Soest • London

Associate Publisher: Richard Mills
Contracts and Licensing Manager: Kristine O'Callaghan
Acquisitions Editor: Denise Santoro Lincoln
Developmental Editor: Tracy Brown
Editor: Susan Hobbs
Production Editor: Jennifer Campbell
Technical Editor: Greg Guntle
Book Designer: Franz Baumhackl
Graphic Illustrator: Tony Jonick
Electronic Publishing Specialist: Nila Nichols
Proofreaders: Laurie O'Connell, Yariv Rabinovitch, Nancy Riddiough
Indexer: Ted Laux
CD Coordinator: Erica Yee
CD Technicians: Keith McNeil, Kevin Ly
Cover Designer: Design Site
Cover Illustrator/Photographer: Jack D. Myers, Design Site

*I would like to dedicate this book to my family—
Maria, Gabrielle and Grayson. I love you all!*

ACKNOWLEDGMENTS

I would like to thank the editors at Sybex who believed in this book idea and were willing to support its publication. Thank you Denise Santoro Lincoln for supporting the idea and congratulations on the new little ones! Thank you Susan Hobbs, Tracy Brown, Greg Guntle, and Jennifer Campbell for providing a great editing job and keeping the schedule on track. And thank you Nila Nichols, Laurie O'Connell, Yariv Rabinovitch, Nancy Riddiough, and Ted Laux for handling the book's production process so flawlessly.

I want to once again thank my wife, Maria, for supporting me through thick and thin, and the writing of this book! I love you! Finally, I thank God for his many blessings.

Noel Jerke

CONTENTS AT A GLANCE

CONTENTS

INTRODUCTION

Building communities on the Web is a hot topic for any organization that has a focused audience with whom to communicate and connect. The Web provides a unique medium for fostering relationships between community members.

This book does not pretend to be the ultimate book on the technical topic of running complex, high-traffic Web sites. That would take many more books. What it does, however, is serve to demonstrate to the programming community how community Web site tools can be designed and constructed using the Microsoft Web technology platform.

By way of background, I am writing this book after having spent nearly six years on the front lines of the Web building battleground, working on heavily community-oriented sites such as Martha Stewart (www.marthastewart.com), American Diabetes Association (www.diabetes.org), Arthritis Foundation (www.arthritis.org), Astronomy (www.astronomy.com), Trains (www.trains.com) and YAPA (www.yapa.com). The technology has come a long way in those six short years. Of course, many people describe "Internet years" like "dog years," so one could argue it has been nearly 42 (and at times it feels like it)! I have tried to distill the core development requirements of a community site into an easy-to-follow set of examples. All of the key processes and tools are covered in the examples, including both the Web visitor interface as well as the administrative tools.

Throughout this book, you will find notes, tips, and warnings that provide more information on specific topics. These sidebars are designed to be helpful guides for any particular issues pertaining to the topic at hand.

Microsoft Tools and Community Building

Nearly every core Microsoft development tool is touched on in the book to help you understand how to build great Windows NT/Windows 2000 based solutions. This platform provides a reasonably priced, scalable, rapid development platform for developing and deploying community solutions.

At times, choosing the right Microsoft tool can be a bit confusing. There are Active Server Pages, Visual Basic with its Internet features, Visual Studio, Microsoft Access, SQL Server, and so on. The beginning chapters of this book review these tools and how they are utilized in both the development and deployment environments.

Finally, just a brief note on technology alternatives. Certainly options of using Sun technology, the up-and-coming Linux operating system, and many other platforms are available. Certainly there are valid arguments that these solutions may be able to scale faster or better in super-scaled sites such as eBay and others. This author can say from experience that Windows and SQL Server can scale to handle significant site traffic if the architecture is designed properly.

Structure of this Book

The book has a total of 14 chapters. The following outlines the basic structure to the chapters.

Chapters 1–2

The first two chapters focus solely on reviewing community concepts. This sets the stage for the tools we will be building.

Chapters 3–5

Chapters 3 through 5 review the Microsoft Toolset and how we utilize it in the book. We also focus on system design and provide guidelines for how to set up the server farm. Finally, we explore an initial programming example to get us started.

Chapters 6–13

Our next set of chapters comprises the bulk of the coding examples for the book. Here we build a full set of community tools, including a site visitor-driven content directory, a full featured guest register, discussion forums, polling tools, and much, much more.

Chapter 14

Our final chapter explores some tuning techniques and best practices to help ensure a successful community Web site.

The Companion CD

The CD provided with the book contains most of the code developed in the book. It is provided in an example code format. This makes it easy to load the code and see it in action as well as follow in the book.

The code primarily consists of three types of formats, as outlined in Table 1.

TABLE 1: Source Code File Formats

Format	Description
SQL DDL scripts (.sql)	These scripts can be run to create the database structure.
Active Server Pages (.asp)	Active Server Pages code files contain a mix of script and HTML code. These can be edited in Visual InterDev.
Images (.gif, .jpg)	Images for the examples are provided with the code on the CD.

The database structure is provided in the SQL scripts sub-folder of each of the examples. This code should be utilized for creating the data structures for the examples. In addition you need the following File DSNs, as shown in Table 2.

TABLE 2: Required File DSNs

Format	Description
Directory	Points to your database for the Directory example
Feedback	Points to the database for the Feedback example
Forums	Points to the database for the Forums example
GuestRegister	Points to the database for the GuestRegister example
Polls	Points to the database for the Polls example

Instructions are provided in the text for setting up the IIS community Web site. Note that the virtual root reference of the examples is always under the community root as

```
http://DOMAINNAME/community/EXAMPLE
```

where DOMAINNAME is replaced with the domain name on which you are developing your site and EXAMPLE is replaced with the root of the example on which you are working.

NOTE All of the code on the CD is provided in the "Community" folder; you can drag this entire folder into the root of your Web server.

References are contained in the ASP code to this structure. If you want to change this, these references have to be changed as well.

NOTE Representing ASP/HTML code on the pages of a book can be challenging because of the difficulty of reproducing long lines of code. Code should therefore be pulled directly from the CD to ensure proper formatting and functioning. The code in the book seldom deviates from the CD and can be followed closely when loading from the CD. Anywhere you see a ↵ symbol on the page means that a long line of code that should not be broken up had to be broken onto more than one line to fit on the page.

How to Reach the Author

If you have questions for me or have difficulties with the book, I would be happy to try to assist. You can reach me at my e-mail address, noeljerke@att.net.

CHAPTER 1

Introduction to Community Building Concepts

- Why a Community Web Site

- Primary Elements of a Web Site

- Building Traffic

- Community Interaction

- Incorporating E-Commerce

- Knowing Your Community

- Designing Your Community

- Managing Your Community

- Outsource Turnkey Solutions

This chapter explores some of the fundamental concepts about building Web sites, specifically community-based Web sites. It takes a look at why you should consider building a community Web site as well as introduces elements such as content and commerce that make a community attractive.

This chapter also explores some basic elements that compose a community as well as how to build traffic, drive transactions, and manage and support your community.

Why a Community Web Site?

You may have heard that you need "community" as part of your Web site to help ensure your success on the Web, but you might not be sure why "community" is important. Typically, a Web site becomes more and more successful with the more Web site traffic it has. And to promote traffic, you need to find a way to draw attention to your site.

To get your site noticed, some kind of promotion is usually required to entice people to type in your Web URL and visit your site. But how do you hold a visitor's attention while they're on your site, and how do you keep them coming back? That is where the role of community comes into play.

Most people remember the tag line in the "Cheers" song, "You want to go where everybody knows your name." That is the idea behind creating a community on the Web. By creating a community, you create a place where visitors can go and "commune" on topics that are of mutual interest. Success in doing this comes through a mix of having the right content and subject matter, and building the right tools to facilitate community interaction.

Primary Elements of a Web Site

You may have heard of the three "Cs" of the Web. Content, community, and commerce (C^3) all work together to build a successful Web site. It is important to understand how community fits within the context of commerce and content. On the Web, you will find these three concepts implemented in different ways, but the ultimate goal is usually to drive transactions of some sort. In this book, we are going to delve into the community aspect that provides the "glue" to bring content, commerce, and traffic (or visitors) together. Ideally, the cycle will continue as the user becomes more engaged with the site

Content first drives interest in the site. A new site visitor will then become involved in the community aspects of a site and interact with other community members. As they become more engaged in the site, they will become more open to interacting with the e-commerce elements of the site, which can range from an online store to advertising, from affiliate links to stores with products targeted at the community. Optimally, the e-commerce offerings will be related to the primary interest of the site.

Content

Content provides the information and ideas that drive community. It provides the topics that are discussed, the polls that are asked, and the fodder for the interaction of site visitors. Content can consist of "traditional" information, such as a magazine article, or it can include product information in an e-commerce store. No matter what composes the content, it is content that is "king" of the Web and drives interest in a Web site.

To build your community, think about from where you will gather your content, how frequently it will be updated, and how you will manage it on the Web site. An entire book can be written on content management alone, and there are some excellent tools in the marketplace for managing content. But, in most cases, the most challenging aspect is actually creating the content itself.

Community

Community is the vehicle through which Web site visitors interact with each other as well as with the site itself, and is built on interactive tools, such as chats, discussion forums, and polls. Community can provide a way for site visitors to generate content that only they can create from their unique perspectives.

In many ways community is the lifeblood of your Web site by making your site interactive and engaging. It is also what keeps the site going on a minute-by-minute, hour-by-hour, and day-by-day basis. Community members discuss the rich content you are providing and, in that process, provide even more interesting information for other site visitors.

Commerce

Commerce, the selling of products over the Web, is in many instances the primary goal of a Web site. Commerce is the means by which you can capitalize on the traffic you are generating in your Web community. The ultimate goal is for site visitors to enact a transaction of some kind, even if it is as simple as viewing a banner ad.

Typically, you must support your community and your business with some kind of commerce transactions. For anyone to know they can purchase from you, they have to engage in the site, which is the purpose of community. Commerce on a community site can take place in many different ways, as discussed in the rest of the chapter.

It is the cross interaction of these three concepts that provides the ingredients for success. Figure 1.1 shows the basic interaction of the C^3 chain.

FIGURE 1.1:

The content, community, and commerce chain

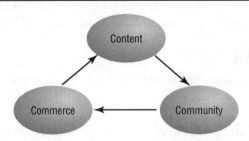

Our first goal is to build a site with attractive content. When community tools are added to attractive content, visitors have a way to engage each other and discuss the content. The community interaction provides a reason for site visitors to return to the site to engage in their community relationships. As they keep returning, the commerce aspect of the Web site provides the necessary transaction opportunities for site visitors to purchase products and ultimately drive revenue.

Building Traffic

Of course, there is one vital precursor to ensuring the success of the C^3 theory. You must make sure that potential site visitors are aware that your Web site exists. This requires a successful marketing campaign.

You are probably familiar with the big advertising budgets dedicated to buy commercial time during the Super Bowl to promote all kinds of dot-com Web sites. You are probably also aware of the extravagant spending for magazine, television, and radio advertising for dot-com promotions. In some cases, first-time site visitors are enticed to shop on a Web site by offering free gifts or substantial discounts on initial purchases. Whatever type of advertising and promotion you choose, the idea is to build awareness of your site to get first-time visitors to check out your offerings.

Bricks and Clicks

The buzz in the media for the year 2001 and beyond is "Bricks and Clicks." The idea is that you need to have both a "physical" presence as well as a "virtual" presence to be successful. Traditional retail storefronts and catalogs combined with an online site provide the right ingredients to breed success. You have the opportunity to drive traffic between the concrete and virtual world and generate transactions at each point. Plus, if you are a traditional business going virtual, you have an existing brand name and business infrastructure to build on, whereas the new virtual company has to build out everything, including the business infrastructure.

The original, primary marketing tools of the Web are the search engines. If you are listed in the search engine database, every time someone searches for a key word(s) that matches your site, then you would show up in the search results. The problem today is that there are millions of Web sites, and the likelihood of another site showing up in your search engine category listing and keywords continues to increase. Plus, it is harder for the search engines to keep up with all the listings.

TIP   You might want to consider using a tool such as submit.com to manage your Web site submissions. It uses a wizard-like interface that will walk you through setting up your meta tags. It also asks all the right questions to submit your site to the top search engines on the Web and then handles making the submissions. You can then schedule for your Web site to be submitted on a regular basis.

There are numerous other methods you can use to build traffic on your site. Affiliate programs, for example, allow you to establish partners who link to your site. To do this, you will typically need to provide some sort of monetary incentive. That may include receiving a fee for each new member who signs up in your community or a commission on a product sale in the e-commerce site of your community. Another method can be as easy as finding partners to cross-link Web banner advertising. Whatever methods you choose, the next step is to convert those first-time visitors into regular visitors. The best way to do that is to ensure you have a rich and valuable content proposition backed up by lots of ways to interact with the Web site via community tools.

Community Interaction

The "magic" behind community is the way in which it engages the site visitor. They are first attracted to the Web site content that interests them. Content needs to be focused on their specific interests so they will have a "natural" reason to want to visit the site regularly.

TIP   One way to make content even more valuable it to target it at a user's specific interests. This is usually done through a method of "profiling," where you gather a user's interests and categorize content based on those interests. This content can then be targeted to them via features such as e-mail or a custom home page.

The goal of a Web community is to build repeat site traffic. For example, if I leave a message posted in a discussion forum that has a topic of which I am particularly interested, the likelihood of my returning to see what the current "conversation" is regarding that topic and the response to my message is very high. Or perhaps I will check back frequently to see the responses to a poll in which I am interested. The bottom line is to ensure that a site visitor has many good reasons to return often.

Community isn't just about forums, polls, and similar tools. Community is also about members contributing content to the Web site. Some of the best examples of this are sites such as GeoCities.com and others where members can actually build their own mini-Web sites. But it can even include concepts as simple as contributing photos, personal stories, and so on. For example, a motorcycle Web site might encourage members to post pictures of their prized, souped-up Harley.

Through all of this interaction, members start to interact with each other and relationships can form. This provides the powerful bond that the Web site facilitates and helps to ensure long-term usage of the Web site. Also, as members become active, they will help to promote the site to people who have not yet visited. This type of promotion provides a significant referral method from a trusted source (a friend or colleague). The process of driving and utilizing community is depicted in Figure 1.2.

FIGURE 1.2:
Driving and utilizing
Community

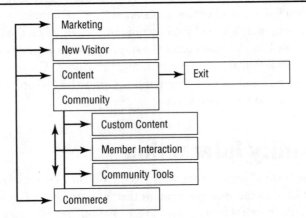

The first step is to implement a marketing program to drive Web site visits. Once you have that initial visit, the goal is to capture them as a "member" of your community. The first step is to ensure you have content that will engage the site visitor. If that content isn't something in which they are interested, then the visitor will likely exit the site and not return.

Once they are engaged with the content, the next step is to drive them into participating in the community, which includes actions such as answering a poll question or jumping into a forum. This cycle of viewing content and participating in community starts to drive an allegiance to the Web site.

Optional Community Building Mediums

In this book we are primarily talking about HTML browser-based community building. It is important, however, that we don't overlook two other mediums—chat and e-mail. E-mail provides an excellent way to "push" content to subscribers of an e-mail list service. These are people who elect to either receive content via e-mail or be a part of a mailing list. As a part of a mailing list, they can push messages to all members of the list and, in this fashion, "conversations" can take place. Chat provides a real-time way to talk in a public space. AOL, of course, is the king of chat rooms, but Internet-based IRC (Internet Relay Chat) is popular, as well.

Incorporating E-Commerce

The last step in the process is the e-commerce aspect. Somehow, all of this content and community building has to be paid for. That means e-commerce. E-commerce functionality can take shape in many different forms on a Web site.

Storefront

Of course, a traditional storefront is an obvious means for selling online. This demands all the requisites of an infrastructure for doing e-commerce.

A great example of a site that combines an e-commerce storefront with content and community is www.MarthaStewart.com. This site features extensive content and community elements, but intermingled throughout each is the ability to buy products in Martha By Mail. All products are related to the topic of the content or the community section.

Affiliates

One of the more popular "viral" marketing methods on the Web is building traffic to a storefront via affiliate links. For example, on your content and community Web site, you could build affiliate links to Amazon.com and link to books that are relevant to the topic of your Web site. If a book were purchased, you would receive a percentage of the sale from Amazon.com.

For example, if you go to the www.Ebizsteps.com Web site for this book, you will see links that enable you to purchase this and other books. This is done through affiliate links to Fatbrain.com. With each book sale, a small transaction fee is paid to me by FatBrain.com. In this way, my site provides content and community, but I don't have to build out the entire e-commerce infrastructure to sell books.

Banner Advertising

Good old banner advertising is another source of revenue if given the right traffic volume. There is hot debate in the industry whether an advertising-only e-commerce model can lead to a profitable Web site. It seems that many successful Web sites include advertising as one of several components to drive transactions on a Web site. Check out online resources such as www.internet.com, www.zdnet.com, and www.cnet.com for more resources.

Miscellaneous

There are all kinds of other options to consider, such as online auctions and classified listings, to derive revenue from your Web site. These options may even include simply driving visitors to more traditional revenue options, such as visiting a storefront or getting a catalog.

With in your business model, consider carefully how you can garner a transaction fee where you are providing additional value that you think the site visitor will be willing to pay for.

B2C Community Building

Building community on a pure Business to Consumer (B2C) Web site can be challenging because you most likely do not have extensive content to engage the site visitor.

Depending on the breadth, depth, and focus of the product being sold, you can implement many community elements with the central "content focus" being the products themselves. Amazon.com has made famous the user product review community aspect. eBay.com moves e-commerce to the community level with online auctions. Implementing community will be easier when a wide range and mix of products is offered, and a "bad" rating for one product will not cast a shadow on the rest of the products. This will be more problematic for a "boutique" Web site with a small product mix.

Know Your Community

One of the most talked-about aspects of conducting business on the Web is the potential ability to understand your visitors on an individual basis and be able to target them based on their specific interests.

WARNING Be careful to ensure that you are following industry standards on privacy issues and fully disclosing your use of profile data. The last thing you want to have happen is to scare away your visitors because they think you are going to act like "Big Brother" by watching and tracking their every move. For more on privacy issues, see sites such as www.internet.com, www .thestandard.com, www.cnet.com, and others.

The first step in understanding your visitors is to understand the traffic patterns of your Web site. This is usually done with traffic statistics packages such as WebTrends and Microsoft Site Server, or through Web sites such as www.mycomputer.com and www .HitBox.com. With these tools you can get data on traffic trends, such as most popular pages, most popular sections (directories), least popular pages, where the site visitor came from, and so on. Through this analysis you will start to get a feel for what is popular on your site and what is not. You can then adjust your strategy to fit your audience.

Statistics can give you a macro overview of what all site visitors are doing, but you need to implement a user profiling method to understand what users with specific characteristics are doing on your Web site.

A profile usually consists of a series of questions that may or may not include personal data, such as name, address, and so on. The questions may include only areas of interest. For example, the registration form at a site such as MarthaStewart.com provides the opportunity to enter in both personal data as well as personal interest data on topics such as gardening, housekeeping, and more, whereas the personalization form at a site such as Diabetes.org only asks about specific content areas of interest.

NOTE   The profiling data is useful only if, upon repeat visits, visitors identify themselves to that profile. That is often done with a cookie being set on their computer so the identification is automatic, or by having them log in with their username and password.

In either case, when the visitor answers the series of questions, you have a way to identify the user and their interests. You then have many options on how to utilize that data. At its simplest, you might highlight new content items on the home page based on their preferences.

At its more complex level, you might start tracking utilization of sections of the site by each user and correlate that to their preferences. For example, on a political site, you might start to see a trend that Democrats are more likely to visit section A where Republicans favor section B. Thus, you might start tailoring the site to include e-commerce targeting based on these preferences.

You also can't forget the personal touch factor as well. Having staff that are heavily involved in your community from day one will help to build a personal touch and relationship from the site managers to the community. Good community tools should provide methods for staff to be able to moderate and be involved in the community.

Designing Your Community

Designing a Web community encompasses many different aspects, ranging from building the site to managing a staff, from maintaining the community to developing the interactive tools used to form the foundation of the community. The first step is to identify the features and functions of your community.

Content Updates

How often will you have new content available for the site? How can this content be utilized to generate visitor interaction? For example, if you are delivering daily news, can a daily poll be generated?

Careful consideration of site content management is a critical step in building a successful community. It is also important to be consistent in ensuring when the content is updated. In some ways you are in a kind of contract with the site visitor. If you provide frequent and updated content, they promise to come back on a frequent basis. If either side doesn't meet the contract, the site will not be successful.

Visit Frequency

How often are site visitors/members able to visit the site? For example, a traveling salesperson may only check in every few days, but an Internet developer might be able to check in a couple times a day.

Understanding your target site member's habits, peccadilloes, interests, and time constraints will help you construct a community that is ready, available, and targeted specifically at their needs.

Staff

What kind of time for content generation and community management will be needed to maintain the community Web site? Can you really support putting up a poll every day, coming up with the questions, tabulating the results, and reporting the findings?

Thinking about the content and community management is similar to managing any other kind of "production," such as a play, magazine, and so on. In fact, some organizations have positions such as "Web producers," community managers, and directors. Organizing and managing this staff will ensure that the site is meeting its daily goals and is supporting a successful community.

Unique Interactions

Are there any unique opportunities for visitors/members to interact with each other and build relationships? For example, a site that connects workers in a given profession might want to develop a mentoring community function to connect seasoned professionals with new entrants. Carefully examine the kinds of relationships that can be established in your community, then look at the techniques outlined in this book to see how you can uniquely connect people in your community.

Competitors

Of course, if you have competitors on the Web, taking a hard look at what their communities provide can help to drive what you need to be and stay competitive. Consider looking at vertical markets that might have similar target audiences.

This book is going to focus on the programmatic elements of building community functions. It will be important to you as the site developer to understand what the impact of specific issues on building the site tools.

The tools demonstrated in this book will provide foundations for building a Web community. They can be expanded easily to meet the needs of what your particular community will require.

Building a Community-Only Web Site

Building community for community's sake with little focus on C^3 can happen in many different situations. One good example is for product support. What better than to have an online community where product owners can interact easily with each other as well as interact with support staff? This is something this author has done for some time to support my books. In many of these cases, there will be little or no e-commerce activity and the only content is the support discussions themselves. Of course the return is happier customers, less costly traditional phone support, and the ability to collaborate personally with many customers and support staff.

Managing Your Community

As alluded to earlier, managing the community is another vital aspect to consider. It is important to understand the dynamic requirements of a community and plan for both the proper management tools as well as the proper personnel requirements.

Table 1.1 demonstrates some possible roles or responsibilities you should consider when planning the management of your community.

TABLE 1.1: Managing Community

Role/Responsibility	Description
Moderator	A moderator helps to facilitate conversation between members of the site. This is common with chat rooms as well as with bulletin boards.
Community Content Editor	A community content editor is responsible for managing the content generated by the community. This may involve keeping a watchful eye on message postings, managing polls, and more.
Project Manager	Often a community will sponsor "events" such as expert chats and online meetings. These require a project manager or coordinator to manage all aspects of the event.
Relationship Manager	One of the key functions of a community is to build relationships. A relationship manager will try to facilitate different members connecting through different discussion areas or other community tools. For example, if there is a discussion thread in one forum topic that relates to a discussion in another forum topic, the relationship manager will point that out to the visitors interacting in those threads.

Managing an active community can be a significant task, depending especially on the volume of content and traffic. Carefully planning this aspect of supporting your community will help to facilitate the proper building and utilization of community tools.

Outsource Turnkey Solutions

Appendix A provides a detailed listing of other resources concerning community building and the tools necessary to assist in this endeavor.

Obviously this book is about developing your own abilities by utilizing the Microsoft Toolset. There are other options to consider that may augment your custom building needs.

Several sites, such as www.mycomputer.com, www.Delphi.com, www.ezboard.com, www.zoomerang.com, www.participate.com, www.peoplelink.com, and others provide turnkey solutions for message boards, polls and surveys and much more. Instead of investing lots of time in programming these solutions, you could consider using one of their solutions. Also, a good Web site for general community building information is www.OnlineCommunityReport.com.

There are tradeoffs to consider with each one of these ready, "out-of-the-box" turnkey solutions, as outlined in Table 1.2.

TABLE 1.2: Community Tool Outsource Considerations

Role/Responsibility	Description
Advertising	Many of these services subsidize their fees to you (or lack of any fee) through ad banners. Your site visitors will be forced to see advertising of the community site builder's choice. If there is no advertising, the fees to use the outsource service are likely much higher.
Branding	More than likely, your Web site will have its own brand image. With some of the less-expensive solutions, you might be able to put your own headers and footers around the solution, but it will likely not match your existing site in terms of layout.
Hosting Management	Any time you turn over the hosting management of part of your site to a third party, you are beholden to their ability to keep the site up and running. This can be a good thing if you think you will have high traffic and they can provide an economy of scale infrastructure that is better than what you can afford to put in place.
Features	Of course, a turnkey solution is just that—turnkey with no customization. You will be stuck with the features that are provided.
General Control	In general an outsourced solution is a two-edged sword. On the upside you pay a basic fee, the service should be taken care of for you, and is immediately available. On the flip side, your ability to customize and control the solution is limited.

Carefully analyzing the trade-offs of buy versus build will help to determine the path you need to take. As will be demonstrated throughout this book, building community tools is certainly well within the ability of any good Visual Basic Script/SQL programmer.

Summary

As we begin to delve into the specifics of programming Web community tools, keep in mind the concepts behind building successful communities to ensure that you are building successful tools.

In the next chapter we begin to examine the specifics of what different kinds of community tools can be built and the different aspects of each. Following that, we dive into the Microsoft Toolset to begin exploring how to build these tools.

CHAPTER 2

Defining Community Elements

- Basic Elements

- Common Tools

- Tracking Community

- Promoting Community

- Other Tools

- Tool Building

The first chapter outlined the core concepts surrounding building a Web site and integrating community into it. This chapter drills down further into the features and functions of a community. It explores some of the elements of a community tool such as interaction and administration. It also looks at specific community tools such as discussion forums and polls/surveys.

It is ultimately the community tools that provide the interaction that makes a community Web site work, but it is the community tools' relationship to the content focus of the site that makes the Web site successful. Understanding the fundamentals of these tools is the first step in building your community Web site.

Basic Elements of a Community Tool

There are basic elements to any community tool that you need to consider including in the tools you will build. As discussed in Chapter 1, community tools come in many different shapes and sizes, but all contain some of the same basic elements. This is outlined in Table 2.1.

TABLE 2.1: Community Tool Elements

Element	Description
User Input	Most of the community-type tools provide for a way for the user to give input into the community. For example, this can be a response in a discussion forum or an answer to a poll question.
Review	Any input by users of the community should be available for easy reviewing and information mining. This can include searching for specific keywords in discussion forum conversations or reviewing a back history of survey data.
Tracking	The owners of the community can track the use of the community. This can be related to a member profile to track community usage based on demographics.
Administration	A community tool will typically need to have some sort of administration for the community owner. This allows the owner to have editorial control over the user's input and content of the site.
External	There are often requirements for the site to reach out externally from the Web community. This may be done through e-mail, list serves, chats, and other means.

It is the interaction of these elements that provides for a rich community tool. Figure 2.1 depicts these elements.

FIGURE 2.1:
Community elements

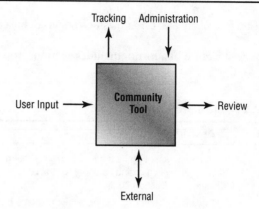

Creating a discussion form related to the current poll of the day is an example of how different community tools can interact with each other. For instance, given the craziness of the 2000 presidential election, there was heated discussion on many site forums with related polls and surveys being taken.

Combining these elements together provides the medium necessary to effect interaction via Web technology. Some of the more common tools are examined in depth in the following section. Some tools will implement aspects of these common elements at different levels and in different ways.

Common Tools

In this section we review some of the more common tools utilized in communities. All are designed to provide the kind of dynamic community interaction needed for success. Keep in mind that these are just basic descriptions of the tools. Much like humans, while all tools are similar, each implementation can be different and unique.

Discussion Forums

Discussion forums are perhaps the most popular of community tools. They provide the most rich and dynamic of interactions between community users and valuable dynamic content.

The fundamental concept behind discussion forums is the capability to have threaded conversations that are stored in a database and displayed in a standard Web page. The beauty of forums over other tools such as e-mail and chat are that they are centrally stored and readily accessible over time. Chat, for example, is instantaneous and short-lived while e-mail doesn't provide a central "gathering place" and it's not easy to review the archive.

TIP   Discussion forums are also called message boards or bulletin boards.

The basic structure of a forum includes sections, topics, and messages. Table 2.2 outlines each.

TABLE 2.2: Forum Structure

Element	Description
Sections	Topical areas set up by the forum owners that provide "rooms" for users to enter. Sections are the primary organizing category for the conversations to take place. An example of a section might be "Election 2000."
Topics	Discussion "themes" created by the message board users. Within the sections, users can create topic threads. In the "Election 2000 section," "Polls" might be a topic for conversation.
Messages	Content the users create. The site users post messages within the topics. Messages would be posted in the "Polls" topic in the "Election 2000" section.

These are the basic structural items of most forums. Depending on the sophistication of the forums, there can be many additional features incorporated. Table 2.3 outlines some of these options.

TABLE 2.3: Forum Features

Feature	Description
Threading	Messages can be cascaded in a "threaded" fashion where responses to specific messages are indented to show the "flow" of the conversation. This is as opposed to simply listing messages in chronological order with no indication of the multiple tiers of responses.
Email Notification	Typically a forum user is interested when other users respond to their messages. The creator of the message receives an e-mail notification when another user responds to the posted message.
Searching	If bulletin boards are utilized extensively, sorting through hundreds or thousands of messages can be a daunting task. A search feature can be helpful in finding topics and messages in which the community user is interested.
Archive/Transcripts	Typically the content of forums eventually becomes outdated and needs to be archived. Forum technology can provide a method of archiving and reviewing transcripts. Archiving can be useful for reviewing that valuable user input.
Registration	Features such as e-mail notifications require the user to register at the Web site. Registration can provide valuable member tracking data, such as display of the user's "handle" and other information.
Moderation	Moderated forums provide a way for the community owner to review and process messages. It also directly interjects the community owner into the process.
Filters	There are often concerns in forums of language use, entering HTML links to unwanted content, and so on. Filters can be built on forums to keep out unwanted content.

Carefully examining the purpose of your forums and how you believe your site visitors will want to interact can help determine what additional features you will need. For example, if you are building a site targeted at children, features such as registration, moderation, and filters will be critical. If you are building a forum where subject experts will be chatting with members, archiving and transcripts will be important.

TIP   Some good examples of how forums can work include: www.delphi.com, www.reba.com/rebanet, and www.MarthaStewart.com/meeting_place/bbs/index.asp.

Administrating forums is a critical requirement to staying on top of what can be a whirring of communication among users. Depending on the size and complexity of the forums, much of the programming development of the forum code can actually be involved in building the administrative functions. Table 2.4 outlines some of the administrative functionality to consider building.

TABLE 2.4:   Forum Administration

Feature	Description
Sections, Threads, and Messages	The capability to add, update, and delete all content input into the forums
Users	Management of users if registration features are provided
Archiving	The capability to selectively archive content

Discussion forums of some type are nearly a requirement in any community-based Web site. Carefully choosing and implementing this feature in your site will be a key to success. Don't overlook the importance of a solid administrative interface.

Polls/Surveys

Interactive questionnaires can provide extensive input from site users on their thoughts and opinions. Those thoughts and opinions can provide useful information and generate interest for the site visitors.

Questionnaires usually take the form of polls or surveys and range from common yes/no quick polls on news Web sites to more sophisticated surveys created to gauge user response.

Like forums, the implementation of question/answer format tools can differ from the most simple yes/no vote to the most complex multi-part surveys. The basic structure of a poll/survey is outlined in Table 2.5.

TABLE 2.5: Polls/Survey Structure

Element	Description
Questions	Questions are the "meat" of the poll/survey. Typically a series of multiple-choice questions are presented for the user to respond to.
Responses	The other side of the coin is the storing of the responses. For polls, the responses are likely shown immediately after the poll is taken. For surveys, the responses are typically not reported.

A good poll/survey engine can provide many extensive capabilities to provide richness to the type of question/answer sessions you put on your site. Table 2.6 outlines some additional options.

TABLE 2.6: Poll/Survey Features

Feature	Description
Question Types	Depending on the sophistication of the poll/survey tool, it may support different question types including multiple response (check boxes), fill in the blank, and commentary. A high-end poll/survey engine will allow you to create polls/surveys on the fly with any type and level of questions.
Personalization	Sophisticated poll/survey engines will allow you to create questions that correlate to a community user's profile. You can target questions specifically based on user's interests and give them a personal poll or survey.
Tracking	As with the discussion forums, you can track responses from a specific member/user and correlate the response to their profile data.

If you want to simply build "quick polls" for your Web site, these extended features are probably not essential. On the other hand, if you want to build extensive surveying techniques by identified site members, all will be critical.

TIP   Some good examples of how polls and surveys can work include: www.devx.com, www.troa.org, and www.zoomerang.com.

As with discussion forums, administration of the poll/survey interface is critical. Not only is building questions an important step, but the sophistication of the types of questions supported as well as analysis and archiving are key as well. Table 2.7 outlines the administrative tools you might want to consider building into your Poll/Survey tool.

TABLE 2.7: Poll/Survey Administration

Feature	Description
Question Setup	The administration capabilities in this area will be crucial to the usefulness of the tool. At a minimum, you should be able to set up a simple yes/no poll question. Beyond that, capabilities to set up multiple questions with different question types and even correlate them to user preferences is possible. Question types can include multiple choice, multiple response, fill in the blank, and commentary. More highly sophisticated tools will also allow the nesting of questions based on response.
Analysis	The statistics behind analyzing responses can be fairly sophisticated, especially when you add user tracking and tie demographics to responses. Minimal analysis would be to simply add up the responses and report them with percentages.
Archiving	Responses to polls and surveys can provide valuable content for community members. The capability to archive this content and make it available is a valuable option.

Quick polls are a great way for users to immediately and easily input their opinions to the site and gauge fellow community members' responses. More sophisticated consumer-type surveys can provide valuable insight into what the members of your community think about your offering.

Guest Registration

The guest register has been a popular part of nearly any type of site since the beginning of the interactive Web. For community Web sites it can evolve into potentially much more than just a "hello, I am here" tool. It is a way to collect demographic data and can evolve into a full site registration tool.

NOTE   Guest registers can go by different names and under different guises. Often a sweepstakes registration will, in effect, profile the user of the site. In some cases, signing up as a "free member" is the same as a registration. Depending on the type of site, it can take the form of a feedback utility. The basic concept is the ability for visitors to a site to register information about themselves and offer feedback.

The features of a guest registration can be dependent upon its utilization on the Web site. Table 2.8 outlines some of the basic elements of guest registration.

TABLE 2.8: Guest Registration Features

Element	Description
Demographic Questions	In addition to basic name and address questions, a guest register can also ask demographic questions based on interests.
Membership Signup	If the site provides a membership area of the community, the guest register functionality can be utilized for the signup.
Personalization	The guest register can be utilized to set personalization options for the site.

These features provide the basic tools for site visitors to identify themselves. It also provides the site owner with valuable information about the people who are visiting the site and are willing to share a little bit of information.

Depending on the sophistication of the guest register, there can be other features incorporated. Table 2.9 outlines some of these options.

TABLE 2.9: Guest Registration Features Options

Feature	Description
Data Editing	If the guest registration data is to be utilized in a proactive fashion, such as for membership and personalization, an option to edit the data can be provided to the user.
Password Reminder	If the user has the option to edit data, they will need a username/password combination. If they forget their password, an option can be provided with either challenge questions to help them remember their password, or e-mail to have their password and username sent to them.

These extended features are usually implemented in cases where the guest registration is utilized to access a "members only" section of the site. This allows users to keep their profile up to date and administer login information.

TIP Some good examples of how forums can work include: www.ebizsteps.com, www .MarthaStewart.com, and www.diabetes.org/publications/guestregister/.

If the registration is going to be utilized for more than just a one-time entry of information, providing tools to edit your registration are important for keeping the user's information current. If the user forgets their access information, providing a secure retrieval method will be important as well.

Of course, a guest register will need administrative capabilities. Table 2.10 outlines the basic functions.

TABLE 2.10: Guest Registration Administration

Feature	Description
Registration Processing	The capability to add, update, and delete all registrations.
Demographic Analysis	Reporting on the demographic preferences, geographic locations, and so on can be provided in Web reports.

The capability to administer the registrations entered for both reporting and updating is important. One of the primary goals of registration is to provide feedback and input to the site owners. Analyzing the input offered by the registrants will provide the kind of reporting that helps gain insight into the users' profiles as well as their attitudes about the site.

Learning more about the visitors to your site is critical to the success of the community. Having a guest register that is not attached to any offer, such as membership or profiling, provides a "no strings attached" way for your site users to provide feedback.

Ask the Expert

Not all members of a community are created equal. In fact, "general" members usually like the opportunity to interact with experts and celebrities in a community.

The challenge is that many members will want to talk to these famous or knowledgeable individuals, and potentially there can be more questions than can be reasonably responded to. An "ask the expert" feature allows for questions to be submitted into a database, which can then be reviewed and the questions responded to. This feature still provides the basic elements of a community tool, but it is not in a direct one-to-one fashion as the earlier tools.

Ask the Expert Discussion Forums and Chats

You can set up discussion forum sections explicitly for interacting with an expert or celebrity, but you have to be careful to gauge the kind of traffic you will get. If you believe you might be flooded with users and their questions , this format will not be as useful and may become overwhelming. The IRC chat format can also be a good medium, but is usually limited to the number of visitors who can reasonably participate (without pandemonium) and will require a transcript to be created after the chat is over for a wider audience to review.

The basic elements of an "ask the expert" feature include those outlined in Table 2.11.

TABLE 2.11: Ask the Expert Features

Element	Description
Question Submission	A core requirement is the ability of the user to post questions. The questions typically are not available for public review. Only the questions that are responded to are seen by the public.
Response Review	After questions are answered, both questions and responses are displayed.

This functionality is fairly straightforward. Something to consider in building this tool is the potential volume of questions. The volume of questions asked of a chemical expert might not be nearly as significant as those asked of a famous celebrity. Ensuring scalability is important.

Depending on the sophistication of the tool, there can be many additional features incorporated. Table 2.12 outlines some of these options.

TABLE 2.12: Ask the Expert Options

Feature	Description
Real Time Responses	IRC chat environments usually provide the best format for a live Q/A session, but a database-driven format can provide the same effect and an easy way to build a transcript.
Search	If responses are extensive, a search feature that provides category, keyword, and date searching can be helpful.
Tracking	As with the other tools, questions can be tracked in relation to a member's profile.

Crafting these additional options will relate to the volume and utilization of the tool. It is important to understand how you think this feature will be utilized and how your site visitors will want to access the content.

TIP Some good examples of how an ask the expert feature can work include: www.reba .com/rebanet/Default.asp and www.msnbc.com/news/spt/askexpert.asp.

Last but not least, the tool requires administration features. Table 2.13 outlines key features.

TABLE 2.13: Ask the Expert Administration

Feature	Description
Question Review and Response	The ability to review all questions and respond to selected questions
Archiving	The ability to archive questions and responses

The "ask the expert" feature is just one example of different variations on how to connect community members of different types together. Another example is to provide a mentoring capability to connect members experienced in the topic of the community with more junior members.

Tracking Community

The tracking of your community activity encompasses storing data related to activity of the user on the site. This can include clicking a link, adding content, or any action that your users can make with community tools. In nearly all of the tools reviewed in this chapter, each one features an option to track the utilization of the tool by the user. The tracking can be done both by all users as well as by the individual. The level of community tracking built into your site can range anywhere from no tracking to extensive tracking of usage patterns.

Planning the tracking elements of your community site up front is crucial to ensuring that you have the kind of data for analysis of your community. This will help to ensure the success and utilization of your community. Tracking enables you to understand what your consumers like and don't like about your community offering.

Tracking community trends using standard Web log files is a key part of the process, but this provides only macro analysis of what is happening on your site, such as most frequently visited pages, top referring sites, and so on. One of the shortcomings of tracking community trends is that many community Web sites are made up of only a few template pages that are dynamically driven from a database. So, statistics such as top pages viewed by site visitors have little meaning and relation to concepts such as what the latest hot topic is in your forums.

The alternative to Web log statistics is database tracking of community utilization. This kind of tracking can take place in a couple of different ways, as outlined in Table 2.14.

TABLE 2.14: Tracking Methods

Feature	Description
Member-Related Tracking	Tracking what a community member does in the Web site can provide valuable trending data related to the demographic information you have on the member. This can help you understand what people like and dislike about the community site.
Function-Related Tracking	Tracking the utilization of the various interactive functions in your community Web site provides an understanding of what functions the site visitors are utilizing and how they are utilizing them. For example, tracking the number of messages posted in sections related to topic A versus topic B can provide good insight. Or, perhaps polling trends related to a day of the week can be tracked. There is almost an unlimited number of possibilities.
Page/Section-Related Tracking	Tracking the utilization of the sections of the Web site can be useful as well. This can include basic click-through tracking as well as tracking of content reviewed, and much more.

As important as the tracking function are the reporting functions. Slicing and dicing the data for statistical analysis is where the insight into visitor utilization of the Web site comes from. Note that you can only do analysis based on the data collected, so it is important to ensure that you are tracking up front on what you will later want to report.

WARNING It is possible to go a little overboard in tracking the use of your site. Remember that each time an action is recorded, a database transaction takes place. If you overload your site with tracking detail, the site may slow down considerably or, at a minimum, require sophisticated caching techniques to be created.

Planning the tracking and analysis of the use of your community Web site will provide the kind of data and insight to understand how visitors interact with it. Taking the time up front to plan the tracking and reporting will pay dividends down the road.

Promoting Community

Tools can be built into your community Web site to help promote the building of community. These important tools can provide value-added functionality, incentives, and ways for community users to attract more members.

Of course, none of these tools can replace good old marketing, but they can enhance the effort and also help to lock in users once you get them. Table 2.15 outlines some of the more common tools for accomplishing community promotion.

TABLE 2.15: Community Promotion Tools

Tool	Description
E-Mail a Friend	If a user sees interesting content, a poll, or a post in a forum, they may want to e-mail a friend to share the information. This is a great way to have your community members pull in people they know.
Affiliates	As discussed earlier, having other sites link to your site is a great way to pull members into your community. Usually, you have to offer the affiliate something to make the link, but sometimes, if they are really gung ho on the community, it will not take much.
Exclusive Clubs	What is true in the real world can certainly be true online. Providing exclusive options for preferred "members" entices more use of the community. An example might include a "frequent flyer" type of program for use of a Web site. Perhaps it is direct access to the community "experts" or other perks.
Greeting Cards	Sending a card to someone with content related to the community Web site can be a very popular feature. And, like e-mail, a card provides a way for existing site users to push your site to people they know.
Sweepstakes	Sweepstakes are always a popular way to have site users give up a little information on themselves for tracking purposes and provide a little excitement. Some sites even increase the user's chances of winning the more they utilize the Web site.

The more ways you can promote your community site and tie site visitors into it, the faster your critical mass of community members will grow. The more you provide tools for community members to promote the site, the more people will be working to help ensure your success.

Other Tools

The reality is that there are all kinds of variations on the tools reviewed in this chapter, as well as many others that can help to build a successful community Web site. Some will be particularly conducive to the type of community, such as a trading community like eBay. Table 2.16 outlines a few options to think about.

TABLE 2.16: Forum Administration

Tool	Description
Site Search	A standard keyword search of content on the site is always a useful tool for users to find what interests them.
Calendars	If your community has events for the site itself or events surrounding the topic at large, a community calendar can be useful.

Continued on next page

TABLE 2.16 CONTINUED: Forum Administration

Tool	Description
Mass E-Mail	Pushing e-mail updates to opt-in members of the community is a powerful tool for staying in front of the member, even when they are not surfing the Web site.
List Servers	List servers provide an alternative format to discussion forums that allow members of the community to group e-mail each other based on the topic of the list.
Chat	Chats provide a real-time communication format in which members can interact. They are also useful for real-time interaction with experts and celebrities.

One way to get ideas for your community site is to visit other sites, including your competitors, to see what they are doing and how they are connecting. Carefully planning all options including "non-standard" ones will help to ensure a successful community.

Tool Building

Building a full community Web site is not within the scope of this book. However, several core elements will be created to demonstrate the steps of building a community Web site using Microsoft tools. Many of the demonstration tools are listed in Table 2.17.

WARNING   The code created in the book is certainly a useful foundation for starting to build a community Web site. It is not recommended, however, that these tools be used "out of the box" without careful review of your specific needs.

TABLE 2.17: Community Tool Examples

Tool	Description
Guest Register	In Chapter 6 we build a guest register that will request basic demographic information. A complete administrative interface will be created to manage the entries.
Forums	A demonstration set of discussion forums will be created that will provide for sections, threads, and messages. An administrative interface will be created for managing the forums.
Poll	A simple poll creation engine will be built to create and administer multiple-choice polls.
Directory	An author and book directory infrastructure will be created to demonstrate member input and tracking. This will allow for authors to register and have their books displayed. It demonstrates an author community being developed as well as a book reader community.
Personalization	In the author directory, book readers will be able to personalize the site to tell them about books in which they are interested.

Continued on next page

TABLE 2.17 CONTINUED: Community Tool Examples

Tool	Description
Tracking	A tracking system will be built to track utilization of the community tools and correlate the usage to the personalization settings of the user.
Rotating News	A simple rotating news tool will be built with a full administration capability.
Affiliate Tracking	An affiliate-tracking program will be built to track a viral marketing program through affiliate links to your community site.

In upcoming chapters, these tools are reviewed in depth. We build basic functionality, but we will explore the full set of possibilities with each tool.

In building these tools, we will look closely at the database design, functional requirements, system planning, and performance enhancements as well as other key aspects of building a community Web site.

Summary

Community tools come in all shapes and sizes, and can be customized to meet the targeted communities' needs, but all tools have the same core elements that facilitate interaction between the users, the site, and the site owners.

Now that we have explored the features and functions of the major community building tools, we can begin to explore the toolset we can utilize to create our community.

CHAPTER 3

The Microsoft Toolset

- The Toolset

- Building the Functionality

Choosing the right tools to build your community Web site is, of course, a critical step. As mentioned in the previous chapters, there are turnkey outsource solutions, such as delphi .com, that you can utilize to add functionality to your Web site. There are also third-party development packages you can utilize as well for adding features to your site.

You most likely wouldn't be reading this book unless you were interested in doing a little programming of your own! The Visual Basic language is a key tool in the community developer's arsenal. There are, however, many tools in the supporting cast that make up a successful community Web site deployment. This chapter explores these tools and, of course, takes an in-depth look at the Visual Basic language and how it will be utilized.

The Toolset

The tools range from server software to programming languages to encryption technology. Each is critical in building the complete solution. An overview of each tool is given in this chapter along with a list of features that are critical for community building.

Presently, Microsoft has taken on a new and significant initiative called ".NET" that seeks to fundamentally change the way Web development is done. The following sections focus on the core NT/2000 tools that are currently available and examines where Microsoft is headed down the road.

Microsoft Windows NT/2000

The Windows NT/2000 platform is the foundation for building a Visual Basic programmed solution. It provides the core Web server, security, TCP/IP functionality, and other fundamental requirements for a Web server operating system. Table 3.1 discusses the key features for community building.

TABLE 3.1: Web Features

Feature	Description
Security	As with any Web server, it is critical to provide solid security to protect the network and operating system from hackers and mischief makers.
TCP/IP networking	TCP/IP is, of course, the standard networking protocol used across the Internet that allows computers to communicate with each other.

Continued on next page

TABLE 3.1 CONTINUED: Web Features

Feature	Description
Component Object Model (COM) support	When using Visual Basic to build the necessary business objects for an e-commerce Web site, COM is a key tool.
Web server	Internet Information Server (IIS) is the server that supports the core Web server functionality. (See the next section.)

There are many excellent book references available for setting up and administering Windows as a Web server.

It is important that Windows is set up properly to ensure security integrity, scalability, and other key issues. Certainly there are differences between the Windows NT and Windows 2000 platforms. Some of the core tools, such as SQL Server, IIS, Active Server Pages (ASP), and so on, are significantly enhanced on the Windows 2000 platform. Windows 2000 also offers more server-side software options for managing your Web site. From a coding development standpoint, however, the work is pretty much the same. The code developed in this book for both SQL Server and ASP will work on either platform.

Internet Information Server

IIS is the Web server that is provided with Windows NT/2000. The latest version on NT is IIS 4.0 and is provided with the Windows NT Option Pack. Windows 2000 comes with IIS 5.0. Table 3.2 gives an overview of the key features of IIS.

TABLE 3.2: IIS Web Server Features

Feature	Description
Index Server	Site content indexing, including HTML pages and Word documents, is supported with Index Server and enables your Web site to have site search functionality.
FTP service	IIS provides the basic functionality to support the File Transfer Protocol (FTP).
HTTP service	IIS provides the basic HTTP service.
SMTP service	IIS provides the support for SMTP mail protocol for sending e-mail from the Web server.
NNTP service	Internet newsgroups can be set up and supported in IIS.
Certificate server	Certificate server allows you to manage your own set of certificates to enable authentication between the server and the client.
Message Queue Server	Microsoft Message Queue Server (MSMQ) is a fast store-and-forward service for Microsoft Windows NT/2000 Server.

Continued on next page

TABLE 3.2 CONTINUED: IIS Web Server Features

Feature	Description
Transaction server	The Option Pack also comes with Microsoft Transaction Server for developing high-performance, mission-critical applications. In Windows 2000 it is integrated into the operating system.
Management console	The management console is the interface for managing the Web server.
Active Server Pages (ASP)	Active Server Pages represent the foundation for Web server development. The ASP engine provides a hosting environment for a number of scripting languages with integrated support for VBScript and JavaScript (JScript). See Table 3.4 for information on what is new in ASP for IIS 5.0.
FrontPage extensions	The FrontPage extensions are key tools for supporting site development in Microsoft FrontPage and Microsoft Visual InterDev. These extensions allow InterDev and Front-Page to manage the Web site over a standard TCP/IP connection.

IIS provides the basic Web server functionality required to serve Web pages. IIS 5.0 has its underpinnings significantly enhanced to be more scalable and stable, but provides the same basic services. The biggest changes for the developer are found in the implementation of ASP.

Active Server Pages/Visual InterDev

The heart of the toolset for building our applications is the ASP component of IIS. Combine that with the Visual InterDev development tool for creating Web pages, working with SQL Server, and building e-commerce applications. Table 3.3 reviews the key features of ASP.

TABLE 3.3: ASP Key Features

Feature	Description
VBScript language	ASP provides the capability to combine client-side HTML code with server-side VBScript, a slightly slimmed-down version of the popular Visual Basic programming language. This code will allow you to access your database, control the code being sent to the client browser, and much more.
Built in objects	IIS has several key objects built in that provide the core functionality for programming from ASP, such as the Response and Request objects. Through these objects you can manage cookies, maintain session state, access other server functions, and more.
COM components	There are a number of COM components that come with ASP, including ADO for accessing data from a range of remote sources, and browser capabilities for checking the user's browser capabilities, managing ad rotation, and much more.

Significant enhancements to the ASP environment in IIS 5.0 are outlined in Table 3.4.

TABLE 3.4: ASP Development Enhancements

Feature	Description
ASP Self Tuning	ASP is now much better at detecting resource bottlenecks, especially with regard to thread allocation. If there is CPU overhead available and requests are backed up, additional threads are allocated. Likewise, if the CPU is being overburdened, threads are de-allocated.
Encoded ASP Scripts	This feature provides basic script encoding so that script logic cannot be easily read. The script code is de-coded during execution.
Application Protection	IIS, in general, provides better protection for Web applications by separating all applications into a segmented memory space from the core IIS processes.
XML Integration	The XML parser provided in Internet Explorer can be utilized to parse XML in your ASP applications.
Windows Script Components	Code written in VBScript can now be compiled into re-usable COM components for use in Web applications.
Flow Control Capabilities	There are now two methods for redirecting a user to another Web page. The traditional method used was the Response object, which sent a message to the browser, and required a trip back to the server. Now the Server object has a redirect option that happens at the server level.
Error Handling	The Server object has a new error handling capability that can help to track down script errors.
Scriptless ASP	Many sites are built with all .ASP pages, even though there may be no script on certain pages. That means even an HTML-only page is run through the ASP parser in IIS 4.0. In IIS 5.0 a check is now done to see if a script is actually included on the page before invoking the ASP parser.
Performance-Enhanced Objects	All of the core objects built into IIS 4.0 are provided, but they have been significantly enhanced for performance.

In IIS 5.0, Microsoft has focused significantly on the performance of aspects of ASP to improve its scalability. In general, they have tuned IIS 5.0 for overall performance. There have been some enhancements for easier coding, with the major change being the capability to compile scripts into COM objects.

Visual InterDev is the key tool utilized throughout this book. It is our primary development environment for building our Active Server Pages–based community. Table 3.5 provides an overview of the key features of Visual InterDev.

TABLE 3.5: Visual InterDev Features

Feature	Description
SQL database tools	Visual InterDev provides an excellent interface when working with remote database environment. Queries can be built, tables managed, stored procedures worked with, and all of the critical functions for building data-driven e-commerce applications can be accomplished.
Remote server site management	Through the use of FrontPage server extensions, you can manage your server-based Web projects remotely with Visual InterDev.
Active Server Pages development	The key use of the tool is for is Active Server Pages, VBScript, or JScript programming.
Team project development/Visual Source Safe integration	In conjunction with Visual Source Safe and the FrontPage server extensions, team project development can be done easily on the same set of pages. Pages that are "checked out" can be locked from use by anyone else.
Client side HTML/script editor	Not only can you work on server-side script development, but you can also work on client-side scripts, DHTML development, cascading style sheets, and so on.
Debugging tools	As is good practice with any development tool, debugging tools are provided for that occasional error a programmer might make.

NOTE   See the Microsoft.NET section later in this chapter to get a peek at what is coming in Visual Studio Studio.net 7.0.

Visual InterDev combined with ASP provides the Microsoft primary programming toolset for Web-based applications. The toolset has been a successful combination that many Web sites are built upon and provides the core tools for the functionality built in this book.

SQL Server

As critical to community building as programming is, even more critical is the database. Without a database to store messages, polls, profiles, and much more, there would be no community at all. Microsoft SQL Server provides a robust development platform for building multi-tier Web applications. You can place as much or as little logic in the database tier as needed. If you are running a multi-server Web farm, then partitioning the client, Web server, and database tier become crucial to ensuring solid performance and balancing server load.

SQL Server can be configured for different security levels, segmentation with replication, programming logic in stored procedures, and so on. With Microsoft's ActiveX Data Objects (ADO) and an OLE DB provider (or ODBC), you can connect from nearly any Microsoft development tool and interface with the underlying e-commerce database.

NOTE   Microsoft Access can be utilized as the database for your community. For a Web site that is going to get any kind of extensive traffic, however, a robust scalable database such as SQL Server should be utilized.

There are three versions of SQL Server still in primary use by developers. SQL Server 6.5 was the first robust version to run on Windows NT 4.0. That was following by SQL Server 7, which provided a significant revamp of the core infrastructure and greatly increased functionality and scalability. The newest version is SQL Server 2000, which is scheduled for release in early 2001. It requires Windows 2000. The SQL Script code developed in this book should work on any of these versions and, with a little work, can be ported to other popular enterprise SQL-based database servers.

In this book, Microsoft SQL Server will be utilized as the database behind the functionality.

NOTE   We assume that you are familiar with setting up and creating SQL Server databases. If you are unfamiliar with this technology, you might want to check out Sybex's *Mastering SQL Server 2000* by Mike Gunderloy and Joe Jorden.

Visual Basic 6

While ASP provides a powerful environment for server-based Web applications in itself through the scripting languages it exposes, it can be further enhanced by the use of compiled code written in a language such as Visual Basic. There are multiple ways in which you can interface from Visual Basic to the Internet, as explored in Table 3.6.

TABLE 3.6: Visual Basic 6 Internet Features

Feature	Description
IIS applications	A new feature has been added to Visual Basic 6. IIS applications enable you to create Visual Basic programs with a standard HTML-based browser as their interface. These applications allow the programmer to utilize all of the familiar tools in VB, such as classes, database programming, and so on. The only difference is that the interface is a browser instead of a standard form. These applications are centrally run on a Web server and can be accessed on your intranet or Internet Web site.

Continued on next page

TABLE 3.6 CONTINUED: Visual Basic 6 Internet Features

Feature	Description
COM objects	A key tool for e-commerce development is the creation of Component Object Model (COM) business objects. For example, in our e-commerce process outlined in Chapter 1, we might build objects for tax and shipping calculations encapsulating existing logic. These COM objects could then be called from our ASP script code.
WIN INET tools/browser control	Of course, there is a traditional capability to create Web applications in a standard Visual Basic forms interface. Visual Basic contains an ActiveX control that can be placed on a form and provides a subset of Internet Explorer. This may be attractive for building management tools for the online store.
ActiveX controls	ActiveX controls can be created in Visual Basic for use in the Internet Explorer browser interface that will run on the client's computer. Again, this may be attractive for encapsulating functionality on the management side of the store.
DHTML applications	In conjunction with IIS applications, DHTML applications are introduced in version 6. DHTML applications allow the Visual Basic programmer to create DHTML interfaces in Internet Explorer, but the language is full-fledged Visual Basic instead of JScript or VBScript. Note that DHTML runs on the client side where IIS applications run on the server side.

This book focuses on building applications in Visual Interdev with Active Server Pages. There might be times, though, when you will want to consider using Visual Basic as part of your Web development arsenal. Usually that is when you need to build complex logic that isn't possible in a scripting context. Often this logic is encapsulated in a COM object and can be used both on the Internet and in a client/server context.

Table 3.7 outlines some of the different situations in which you might want to utilize Visual Basic.

TABLE 3.7: Visual Basic Utilization

Feature	Description
Legacy Code Migration	If you have existing code building in Visual Basic, then utilizing it in a Web application environment is possible with Visual Basic's Internet capabilities.
Performance	Generally speaking, compiled code will execute much more quickly than script code. You can develop extensive COM objects in Visual Basic for performance gains and then utilize them in ASP.

Continued on next page

TABLE 3.7 CONTINUED: Visual Basic Utilization

Feature	Description
Logic Segmentation	Visual Basic provides a full-featured object-based development environment complete with many of the features of object-oriented development. The Visual Basic development environment provides a much more robust development interface and programming language.
Mixed Functionality	If you are building a LAN-based application that also needs to have a Web-based intranet-type interface, Visual Basic can provide the capability to do both right out of the box.

The good news is that the Visual Basic developer has options for what implementation of Visual Basic to utilize and can "right-size" the solution appropriately.

Microsoft Site Server 3.0

Microsoft's Site Server 3.0 is the big gun in Microsoft's arsenal for developing extended community and e-commerce applications. Site Server 3.0 provides a number of tools, including the core programming environment for directory level security, site personalization, membership tracking, site log file analysis, staging and development server support, and much more. With this toolset that is built on an ASP programming foundation and SQL Server, high-end, feature-rich Web sites can be built. Sample sites include those of Dell Computers (www.dell.com), Martha Stewart (www.MarthaStewart.com), and Ulla Popken (www.ullapopken.com).

In reality, it is important to point out that Site Server is primarily a framework of COM objects and applications that support the commerce and community processes. Table 3.8 gives an overview of the key feature set of Site Server, Commerce Edition. If your goal is to start out developing in Site Server, it is still important to understand all the concepts and programming techniques outlined in this book. If you are going to be building a significant e-commerce aspect to your site, then using Site Server 3.0, Commerce Edition (SSCE) will provide the commerce development foundation.

TABLE 3.8: Site Server 3.0 Key Features

Feature	Description
Membership Server	Membership Server provides a way to create a membership-based site with appropriate security and tracking. Security can be based on a database or on the Lightweight Directory Access Protocol (LDAP) used by the Windows 2000 Active Directory among others.
Personalization Server	Personalization Server offers a way to provide targeted content to the user based on the user's membership profile.
Commerce Server (SSCE Only)	Commerce Server is the key toolset for building e-commerce applications. The Commerce Interchange Pipeline (CIP) provides a series of COM objects to manage the purchasing process and can support business-to-business integration as well.
Ad Server (SSCE Only)	Ad Server provides the ability to manage banner ad campaigns on a Web site. A complete Web-based management interface is provided for adding, updating, and deleting ad campaigns and, in particular, tracking the success (or failure) in terms of "click-throughs."
Site Analysis	As mentioned in earlier chapters, site traffic analysis is an important aspect of understanding your community Web site. Site Server provides Web log analysis tools to analyze traffic patterns.

Commerce Server 3.0

Microsoft's Commerce Server 2000 product for the Windows 2000 platform is scheduled to be released in the near future (at the time of this writing), probably around the same time this book will be available. It is the next generation of the Site Server product. Table 3.9 provides a breakdown of its main features.

TABLE 3.9: Commerce Server 2000

Feature	Description
Profile and Targeting	Site Server 3.0 provides a profile and targeting solution. The new twists in Commerce Server 2000 are much more e-commerce focused and built on the underpinnings of the Windows 2000 platform.
Product Catalog	Based on SQL Server, the new Product Catalog System helps create catalogs, and import and export from existing data sources. Integrated and powerful search capabilities also make product information easy to find.
Analysis	Provides extended features including Web log file analysis as well as integrating in actual activity based on the Web site database.
Advertising	Banner advertising is provided as a type of business processing pipeline similar to the commerce pipelines for purchasing.

There is certainly much more available in the product; for additional information, check out www.microsoft.com/CommerceServer/. Commerce Server 2000 is a significant overhaul of the Site Server platform, but it does require Windows 2000. Making a careful selection between Commerce Server 2000 and Site Server will have a significant impact on your development requirements down the road. Either way, both have significant features, especially in an e-commerce context, to build community.

Secure Sockets Layer (SSL)/Verisign Certificates

Security on an e-commerce Web site is crucial for securing private data—especially credit card data. On the management side, passwords and other business-critical data should be encrypted between the browser and the server.

IIS 4 supports SSL 3. There is a simple process for requesting a certificate on the server and then submitting the certificate request to an authority, such as Verisign (http://www.verisign.com). Once the certificate request is made, the keys will be sent back installed on the server.

Miscellaneous Tools

There are many other tools available for Internet development. Certainly many non-Microsoft tools are available for development on Windows NT or on any other operating system.

Table 3.10 reviews other Microsoft tools.

TABLE 3.10: Microsoft's Web-Enabled Tools

Feature	Description
Microsoft Exchange Server	If you want to build extended e-mail capabilities to e-mail targeting, provide e-mail boxes for customer support, and other related functions, Exchange Server provides a robust e-mail platform.
Microsoft FrontPage 2000	While Visual InterDev does provide WYSIWYG editing, FrontPage 2000 is an excellent WYSIWYG HTML editing tool for creating static content on the Web site.
Microsoft Office	Microsoft Office provides extended tools for working with the Web. Microsoft Word can also be utilized for creating and editing Web page documents. Microsoft Access can be an excellent database tool to use in conjunction with Microsoft SQL Server.

Continued on next page

TABLE 3.10 CONTINUED: Microsoft's Web-Enabled Tools

Feature	Description
Internet Explorer	Internet Explorer provides much more than a standard Web page display. There are a number of tools provided along with the browser itself. Remote Data Service (RDS) objects are provided for interfacing with data on the Web server via HTTP, ActiveX controls can run in the browser interface, and there is the capability to create client-side scripting in VBScript and Jscript.
Visual Source Safe	Visual Source Safe provides a source code control toolset for storing source code and related files in a source database. It provides source code version management as well as an infrastructure for checking code in and out. This is particularly useful for avoiding version conflicts in team-based environments.
Remote Data Services (RDS)	RDS provides a toolset for querying databases across the Internet via HTTP. It provides a direct link between the browser and the database without having to make a trip to the server to work through ASP or some other server-side development tool.
Microsoft Visual Studio	Two tools included in Visual Studio have already been mentioned: Visual InterDev and Visual SourceSafe. Also included are Visual C++ and Visual J++ along with other development tools, such as Visual Modeler. All of these may be useful at various points in the development process. In Visual Studio.NET, the next generation of C++ programming environment, C# will be introduced.
BizTalk Server 2000	BizTalk makes it easy to integrate applications and businesses together with graphical tools for building Extensible Markup Language (XML) schema, performing schema transformation, establishing trading partner relationships over the Internet, as well as tracking and analyzing data and documents that are exchanged. BizTalk Server 2000 extends the features of traditional e-commerce and electronic data interchange (EDI).
Application Center	Application Center 2000 is Microsoft's deployment and management tool that makes managing groups of servers as simple as managing a single computer. It provides a complete toolset for managing Web server farms. For large community Web sites with extensive server farms, this is an invaluable tool.

Microsoft continues to enhance and hone its overall product offering for the Internet. Which Microsoft or third-party solutions you utilize will greatly depend on the scope and scale of the Web application you are building. The next section takes a look at Microsoft's much-promoted .NET initiative.

Microsoft .NET

In mid-1999 Microsoft announced a significant shift in its Internet strategy, called ".NET". Bill Gates and Steve Ballmer likened it to the decision to move from DOS to Windows, or when Microsoft made its infamous Internet strategy shift in the 1990s. It is important to understand that this isn't a shift that happens overnight. It will be a progression over many years.

The expansiveness of the .NET strategy touches nearly every piece of software that Microsoft produces, which is a bit beyond the scope of this book to explain. For more information, check out www.microsoft.com/net/.

For developers, there are significant initiatives that need to be considered. Table 3.11 outlines some of the highlights.

TABLE 3.11: Microsoft's .NET Development Initiatives

Feature	Description
Web Services	Web Services are building blocks for constructing distributed Web-based applications in a platform, object model, and multi-language manner. Web Services are based on open Internet standards, such as HTTP and XML, and form the basis of Microsoft's vision of the programmable Web. In other words, it's a URL-addressable resource that programmatically returns information to clients who want to use it. One important feature of Web Services is that clients don't need to know how a service is implemented. They communicate through using standard Web protocols and data formats, such as HTTP and XML.
Visual Studio	Visual Studio.NET includes exciting features, some of which are enhancements to previous versions and some of which are brand new. A few of the most significant additions include the new Microsoft programming language called C#; a new, smarter, integrated development environment; new object-oriented features in Visual Basic .NET; and development life-cycle tools.
ASP+	ASP+ is a new version of ASP that has been rebuilt from the ground up. ASP+ provides for cleaner code that is easier to write, and simple to reuse and share. ASP+ boosts performance and scalability by offering access to complied languages; development is more intuitive with Web Forms, and an object-oriented foundation facilitates reuse. Other important features include page events, Web controls, and caching. Server controls and improvements in data binding are also new with ASP+. Libraries for use with ASP+, and the Microsoft .NET Framework that allows custom business functions to be exposed over the Web, provide more new development opportunities.
Web Forms	ASP+ Web Forms are Web pages that enable you to write code just as you do for ASP today. More than that, though, ASP+ Web Forms are designed on top of an object-oriented programming model, enabling code reuse and separation of the application code from page content. In Visual Basic you draw the controls on a form, then implement the event procedures underneath. In traditional ASP this isn't possible because there's no link between the controls and their server-side code. In ASP+, however, there is a link; instead of having to manually pull out values from the form variables, you can write code directly.
ADO+	ADO+ is the new set of data access services for the .NET Framework. ADO+ is a natural evolution of ADO, built around n-tier development and architected with XML at its core. Two key enhancements are extensive support for the disconnected programming model and rich XML integration.

Extensible Markup Language (XML)

Woven throughout the .NET platform is XML for data sharing. Extensible Markup Language (XML) is a meta-markup language that provides a format for describing structured data. This facilitates more precise declarations of content and more meaningful search results across multiple platforms. XML enables Web-based data viewing and manipulation applications.

In XML you can define an unlimited set of tags. While HTML tags can be used to display a word in bold or italic, XML provides a framework for tagging structured data. An XML element can declare its associated data to be a retail price, a sales tax, a book title, the amount of precipitation, or any other desired data. With XML there is the capability to search for and manipulate data regardless of the applications within which it is found. Once data has been located, it can be presented in a browser, such as Internet Explorer, in any number of ways, or it can be handed off to other applications for further processing and viewing. More information can be found at http://msdn.microsoft.com/xml/. Over the next several months, Microsoft will be fleshing out the vision and direction for all of its tools.

The goal of this book is to explore the development techniques behind building community based functionality. This will be primarily done through the use of VBScript code created in Visual Interdev and SQL code in Microsoft SQL Server.

Browsers

There are two primary browsers utilized on the Internet. The first is Internet Explorer 5.x and the second is Netscape Navigator (or Communicator) 6.x; Figures 3.1 and 3.2 show the two browsers, respectively. Even though Internet Explorer has seen strong growth in utilization, Netscape is still a significant player in the marketplace.

FIGURE 3.1:

Internet Explorer 5

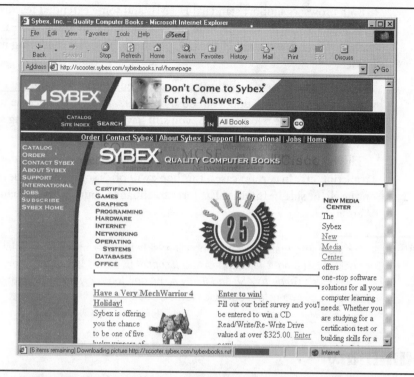

FIGURE 3.2:

Netscape Navigator 4

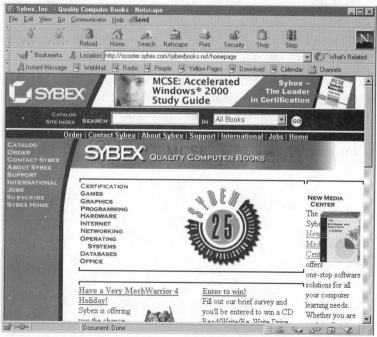

Both browsers support standard HTML and some extended features, such as cascading style sheets, dynamic HTML, and JavaScript. The only thing you can be sure will work in both, however, is standard HTML. Even then, the visual rendering might be a little different in each.

Trying to design a truly unique and advanced interface on the client side can be tricky when trying to ensure support in both browsers. Even if you decide to build two different interfaces for those two browsers, you still have issues of supporting smaller segment browsers, such as earlier versions, specialized browsers, and so on.

This book does not explore the difficult issues of cross-browser development of client-side JavaScript, etc. In certain cases, this book will offer some specific development with VBScript on the client side in Internet Explorer to enhance your ability to maintain the community Web site.

NOTE   For more information on building client-side browser-based applications, see the following books: *Mastering™ JavaScript® and JScript™* by James Jaworski (Sybex, 1999), *Visual Basic® Developer's Guide to ASP and IIS* by A. Russell Jones (Sybex, 1999), and *Mastering™ Visual Basic® 6* by Evangelos Petroutsos (Sybex, 1998).

Summary

The primary browser utilized Internet Explorer 5.0, but the applications will run in Netscape 6.x as well with no problem. The primary foundation for all of the development is Windows NT with SQL Server 7.0. Again, all of the code developed will run properly on a Windows 2000/SQL Server 2000 platform, as well.

The Microsoft platform provides a rich Internet development environment. At its core is the SQL Server database and the Visual Basic Script programming environment. Careful planning based on the size and scope of your site will help to determine what additional tools you need. In the next chapter, we build a simple application to demonstrate the use of Visual InterDev for developing ASP pages.

CHAPTER 4

System Configuration

- Designing the Server Farm
- Server Management

It is crucial to the success of a Web site to have the system configured properly for running the community Web site. The "server farm" can include any number of servers, from one to dozens. It consists of all the hardware required to make the site available on the Internet for a targeted traffic load. Designing and setting up the server farm properly is of great importance, whether the community is simple and meant for a small audience, or complex and intended for an audience of millions.

Related issues such as backups, the development environment, product staging, and source code control become critical in a 24/7/365 real-time production environment where any downtime may mean loss of dollars, not to mention loss of confidence by your site visitors. This chapter introduces the core issues related to designing a system for your community Web site.

Designing the Server Farm

The server farm consists of all the servers required to run the site and can include one server, or many servers with different roles such as database management, Web site serving, and more. You need to consider many aspects of setting up the server farm when developing a community system. Knowing what servers you need for your applications is a little bit of a chicken and egg scenario as the complexity of the applications and volume will define the server needs. Adding multiple servers can become an expensive option and may be set by budget limits which, in turn, may drive the complexity of the applications that can be built.

In the server farm, there are multiple servers that play different roles. Running all of the functions on one server could compromise security and performance. Let's explore the options for building a server farm by analyzing each type of server that can be found in the farm.

Community Servers

The community site should run on a Windows NT/2000 Web server. For our ASP based examples, you also need Internet Information Server 4.0/5.0.

A Web site often encompasses more than just the community site. Other features might be more content focused and not necessarily interactive in nature, or can include e-commerce functionality. When planning your Web server needs, be sure to take these other features into account.

Typically the community Web server is set up separately from the database server and the Web server. Only in cases of very simple minimal traffic sites should all three be combined.

There are some key requirements to consider, including where secure community administration functionality will be placed and database security. Table 4.1 reviews each.

TABLE 4.1: Community Site Configuration Requirements

Requirement	Description
Community management interface	A management interface is built for the various functions of the community site. Security is essential, so the management interface URL should be distinct (for example, `admin.communitysite.com`) from that of the user side of the site (for example, `www.communitysite.com`). Security can be implemented in a number of ways. NT Challenge and Response authentication can be required with directory-level security. Or, as will be explored later in the book, a database-driven security system can be implemented.
Secure Sockets Later (SSL) security	Secure Sockets Later security is required for encrypting private data between the browser and the server.
Database connection	Presuming the database server is not on the same machine, an ODBC link to the database is needed on the community Web server. That also presumes that the database server is easily accessible on the network.

The community Web server is like any other Web server. Unlike a server that is primarily serving static pages, however, this Web server will be delivering primarily template- and data-driven Web pages.

Standard Web Server

If a Web server for the "home site" that is separate from the community server is required, it should be configured in much the same way as the community Web server. The primary requirement is an appropriate link to the community site. An excellent example of how this type of server management is done can be found on the Yahoo! Web site. The primary Web site is at www.yahoo.com. The chat site is hosted at chat.yahoo.com.

Database Server

Typically you do not want the database server to be accessible to the outside world. Placing a database server directly on the Internet removes a layer of security for your private community data.

The database server should sit behind a firewall where it is accessible via the LAN environment. If the Web server and the database server are on the same machine, then the database is exposed to outside access. This has the potential of permitting access to private data, such as credit cards. While certainly SQL Server does provide login access security and other means of locking down the database, making the database publicly inaccessible helps to ensure security.

Multiple Server Support

As mentioned in the Introduction, the simplest of Web sites could be one single Web server that includes all functionality (as shown in Figure 4.1).

FIGURE 4.1:

Single server farm

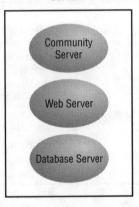

Server 1

The next level of division, as shown in Figure 4.2, is to separate any Web server support from database support. This would require a minimum of two servers in the data farm. The figure shows a primary Web site and the community Web site split into two servers with a third database server.

FIGURE 4.2:

Multiple server farm

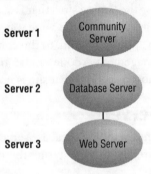

The next challenge comes when multiple Web servers and database servers are needed to support transaction volume, as shown in Figure 4.3. While the fundamental coding and database functionality is the same, there are issues of data synchronization, content synchronization, load balancing, and more that need to be addressed. Tackling those specific issues is beyond the scope of this book, but careful consideration should be given to these issues before launching a potentially high transaction volume Web site to the public. Note that Figure 4.3 simply indicates that the Web servers, community servers, and database servers could be linked in any number of ways depending on the needs of the Web site.

FIGURE 4.3:

High transaction volume
server farm

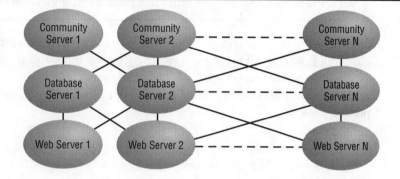

TIP

For development purposes, there is no problem with having all of the functionality on a single server, but it is important to stage the full server farm to ensure that all items are linking up properly.

WARNING

When the requirement for balancing traffic over multiple servers (such as load balancing) comes into play in a multiple-server environment, additional functionality is needed to handle serving the Web requests to the different servers. It is also important to ensure that the server to where the Web visitor is initially sent is the same server the visitor continues to interact with during their visit. If the site visitor ends up going to different Web servers, tracking their vital data will be next to impossible.

It is also important to point out that as Web sites grow and different levels of traffic spiking occur, the server farm configuration may change. Ensuring up front that the foundation development of the community is done properly for future growth is critical.

NOTE

For more information on server management see *Web Server Technology: The Advanced Guide for World Wide Web Information Providers* by Nancy Yeager and Robert McGrath (Morgan Kaufmann, 1996) and *Administrating Web Servers, Security and Maintenance* by Eric Larson and Brian Stephens (Prentice Hall, 1999).

Staging and Development Server Management

While much of the attention is given to the production Web server farm, consideration should also be given to development server and staging server management. The development server is where ongoing development takes place for new functionality on the community Web server.

The staging server is utilized for staging Web site updates into the Web server farm to ensure all is working. This phase is especially critical if updates are ongoing and frequent, especially in a multi-server production environment. If the updates to the site are significant, it can be critical to perform proper load testing to ensure the changes do not fail under a full production load.

TIP   The type and quantity of development and staging servers do not have to match the production environment, but they do need to provide a reasonable simulation of the production environment to provide a good development and test bed.

Server Management

Many of the traditional challenges of managing a client/server server farm environment are also inherent in managing a Web server farm. Key aspects of any good development and production management process include source code control, backups, and so on. In this section, we review some of those requirements. We also review the basics of setting up the Web site so we can kick off our development in the next chapter.

Development Environment

Building a community site is not significantly different than building an internal client/server application. Good development techniques and tools are critical for this activity.

Visual SourceSafe is an excellent tool for managing source code for a project. It does an excellent job of managing code check-in and check-out in a group project development environment. The SourceSafe database can reside on the development server or, more preferably, on a separate server on the network.

A development requirement unique to a community Web server development environment is that all of the source code files must be worked on in a central development server. Figure 4.4 shows the basic development process for working in Visual InterDev on the development Web server.

FIGURE 4.4:

Active Server Pages
development environment

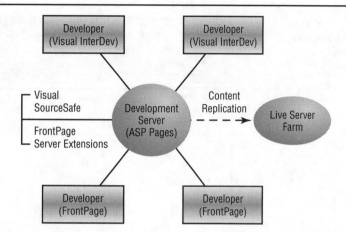

The developer in this environment connects to the Web server via Visual InterDev. The FrontPage extensions need to be installed on the Web server for the IP address of the development Web site. InterDev then connects via that IP address.

Web Server Setup

To create our development environment, let's go through the steps necessary to configure Internet Information Server and FrontPage Extensions, and then connect via Visual InterDev.

NOTE   These steps are for Windows NT 4.0 Server. Setting up IIS in Windows 2000 is a little different, but follows nearly the same steps and concepts.

1. Start Internet Information Server (IIS). The Microsoft Management Console (MMC) is utilized for managing processes on the server and is launched with IIS. In this case, snap-ins are used for configuring the Internet services, including FTP, Web, and SMTP. Figure 4.5 shows the MMC.

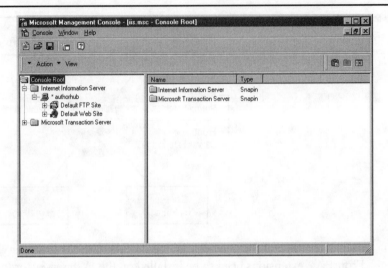

2. Configure the Web site next. In the example in this book, the Web site runs off the default Web site installed with IIS. A new Web site can be created and an IP address applied to it. Figure 4.6 shows the properties tab for the Web site. Use the localhost IP of 127.0.0.1 for a local Web site on the machine.

FIGURE 4.6:

The Web site configuration
pane for our Web site

3. Now configure the home directory to ensure that the proper settings for our Web site are set. Click on the Home Directory tab. The home directory tab is shown in Figure 4.7. The FrontPage Web option must be checked to ensure the site supports FrontPage extensions. The rest of the defaults should be fine.

FIGURE 4.7:

The Web site configuration pane for our Web site's home directory

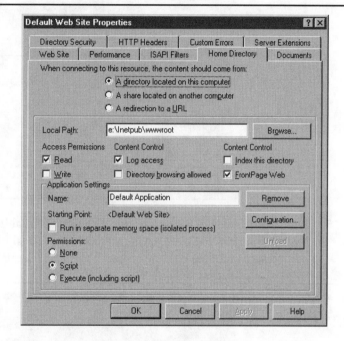

4. The basics of the Web site are now set up. Next, install the FrontPage extensions on the site. Start FrontPage Server Administrator in the Windows NT 4 Option Pack program group. Figure 4.8 shows the FrontPage Server Administrator. From the list box, select the new Web site you have created, and then select Install to create the extensions on that Web server.

FIGURE 4.8:
Configuring the Web site
FrontPage extensions

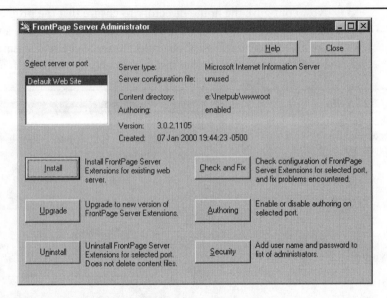

5. Now we are ready to connect to the Web site in Visual InterDev. Figure 4.9 shows InterDev at startup. Select the New tab, choose Visual InterDev Projects to create a new project, and then give the project a name. Click the Open button to continue.

FIGURE 4.9:
Visual InterDev at startup

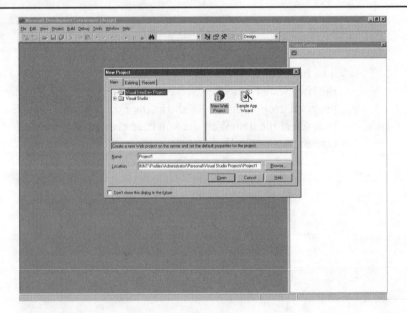

6. Visual InterDev now prompts for the IP address of the Web site to which to connect. If it is the local site on the Web server, the IP is 127.0.0.1 or localhost. Figure 4.10 shows the dialog box.

FIGURE 4.10:

Prompt for the IP address of the Web

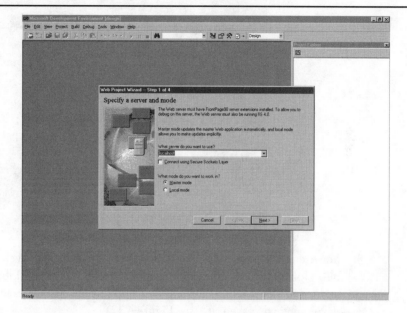

7. Once the Web site is selected, Visual InterDev asks what virtual Web or Web application we want to connect to. In this case, create a new one called Community. Figure 4.11 shows the settings.

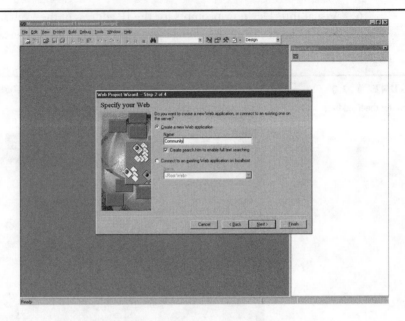

8. You are now connected to your Web site. When the new Web application is created, a new global.asa file is created. The global.asa file contains global settings for application and session level actions for our Web application. At this stage, you are ready to begin developing your Web site (see Figure 4.12).

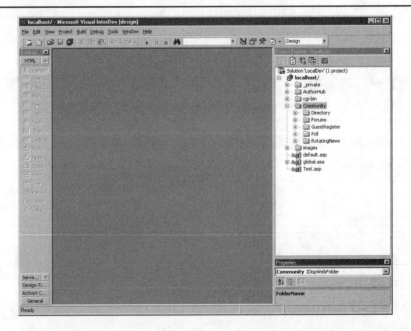

Server Backups

Backing up server data is, of course, critical. Perhaps backups are even more crucial on the Web due to the transactional nature of the Web site and the need to have 24x7x365 capability. Table 4.2 offers an overview of the key items to back up.

TABLE 4.2: Server Backup Considerations

Requirement	Description
ASP and other key Web files	Code, images, HTML pages, and other files on the Web site should be backed up frequently. Keeping backups over time may be important as well, in case past content needs to be resurrected.
COM objects	Any business objects created in Visual Basic 6 should be backed up on a frequent basis. The source code for these objects (stored in Visual SourceSafe) should be backed up, as well.
SSL certificates	Often missed in the backup process is the requirement to store the SSL certificates in a backed-up location. If the certificates are lost, there is no choice but to request a new set of certificates.
ODBC DSNs	Another often-missed item is backing up the settings of ODBC DSNs on the Web server. If you are using File DSNs, the actual DSN can be backed up.
IIS configuration settings	If you are making changes to the default IIS configuration settings, those should also be noted and saved in case the Web server needs to be rebuilt.
SQL Server configuration settings	The same goes for the SQL Server configuration settings as with the IIS configuration settings.
Operating system and other server files	As with any good, standard backup, and for a quick recovery, the full system should be backed up frequently.

Backing up Web sites can happen at multiple levels. The first is a time factor—backups can be done daily, weekly, monthly, and so on. In the event of a system crash, the latest data will only be as fresh as the last backup. You can go to extended extremes, such as backing up database transaction logs on an hourly or more frequent basis. Finding the right backup solution will depend on your willingness to spend funds on expensive backups and backup timing requirements.

Security

As mentioned earlier in this chapter, security is a key issue when configuring the Web site. We can secure our Web site directly at the Web level in IIS. This is opposed to implementing database security and not allowing access to content via ASP coding.

Figure 4.13 shows the Authentication Methods dialog box that manages the security of IIS for the Web site. In general, anonymous access is the setting for providing public access to a Web site. If a particular virtual root or directory needs to be locked down further, you can implement basic authentication and Windows NT Challenge/Response. Basic Authentication sends passwords across the Internet in clear text. In Windows NT Challenge/Response, you have to use Internet Explorer to gain access to the Web site. In either case, the user is prompted with a user name and password dialog box.

FIGURE 4.13:

Security settings for the
Web site

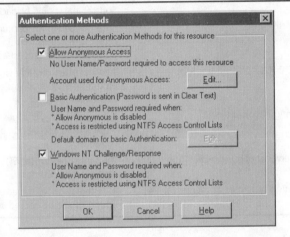

Also on the security front, management of SSL certificates is critical. The Key Manager icon is found on the primary management interface of the IIS management console. Clicking the icon displays the Key Manager interface, as shown in Figure 4.14.

NOTE   Windows 2000 management of SSL certificates is quite different than Windows NT.

FIGURE 4.14:

Key Manager interface

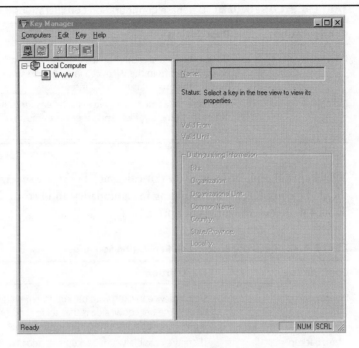

In the Key Manager you can create a new key, install certificates from a certificate authority (such as Verisign), import certificates, and back up certificates.

Database Setup

Configuring the database is as important as setting up the Web server. While it is out of the scope of this book to go through all of the ins and outs of database configuration, a few items to consider are shown in Table 4.3.

TABLE 4.3: Database Configuration Considerations

Configuration	Description
Peak loading	Unlike the business environment where the peak spike load may be a moderate blip on the radar, Web sites can often have peaks at unusual times that will require far more resources than day-to-day loading. Holidays, sales promotions, and other events can provide significant loading requirements. Ensure the Web server can support extended connections and data objects. Each of these will impact the server configuration requirements, and so on.

Continued on next page

TABLE 4.3 CONTINUED: Database Configuration Considerations

Configuration	Description
Drive space	Transaction logs and other space requirements, including sheer data storage of information collected from the Web, can impact drive storage requirements. Continuing to monitor the drive utilization is critical.
Multiple server support	If multiple database servers are in place, ensuring the synchronization of product data, orders, customer profiles, and other issues must be addressed up front in the basic system design.

Backup and replication is also a critical issue. There are several different scenarios that should be considered when building in redundancy and backup for the database server. Table 4.4 reviews the different options.

TABLE 4.4: Database Backup and Replication Scenarios

Configuration	Description
Device backup	Simple device backup with backup to tape nightly can provide basic backup capabilities. The only downside is that there is no real-time backup to ensure the Web site will stay up without significant downtime.
Warm backup	There are possible warm backup scenarios where the database data is transferred or replicated on an infrequent basis (perhaps hourly or less). If the database server should go down, a simple reconfiguration of ODBC settings to point at the warm backup will keep the Web site up and functioning.
Real-time replication	The best of all worlds is real-time replication between database servers. Putting this kind of requirement on the database server calls for significant planning for resource loading, depending on the different transaction levels.

Another critical issue is supporting database development that ensures live site synchronization and updates go smoothly. Any time updates are made to the production database server from the development server, issues such as ensuring peak loading will not be affected and providing security will become critical to the Web site's success.

Load Planning

As intertwined throughout many of the discussions in this chapter on system design, load planning is a vital issue. Coding of the community site for core functionality may have a minimal impact, but if significant load is being anticipated, ensuring the code is solid and designed to handle multiple server requirements is important.

There are excellent load-planning tools on the Web. If you are working with an ISP to run and manage the server farm, the ISP will typically have load-testing capabilities to assist in planning for different traffic loads. In these tests, it is important to ensure that key code-heavy sections of the site are tested properly.

Browser Considerations

Finally, an integral part of system planning is understanding the browser requirements that need to be supported by the system. While much of this relates to design, in some cases the type of browser may be dictated if certain parts of the site are coded to use extended browser features (such as ActiveX or DHTML). An example of this could include a community manager that is developed to use a specific browser for extended functionality. In some cases, Internet Explorer may be required for NT Challenge/Response. In rare cases, Internet Explorer Remote Data Services (RDS) may be needed.

Summary

System design for a Web site is critical to ensuring success of all the hard work that goes into the code development of the Web site. In some respects the issues are not all that different than designing a client/server server farm. The primary differences are in planning for different server loads, a somewhat different set of tools, different clients, and the potential for the environment to change rapidly.

CHAPTER 5

Sample Application

- Building the Data Table

- Building the HTML Form

- Programming the Script Code

- Testing the Application

Before going full bore into the community site development process, this chapter demonstrates how to build a simple feedback application based on Active Server Pages (ASP) and SQL Server. This will help to get your feet wet with the ASP development environment.

The sample application used in this chapter is a simple form designed to provide a way for site users to send feedback to selected personnel. This form will take in the name, e-mail address, recipient, subject, and text of the feedback.

Building the Data Table

The core of any interactive Web site is a well-designed database. Before you jump into programming the feedback form, you need to know the data structure to utilize behind this database-driven application.

NOTE   Learning to utilize SQL Server is a complete topic for another book. We are assuming in this book that you are familiar with SQL-based relational databases and the key components, including tables and stored procedures.

Utilizing a SQL-based Relational Database

As mentioned in previous chapters, we are using Microsoft's enterprise-level database, Microsoft SQL Server 6.5/7.0/2000. SQL Server provides a robust relational database architecture for building high-transaction community Web sites. It is the database server technology behind high-profile community Web sites such as Reba McEntire.com, diabetes.org, Arthritis.org, and many others.

In this chapter, the primary tools utilized for interfacing with SQL Server are Visual Studio and, specifically, the data tools included with Visual InterDev. For direct development, SQL Enterprise Manager is utilized. SQL Enterprise Manager provides powerful administration tools that are used to manage multiple servers, configure, start and stop SQL Servers, monitor current server activity, and view the SQL Server error log. By using SQL Enterprise Manager, you can create and mange devices and databases, and also manage security, including logins, database users, and permissions.

NOTE   Microsoft SQL Server supports the Transact-SQL (T-SQL) language, which is a superset of the Structured Query Lange (SQL), a leading standard for querying relations databases. T-SQL has been certified as compliant with the ANSI SQL-92 standard, but any code taking advantage of proprietary extensions will, of course, not be easily portable. As much as possible, the SQL code written in this book will be ANSI compliant.

Designing the Database Table

For our sample application, we first need to create a simple database table into which we can insert our feedback data. Listing 5.1 shows the SQL code to create the database structure.

Listing 5.1   Feedback Database Table

```
CREATE TABLE dbo.Feedback (
    idFeedBack int IDENTITY (1, 1) NOT NULL ,
    chrName varchar (255) NOT NULL ,
    chrEmail varchar (255) NULL ,
    chrRecipient varchar (255) NOT NULL ,
    chrSubject varchar (255) NOT NULL ,
    txtMessage text NOT NULL ,
    dtEntered datetime NOT NULL
)
```

Our table has the obvious fields for name, e-mail, recipient, subject, and message. It also includes a unique identity column that will assign a new id number for each feedback entry. This is utilized to ensure that we can uniquely identify any entry into the feedback database and also serves as our primary key.

We also have included a date entered field, dtEntered. When building the table, be sure to set it to default to the current date and time by using the SQL GetDate() function. That way the system time is utilized for each entry into the feedback database.

Building Stored Procedures

To interact with our database table, we need to build stored procedures that act as the interface with our data from the ASP script code we write. Stored procedures are a good way to build in a layer of abstraction from the underlying relational table data structure and the ASP script coding. Should the underlying table structure need to change, the stored procedures can be updated to reflect these changes and, in many cases, very minimal ASP script code updating will need to be done.

For our feedback table, we build two stored procedures. The first is utilized to insert data into the table. The second retrieves the full set of data in the table.

NOTE   There are many additional procedures that can be built to manage the feedback entries, including archiving and deleting them.

The first stored procedure shown in Listing 5.2 simply executes a SQL statement to get all rows in the feedback database.

Listing 5.2	sp_GetFeedback Stored Procedure

```
/* Stored procedure to retrieve feedback
   entries */
CREATE PROCEDURE sp_GetFeedback AS

/* Select statement */
select * from feedback
GO
```

Listing 5.3 is our stored procedure for inserting a new set of feedback into the database. Note that the name, e-mail address, recipient selection, subject, and message are all passed in as parameters of the stored procedure. A SQL insert statement is then created to insert the data.

Listing 5.3	sp_InsertFeedback Stored Procedure

```
/* Stored procedure to insert feedback
   entries into the database */
CREATE PROCEDURE sp_InsertFeedback

/* Variables containing the feedback
   data */
@chrName    varchar(255),
@chrEmail   varchar(255),
@chrRecipient   varchar(255),
@chrSubject   varchar(255),
@txtMessage   text

AS

/* Insert statement for the feedback data */
insert into feedback(chrName, chrEmail, chrRecipient,
          chrSubject, txtMessage)
      values(@chrName, @chrEmail, @chrRecipient,
          @chrSubject, @txtMessage)
GO
```

The data table and these stored procedures combine to form the data tier of our ASP feedback application. Next we take a look at the building of the HTML form where the user enters the data.

Building the HTML Form

Using what you learned in the last chapter, create a new Visual InterDev project on your Web server. Once you have that set up, we are ready to begin adding pages to our new project.

In the Project Explorer windows in Visual InterDev, select Add, on the menu. On the submenu select Active Server Page, as shown in Figure 5.1, to open the Add New Page dialog box. Enter Feedback.asp as the name of the feedback Active Server Page.

FIGURE 5.1:

Adding an active
server page

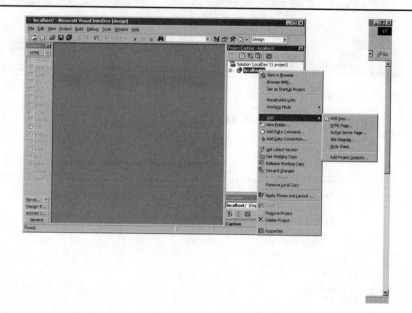

Once that is done, a new file is created on the Web server and we are ready to begin building the HTML structure of the page. A basic template for the page is created when the ASP page is created. We can now begin editing in Visual InterDev. We have three view options—Design, Source and Quick view. In general, Source view is utilized for all development. Design view is used for WYSIWYG HTML building. Quick view is utilized for viewing the HTML in a browser interface, but note that no ASP code is processed.

NOTE   You also need to create pages for *AdminFeedback.asp* and *ProcessFeedback.asp* using the same techniques as adding *Feedback.asp*.

To build the HTML page, we need to create an HTML form and HTML elements on the page. We then can build a script page to process the data entered by the user.

The first part of the page is straightforward, as shown in Listing 5.4. The standard HTML headers for the page are created. We also start out the form by setting it to post results of the ProcessFeedback.asp page, which processes the feedback.

Code Documenting Standards

There are certainly a number of different ways to document your code. In this book, we perform basic documentation procedures. Each page uses "Option Explicit" to force variable declaration. Also, each page has a header with the name of the page and a brief description. In general, every significant section of the page is commented. It is important to ensure that some level of documentation procedure is followed and is followed consistently.

Listing 5.4   Feedback.asp

```asp
<%@ Language=VBScript %>
<%Option Explicit%>
<%
'*****************************************************
'** Feedback.asp
'**
'** Displays the feedback form
'*****************************************************
%>
<HTML>
<HEAD>
</HEAD>
<BODY>

<!- Build a form to post the data ->
<form method="post" action="ProcessFeedBack.asp">

<!- Begin the table to display the form ->
<table>

<!- Input for the person's name ->
<tr>
   <td align="right">Name:</td>
   <td>
    <input type="text" name="chrName" value="" size="40">
   </td>
</tr>

<!- Input for the person's email address ->
<tr>
   <td align="right">Email:</td>
   <td>
    <input type="text" name="chrEmail" value="" size="40">
   </td>
</tr>
```

```
<!- Select a targeted recipient ->
<tr>
  <td align="right">Recipient:</td>

  <td>
   <select name="chrRecipient">
   <option value="TomBond">Tom Bond - Customer Service
   <option value="KaylaRocker">Kayla Rocker - Billing
   <option value="JennyNinny">Jenny Ninny ⏎
        - Administration
   <option value="WillieWinifred">Willie Winifred ⏎
        - Marketing
   </select>
  </td>
</tr>

<!- Input the subject of the email ->
<tr>
  <td align="right">Email Subject:</td>
  <td>
   <input type="text" name="chrSubject" value=""
     size="40">
  </td>
</tr>

<!- Input the message ->
<tr>
  <td align="right">Message:</td>
  <td>
   <textarea name="txtMessage" cols="60" ⏎
        rows="20"></textarea>
  </td>
</tr>

<!- The submit button ->
<tr>
  <td colspan="2" align="center">
   <input type="submit" value="Submit" name="Submit">
  </td>
</tr>

</form>

</BODY>
</HTML>
```

After the opening HTML form tag, all of the fields of the form are created using standard HTML input field tagging. A submit button is created to execute the form when the user is ready. The fields are all formatted into a table for easy viewing by the end user. Note that on each of the input fields, we specify a field length for display.

Programming the Script Code

Now that the primary page the Web site visitor sees is built, we need to construct the page that processes their input. We also need to construct a page for a site administrator to retrieve their feedback.

End User Interaction

Now the real programming fun begins as we can begin work on processing the feedback submission. Our goal in this page is to retrieve the data and insert it into the database. We also want to thank the user for submitting the feedback.

Listing 5.5 shows the code for the ProcessFeedback.asp page. The page starts out with the Option Explicit declaration, followed by the header documentation for the page. A thank-you note in standard HTML on the page is also included.

One of the powerful features of ASP programming is its capability to mix HTML and script code in the same page. Immediately following the thank you message in this page, we see the script code to grab the data from the HTML input form and insert it into the database.

Listing 5.5   ProcessFeedback.asp

```
<%@ Language=VBScript %>
<%Option Explicit%>
<%
'*****************************************************
'** ProcessFeedback.asp
'**
'** Inserts the feedback data into the database
'*****************************************************
%>
Thank you for your feedback. We will follow up shortly.

<HTML>
<head>

</head>
<BODY BGCOLOR="WHITE">

<%

' Declare the variables
Dim dbFeedback          ' database connection
```

```
Dim SQL           ' string
Dim chrName       ' string
Dim chrSubject    ' string
Dim txtMessage    ' string

' Create an ADO database connection
set dbFeedback = _
   server.createobject("adodb.connection")

' Open the connection using our ODBC file DSN
dbFeedback.open("filedsn=Feedback")

' If any of our fields have a single quote, we will
' need to double it to insert it into the database
chrName = replace(request("chrName"), "'", "''")
chrSubject = replace(request("chrSubject"), "'", "''")
txtMessage = replace(request("txtMessage"), "'", "''")

' SQL insert statement to insert the feedback
' data into the database
sql = "execute sp_InsertFeedback '" & _
    chrName & "', '" & _
    request("chrEmail") & "', '" & _
    request("chrRecipient") & "', '" & _
    chrSubject & "', '" & _
    txtMessage & "'"

' Execute the SQL statement
dbFeedback.execute(sql)

' Close the database connection
dbFeedback.Close

%>

</body>

</html>
```

The first thing we do in the script code is declare our variables. Then we open a database connection to the SQL server. The "Feedback" file DSN is utilized to connect to the database.

WARNING You need to have to have an ODBC Data Source Name (DSN) pointing to the database to connect to it. In our code throughout this book, we utilize File DSNs as an easy way to manage our DSNs. But a standard system DSN can be substituted as well with a small VBScript code change.

When inserting data into the SQL database, we have to ensure that any single quotes (')
are doubled up so that SQL will know they are to be inserted versus signifying the end of a

text string. We utilize the Replace function on the name, subject, and message to ensure that all single quotes are replaced with two single quotes ('').

Once we have our data prepared, we are ready to insert it into the database. The sp_Insert-Feedback stored procedure we created earlier is utilized to insert the data. Each of the data elements of the input form is passed to the stored procedures as the parameters that are required.

Finally, it is always good coding practice to ensure that you close out any database connections to free up resources. This is done as the last step in the script code.

Administrative Reporting

We next need to build some kind of reporting functionality so that a site administrator can retrieve feedback data. As we see in later chapters, this kind of reporting can get complicated by adding archiving, searching, and deletion capabilities. For our starter example, we build a simple HTML table formatted report of the feedback data.

Listing 5.6 shows the code for a report generator that lists each feedback entry in a displayed table. The standard page header that we see throughout this book starts out the page. The variables are then declared.

As with the feedback-processing page, a database connection is created and opened. In this case, we create an ADO record set, rsFeedback, that holds the results of our query.

Listing 5.6   AdminFeedback.asp

```
<%@ Language=VBScript %>
<%Option Explicit%>
<%
'*******************************************************
'** AdminFeedback.asp
'**
'** Displays the feedback entries
'*******************************************************
%><HTML>
<HEAD>
</HEAD>
<BODY>

<%

' Declare the variables
Dim dbFeedback          ' database connection
Dim rsFeedback          ' record set
Dim SQL                 ' string
```

```
Dim txtMessage          ' string
Dim dtEntered

' Create an ADO database connection
set dbFeedback = _
   server.createobject("adodb.connection")

' Open the connection using our ODBC file DSN
dbFeedback.open("filedsn=Feedback")

' SQL insert statement to retrieve the
' feedback entries
sql = "execute sp_GetFeedback"

' Execute the SQL statement
set rsFeedback = dbFeedback.execute(sql)

%>

<!- Build a table to display the feedback ->
<table border="1" cellspan="3">

<tr>
   <th>Name</th>
   <th>Email</th>
   <th>Recipient</th>
   <th>Subject</th>
   <th>Date</th>
   <th>Message</th>
</tr>

<%
' Loop through the feedback
do until rsFeedback.eof

txtMessage = rsFeedback("txtMessage")
dtEntered = rsFeedback("dtEntered")

%>

<!- Build a row to display the feedback. ->
<tr>
   <td><%=rsFeedback("chrName")%></td>
   <td><%=rsFeedback("chrEmail")%></td>
   <td><%=rsFeedback("chrRecipient")%></td>
   <td><%=rsFeedback("chrSubject")%></td>
   <td><%=rsFeedback("dtEntered")%></td>
   <td><%=txtMessage%></td>
</tr>

<%
```

```
' Move to the next record
rsFeedback.movenext

' Loop back
loop

%>

</table>
<%

' Close the database connection
dbFeedback.Close

%>
</BODY>
</HTML>
```

To retrieve the feedback data, the sp_GetFeedback stored procedure is utilized. The stored procedure is only returning data and does not need any parameters.

The resulting set of rows is stored in the rsFeedback record set. We can loop through each row in the record set and display the data. A table header is created before we loop through the data. Then with each iteration, a new table row is created and the data displayed. Once the row has been built, the MoveNext function of the record set is utilized to advance to the next row. Once the last row has been processed, the record set is at the end and our Do Loop is completed.

Finally, when the loop is completed, we close out the table and the page. That does it for the scripting of our simple feedback form. Now let's take a look at all of the pages in action.

Testing the Application

To test the application, open a browser and put in the URL for the Web page. In this case, it will be the domain name (such as localhost, if browsing on the same machine) plus the directory structure (such as community/feedback) plus the name of the page. So, for the Feedback.asp example, the URLs could be as shown in Listing 5.7.

Listing 5.7   Sample URLs for the Feedback Application

```
http://localhost/community/feedback/feedback.asp
http://SOMEDOMAIN/feedback/feedback.asp
```

This is dependent upon how you set up your Web server. Once you have the page pulled up, it should look like Figure 5.2.

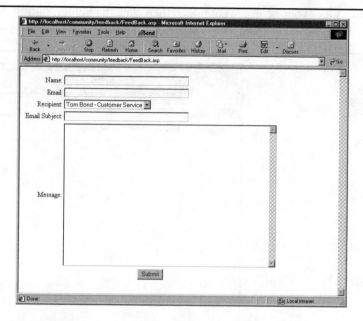

Now we need to enter data into the form by filling in every field with appropriate entries. Figure 5.3 shows a completed sample of the form.

FIGURE 5.3:

The feedback form with entries

Once your fields are complete, then click the Submit button. When you submit the page, the ProcessFeedback.asp page is called and processed. Figure 5.4 shows a sample of the page.

FIGURE 5.4:

The processed feedback page

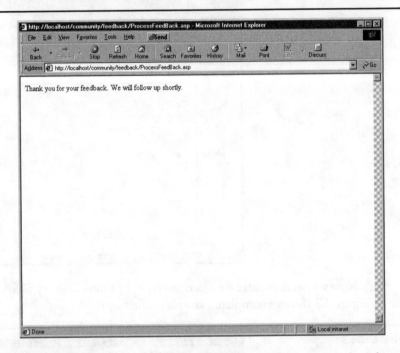

The data has now been entered into our SQL database table. At this stage, make a few more entries with various data so we can see how the information is processed and reported.

We are now ready to test the reporting functionality. We placed the reporting page, Adminfeedback.asp, in the same directory as the other ASP pages.

Securing Administrative Pages

In general, you do not want your administrative pages placed in the same directory as your other user pages. You also want to ensure they are password protected. For this simple example we left everything in the same directory and unprotected. Later in the book we segment the pages and show some security techniques.

Figure 5.5 shows the report of the feedback entries. Each entry is listed in a row with each of the fields displayed. Note that the date field is filled in with the time the entry was made into the database even though it was not entered into the browser. This was accomplished with a default setting for that field and using the SQL GetDate() function.

FIGURE 5.5:

The feedback report

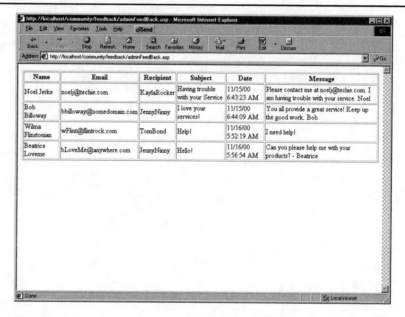

That does it for testing our sample application. As mentioned earlier, we don't have any archiving or deleting functions in the administrative portion. These could be added easily, and later in the book we show techniques to demonstrate this type of functionality.

Summary

Our sample application hits on the key tools we utilize for development—ASP, SQL Server, HTML, and a browser. For a site that needs a simple way to get feedback from the user, this type of form will be more than adequate. One other feature you may want to add to the form is an e-mail notification to the appropriate recipient that they have feedback waiting for them, and a link to a list of feedback for them specifically. Regardless of how you implement it, providing an easy method for feedback to be delivered from your community will be important.

CHAPTER 6

Guest Register

- Guest Registration Basics
- Building the Database
- Building the User Interface
- Building the Management Interface
- Testing the Application

Now we are ready to dive into our first full community application. One of the most important features of a community Web site is the ability for visitors to identify themselves. This can be utilized as the basis of profiling the visitor as well as being the central repository for community member information.

The sample guest register created in this chapter is fairly straightforward in terms of demographic data collection. And, unlike the feedback form, a full administrative interface for the guest register is built out.

This chapter examines the basics of how the guest register is structured. It looks at the underlying database structure and functionality. This chapter also goes through the ASP coding and testing of the application.

Guest Registration Basics

The primary purpose of the guest register is to collect demographic information about the site visitor. In this chapter, we build a sample site called "Authors R Us" that provides a way for readers and authors to connect in a community setting.

The guest register's role in the community is for site visitors to identify themselves and indicate what primary topic areas they are interested in (such as business applications, certifications, and so on.). Our sample application will collect only demographic data and will not require a username and password. It easily could include more data and provide a simple profiling functionality for a password-protected community Web site.

One of the important demonstrations in this chapter is the administrative functionality of the guest register. We go far beyond the simple reporting page in the feedback sample built in Chapter 5. Our guest register allows us to process new registrations, archive registrations, and search and sort registrations.

In addition, error checking is performed on the registration page. We ensure that appropriate fields have been validated and, if not, error messages reported to the user.

Building the Database

As with the feedback application, we need to create a set of database tables and stored procedures to support the guest register. In this case we move beyond a simple one table structure and a couple of stored procedures to two tables and multiple stored procedures.

Designing the Relational Data Structure

Our guest register is designed to store basic name and address type of data, but we also want to collect the primary interests of the registrant as well. To do this properly, we need a lookup table of interest topics that can be selected by the registrant. Thus, we will have two tables with a lookup link combining them.

Figure 6.1 shows the basic structure of the database tables.

FIGURE 6.1:

Guest register database structure

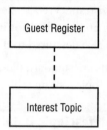

Our primary table is the GuestRegister table. The values for the interest topics that the user can select are stored in the InterestTopic table. The users are allowed to select two interest types. To implement the lookup, two fields in the GuestRegister table store the ID of the interest topic.

Listing 6.1 shows the SQL code to create the GuestRegister. We have our standard identity column, idGuestRegister, that automatically increments and assigns a unique primary key value for each record. Also, be sure and set a default data entered (dtEntered) by using the GetDate() function in SQL Enterprise manager.

Listing 6.1   GuestRegister Database Table

```
CREATE TABLE dbo.GuestRegister (
    idGuestRegister int IDENTITY (1, 1) NOT NULL ,
    chrFirstName varchar (100) NULL ,
    chrLastName varchar (100) NULL ,
    chrAddress varchar (200) NULL ,
    chrCity varchar (150) NULL ,
    chrState varchar (150) NULL ,
    chrProvince varchar (150) NULL ,
    chrCountry varchar (150) NULL ,
    chrZipPostal varchar (20) NULL ,
    chrPhone varchar (25) NULL ,
    chrEmail varchar (100) NULL ,
    intPrimeInterest int NULL ,
    intSecondInterest int NULL ,
    txtComments text NULL ,
    bitProcessed bit NOT NULL CONSTRAINT
```

```
         DF_GuestRegis_bitProcesse1__12 DEFAULT (0),
     dtEntered datetime NULL CONSTRAINT
         DF_GuestRegis_dtEntered_2__12 DEFAULT (getdate())

)
GO
```

Our relational link to the interest topic table is created by the intPrimeInterest and intSecondInterest fields in the table. These contain the IDs of the primary and secondary topics of interest to the site registrant. We also have a field called "bitProcessed" that is utilized to flag a guest registration as processed or not in the administrative interface of our application. Note that this field is also defaulted to 0.

The rest of the fields are standard name and address kinds of information. Next, we need to define the InterestTopic lookup table. Listing 6.2 shows the SQL code to create this table.

Listing 6.2   InterestTopic Database Table

```
CREATE TABLE dbo.InterestTopic (
    idInterestTopic int IDENTITY (1, 1) NOT NULL ,
    chrName varchar (255) NULL
)
GO
```

This table is fairly simple. We have an identity column that provides a unique identifier for each topic of interest, and the chrName field is where the name of the topic is entered. For the purpose of this example, Table 6.1 shows the values with which you want to populate the database.

TABLE 6.1: Data for Populating the InterestTopic Database Table

Identity Value	Topic
1	Certification
2	Computer Science
3	Graphics Software
4	Networking & OS
5	New to Computing
6	Programming
7	Web Development
8	Hardware
9	Internet
10	E-Commerce
11	Business Applications

We are now ready to review our stored procedures utilized to interface with our data tables. We have a series of 10 stored procedures that we create for the functionality needs in this example.

Building the Stored Procedures

The first stored procedure is the sp_InsertGuestRegister, as shown in Listing 6.3. This stored procedure is responsible for inserting a new registration record into the database. The data entered by the user is passed into the stored procedure.

Note that the dtEntered and bitProcessed field values are not passed in, nor inserted into the table. This is because these fields have default values for any new record inserted. Note also that the values for the InterestTopic fields are passed in as well. These will just be the unique ID values and not the actual topic title.

Listing 6.3	sp_InsertGuestRegister Stored Procedure

```
CREATE PROCEDURE sp_InsertGuestRegister

/* Declare the parameters to be
   passed into the stored procedure */
@chrFirstName varchar(255),
@chrLastname varchar(255),
@chrAddress varchar(255),
@chrCity varchar(255),
@chrState varchar(255),
@chrProvince varchar(255),
@chrZipPostal varchar(255),
@chrPhone varchar(255),
@chrEmail varchar(255),
@intPrimeInterest int,
@intSecondInterest int,
@txtComments text

AS

/* Build the SQL Insert statement
   to add the new data */
insert into guestregister(
    chrFirstName, chrLastname, chrAddress,
    chrCity, chrState, chrProvince,
    chrZipPostal, chrPhone, chrEmail,
    intPrimeInterest, intSecondInterest,
     txtComments)
values (
    @chrFirstName, @chrLastName, @chrAddress,
    @chrCity, @chrState, @chrProvince,
    @chrZipPostal, @chrPhone, @chrEmail,
```

```
      @intPrimeInterest, @intSecondInterest,
        @txtComments)
GO
```

Our next three stored procedures all relate to the processing of registrations. With the bitProcesses field, we are differentiating between registrations that have been viewed and processes in some fashion (for example, printed out or reviewed) and those that are newly entered into the database.

The first stored procedure, sp_ProcessRegistrations shown in Listing 6.4, updates all of the bitProcessed fields in the database to a value of "1" so that all are flagged as processed. This is initiated when any new registrations are processed by the administrative user.

Listing 6.4   sp_ProcessRegistrations Stored Procedure

```
CREATE PROCEDURE sp_ProcessRegistrations

/* Declare our parameters */
@idRegistration int

AS

/* Build an update statement to update the
   bitProcessed parameter to 1 based on the
   ID of the registration. Note that ALL
   registration IDs smaller than the one
   passed in will be set to 1. */
update guestregister set bitProcessed = 1
where idGuestRegister <= @idRegistration
GO
```

Our second stored procedure, sp_RetrieveAllRegistrations shown in Listing 6.5, is straightforward and returns all registrations in the database. sp_RetrieveUnProcRegistrations, shown in Listing 6.6, retrieves all registrations where the bitProcessed field is set to 0. This returns any new entries into the database since the last time new entries were processed.

Listing 6.5   sp_RetrieveAllRegistrations Stored Procedure

```
CREATE PROCEDURE sp_RetrieveAllRegistrations AS

/* Retrieve all registrations */
select * from GuestRegister
GO
```

Listing 6.6   **sp_RetrieveUnProcRegistrations Stored Procedure**

```
CREATE PROCEDURE sp_RetrieveUnProcRegistrations AS

/* Retrieve all registrations that are un
   processed by checking the bitProcessed
   field */
select * from guestregister where bitProcessed = 0
GO
```

The next set of stored procedures is utilized for searching the registrations database. We want to provide a rich set of registration search features to make it easy to find specific entries.

The first stored procedure, sp_SearchByDateRange shown in Listing 6.7, returns all matching records that are inserted into the database in the given date range. Note that the start and end dates are passed in as parameters to the stored procedure.

Listing 6.7   **sp_SearchByDateRange Stored Procedure**

```
CREATE PROCEDURE sp_SearchByDateRange

/* Declare our parameters for the stored
   procedure */
@begindate datetime,
@enddate datetime

AS

/* Build a SQL statement to retrieve all the
   registrations in the given date range. */
select * from guestregister
where dtEntered >= @begindate and
    dtEntered <= @enddate
GO
```

Next, we have a stored procedure, shown in Listing 6.8, that allows us to retrieve registrations by e-mail address. This can be valuable when the administrator needs to find a registration based on an e-mail they have received. The sp_SearchByEmail stored procedure takes one parameter, which is the e-mail address. Note that only part of an e-mail address has to be passed in. The query uses the "like" SQL function to find addresses that contain text in the @e-mail variable. Thus, you could search on "noelj" and get the address "noelj@techie.com" returned.

Listing 6.8   **sp_SearchByEmail Stored Procedure**

```
CREATE PROCEDURE sp_SearchByEmail

/* Declare the parameters to be passed in */
@email varchar

AS

/* Retrieve the registration where the email
   contains the parameter passed in. */
select * from guestregister
where chrEmail like '%' + @email + '%'
GO
```

Finally, we have a stored procedure, sp_SearchByInterestTopic shown in Listing 6.9, that retrieves all registrations by the selected interest topics. This can be especially useful if the administrator is interested in sending out a mailing or survey to people with selected interest, or is simply wanting to analyze people's interests. The ID of the topic is passed in to the stored procedure. Then both the intPrimeInterest and intSecondInterest fields are searched to find matches.

Listing 6.9   **sp_SearchByInterestTopic Stored Procedure**

```
CREATE PROCEDURE sp_SearchByInterestTopic

/* Declare the parameters to be passed in */
@idInterest int

AS

/* Build a SQL statement that checks for registrations
   that have as either the primary or secondary
   interest the ID passed in. */
select * from guestregister
where intPrimeInterest = @idInterest or
   intSecondInterest = @idInterest
GO
```

The last search stored procedure provides a method for searching by last name. As with the e-mail search stored procedure, this query utilizes the SQL "like" function to find matches to the passed in text. For example, you could search for "John" and get all the "Johnsons" returned. The text of the sp_SearchByLastName stored procedure is shown in Listing 6.10.

Listing 6.10   sp_SearchByLastName Stored Procedure

```
CREATE PROCEDURE sp_SearchByLastName

/* Declare the parameters to be passed in */
@name varchar

AS

/* Retrieve registrations where the last name
   contains the data passed in. */
select * from guestregister
where chrLastName like '%' + @name + '%'
GO
```

Our last two stored procedures work with the InterestTopic table. The first stored procedure, sp_RetrieveInterestTopicById shown in Listing 6.11, retrieves a topic specified by a passed in ID and the selected value is returned. The second stored procedure, sp_RetrieveInterestTopics shown in Listing 6.12, returns all of the current topics in the table.

Listing 6.11   sp_RetrieveInterestTopicByID Stored Procedure

```
CREATE PROCEDURE sp_RetrieveInterestTopicByID

/* Declare the parameters for the
   stored procedure */
@idInterestTopic int

AS

/* SQL statement to retrieve the interest topic
   based on the ID passed in. */
select * from InterestTopic

where idInterestTopic = @idInterestTopic
GO
```

Listing 6.12   sp_RetrieveInterestTopics Stored Procedure

```
CREATE PROCEDURE sp_RetrieveInterestTopics AS

/* Retrieve all interest topics in the table
   and order them by name */
select * from InterestTopic order by chrName
GO
```

That does it for building the data side of our guest registration application. We now need to put the data structure and stored procedures into use with the ASP scripting interface.

Building the User Interface

The user interface for our guest register is fairly straightforward. It consists of a data entry form and a processing page. Unlike our feedback application demonstrated in the last chapter, this application has extensive data validation and user feedback.

Let's first take a look at the data entry form. Listings 6.13 through 6.15 show the code for the page. As appropriate, the page starts out with the correct header information. The core of the form consist of the table formatting with the data entry fields for name, address, city, state, zip code, phone, e-mail, and comments.

Listing 6.13   GuestRegister.asp

```
<%@ Language=VBScript %>
<% Option Explicit %>

<HTML>
<HEAD>
<%
'*****************************************************
'** GuestRegister.asp
'**
'** Input form for a new guest registration
'*****************************************************
%>
</HEAD>
<BODY>
<%

' Declare variables
Dim chrCountry            ' String
Dim dbGuestRegister       ' Database Connection
Dim rsGuestRegister       ' Record Set
Dim SQL                   ' String
Dim Selected              ' String

%>
<BR><BR>

<center>

<!- Setup the Header ->
<font size="4" color="blue"><b>
Author's R Us - Guest Register
</b></font>
```

Our page posts to the ProcessGuestRegister.asp page, as shown in Listing 6.13. That page processes the results and provides data validation. Note that we are using session variables in each of the data entry fields to set the value. These session variables are set if there is a problem in validating the data entered by the user. Thus, the user does not have to reenter data already typed into these fields when they return to make the corrections.

Listing 6.14   GuestRegister.asp continued

```
<!- Start the form that will post to the
    ProcessGuestRegister.asp page.
->
<form method="post" action="ProcessGuestRegister.asp">

<!- Next the table starts that will layout the
    data entry form
->
<table border=0>

<!- First Name ->
<tr>
 <td align="right">First Name:</td>
 <!- Input field for the first name ->
 <td><input type="text"
         value="<%=session("chrFirstName")%>"
          name="chrFirstName"
         size="50">
 </td>
</tr>

<!- Last Name ->
<tr>
 <td align="right">Last Name:</td>
 <!- Input field for the last name ->
 <td><input type="text"
         value="<%=session("chrLastName")%>"
         name="chrLastName"
         size="50">
 </td>
</tr>

<!- Address ->
<tr>
 <td align="right">Address:</td>
 <!- Input field for the address ->
 <td><input type="text"
         value="<%=session("chrAddress")%>"
         name="chrAddress"
         size="50">
 </td>
```

```
 </tr>

<!- City->
<tr>
 <td align="right">City:</td>
 <!- Input field for the city ->
 <td><input type="text"
            value="<%=session("chrCity")%>"
            name="chrCity"
            size="50">
 </td>
</tr>

<!- State ->
<tr>
 <td align="right">State:</td>
 <!- Input field for the state ->
 <td><input type="text"
            value="<%=session("chrState")%>"
            name="chrState"
            size="2">
 </td>
</tr>

<!- Province for International ->
<tr>
 <td align="right">Province:</td>
 <!- Input field for Province ->
 <td><input type="text"
            value="<%=session("chrProvince")%>"
            name="chrProvince"
            size="50"></td>
</tr>

<!- Country ->
<tr>
 <td align="right">Country:</td>
 <%
 ' Check to see if we are entering a
 ' country for the first time. If so
 ' then default to USA.
 if session("chrCountry") = "" then
   chrCountry = "USA"
 end if
 %>
 <!- Input field for country ->
 <td><input type="text" value="<%=chrCountry%>"
            name="chrCountry" size="50">
 </td>
</tr>
```

```
<!- Zip/Postal Code ->
<tr>
 <td align="right">Zip/Postal Code:</td>
 <!- Input field for the zip/postal code ->
 <td><input type="text"
            value="<%=session("chrZipPostal")%>"
            name="chrZipPostal">
 </td>
</tr>

<!- Phone Number ->
<tr>
 <td align="right">Phone:</td>
 <!- Input field for the phone number ->
 <td><input type="text" value="<%=session("chrPhone")%>"
            name="chrPhone">
 </td>
</tr>

<!- Email Address ->
<tr>
 <td align="right">Email Address:</td>
 <!- Input field for the email address ->
 <td><input type="text" value="<%=session("chrEmail")%>"
        name="chrEmail" size="50">
 </td>
</tr>
```

To populate the select input boxes with the primary interest topics, we have to create a new database connection and query the data from the InterestTopic table. To do this, the sp_RetrieveInterestTopics stored procedure is utilized.

Session Variables

In standard Web technology, there is no simple way of remembering user "state" data between Web pages. This would include data about what the user is doing that, in a typical client/server application, would be stored in global variables. For example, if the shopper enters in a zip code and then starts browsing through the rest of the site, we would have to do a lot of work to track the data on the URL or through the use of hidden HTML elements. Fortunately, in IIS/ASP, Microsoft built in the Session variable capability. This allows us to save data in a variable that stays active for the user's entire visit to the Web site. All we do is set the variable on one page and then retrieve the value as needed on subsequent pages. Note that the sessions have a time out setting that is defaulted to 30 minutes. In reality, we never know when the visitor has left the site, so we want the session data to disappear if there is no activity for that session for the specified timeout period.

We start the loop to list the interest topics. If users are coming back to the page because of an error, we need to be able to default the HTML select box back to their original selection. This is done by checking the session variable against the current row in the record set. If they match, then the Selected variable is set to a value of "selected" and that entry in the select box will be set at the default. The same process is followed for the secondary interest as well.

Listing 6.15   GuestRegister.asp continued

```
<!- Primary Topic Interest ->
<tr>
 <td align="right">Primary Topic Interest:</td>
 <!- Input field for the primary topic interest ->
 <td>

<%

' Create an ADO database connection
set dbGuestRegister = _
   server.createobject("adodb.connection")

' Create a record set
set rsGuestRegister = _
   server.CreateObject("adodb.recordset")

' Open the connection using our ODBC file DSN
dbGuestRegister.open("filedsn=GuestRegister")

' Retrieve the list of interest topics
sql = "execute sp_RetrieveInterestTopics"

' Execute the SQL statement
set rsGuestRegister = dbGuestRegister.execute(sql)

%>

   <!- Start the select list ->
   <select name="intPrimeInterest">

<%

' Loop through the list
do until rsGuestRegister.EOF

   ' Check to see if a previous interest topic
   ' was selected (when the user is kicked back to
   ' to an error).
   if int(session("intPrimeInterest")) = _
     rsGuestRegister("idInterestTopic") then
```

```
              ' If the current topic was selected then set
              ' the selected variable
              selected = "selected"
         else
              ' Clear the variable
              selected = ""
         end if

%>
     <!- Build the option. Note the selected variable
         is output. When set to "selected" that option
         will be the default.  ->
     <option value="<%=rsGuestRegister("idInterestTopic")%>"
     <%=selected%>><%=rsGuestRegister("chrName")%>
<%

     ' Move to the next row
     rsGuestRegister.movenext

' Loop back
loop
%>
 </select>

 </td>
</tr>

<!- Secondary Topic Interest ->
<tr>
 <td align="right">Secondary Topic Interest:</td>
 <td>

 <select name="intSecondInterest">

<%

' Move to the beginning of the record set to loop
' again
rsGuestRegister.MoveFirst

' Logic follows the same as the primary interest topic
do until rsGuestRegister.EOF

    if int(session("intSecondInterest")) = _
       rsGuestRegister("idInterestTopic") then

       selected = "selected"
    else
       selected = ""
    end if
```

```
%>

    <option value="<%=rsGuestRegister("idInterestTopic")%>"
          <%=selected%>><%=rsGuestRegister("chrName")%>
<%

    rsGuestRegister.movenext

loop

dbGuestRegister.Close

%>

 </select>

 </td>
</tr>

<!- Comments ->
<tr>
 <td align="right">Comments:</td>
 <!- Input field for the email address ->
 <td><textarea name="txtComments"
            cols="50"
             rows="5"><%=session("txtComments")%>
     </textarea>
 </td>
</tr>

<!- Submit ->
<tr>
 <td colspan="2" align="center">
 <input type="submit" value="Submit" name="submit">
 </td>
</tr>

</table>

</center>

<!- Closing tag for the end of the form ->
</form>

</BODY>
</HTML>
```

Finally, the page closes out with the appropriate closing tags for the table, form, and page. We are now ready to review the processing page.

Listings 6.16 through 6.19 show the code for ProcessGuestRegister.asp. This page is broken up into three major sections—page set up, data validation, and data insertion. The first section is the header for the page and the declaration of variables, as shown in Listing 6.16. We need to be able to retrieve all of the input fields from the GuestRegister.asp page and process them for validation.

Listing 6.16   ProcessGuestRegister.asp

```
<%@ Language=VBScript %>
<%Option Explicit%>

<HTML>
<head>
<%
'*****************************************************
'** ProcessGuestRegister.asp
'**
'** Verifies the data enter for the new
'** registration. It then reports errors or
'** inserts the data.
'*****************************************************
%>
</head>
<BODY BGCOLOR="WHITE">

<%

' Declare the variables
Dim chrFirstName       ' string
Dim chrLastName        ' string
Dim chrAddress         ' string
Dim chrCity            ' string
Dim chrState           ' string
Dim chrProvince        ' string
Dim chrZipPostal       ' string
Dim chrPhone           ' string
Dim chrEmail           ' string
Dim intPrimeInterest   ' integer
Dim intSecondInterest  ' integer
Dim txtComments        ' comments
Dim strError           ' string
Dim dbInterests        ' database connection
Dim rsInterests        ' record set
Dim SQL                ' string
Dim dbGuestRegister    ' database connection
Dim rsGuestRegister    ' record set

' Retrieve all of the data that the user entered.
chrFirstName = request("chrFirstName")
```

```
chrLastName = Request("chrLastName")
chrAddress = Request("chrAddress")
chrCity = Request("chrCity")
chrState = Request("chrState")
chrProvince = request("chrProvince")
chrZipPostal = Request("chrZipPostal")
chrPhone = Request("chrPhone")
chrEmail = Request("chrEmail")
intPrimeInterest = Request("intPrimeInterest")
intSecondInterest = Request("intSecondInterest")
txtComments = Request("txtComments")
```

Next, we need to validate the data entered by the user by checking the name fields and e-mail addresses. If a check fails, we need to set a variable, *strError*, to display the appropriate error message.

NOTE   Additional validation could be done on any fields deemed required or important. You can even get as detailed as doing a city/zip code validity check with an appropriate zip code lookup database.

The e-mail address validation not only checks to see if an address was entered, but we also check to ensure that an "@" symbol and a "." were entered appropriately.

If the *strError* variable is not NULL, then the error message is displayed in red. This is followed by a message indicating that the user needs to go back to the Guest Register page and correct any errors.

TIP   To build an even more sophisticated error engine, we could flag which fields were the problem fields using session variables. By doing this on the GuestRegister.asp page, we could highlight the problem fields to provide support feedback to the user. If the e-mail address was invalid on the GuestRegister.asp page, that field might be displayed in bold-red.

Listing 6.17   ProcessGuestRegister.asp continued

```
' Check to see if the first name was entered.
if chrFirstName = "" then

    ' Give an error if not.
    strError = "You did not enter in your first name.<BR>"

end if

' Check to see if a last name was entered.
if chrLastName = "" then
```

```
    strError = strError & _
        "You did not enter in your last name.<BR>"

end if

' Check to see if a valid email address was entered.
if chrEmail <> "" then

    ' Check for @ symbol and a period in the
    ' email address
    if instr(1, chrEmail, "@") = 0 or _
      instr(1, chrEmail, ".") = 0 then

    strError = strError & _
        "You did not enter in a valid email address.<BR>"

    end if

else

    strError = strError & _
        "You did not enter in your email address.<BR>"

end if


' Now we check to see if there are any errors.
if strError <> "" then

%>

    <!- Note the error ->
    <B><font color="red">
        There is an error in your guest registration:<BR><BR>
    </b></font>

<%

    ' Write out the error messages
    Response.Write strError

%>

<!- Link back to the registration page ->
<BR>
Click <a href="GuestRegister.asp">here</a> to update.

<%

' Set session variables so the guest register form can be
' re-populated
```

```
session("chrFirstName") = chrFirstName
session("chrLastName") = chrLastName
session("chrAddress") = chrAddress
session("chrCity") = chrCity
session("chrState") = chrState
session("chrProvince") = chrProvince
session("chrZipPostal") = chrZipPostal
session("chrPhone") = chrPhone
session("chrEmail") = chrEmail
session("intPrimeInterest") = intPrimeInterest
session("intSecondInterest") = intSecondInterest
session("txtComments") = txtComments

else

%>
```

If there was no error in the data validation, then we are ready to process the data and insert it into the database. As a way of providing feedback to the user, we display the entries and thank the user. This provides a nice, reinforcing visual to the user to reassure them the data was collected.

This display includes showing the interest topics they selected. This can only be done by querying the InterestTopic table and retrieving the name of the topic based on the ID. This is done using the sp_RetrieveInterestTopicByID stored procedure.

Listing 6.18   ProcessGuestRegister.asp continued

```
<!- Thank the customer for the entry ->
<font size="4" color="blue">
Thank you for your entry!</font>

<!- Redisplay the data entered into the registration ->
<BR><BR>
<Table>

<!- Show a combined name ->
<tr><td align="right"><B>Name:</b></td>
<td><i>
    <% = chrFirstName & " " & chrLastName %></i>
</td></tr>

<!- Show the address, phone, and email ->
<tr><td align="right"><B>Address:</b></td>
<td><i> <% = chrAddress %></i></td></tr>

<tr><td align="right"><B>City:</b></td>
<td><i> <% = chrCity %></i></td></tr>
```

```
<tr><td align="right"><B>State:</b></td>
<td><i> <% = chrState %></i></td></tr>

<tr><td align="right"><B>Zip Code:</b></td>
<td><i> <% = chrZipPostal %></i></td></tr>

<tr><td align="right"><B>Phone:</b></td
><td><i> <% = chrPhone %></i></td></tr>

<tr><td align="right"><B>Email:</b></td>
<td><i> <% = chrEmail %></i></td></tr>

<%

' Create an ADO database connection
set dbInterests = _
   server.createobject("adodb.connection")

' Create a record set
set rsInterests = _
   server.CreateObject("adodb.recordset")

' Open the connection using our ODBC file DSN
dbInterests.open("filedsn=GuestRegister")

' Retrieve the name of the primary interest
sql = "execute sp_RetrieveInterestTopicByID " & _
intPrimeInterest

' Execute the SQL statement
set rsInterests = dbInterests.execute(sql)

%>

<!- Display the primary interest ->
<tr><td align="right"><B>Primary Interest Topic:
   </b></td>
<td><i> <% = rsInterests("chrName") %></i></td></tr>

<%

' Get the second interest name
sql = "execute sp_RetrieveInterestTopicByID " & _
   intSecondInterest

' Execute the SQL statement
set rsInterests = dbInterests.execute(sql)

%>
```

```
<!- Display the second interest ->
<tr><td align="right"><B>Secondary Interest Topic:
   </b></td>
<td><i> <% = rsInterests("chrName") %></i></td></tr>

<!- Display the comments ->
<tr><td align="right"><B>Comments:</b></td>
<td><i> <% = txtComments %></i></td></tr>

</table>

<%

' Close the database connection.
dbInterests.Close
```

We first need to check for any fields where an apostrophe (') could be entered by the user and ensure the apostrophe is doubled up for insertion into the data table.

Once we have checked for apostrophes, we are ready to utilize the sp_InsertGuestRegister stored procedure to insert the registration into the database. Each of the fields on the guest registration form is utilized as the parameters for the stored procedure.

Listing 6.19   ProcessGuestRegister.asp continued

```
' Create an ADO database connection
set dbGuestRegister = _
   server.createobject("adodb.connection")

' Open the connection using our ODBC file DSN
dbGuestRegister.open("filedsn=GuestRegister")

' If any of our fields have a single quote, we will
' need to double it to insert it into the database
chrFirstName = replace(chrFirstName, "'", "''")
chrLastName = replace(chrLastName, "'", "''")
chrAddress = replace(chrAddress, "'", "''")
chrCity = replace(chrCity, "'", "''")
chrProvince = replace(chrProvince, "'", "''")
txtComments = replace(txtComments, "'", "''")

' SQL insert statement to insert the registration
' data into the database
sql = "execute sp_InsertGuestRegister '" & _
    chrFirstName & "', '" & _
    chrLastName & "', '" & _
    chrAddress & "', '" & _
    chrCity & "', '" & _
    chrState & "', '" & _
```

```
        chrProvince & "', '" & _
        chrZipPostal & "', '" & _
        chrPhone & "', '" & _
        chrEmail & "', " & _
        intPrimeInterest & ", " & _
        intSecondInterest & ", '" & _
        txtComments & "'"

    ' Execute the SQL statement
    dbGuestRegister.execute(sql)

    ' Close the database connection
    dbGuestRegister.Close

end if

%>

</body>

</html>
```

Once the data is inserted, the database connections are closed and the page is finished. That takes care of the user end of our guest register. We have enhanced the process demonstrated by the feedback functionality in the last chapter with data validation and better user management. In the next section we see that a much more sophisticated administrative interface can be built, rather than the simple report in the feedback application.

Building the Management Interface

The management interface for our guest register application consists of three pages and six primary functions. The goal is to provide a number of ways for a site administrator to process and find registrations.

Table 6.2 outlines the primary functions provided in the management interface.

TABLE 6.2: Management Functions

Function	Description
Process New Registrations	Retrieves all new registrations posted
Retrieve All Registrations	Retrieves all registrations in the database
Last Name Search	Searches by last name
Email Address Search	Searches by email address

Continued on next page

TABLE 6.2 CONTINUED: Management Functions

Function	Description
Date Range Search	Searches by date range
Interest Area Topic Search	Searches by topic of interest

ProcessGuestRegisterAdmin.asp, the first page in our management interface, provides a menu listing of management options. Listings 6.20 through 6.22 show the code for the page.

Listing 6.20   GuestRegisterAdmin.asp

```
<%@ Language=VBScript %>
<% Option Explicit %>
<HTML>
<HEAD>
<%
'*********************************************************
'** GuestRegisterAdmin.asp
'**
'** Provides options for reporting registrations
'*********************************************************
%>
</HEAD>
<BODY>

<!-- Header ->
<font color="blue">
<center><h1>Guest Register Administration</h1></center>
</font>

<%

' Declare Variables
Dim dbGuestRegister      ' Database Object
Dim rsGuestRegister      ' Record Set Object
Dim SQL                  ' String
Dim Selected             ' String

%>
```

After the basic header and variable declarations, we are ready to build the table that will display the administrative options. All of the links and forms connect to the GuestRegister-Report.asp page. With each option, an ID is passed on the URL or as a hidden form variable to identify the type of report to be displayed since one page handles all of the various reporting options.

Listing 6.21   GuestRegisterAdmin.asp continued

```
<B>Please make your selection:</b><BR><BR>

<!- Build table of report options ->
<table border="1" cellpadding="5" cellspacing="5">

<!- Option for seeing new registrations ->
<tr>
   <td align="right"><b>New Registrations</b></td>
   <td valign="center">
      <a href="guestregisterreport.asp?id=1">Process</a>
   </td>
</tr>

<!- Option for reporting all registrations ->
<tr>
      <td align="right"><b>All Registrations</b></td>
   <td valign="center">
      <a href="guestregisterreport.asp?id=2">Retrieve</a>
   </td>
</tr>

<!- Option for searching by last name ->
<tr>
   <td align="right"><B>Search by Last Name</b></td>
   <td valign="center">
      <form method="post" ↵
      action="guestregisterreport.asp?id=3">
      <input type="text" value="" name="name">
      <input type="submit" value="Submit" name="submit">
      </form>
   </td>
</tr>

<!- Option for searching by email address ->
<tr>
      <td align="right"><B>Search by Email Address</b></td>
      <td>
      <form method="post" ↵
      action="guestregisterreport.asp?id=4">
      <input type="text" value="" name="email">
      <input type="submit" value="Submit" name="submit">
      </form>
   </td>
</tr>

<!- Option for searching by date range ->
<tr>
   <td align="right"><B>Search by Date Range</b></td>
```

```
<td>
  <form method="post" ⏎
   action="guestregisterreport.asp?id=5">
   Beginning Date:<input type="text" value=""
       name="dtBegin">
   Ending Date:<input type="text" value="" name="dtEnd">
   <input type="submit" value="Submit" name="submit">
   </form>
  </td>
</tr>
```

For the topic reporting we need to retrieve a list of topics in the database. A database connection is opened to retrieve all of the entries in the InterestTopic table and list them for searching. Note that we don't differentiate between primary and secondary interest.

Listing 6.22   GuestRegisterAdmin.asp continued

```
<!- Option for searching by interest topic ->
<tr>
    <td align="right"><B>Search by Interest Area</b></td>
    <td>
        <form method="post" ⏎
        action="guestregisterreport.asp?id=6">
        Topic:
        <%

        ' Create an ADO database connection
        set dbGuestRegister = _
            server.createobject("adodb.connection")

        ' Create record set
        set rsGuestRegister = _
            server.CreateObject("adodb.recordset")

        ' Open the connection using our ODBC file DSN
        dbGuestRegister.open("filedsn=GuestRegister")

        ' Retrieve all interest topics
        sql = "execute sp_RetrieveInterestTopics"

        ' Execute the SQL statement
        set rsGuestRegister = dbGuestRegister.execute(sql)

        %>

        <!- Build select box ->
        <select name="intInterest">
```

```
<%

    ' Loop through registrations
    do until rsGuestRegister.EOF

%>

    <!- Build option ->
    <option ⌐
value="<%=rsGuestRegister("idInterestTopic")%>"> ⌐
    <%=rsGuestRegister("chrName")%>

<%

    ' Move to the next record
    rsGuestRegister.movenext

    ' Loop back
    loop

    ' Close the database connection
    dbGuestRegister.Close

%>
    </select>
    <input type="submit" value="Submit" name="submit">
    </form>
</td>
</tr>
</table>

</BODY>
</HTML>
```

Finally the page is closed out and all database connections are closed. Now we are ready to move on to the registrations reporting.

The GuestRegisterReport.asp page is a complex page that encompasses all of the different reports as well as provides a three-column reporting format. The code for the page is shown in Listings 6.23 through 6.28.

Listing 6.23   GuestRegisterReport.asp

```
<%@ Language=VBScript %>
<% Option Explicit %>

<HTML>
<HEAD>
```

```
<%
'*******************************************************
'** GuestRegisterReport.asp
'**
'** Process registration report requests
'*******************************************************
%>
</HEAD>
<BODY>

<%

' Declare Variables
Dim dbGuestRegister      ' Database connection
Dim dbInterests          ' Database connection
Dim rsGuestRegister      ' Record set
Dim rsInterests          ' Record set
Dim id                   ' integer
Dim SQL                  ' string
Dim idRegistration       ' integer
Dim NoResultsFlag        ' Integer
Dim idGuestRegister1     ' Integer
Dim Name1                ' string
Dim Address1             ' string
Dim Location1            ' string
Dim Phone1               ' string
Dim Email1               ' string
Dim txtComments1         ' string
Dim PrimeInterest1       ' string
Dim SecondInterest1      ' string
Dim dtEntered1           ' datetime
Dim idGuestRegister2     ' integer
Dim Name2                ' string
Dim Address2             ' string
Dim Location2            ' string
Dim Phone2               ' string
Dim Email2               ' string
Dim txtComments2         ' string
Dim PrimeInterest2       ' string
Dim SecondInterest2      ' string
Dim dtEntered2           ' datetime
Dim idGuestRegister3     ' integer
Dim Name3                ' string
Dim Address3             ' string
Dim Location3            ' string
Dim Phone3               ' string
Dim Email3               ' string
Dim txtComments3         ' string
Dim PrimeInterest3       ' string
Dim SecondInterest3      ' string
Dim dtEntered3           ' datetime
```

The first thing we do in the page is open up the appropriate database connections that are utilized for the reporting. We also have to determine the type of report that the user selected. The "ID" value is read from the URL.

Listing 6.24   GuestRegisterReport.asp continued

```
' Create an ADO database connection
set dbGuestRegister = _
   server.createobject("adodb.connection")

' Create record set
set rsGuestRegister = _
   server.CreateObject("adodb.recordset")

' Open the connection using our ODBC file DSN
dbGuestRegister.open("filedsn=GuestRegister")

' Create an ADO database connection
set dbInterests = _
   server.createobject("adodb.connection")

' Create record set
set rsInterests = _
   server.CreateObject("adodb.recordset")

' Open the connection using our ODBC file DSN
dbInterests.open("filedsn=GuestRegister")

' Retrieve the report identifier
id = Request("id")
```

Based on the ID selected, we can build the appropriate SQL statement. In each case, we call one of our stored procedures created earlier. And, when appropriate, we retrieve the user input values on the administrative page.

Once the SQL statement is created, execute the query to retrieve the results. Note that we check to see if we are processing new entries. If there are no new entries, we do not want to show a link to clear them.

Listing 6.25   GuestRegisterReport.asp continued

```
' Execute select statement on the report type to
' build the appropriate query.
select case id

    ' Unprocessed registrations report
    case 1
```

```
                sql = "execute sp_RetrieveUnProcRegistrations"

        ' All registrations report
        case 2
            sql = "execute sp_RetrieveAllRegistrations"

        ' Search for registrations by last name
        case 3
            sql = "execute sp_SearchByLastName '" & _
                request("name") & "'"

        ' Search by email address
        case 4
            sql = "execute sp_SearchByEmail '" & _
                request("email") & "'"

        ' Search by date range
        case 5
            sql = "execute sp_SearchByDateRange '" & _
                request("dtBegin") & "', '" & _
                request("dtEnd") & "'"

        ' Search by interest topic
        case 6
            sql = "execute sp_SearchByInterestTopic " & _
                request("intInterest")

    end select

    ' Execute the statement and retrieve the record set
    set rsGuestRegister = dbGuestRegister.Execute(sql)

    ' Check to see if we are processing new registrations
    if id = 1 then

        ' If nothing is returned then later on the page we
        ' do not want to give the user an option to clear
        ' the unprocessed registrations (since there aren't
        ' any).
        if rsGuestRegister.EOF = true then NoResultsFlag = 1

    end if


%>
```

We are now ready to start the display of the results. A table is started that structures the output. Perform some initial checking to see if we have any registrations to display; if not, then indicate that to the user.

If there are registrations, begin to loop through the data. We have a challenge in presenting our data, we cannot simply loop and display row upon row if we are going to have three registrations per row in three columns. We have to retrieve all three columns of data before looping to the next row.

In essence, do this by moving to each subsequent row and storing the data into variables. The data is rolled up into appropriate variables, such as name and location. For the topics in which the registrant was interested, we have to query the InterestTopic table to get the text name of the topic. The e-mail address is also built into a clickable link.

We also have to be careful that with each retrieval, we are not at the end of the record set and cause a scripting error. If we are at the end of the record set, then blank entries are built for the variables.

Listing 6.26   GuestRegisterReport.asp continued

```
<!- Start the table to display the registrations ->
<Table border="1" cellpadding="2" cellspacing="2">

<%

    ' Check to see if no registrations are returned
    if rsGuestRegister.EOF then

        ' If so, then write an appropriate message
        Response.Write "No registrations to report."

    else

    ' Loop through the regostrations
    do until rsGuestRegister.eof

    ' Retrieve all the data fields
    txtComments1 = rsGuestRegister("txtComments")
    idGuestRegister1 = _
        rsGuestRegister("idGuestRegister")

    idRegistration = rsGuestRegister("idGuestRegister")

    ' Build a combined name field
    Name1 = rsGuestRegister("chrFirstName") & " " & _
        rsGuestRegister("chrLastName")

    Address1 = rsGuestRegister("chrAddress")

    ' Build a combined second address line field
    ' Note we handle differently for US and non-US
    ' entries
```

```
if rsGuestRegister("chrState") = "" then
    Location1 = rsGuestRegister("chrCity") & ", " & _
        rsGuestRegister("chrState") & " " & _
        rsGuestRegister("chrZipPostal")
else
    Location1 = rsGuestRegister("chrCity") & ", " & _
        rsGuestRegister("chrProvince") & " " & _
        rsGuestRegister("chrZipPostal") & " " & _
        rsGuestRegister("chrCountry")
end if

Phone1 = rsGuestRegister("chrPhone")

' Retrieve the email address and build a mailto
' link to the address so they can be easily emailed
Email1 = "<a href=""mailto:" & _
    rsGuestRegister("chrEmail") & """>" & _
    rsGuestRegister("chrEmail") & "</a>"

' Execute the stored procedure to retrieve
' an interest topic by ID
sql = "execute sp_RetrieveInterestTopicByID " & _
    rsGuestRegister("intPrimeInterest")

' Execute the SQL statement
set rsInterests = dbInterests.execute(sql)

' Get the primary interest topic name
PrimeInterest1 = rsInterests("chrName")

' Execute the stored procedure again
sql = "execute sp_RetrieveInterestTopicByID " & _
    rsGuestRegister("intSecondInterest")

' Execute the SQL statement
set rsInterests = dbInterests.execute(sql)

' Get the second interest topic
SecondInterest1 = rsInterests("chrName")

' Get the date the entry was made
dtEntered1 = rsGuestRegister("dtEntered")

'*****************************************************
' Retrieve second report column
'*****************************************************

' Move to the next record
rsGuestRegister.MoveNext

' Ensure we are not at the end of the record set
```

```
if not rsGuestRegister.eof then

    ' Retrieve the data elements the same as above

    txtComments2 = rsGuestRegister("txtComments")
    idGuestRegister2 = _
        rsGuestRegister("idGuestRegister")

    idRegistration = rsGuestRegister("idGuestRegister")

    Name2 = rsGuestRegister("chrFirstName") & " " & _
        rsGuestRegister("chrLastName")

    Address2 = rsGuestRegister("chrAddress")

    if rsGuestRegister("chrState") = "" then
        Location2 = rsGuestRegister("chrCity") & _
            ", " & rsGuestRegister("ChrState") & _
            " " & rsGuestRegister("chrZipPostal")
    else
        Location2 = rsGuestRegister("chrCity") & ", " & _
            rsGuestRegister("chrProvince") & " " & _
            rsGuestRegister("chrZipPostal") & " " & _
            rsGuestRegister("chrCountry")
    end if

    Phone2 = rsGuestRegister("chrPhone")

    Email2 = "<a href=""mailto:" & _
        rsGuestRegister("chrEmail") & _
        """>" & rsGuestRegister("chrEmail") & "</a>"

    sql = "execute sp_RetrieveInterestTopicByID " & _
        rsGuestRegister("intPrimeInterest")

    ' Execute the SQL statement
    set rsInterests = dbInterests.execute(sql)

    PrimeInterest2 = rsInterests("chrName")

    sql = "execute sp_RetrieveInterestTopicByID " & _
        rsGuestRegister("intSecondInterest")

    ' Execute the SQL statement
    set rsInterests = dbInterests.execute(sql)

    SecondInterest2 = rsInterests("chrName")

    dtEntered2 = rsGuestRegister("dtEntered")

    rsGuestRegister.MoveNext
```

```
else

    ' Clear the variables if there is no current
    ' record set
    txtComments2 = " "
    idGuestRegister2 = " "
    Name2 = " "
    Address2 = " "
    Location2 = " "
    Phone2 = " "
    Email2 = " "
    PrimeInterest2 = " "
    SecondInterest2 = " "
    dtEntered2 = " "

end if

'*****************************************************
' Retrieve third report column
'*****************************************************

' Logic follows the same as above

if not rsGuestRegister.EOF then

    txtComments3 = rsGuestRegister("txtComments")
    idGuestRegister3 = _
        rsGuestRegister("idGuestRegister")

    idRegistration = rsGuestRegister("idGuestRegister")

    Name3 = rsGuestRegister("chrFirstName") & " " & _
        rsGuestRegister("chrLastName")

    Address3 = rsGuestRegister("chrAddress")

    if rsGuestRegister("chrState") = "" then
      Location3 = rsGuestRegister("chrCity") & ", " & _
          rsGuestRegister("chrState") & " " & _
          rsGuestRegister("chrZipPostal")
    else
      Location3 = rsGuestRegister("chrCity") & ", " & _
          rsGuestRegister("chrProvince") & " " & _
          rsGuestRegister("chrZipPostal") & " " & _
          rsGuestRegister("chrCountry")
    end if

    Phone3 = rsGuestRegister("chrPhone")

    Email3 = "<a href=""mailto:" & _
        rsGuestRegister("chrEmail") & """>" & _
```

```
                      rsGuestRegister("chrEmail") & "</a>"

            sql = "execute sp_RetrieveInterestTopicByID " & _
                rsGuestRegister("intPrimeInterest")

            ' Execute the SQL statement
            set rsInterests = dbInterests.execute(sql)

            PrimeInterest3 = rsInterests("chrName")

            sql = "execute sp_RetrieveInterestTopicByID " & _
                rsGuestRegister("intSecondInterest")

            ' Execute the SQL statement
            set rsInterests = dbInterests.execute(sql)

            SecondInterest3 = rsInterests("chrName")

            dtEntered3 = rsGuestRegister("dtEntered")

            ' Move to the next registration
            rsGuestRegister.MoveNext

        else

            txtComments3 = " "
            idGuestRegister3 = " "
            Name3 = " "
            Address3 = " "
            Location3 = " "
            Phone3 = " "
            Email3 = " "
            PrimeInterest3 = " "
            SecondInterest3 = " "
            dtEntered3 = " "

        end if

    %>
```

We are now ready to begin displaying the registration data. This is done on a row-by-row basis with three columns. We include one column that tags the data that is displayed. There is also a blank separator row between each "row" of registrations.

Listing 6.27   GuestRegisterReport.asp continued

```
<!- Display the Registration ID ->
<TR>
<TD align="right"><B>Registration ID:</b></TD>
```

```
<TD>    <%=idGuestRegister1%></TD>
<TD>    <%=idGuestRegister2%></TD>
<TD>    <%=idGuestRegister3%></TD>
</TR>

<!- Display the name data ->
<TR>
<TD align="right"><B>Name:</b></TD>
<TD>    <%=Name1%></TD>
<TD>    <%=Name2%></TD>
<TD>    <%=Name3%></TD>
</TR>

<!- Display the address data ->
<TR>
<TD align="right"><B>Address:</b></TD>
<TD>    <%=Address1%></TD>
<TD>    <%=Address2%></TD>
<TD>    <%=Address3%></TD>
</TR>

<!- Display the city data ->
<TR>
<TD align="right"><B>City:</b></TD>
<TD>    <%=location1%></TD>
<TD>    <%=location2%></TD>
<TD>    <%=location3%></TD>
</TR>

<!- Display the phone data ->
<TR>
<TD align="right"><B>Phone:</b></TD>
<TD>    <%=Phone1%></TD>
<TD>    <%=Phone2%></TD>
<TD>    <%=Phone3%></TD>
</TR>

<!- Display the email data ->
<TR>
<TD align="right"><B>Email:</b></TD>
<TD>    <%=Email1%></TD>
<TD>    <%=Email2%></TD>
<TD>    <%=Email3%></TD>
</TR>

<!- Display the primary interest data ->
<TR>
<TD align="right"><B>Primary Interest Topic:</b></TD>
<TD>    <%=PrimeInterest1%></TD>
<TD>    <%=PrimeInterest2%></TD>
<TD>    <%=PrimeInterest3%></TD>
</TR>
```

```
        <!- Display the secondary interest data ->
        <TR>
        <TD align="right"><B>Secondary Interest Topic:</b></TD>
        <TD>    <%=SecondInterest1%></TD>
        <TD>    <%=SecondInterest2%></TD>
        <TD>    <%=SecondInterest3%></TD>
        </TR>

        <!- Display the comments data ->
        <TR>
        <TD align="right"><B>Comments:</b></TD>
        <TD>    <%=txtComments1%></TD>
        <TD>    <%=txtComments2%></TD>
        <TD>    <%=txtComments3%></TD>
        </TR>

        <!- Display the date entered data ->
        <TR>
        <TD align="right"><B>Date Entered:</b></TD>
        <TD>    <%=dtEntered1%></TD>
        <TD>    <%=dtEntered2%></TD>
        <TD>    <%=dtEntered3%></TD>
        </TR>

        <!- Build a blank row seperator ->
        <TR>
        <TD> </TD>
        <TD> </TD>
        <TD> </TD>
        <TD> </TD>
        </TR>

    <%

    loop

    end if

    ' Close our data base connections
    dbGuestRegister.Close
    dbInterests.close

    %>

    </table>

<BR><BR>
```

If we are showing new registrations, we need to provide a link for the administrator to flag them as processed. That way, the next time the administrator comes in to report new registrations, they see only the registrations entered since they last reviewed the report.

Listing 6.28   GuestRegisterReport.asp continued

```
<%

' Check to see if we are processing registrations
' and if there was something to be processed.
if id = 1 and NoResultsFlag <> 1 then

%>

<!- Link to this page with the last registration ID ->
Click
<a href="ClearRegistrations.asp?idRegistration= ↵
    <%=idRegistration%>">
here</a> to clear this report.

<%
end if
%>

</BODY>
</HTML>
```

That does it for the reporting of the registrations. The final piece of functionality in our administrative interface is the clearing of the new registrations. Listing 6.29 shows the code for the page.

Listing 6.29   ClearRegistrations.asp

```
<%@ Language=VBScript %>
<%Option Explicit %>
<HTML>
<HEAD>
<%
'*****************************************************
'** ClearRegistrations.asp
'**
'** Flags all unprocessed registrations as
'** Processed
'*****************************************************
%>
</HEAD>
<BODY>
```

```
<%

' Declare our Variables
Dim dbGuestRegister    ' database connection
Dim rsGuestRegister    ' Record set
Dim SQL                ' String

   ' Create an ADO database connection
   set dbGuestRegister = _
      server.createobject("adodb.connection")

   ' Create a record set
   set rsGuestRegister = _
      server.CreateObject("adodb.recordset")

   ' Open the connection using our ODBC file DSN
   dbGuestRegister.open("filedsn=GuestRegister")

   ' Create a SQL statement to process all registrations
   ' up to the the ID passed into the stored procedure
   sql = "execute sp_ProcessRegistrations " & _
      request("idRegistration")

   ' Execute the statement
   dbGuestRegister.Execute sql

   ' Close the connection
   dbGuestRegister.Close
%>

All open registrations have been marked as processed.
Click <a href="GuestRegisterAdmin.asp">here</a>
to continue.

</BODY>
</HTML>
```

A database connection is opened and a SQL statement is created that calls the sp_Process-Registrations stored procedure. The ID of the last registration displayed on the reporting page is passed on the URL to this page. That ID is then passed as a parameter to the stored procedure. This ensures that if a user has added any new registrations while we are working on the reporting, they don't accidentally get cleared. By passing the ID of the last, viewed, new registration, we ensure any registrations with a higher ID will not be cleared.

That does it for the administrative functionality for the guest register. The only missing piece of functionality is some form of security access coding to utilize the administrative pages. We wouldn't want an end user accidentally "stumbling" across these administrative pages. This kind of security will be explored in later chapters.

Testing the Application

To test the application, we need to open a browser and put in the URL for the Web page. In this case it will be the domain name (such as localhost, if browsing on the same machine) plus the directory structure such as community/guestregister) plus the name of the page—GuestRegister.asp.

Figure 6.2 shows the registration page with all of the appropriate fields. The first step is to enter in data. Fill out all of the fields appropriately except for the e-mail field. Enter an invalid e-mail address (for example, one that is missing an @ or a dot), and then submit the form.

FIGURE 6.2:

Guest registration page

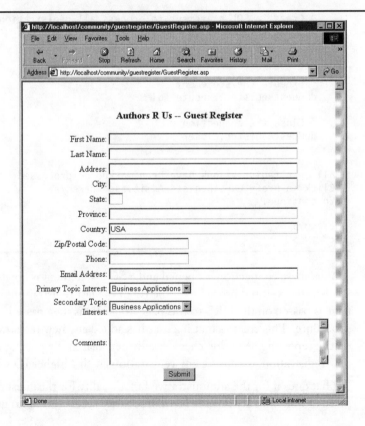

After retrieving the data and processing it, you should get an error indicating that the e-mail address is invalid, as shown in Figure 6.3. Click the link to return to the registration page.

FIGURE 6.3:

Guest registration error page

As shown in Figure 6.4, all of the fields are re-populated with your original selections. Even the primary topics of interests are reset to default to your selections. You can now correct the e-mail address entry and resubmit the form.

FIGURE 6.4:

Guest registration page
populated after errors

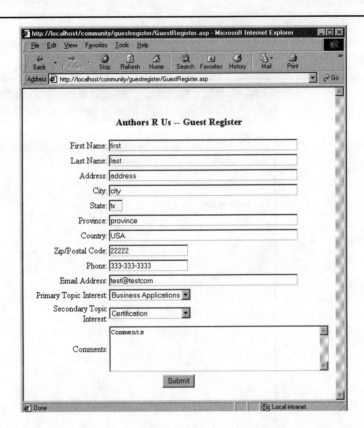

Now that the e-mail address is formatted properly, the data is processed and inserted into the database. Figure 6.5 shows the displayed results of the ProcessGuestRegister.asp page.

FIGURE 6.5:

Processed guest
registration page

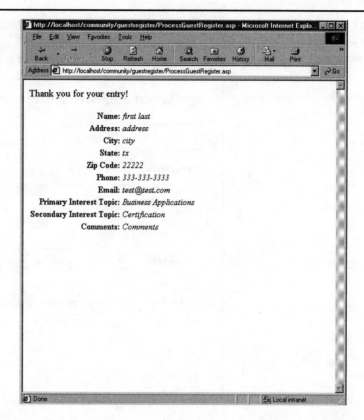

FIGURE 6.5:

Processed guest
registration page

That does it for the user interface side of our guest register. Now we are a ready to take a look at the administrative functionality. We need to change URL to access the administrative Web page. In this case it will be the domain name (such as localhost, if browsing on the same machine) plus the directory structure (such as community/guestregister/admin) plus the name of the page—GuestRegisterAdmin.asp. Figure 6.6 shows the guest registration administrative options.

FIGURE 6.6:

Guest registration
administration page

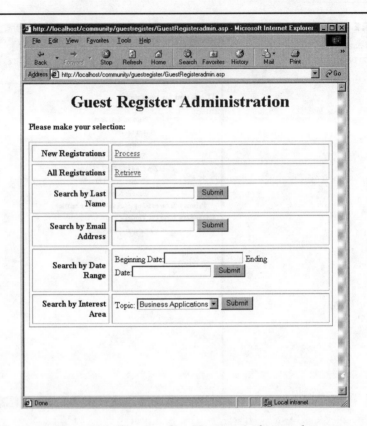

Let's first look at the new registrations functionality. Ensure you have at least one new un-processed registration in the database and click the Process link. Figure 6.7 shows the report of all unprocessed registrations. In this case, we have only one.

FIGURE 6.7:

New registrations report

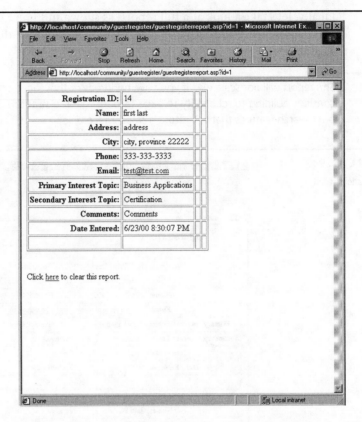

FIGURE 6.7:

New registrations report

Click the link at the bottom of the page to clear the report. Figure 6.8 shows the Clear-Registrations.asp page with the corresponding message indicating that registrations have been marked as processed. Click the link to return to the administrative page.

FIGURE 6.8:

New registrations
processed

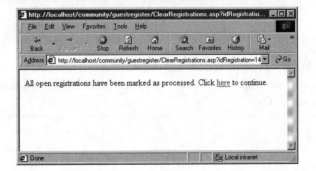

Finally, let's take a look at a full report, as shown in Figure 6.9. Click the Retrieve link on the "All Registrations" row. A report will come up of all the registrations entered into the database.

NOTE   This report will not scale well if you have hundreds or thousands of registrations. In that case, consider building functionality to page through the registrations. Another option is to only offer search features that will return a smaller record set.

FIGURE 6.9:

All registrations report

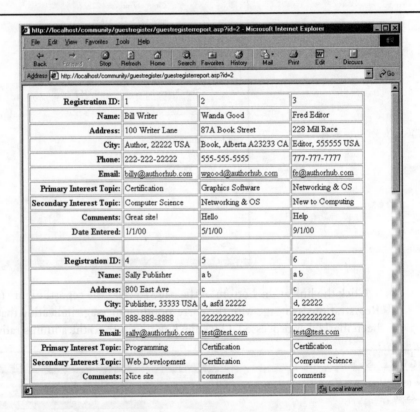

We have completed testing the interface of our new guest registration functionality. This type of development methodology serves us well in building out the rest of our community functionality.

Summary

At this stage we have built two of the entry components of our community Web site—a feed-back form and a guest registration page. This guest registration outlined here can be the basis of a full-featured profiling functionality of a community Web site.

In the next chapter, we begin our journey into building interactive community functions of a Web site. The first step is to build a way for authors to set up profiles and provide targeted community content.

SUMMARY

...

CHAPTER 7

User Content Contributions

- Designing the Application
- Building the Database
- Building the User Interface
- Testing the Application

Enabling users to contribute unique content to your community Web site is part of what makes a site successful. The next few chapters discuss how to build out an author and book directory that allows authors to list their books on the Web site. Authors can update and administrate their entries. This basic user content contribution forms the basis around which the rest of our community tools are built.

Once the author administration tools are built, we can build search, personalization, and promotion tracking features on top of the basic directory. In addition, we can explore all of the necessary administrative features to support these tools.

Designing the Application

Our author and book directory has an interface for an author to add personal information as well as list the books they have written. To ensure protection of their content, the author needs to sign in with a username and password that will allow them to log back in and administrate the information.

An author can add multiple books into their profile. Figure 7.1 shows the basic application structure.

FIGURE 7.1:

Author and book content
relationship structure

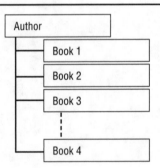

The application needs to allow authors to enter in all of the data for their bios as well as their books. It also should provide a method for them to be able to update all of this information.

Ultimately, this data will be available on the general directory Web site for searching and browsing. We build this interface in the next chapter.

To set up the Web site, we need to create a new directory called, appropriately enough, "directory." Under this directory, we add an additional directory called "author." That is where these pages will be placed.

Building the Database

Our database consists of four tables and eleven stored procedures. This database will continue to grow over the next several chapters. This initial structure, however, supports the functionality we build in this chapter.

Designing the Relational Data Structure

The relational database structure contains four tables, although only three are "key." There is one table to hold the author data, one to hold the book data, one to make the relationship link between the two tables, and a final table to hold publisher lookup data. Figure 7.2 shows the relationship between the three key tables.

FIGURE 7.2:
Author, BookAuthor, and Book table structure

Each author will have one personal entry, although can have multiple book entries. The BookAuthor table links the ID of the author with the IDs of the books they have entered.

Listing 7.1 show the SQL code to create the Author table. An identity column creates a primary key for each author where the author can enter biographical data. The author also has to enter a username and password that they will utilize to log in later and update their data.

Listing 7.1   Author Table

```
CREATE TABLE dbo.Author (
    idAuthor int IDENTITY (1, 1) NOT NULL ,
    chrFirstName varchar (100) NULL ,
    chrLastName varchar (100) NULL ,
    chrCompany varchar (150) NULL ,
    chrEmail varchar (50) NULL ,
    chrImageLink varchar (150) NULL ,
    chrURL varchar (150) NULL ,
    txtAuthorBio text NULL ,
    chrUserName varchar (50) NULL ,
    chrPassword varchar (50) NULL
)
GO
```

Our next listing shows the SQL code to create the Book table. Even though the author can enter in an ISBN, which is unique for each title, we need to generate an ID primary key to ensure we have a unique record for each book entry in case of user error.

We can store three lookup values in our book table. Listing 7.2 shows the SQL Script to create the table. The first two, intPrimeInterest and intSecondInterest, assign the book to two topic categories using the same lookup data outlined in Chapter 6 for setting guest topic interests. The idPublisher field will store the ID of the publisher of the book. That data is pulled from the Publisher table.

Listing 7.2   Book Table

```
CREATE TABLE dbo.Book (
    idBook int IDENTITY (1, 1) NOT NULL ,
    chrISBN varchar (150) NULL ,
    intPrimeInterest int NULL ,
    intSecondInterest int NULL ,
    chrTitle varchar (255) NULL ,
    txtDescription text NULL ,
    txtTOC text NULL ,
    chrImageLink varchar (150) NULL ,
  dtCreated datetime NULL CONSTRAINT
  DF_Book_dtCreated_3__10 DEFAULT (getdate()),
    idPublisher int NULL
)
GO
```

The BookAuthor table, as shown in Listing 7.3, stores the relationship between the Book and Author tables. A primary key table is created to ensure the uniqueness of each record. The ID of the author and the ID of the book are stored in the record, as well.

Listing 7.3   BookAuthor Table

```
CREATE TABLE dbo.BookAuthor (
    idAuthor int NOT NULL ,
    idBook int NOT NULL ,
    idAuthorBook int IDENTITY (1, 1) NOT NULL
)
GO
```

Our final table is the Publisher table, as shown in Listing 7.4. This table is utilized as a lookup for setting up the author's books. We have one identity column and a character field to insert the publisher's name.

Listing 7.4   Publisher Table

```
CREATE TABLE dbo.Publisher (
    idPublisher int IDENTITY (1, 1) NOT NULL ,
    chrPublisher varchar (255) NULL
)
GO
```

Note that nowhere in the example code are any administrative tools provided to manage this table. Table 7.1 provides sample data to be inserted for the code examples.

TABLE 7.1: Publisher Sample Data

ID	Publisher
1	Sybex
2	Musical Books
3	Meta Books
4	Databases R Us
5	Cook Waves
6	Back to the Future Publishers

That does it for our data structure for our author content contribution functionality. As you can guess, we have a slew of stored procedures that will be needed to manage the data in the tables.

Building the Stored Procedures

The stored procedures break down into four categories: managing the author data, managing the book data, managing the authentication data, and the utility stored procedures.

Our first stored procedure shown in Listing 7.5, sp_InsertAuthor, manages the insertion of a new author into the database. The appropriate parameters are passed into the stored procedure and the SQL statement executes the insert.

Listing 7.5 **sp_InsertAuthor Stored Procedure**

```
CREATE PROCEDURE sp_InsertAuthor

/* Pass in all of the data for a new
   author */
@chrFirstName varchar(255),
@chrLastName varchar(255),
@chrCompany varchar(255),
@chrEmail varchar(255),
@chrURL varchar(255),
@txtAuthorBio text,
@chrUserName varchar(255),
@chrPassword varchar(255)

AS

/* Insert the author data into the table */
```

```
insert into Author(chrFirstName, chrLastName,
        chrCompany, chrEmail,
        chrURL, txtAuthorBio,
        chrUserName, chrPassword)
    values(@chrFirstName, @chrLastName,
        @chrCompany, @chrEmail,
        @chrURL, @txtAuthorBio,
        @chrUserName, @chrPassword)
GO
```

Through the management interface we are building, authors can update their bio data. The sp_UpdateAuthor stored procedure, shown in Listing 7.6, takes in the updated parameter data and then executes an SQL update statement to update the record. Note that the ID of the author to be updated is passed as a parameter.

Listing 7.6   sp_UpdateAuthor Stored Procedure

```
CREATE PROCEDURE sp_UpdateAuthor

/* Pass in the fields to be updated
   in the profile */
@chrFirstName varchar(255),
@chrLastName varchar(255),
@chrCompany varchar(255),
@chrEmail varchar(255),
@chrURL varchar(255),
@txtAuthorBio text,
@chrUserName varchar(255),
@chrPassword varchar(255),
@idAuthor integer

AS

/* Update the author data */
update author set
    chrFirstName = @chrFirstName,
    chrLastName = @chrLastName,
    chrCompany = @chrCompany,
    chrEmail = @chrEmail,
    chrURL = @chrUrl,
    txtAuthorBio = @txtAuthorBio,
    chrUserName = @chrUserName,
    chrPassword = @chrPassword
  where idAuthor = @idAuthor
GO
```

Finally, to retrieve an author from the database, the sp_RetrieveAuthor stored procedure shown in Listing 7.7 retrieves the data. The ID of the author to be retrieved is passed in as a parameter and a SQL select statement returns the data.

Listing 7.7   sp_RetrieveAuthor Stored Procedure

```
CREATE PROCEDURE sp_RetrieveAuthor

/* Pass in the ID of the author */
@idAuthor integer

AS

/* Retrieve the specified author ID */
select * from author
 where idAuthor = @idAuthor
GO
```

We next move to the stored procedures for managing the book data. The first is the sp_InsertBook stored procedure. We have two actions taking place in this stored procedure. The first is the insertion of the book data, and the second is the linking of the book to the author.

All of the data for the author's book are passed in as parameters to the stored procedure. This includes the two assigned topics, the ID of the publisher to whom it is linked, and the ID of the author of the book. The book is inserted into the database first.

The resulting unique ID is retrieved using the SQL @@Identity variable, which returns the last unique identifier created in the table. The ID of the book and the ID of the author are passed in as parameters and are then inserted into the BookAuthor table to make the relationship, as shown in Listing 7.8.

Listing 7.8   sp_InsertBook Stored Procedure

```
CREATE PROCEDURE sp_InsertBook

/* Pass in all of the data for the
   new book. Also pass in the ID
   of the author to link the book
   to. */
@chrTitle varchar(255),
@chrISBN varchar(255),
@intPrimeInterest integer,
@intSecondInterest integer,
@chrImageLink varchar(255),
@txtDescription text,
```

```
@idPublisher integer,
@txtTOC text,
@idAuthor integer

AS

/* Declare a variable for storing
   the new book ID from our insert */
declare @idBook integer

/* Insert the book into the database */
insert into book(chrTitle, chrISBN,
        intPrimeInterest, intSecondInterest,
        chrImageLink, txtDescription,
        idPublisher, txtTOC)
    values(@chrTitle, @chrISBN,
        @intPrimeInterest, @intSecondInterest,
        @chrImageLink, @txtDescription,
        @idPublisher, @txtTOC)

/* Retrieve the ID of the book just inserted */
select @idBook = @@identity

/* Build the relationship of the book to the
   author */
insert into BookAuthor(idBook, idAuthor)
        values(@idBook, @idAuthor)
GO
```

Our next book stored procedure, shown in Listing 7.9, handles updating book data. The standard parameters are created to accept the data, and the ID of the book is passed in to identify the book to be updated. Note that the ID of the author is not passed in because there is no way for a book to be assigned to a new author in the administrative interface (something that could be added).

Listing 7.9   sp_UpdateBook Stored Procedure

```
CREATE PROCEDURE sp_UpdateBook

/* Pass in the book data to be update */
@chrTitle varchar(255),
@chrISBN varchar(255),
@intPrimeInterest integer,
@intSecondInterest integer,
@chrImageLink varchar(255),
@txtDescription text,
@idPublisher integer,
@txtTOC text,
@idBook integer
```

```
AS

/* Update the book data for the specified
   book. */
update book set
   chrTitle=@chrTitle, chrISBN=@chrISBN,
   intPrimeInterest=@intPrimeInterest,
   intSecondInterest=@intSecondInterest,
   chrImageLink=@chrImageLink,
   txtDescription=@txtDescription,
   idPublisher=@idPublisher,
   txtTOC=@txtTOC
 where idBook = @idBook
GO
```

Authors do have the ability to delete a book in their list. Listing 7.10 shows the sp_Delete-Book stored procedure. The ID of the book is passed in and a SQL delete statement is executed.

Listing 7.10   sp_DeleteBook Stored Procedure

```
CREATE PROCEDURE sp_DeleteBook

/* Pass in the ID of the book */
@idBook integer

AS

/* Delete the specified book */
delete from book where idBook = @idBook
GO
```

The last book stored procedure, sp_RetrieveBook, retrieves specified book by ID, as shown in Listing 7.11.

Listing 7.11   sp_RetrieveBook Stored Procedure

```
CREATE PROCEDURE sp_RetrieveBook

/* Pass in the ID of the book */
@idBook integer

AS

/* Retrieve the book data for the
   specified book */
select * from book
 where idBook = @idBook
GO
```

The next two stored procedures handle the authentication process of an author logging into their administrative area and updating their authentication data.

Listing 7.12 shows the sp_RetrieveAuthentication stored procedure. It retrieves any records that match the username and password entered in by the user. This stored procedure is used to authenticate users as well as ensure that duplicate usernames and passwords are not entered.

Listing 7.12   sp_RetrieveAuthentication Stored Procedure

```
CREATE PROCEDURE sp_RetrieveAuthentication

/* The username and password are passed in */
@chrUsername varchar(255),
@chrPassword varchar(255)

AS

/* Retrieves all author profiles that
   have a matching username and password */
select * from author
 where chrUsername = @chrUsername and
    chrPassword = @chrPassword
GO
```

The sp_CheckAuthentication stored procedure, shown in Listing 7.13, checks to see if there are any other records in the database that match the username and password that do *not* match the passed-in author ID. This is utilized when authors update their username and password data, we need to ensure they are not duplicating another author's record.

Listing 7.13   sp_CheckAuthentication Stored Procedure

```
CREATE PROCEDURE sp_CheckAuthentication

/* Pass in the username, password and
   the ID of the author */
@chrUsername varchar(255),
@chrPassword varchar(255),
@idAuthor integer

AS

/* Search for a record that matches the specified
   username and password but isn't the record of
   the specified user */
select * from author
 where chrUsername = @chrUsername and
```

```
             chrPassword = @chrPassword and
             idAuthor <> @idAuthor
      GO
```

Next we have two utility stored procedures. The first, sp_RetrieveAuthorBooks shown in Listing 7.14, retrieves all of the books assigned to the specified author. An SQL select statement joins the two tables together and returns the related books.

Listing 7.14   sp_RetrieveAuthorBooks Stored Procedure

```
CREATE PROCEDURE sp_RetrieveAuthorBooks

/* Pass in the ID of the author */
@idAuthor integer

AS

/* Retrieve all of the books related to the
   specified author */
select *
 from book, bookauthor
where bookauthor.idAuthor = @idAuthor and
   book.idbook = bookauthor.idbook
GO
```

The last stored procedure shown in Listing 7.15, sp_RetrievePublishers, retrieves all of the publishers in the Publisher table. This is utilized to populate a select box to assign a book to a publisher.

Listing 7.15   sp_RetrievePublishers Stored Procedure

```
CREATE PROCEDURE sp_RetrievePublishers AS

/* Retrieve the publisher data and
   order by publisher name */
select * from publisher
 order by chrPublisher
GO
```

That does it for building the database structure for our author contribution interface. Now we are ready to build the VBScript code tools for authors to use to sign up and manage their data.

Building the User Interface

In this chapter we build the interface pages for authors to sign up and manage their data, though we will not build any site administrator pages until Chapter 11. These pages are to be utilized strictly by authors to contribute content to the Web site author and book directory.

Our page code falls into four categories: the management of signing up new authors, the management of author login and validation, author management interface, and updating author data. The final one is managing book data. The combination of these pages provide the tools for authors to manage the data that appears on the author and book directory we will build in the next chapter.

Author Sign Up

The first page we need to build is for a new author to sign up. This gets the ball rolling with authors being able to get their bio data into the database.

Listings 7.15 through 7.17 show the code for the AuthorSignUp.asp page. As in the previous two chapters, the pages in this chapter have the appropriate header information, including the Option Explicit setting as well as the comment header.

Listing 7.15   AuthorSignUp.asp

```
<%@ Language=VBScript %>
<%Option Explicit%>
<%
'*******************************************************
'** AuthorSignUp.asp
'**
'** Builds a form for a new author to sign up
'*******************************************************
%>
<HTML>

<BODY bgcolor="white">

<b>Enter in your author information:<BR><BR></b>
```

As you would expect, this page is primarily a data entry form for authors to enter in their data. The requisite first name, last name, company, and e-mail fields are created. The form posts to the AddAuthor.asp page.

Listing 7.16   AuthorSignUp.asp continued

```
<!- Build a form to sign up an author to the
    database ->
<form method="post" action="AddAuthor.asp">

<!- Build a table for the form ->
<table border="0" cellpadding="3" cellspacing="3">

<!- Build a field for the first name ->
<tr>
   <td align="right">First Name:</td>
   <td>
    <input type="text" value="" name="chrFirstName">
   </td>
</tr>

<!- Build a field for the last name ->
<tr>
   <td align="right">Last Name:</td>
   <td>
    <input type="text" value="" name="chrLastName">
   </td>
</tr>

<!- Build a field for the company ->
<tr>
   <td align="right">Company:</td>
   <td>
    <input type="text" value="" name="chrCompany"
       size="40">
   </td>
</tr>

<!- Build a field for the email address ->
<tr>
   <td align="right">Email Address:</td>
   <td>
    <input type="text" value="" name="chrEmail"
       size="40">
   </td>
</tr>
```

Next we need to add several fields that are specific to the author's bio. The first field is a URL the author might want to display that links to a personal Web site, a book Web site, the publisher, and so on. The next field is a text box that allows the author to enter in a short biography.

Finally we have the username and password fields. As is customary, users should type in the password twice to ensure that they don't make a typo on the first entry. Note that the password fields are of type "password" so that the data is not displayed on the screen.

Listing 7.17   AuthorSignUp.asp continued

```
<!- Build a field for the URL ->
<tr>
   <td align="right">URL:</td>
   <td>
    <input type="text" value="" name="chrURL"
        size="40">
   </td>
</tr>

<!- Build a field for the author bio ->
<tr>
   <td align="right">Author Bio:</td>
   <td>
    <textarea name="txtAuthorBio" cols="40" ↵
    rows="10"></textarea>
   </td>
</tr>

<!- Build a field for the username ->
<tr>
   <td align="right">Username:</td>
   <td>
    <input type="text" value="" name="chrUserName">
   </td>
</tr>

<!- Build a field for the password ->
<tr>
   <td align="right">Password:</td>
   <td>
    <input type="password" value="" name="chrPassword1">
   </td>
</tr>

<!- Build a field for the password ->
<tr>
   <td align="right">Password:</td>
   <td>
    <input type="password" value="" name="chrPassword2">
   </td>
</tr>

<tr>
   <td align="center" colspan="2">
```

```
      <input type="submit" value="Submit" name="Submit">
      </td>
</tr>

</form>

</table>

</body>

</HTML>
```

The page closes out with the appropriate submit button and closing tags for the page. Now we are ready to process the data posted to the AddAuthor.asp page.

The AddAuthor.asp page, shown in Listings 7.18 through 7.21, begins with the standard header. The first step in the page is to validate the data entered in by the prospective author. They are required to enter in a first name, last name, and e-mail address.

Listing 7.18   AddAuthor.asp

```
<%@ Language=VBScript %>
<%Option Explicit%>
<%
'*****************************************************
'** AddAuthor.asp
'**
'** Inserts a new author into the database
'*****************************************************
%>
<HTML>
<Body>

<!- #include file="navigation.asp" ->

<%

Dim dbAuthor    ' Database Connection
Dim rsAuthor    ' Record Set
Dim sql         ' String
Dim strError    ' String

' Check to see if a fist name was entered
if request("chrFirstName") = "" then

    strError = "You did not enter in your first name.<BR>"

end if
```

```
' Check to see if a last name was entered
if request("chrLastName") = "" then

   strError = strError & _
      "You did not enter in your last name.<BR>"

end if

' Check to see if an email address was entered
if request("chrEmail") = "" then

   strError = strError & _
      "You did not enter in your email address.<BR>"

end if
```

Next, we check the username and password data. The author has to enter in a username. And, we need to ensure that the two password entries match up. If any error is produced, the error string created throughout the validation is displayed and the users are asked to click the Back button to correct their entries.

Listing 7.19   AddAuthor.asp continued

```
' Check to see if a username was entered
if request("chrUserName") = "" then

   strError = strError & _
      "You did not enter in a user name.<BR>"

end if

' Check to see if the first password was entered
if request("chrPassword1") = "" then

   strError = strError & _
      "You did not enter in a password.<BR>"

end if

' Check to see if the two passwords entered match
if request("chrPassword1") <> request("chrPassword2") then

   strError = strError & _
      "Your password entries did not match.<BR>"

end if

' See if an error was entered
if strError <> "" then
```

```
' Write out the error
Response.Write "<i>" & strError & "</i>"

%>
<BR>
<b>Please hit your browser Back
  button to update your data.</b>

<%

else
```

If all of the data is valid to this stage, we then have to check the username and password combination to ensure that it is not already being used. A database connection is open and we use the sp_RetrieveAuthentication query to see if the username and password combination is currently in use. If it is, then a message is displayed to users indicating they need to choose a different combination.

Listing 7.20   AddAuthor.asp continued

```
' Create an ADO database connection
set dbAuthor = _
   server.createobject("adodb.connection")

' Create record set
set rsAuthor = _
   server.CreateObject("adodb.recordset")

' Open the connection using our ODBC file DSN
dbAuthor.open("filedsn=Directory")

' Check to see if the username and password
' were previously entered
sql = "execute sp_RetrieveAuthentication '" & _
   request("chrUserName") & "', '" & _
   request("chrPassword1") & "'"

' Execute the statement and retrieve the record set
set rsAuthor = dbAuthor.Execute(sql)

' Check to see if a record was returned
if not rsAuthor.EOF then

%>

<!- Indicate that the username and password
   combination is in use ->
<b>The username and password combination you
  have selected is already taken. Please hit
```

```
    your browser Back button to update your data.</b>

    <%

    else
```

Finally, we are ready to insert the data showing that everything has been properly validated. An SQL statement is built to call the sp_InsertAuthor stored procedure. As we have done in the past, we have to ensure that any single quotes are doubled using the Replace command. This includes the username and password fields. The SQL command is then executed and the database connection is closed.

Listing 7.21　AddAuthor.asp continued

```
' Build the SQL statement to insert the author
sql = "execute sp_InsertAuthor '" & _
replace(request("chrFirstName"), "'", "''") & "', '" & _
replace(request("chrLastName"), "'", "''") & "', '" & _
replace(request("chrCompany"), "'", "''") & "', '" & _
replace(request("chrEmail"), "'", "''") & "', '" & _
replace(request("chrURL"), "'", "''") & "', '" & _
replace(request("txtAuthorBio"), "'", "''") & "', '" & _
replace(request("chrUserName"), "'", "''") & "', '" & _
replace(request("chrPassword1"), "'", "''") & "'"

' Execute the statement and retrieve the record set
set rsAuthor = dbAuthor.Execute(sql)

' Close the database connection
dbAuthor.Close

%>

Thank you for your entry! Click
<a href="default.asp">here</a> to log in.

<%

    end if

end if

%>

</body>
</html>
```

Finally, usesr are given a link to the login page. This enables them to enter their book data to go with their profile.

Author Login and Validation

Now that we have a way for an author to sign up, we are ready to build the login and validation functionality to enable the author to access the author management area. The first page is the Default.asp page, shown in Listing 7.22, that provides username and password login fields. This page also provides a link to the new author sign up page we just reviewed.

Note that at the beginning of the page, a check is done to see if there is an "idError" parameter. If so, and the value is 1, we indicate to users that they have not successfully logged in.

Listing 7.22   Default.asp

```
<%@ Language=VBScript %>
<%Option Explicit%>
<%
'*****************************************************
'** Default.asp
'**
'** Builds a login screen for the user to enter
'** their username and password
'*****************************************************
%>
<HTML>

<BODY bgcolor="white">

<BR><BR>

<%

' See if an error happened
if request("idError") = 1 then

%>

<!- Indicate an invalid login ->
<font size="4" color="red">
 <B>You were not successfully logged in.</b>
</font><BR><BR>
<%

end if

%>

<!- Build a link to sign up an author ->
```

```
<A href="AuthorSignUp.asp">Login as a new author!</a>

<BR><BR>

<!- Build a form for the login ->
<form method="post" action="Login.asp">

<!- Build a table for the form ->
<table border="0" cellpadding="3" cellspacing="3">

<!- Build a field for the username ->
<tr>
   <td align="right">Username</td>
   <td>
    <input type="text" value="" name="chrUserName">
   </td>
</tr>

<!- Build a field for the password ->
<tr>
   <td align="right">Password</td>
   <td>
    <input type="password" value="" name="chrPassword">
   </td>
</tr>

<tr>
   <td align="center" colspan="2">
   <input type="submit" value="Submit" name="Submit">
   </td>
</tr>

</form>

</table>

</body>

</HTML>
```

The form posts to the Login.asp page, shown in Listings 7.23 and 7.24, which will validate the username and password entered on the Default.asp page. This page will check the database against the entry and then either send the user into the author management area with them identified or indicate that an invalid entry was made.

Listing 7.23   Login.asp

```
<%@ Language=VBScript %>
<%Option Explicit%>
<%
'****************************************************
'** Login.asp
'**
'** Processes the request for the author to login
'****************************************************
%>
<%

Dim dbAuthor      ' Database Connection
Dim rsAuthor      ' Recordset
Dim SQL           ' String

' Create an ADO database connection
set dbAuthor = _
   server.createobject("adodb.connection")

' Create record set
set rsAuthor = _
   server.CreateObject("adodb.recordset")

' Open the connection using our ODBC file DSN
dbAuthor.open("filedsn=Directory")
```

The sp_RetrieveAuthentication stored procedure is utilized to retrieve any records that match the username and password. If there is no match, the user is redirected to the Default.asp page with a parameter of "iderror=1" passed to indicate a login error.

If a record was found, then a session variable, Validated, is set to "Yes" and can be checked on the subsequent manager pages to ensure that the person accessing those pages has been validated. Also, the idAuthor session variable is set to the record ID returned from the query. That is how we will know what author is accessing the site.

Listing 7.24   Login.asp continued

```
' Check to see if the user has entered the correct
' username and password
sql = "execute sp_RetrieveAuthentication '" & _
   request("chrUserName") & "', '" & _
   request("chrPassword") & "'"

' Execute the statement and retrieve the record set
set rsAuthor = dbAuthor.Execute(sql)
```

```
' See if a valid record was returned
if rsAuthor.EOF then

    ' If not close the database connection and
    ' send the user back to the default page
    dbAuthor.Close

    response.redirect "Default.asp?idError=1"

else

    ' Indicate that the user has been validated
    session("Validated") = "Yes"

    ' Store the author ID in a session variable
    session("idAuthor") = rsAuthor("idAuthor")

    ' Close the database connection
    dbAuthor.Close

    ' Send the user to the author manager
    Response.Redirect "AuthorManager.asp"

end if

%>
```

As part of our security code, we need to create a file that is included on the top of all the author management pages. CheckCode.asp, shown in Listing 7.25, will look at the Validated session variable and ensure it is set to "Yes," which means the current user has been validated. If not, then the user is redirected to the Default.asp page to login.

NOTE   If a session stays inactive for 30 minutes, the session variable is cleared and the user is sent to the login page, even though they may have been previously validated.

Listing 7.25   CheckCode.asp

```
<%
'*****************************************************
'** CheckCode.asp
'**
'** Code to ensure the user is validated to be
'** in the author manager
'*****************************************************
%>
<%
```

```
' Check to ensure the user has been validated
if session("Validated") <> "Yes" then

    ' If not then send them to the login page
    Response.Redirect "Default.asp"

end if
%>
```

This set of pages takes care of the login and authentication of the user. Authors now have the ability to sign up and to be validated, and are finally ready to move to the author management pages.

Author Management

Now we are ready to build our set of pages that provide tools for authors to manage their profile data. This includes being able to add, update, and delete book data as well as update author bio data. The first page, AuthorManager.asp, is shown in Listings 7.26 through 7.28.

The first page we need is a menu of options for the authors. This includes the list of current books as well as a link to update their bio data. Note the top of the page includes the CheckCode.asp code to ensure the author has been validated.

Listing 7.26   AuthorManager.asp

```
<%@ Language=VBScript %>
<%Option Explicit%>
<%
'*****************************************************
'** AuthorManager.asp
'**
'** Provides a set of options for the author to
'** manager their data and books
'*****************************************************
%>
<!- #include file="checkcode.asp" ->

<%
Dim dbBook    ' Database connection
Dim rsBook    ' Recordset
Dim SQL    ' string

%>
<HTML>
<HEAD>
</HEAD>
<BODY>
```

A table with two sections is created. The first section is a link to the UpdateAuthor.asp page where authors can update their bio data. The second section is where the book data is administrated. The first link is to the AddBook.asp page where a new book can be added to their profile. We then open a database connection to prepare to query the list of books the authors have entered.

Listing 7.27   AuthorManager.asp continued

```
Welcome to the author management center:<BR><BR>

<!- Build a table to display the
    management options ->
<table cellpadding="5" cellspacing="5" border="1">
<tr>
    <td>Author Data</td>
    <td>
        <!- Build a link to update the
            author data ->
        <a href="UpdateAuthor.asp">Update</a>
    </td>
</tr>
<tr>
    <td colspan="2"> </td>
</tr>
<tr>
    <td>Manage Books</td>
    <td>
        <!- Build a link to add a new
            book ->
        <a href="AddBook.asp">Add New Book</a>
    </td>
</tr>

<%

' Create an ADO database connection
set dbBook = _
    server.createobject("adodb.connection")

' Create record set
set rsBook = _
    server.CreateObject("adodb.recordset")

' Open the connection using our ODBC file DSN
dbBook.open("filedsn=Directory")
```

The list of books will be retrieved with the sp_RetrieveAuthorBooks stored procedure. The ID of the author is passed in as a parameter to the stored procedure which is retrieved from the idAuthor session variable.

Listing 7.28   AuthorManager.asp continued

```
' Retrieve the existing books for the author
sql = "execute sp_RetrieveAuthorBooks " & _
      session("idAuthor")

' Execute the statement and retrieve the record set
set rsBook = dbBook.Execute(sql)

' Loop through the books
do until rsBook.EOF

%>

<tr>
   <td> </td>
   <td>
      <!- Build a link to update the book ->
      <a href="UpdateBook.asp?idBook= ↵
   <%=rsBook("idBook")%>"><%=rsBook("chrTitle")%></a>
   </td>
</tr>

<%

' Move to the next row
rsBook.MoveNext

Loop

' Close the database connection
dbBook.Close

%>

</table>

</BODY>
</HTML>
```

The list of books retrieved from the database is looped through and listed in the table. Each book is hyperlinked to the UpdateBook.asp page and the ID of the book is passed as a parameter on the URL.

To make our author management interface easy to navigate, we build an include page called Navigation.asp, shown in Listing 7.29, that will have a link back to the author manager page. By building this into an include, we can expand the navigation menu options down the road and have them show up through out the rest of the author manager pages by updating this one file.

Listing 7.29   Navigation.asp

```
<%
'****************************************************
'** Navigation.asp
'**
'** Builds the navigation options for the author
'** manager
'****************************************************
%>
<!- Build a navigation bar for the author manager ->
| <a href="AuthorManager.asp">AuthorManager</a> |
<HR><BR>
```

The next author management page is for authors to be able to update their bio data. UpdateAuthor.asp is shown in Listing 7.30 through 7.32. The page has the standard header and, in this case, includes both the CheckCode.asp and Navigation.asp. Thus, we have a standard navigation header and validation.

Listing 7.30   UpdateAuthor.asp

```
<%@ Language=VBScript %>
<%Option Explicit%>
<%
'****************************************************
'** UpdateAuthor.asp
'**
'** Build a pre-populated form for updating the
'** existing author data
'****************************************************
%>
<!- #include file="checkcode.asp" ->

<HTML>

<BODY bgcolor="white">

<!- #include file="navigation.asp" ->

<%
```

```
Dim dbAuthor      ' Database Connection
Dim rsAuthor      ' Recordset
Dim SQL           ' String
Dim txtAuthorBio   ' String
Dim chrUserName    ' String
Dim chrPassword    ' String
```

The first step in the page is to open a database connection so we can retrieve the author's current bio data in the database. The sp_RetrieveAuthor stored procedure is utilized with the ID of the author passed in. Once the data is retrieved, we can populate the form with the current data. The form posts to the UpdateAuthorData.asp page.

Listing 7.31   UpdateAuthor.asp continued

```
' Create an ADO database connection
set dbAuthor = _
    server.createobject("adodb.connection")

' Create record set
set rsAuthor = _
    server.CreateObject("adodb.recordset")

' Open the connection using our ODBC file DSN
dbAuthor.open("filedsn=Directory")

' Retrieve the author data
sql = "execute sp_RetrieveAuthor " & session("idAuthor")

' Execute the statement and retrieve the record set
set rsAuthor = dbAuthor.Execute(sql)

' Retrieve the record set values
txtAuthorBio = rsAuthor("txtAuthorBio")
chrUserName = rsAuthor("chrUserName")
chrPassword = rsAuthor("chrPassword")

%>

<BR><BR>

<!- Build a form to update the author data ->
<form method="post" action="UpdateAuthorData.asp">

<!- Build a table to display the author data ->
<table border="0" cellpadding="3" cellspacing="3">

<!- Display the first name ->
<tr>
    <td align="right">First Name:</td>
```

```
   <td><input type="text"
        value="<%=rsAuthor("chrFirstName")%>"
        name="chrFirstName"></td>
</tr>

<!- Display the last name ->
<tr>
   <td align="right">Last Name:</td>
   <td><input type="text"
        value="<%=rsAuthor("chrLastName")%>"
        name="chrLastName"></td>
</tr>

<!- Display the company ->
<tr>
   <td align="right">Company:</td>
   <td><input type="text"
        value="<%=rsAuthor("chrCompany")%>"
        name="chrCompany" size="40"></td>
</tr>

<!- Display the email address ->
<tr>
   <td align="right">Email Address:</td>
   <td><input type="text"
        value="<%=rsAuthor("chrEmail")%>"
        name="chrEmail" size="40"></td>
</tr>

<!- Display the URL ->
<tr>
   <td align="right">URL:</td>
   <td><input type="text"
        value="<%=rsAuthor("chrUrl")%>"
        name="chrURL" size="40"></td>
</tr>

<!- Display the author bio ->
<tr>
   <td align="right">Author Bio:</td>
   <td>
    <textarea name="txtAuthorBio" cols="40" ⏎
   rows="10"><%=txtAuthorBio%></textarea>
   </td>
</tr>
```

The current username and password are displayed in the form. Again two fields are used for the password using the "password" field type. The users can change their username and password in this form as well.

Listing 7.32   UpdateAuthor.asp continued

```
<!- Display the username ->
<tr>
   <td align="right">Username:</td>
   <td>
   <input type="text"
       value="<%=rsAuthor("chrUserName")%>"
       name="chrUserName">
   </td>
</tr>

<!- Display the password ->
<tr>
   <td align="right">Password:</td>
   <td>
    <input type="text"
       value="<%=rsAuthor("chrPassword")%>"
       name="chrPassword1">
   </td>
</tr>

<!- Display the password ->
<tr>
   <td align="right">Password:</td>
   <td>
    <input type="text"
       value="<%=rsAuthor("chrPassword")%>"
       name="chrPassword2">
   </td>
</tr>

<tr>
   <td align="center" colspan="2">
   <input type="submit" value="Submit" name="Submit">
   </td>
</tr>

</form>

</table>

<%

' Close the database connection
dbAuthor.Close

%>

</body>

</HTML>
```

Finally, the page is closed out with the appropriate Submit button, table, and form tags. The database connection closes. We can now update the author data.

As when the author signed up on the site, we will need to validate the data entered by the user. UpdateAuthorData,asp, shown in Listings 7.33 through 7.35, handles this functionality. The first name, last name, and e-mail address are validated to ensure an entry has been made.

Listing 7.33   UpdateAuthorData.asp

```
<%@ Language=VBScript %>
<%Option Explicit%>
<%
'***************************************************
'** UpdateAuthorData.asp
'**
'** Updates the entered author data for the
'** specified author
'***************************************************
%>
<!- #include file="checkcode.asp" ->

<HTML>
<Body>

<!- #include file="navigation.asp" ->

<%

Dim dbAuthor      ' Database Connection
Dim rsAuthor      ' Record Set
Dim sql           ' String
Dim strError      ' String
Dim idAuthor      ' integer

' Check to ensure a first name was entered
if request("chrFirstName") = "" then

    strError = "You did not enter in your first name.<BR>"

end if

' Check to ensure a last name was entered
if request("chrLastName") = "" then

    strError = strError & _
    "You did not enter in your last name.<BR>"

end if

' Check to ensure an email address was entered
```

```
if request("chrEmail") = "" then

    strError = strError & _
     "You did not enter in your email address.<BR>"

end if
```

The username and password are validated again, as well. This time around, however, we utilize the sp_CheckAuthentication stored procedure to validate that there is no other username and password combination in use that matches the user's entry.

The sp_RetrieveAuthentication stored procedure checks all entries in the database to see if there is a match. In this case, however, if users entered in the same username and password as they previously utilized, (that is, no changes) then there will indeed be a match in the database which is specifically their record. The sp_CheckAuthentication stored procedure checks all other entries but the current author's, which is why the ID of the author is passed into the stored procedure.

Listing 7.34   UpdateAuthorData.asp continued

```
' Check to ensure a username was entered
if request("chrUserName") = "" then

    strError = strError & _
     "You did not enter in a user name.<BR>"

end if

' Check to ensure the first password was entered
if request("chrPassword1") = "" then

    strError = strError & _
     "You did not enter in a password.<BR>"

end if

' Check to ensure the first password and
' second password match was entered
if request("chrPassword1") <> request("chrPassword2") then

    strError = strError & _
     "Your password entries did not match.<BR>"

end if

' Check to see if an error was generated
if strError <> "" then
```

```
        ' Write out the error
        Response.Write "<i>" & strError & "</i>"

    %>
    <BR>
    <b>Please hit your browser back
       button to update your data.</b>

    <%

else

    ' Create an ADO database connection
    set dbAuthor = _
        server.createobject("adodb.connection")

    ' Create record set
    set rsAuthor = _
        server.CreateObject("adodb.recordset")

    ' Open the connection using our ODBC file DSN
    dbAuthor.open("filedsn=Directory")

    ' Check to see if the username and password entered
    ' by the user is already in use.
    sql = "execute sp_CheckAuthentication '" & _
        request("chrUserName") & "', '" & _
        request("chrPassword1") & "', " & _
        session("idAuthor")

    ' Execute the statement and retrieve the record set
    set rsAuthor = dbAuthor.Execute(sql)

    ' If a record was returned then it is in use
    if not rsAuthor.EOF then

    %>

        <!- Indicate to the user that the username
            and password are in use ->
        <b>The username and password combination
        you have selected is already taken. Please
        hit your browser Back button to update your
        data.</b>

    <%

    else
```

Finally, if all of the validation passes with out a problem, we are ready to update the author's record. This is done with the sp_UpdateAuthor stored procedure with all of the appropriate parameters being passed in. Once the update has been performed, the user is given a link back to the AuthorManager.asp page.

Listing 7.35   UpdateAuthorData.asp continued

```
' Build a SQL statement to update the author data
sql = "execute sp_UpdateAuthor '" & _
replace(request("chrFirstName"), "'", "''") & "', '" & _
replace(request("chrLastName"), "'", "''") & "', '" & _
replace(request("chrCompany"), "'", "''") & "', '" & _
replace(request("chrEmail"), "'", "''") & "', '" & _
replace(request("chrURL"), "'", "''") & "', '" & _
replace(request("txtAuthorBio"), "'", "''") & "', '" & _
replace(request("chrUserName"), "'", "''") & "', '" & _
replace(request("chrPassword1"), "'", "''") & "', " & _
session("idAuthor")

' Execute the statement and retrieve the record set
set rsAuthor = dbAuthor.Execute(sql)

%>

Your data has been updated! Click
<a href="AuthorManager.asp">here</a> to
continue.

<%

end if

end if

' Close the database connection
dbAuthor.Close

%>

</body>
</html>
```

Finally, the database is closed and the page is ended. We have now come full circle on the author data. Authors can sign up, login, and edit their data. Next, we move to the book management portion of the author management interface.

Book Management

Our book management interface is comprised of three primary functions: adding a book, updating book information, and deleting book information. In managing the books, we run into some additional complexity in that we have to allow the users to assign their books to topic areas as well as assign them to a publisher. The data for both of these will have to be retrieved from other tables.

The first function we provide is the ability to add a book. The AddBook.asp page, shown in Listings 7.36 through 7.38, provides an input form for the users to enter in their book data. The page starts out with the standard header. We are also including both the Check-Code.asp page for security and the Navigation.asp for the navigation menu.

Listing 7.36   AddBook.asp

```
<%@ Language=VBScript %>
<%Option Explicit%>
<%
'*****************************************************
'** AddBook.asp
'**
'** Builds a form for the author to enter in a
'** new book
'*****************************************************
%>
<!- #include file="checkcode.asp" ->

<HTML>

<BODY bgcolor="white">

<!- #include file="navigation.asp" ->

<b>Add Book:</b>

<BR><BR>
```

We create a form to post the new book data to the InsertBook.asp page, complete with form fields for book title and ISBN. We then have two select boxes for the assigned topics for the book. In this case, we need to query the InterestTopic table with the sp_RetrieveInterestTopics stored procedure to return all of the current topics in the database. A select box with options for each topic is created. The value of each option is the ID of the topic.

NOTE   Since the InterestTopic table was created in the Guest Register database, the database connection and file DSN here are labeled with the Guest Register name to clarify the connection.

Listing 7.37 AddBook.asp continued

```
<!- Build a table to display the book form ->
<table border="0" cellpadding="5" cellspacing="5">

<form method="post" action="InsertBook.asp">

<!- Build an input field for the book title ->
<tr>
   <td align="right">Title:</td>
   <td>
    <input type="text" value=""
       name="chrTitle" size="40">
   </td>
</tr>

<!- Build an input field for the book ISBN ->
<tr>
   <td align="right">ISBN:</td>
   <td>
    <input type="text" value="" name="chrISBN">
   </td>
</tr>

<!- Build an input field for the primary interest
   topic ->
<tr>
   <td align="right">Primary Interest Category:</td>
   <td>

<%

Dim dbGuestRegister    ' Database Connection
Dim rsGuestRegister    ' Recordset
Dim SQL                ' String
Dim Selected           ' String
Dim dbPublisher        ' String
Dim rsPublisher        ' String

' Create an ADO database connection
set dbGuestRegister = _
   server.createobject("adodb.connection")

' Create a record set
set rsGuestRegister = _
   server.CreateObject("adodb.recordset")

' Open the connection using our ODBC file DSN
dbGuestRegister.open("filedsn=GuestRegister")
```

```
' Retrieve the list of interest topics
sql = "execute sp_RetrieveInterestTopics"

' Execute the SQL statement
set rsGuestRegister = dbGuestRegister.execute(sql)

%>

  <!- Start the select list ->
  <select name="intPrimeInterest">

  <%

  ' Loop through the list
  do until rsGuestRegister.EOF

  %>
    <!- Build the option. Note the selected variable
        is output. When set to "selected" that option
        will be the default.  ->
   <option value="<%=rsGuestRegister("idInterestTopic")%>"⌐
      <%=selected%>><%=rsGuestRegister("chrName")%>
   <%

    ' Move to the next row
    rsGuestRegister.movenext

  ' Loop back
  loop
  %>
 </select>

  </td>
</tr>
<tr>
  <td align="right">Second Interest Category:</td>
  <td>

  <!- Start the select list ->
  <select name="intSecondInterest">

  <%

  ' Move to the first record
  rsGuestRegister.MoveFirst

  ' Loop through the list
  do until rsGuestRegister.EOF

  %>
    <!- Build the option. Note the selected variable
```

```
            is output. When set to "selected" that option
            will be the default.  ->
    <option value="<%=rsGuestRegister("idInterestTopic")%>"⏎
      <%=selected%>><%=rsGuestRegister("chrName")%>
    <%

        ' Move to the next row
        rsGuestRegister.movenext

      ' Loop back
      loop

      ' Close the databse connection
      dbGuestRegister.Close

    %>
  </select>

    </td>
</tr>
```

We now need to create an image link field on our form. The image link can be a URL to the book image, and is followed by a text input field where the author can enter a description of the book as well as assign a publisher. A select box is created by querying all of the current publishers in the database using our sp_RetrievePublishers stored procedure. The ID of the publisher is stored with each option.

Listing 7.38   AddBook.asp continued

```
<!- Build an input field for the book
    image link ->
<tr>
   <td align="right">Image Link</td>
   <td>
    <input type="text" value=""
       name="chrImageLink" size="40">
   </td>
</tr>

<!- Build an input field for the description ->
<tr>
   <td align="right">Description</td>
   <td>
    <textarea name="txtDescription" cols="60" ⏎
    rows="5"></textarea>
   </td>
</tr>

<tr>
```

```
        <td align="right">Publisher:</td>
        <td>

<%

' Create an ADO database connection
set dbPublisher = _
   server.createobject("adodb.connection")

' Create a record set
set rsPublisher = _
   server.CreateObject("adodb.recordset")

' Open the connection using our ODBC file DSN
dbPublisher.open("filedsn=Directory")

' Retrieve the list of publishers
sql = "execute sp_RetrievePublishers"

' Execute the SQL statement
set rsPublisher = dbPublisher.execute(sql)

%>

        <!- Start the select list ->
        <select name="idPublisher">

        <%

        ' Loop through the list
        do until rsPublisher.EOF

        %>
         <!- Build the option. Note the selected variable
            is output. When set to "selected" that option
            will be the default.  ->
         <option value="<%=rsPublisher("idPublisher")%>">↵
         <%=rsPublisher("chrPublisher")%>
         <%

            ' Move to the next row
            rsPublisher.movenext

         ' Loop back
         loop

         ' Close the database connection
         dbPublisher.Close
         %>
        </select>
```

```
        </td>
    </tr>

    <!- Build an input field for TOC ->
    <tr>
        <td align="right">Table of Contents:</td>
        <td>
         <textarea name="txtTOC" cols="60" rows="5"></textarea>
        </td>
    </tr>
    <tr>
        <td colspan="2">
         <input type="Submit" value="Add Book"
             name="Submit">
        </td>
    </tr>

    </form>

    </table>

    </body>

    </HTML>
```

Finally, the last field on the form is a text box where the author can enter a table of contents for the book. The page is then closed out with a Submit button and the appropriate closing tags.

Next, the InsertBook.asp page, shown in Listings 7.39 through 7.40, processes the data input by the author. We want to ensure that the appropriate information was entered by validating the title, ISBN, topic, and description fields. We need to ensure that the book is assigned to a topic so it will show up by topic category, and we also need to ensure a title and description are entered for listing and searching. If there is a validation issue, the user is asked to browse back to the data entry page and fix any incorrect entries.

Listing 7.39   InsertBook.asp

```
<%@ Language=VBScript %>
<%Option Explicit%>
<%
'*****************************************************
'** InsertBook.asp
'**
'** Inserts the new book into the database
'*****************************************************
%>
<!- #include file="checkcode.asp" ->
```

```
<HTML>
<Body>

<!- #include file="navigation.asp" ->

<%

Dim dbBook      ' Database Connection
Dim rsBook      ' Record Set
Dim sql         ' String
Dim strError    ' String

' Check to ensure a book title was entered
if request("chrTitle") = "" then

    strError = "You did not enter in a title on the book.<BR>"

end if

' Check to ensure a book ISBN was entered
if request("chrISBN") = "" then

    strError = strError & _
      "You did not enter in an ISBN number.<BR>"

end if

' Check to ensure a primary interest was
' selected
if request("intPrimeInterest") = "" then

    strError = strError & _
      "You did not enter in a primary interest ↵
    category.<BR>"

end if

' Check to ensure a secondary interest was
' selected
if request("intSecondInterest") = "" then

    strError = strError & _
      "You did not enter in a secondary interest ↵
    category.<BR>"

end if

' Check to ensure a book description was
' entered
if request("txtDescription") = "" then
```

```
      strError = strError & _
        "You did not enter in a description.<BR>"

  end if

  ' See if an error was generated
  if strError <> "" then

     ' Write out the error
     Response.Write "<i>" & strError & "</i>"

  %>
  <BR>
  <b>Please hit your browser Back
     button to update your data.</b>

  <%

  else
```

If all was entered properly, we are ready to insert the data into the database. For this, the sp_InsertBook stored procedure is utilized. The data entered by the author is sanitized for single quotes and passed as parameters to the stored procedure. Note that the ID of the author is passed into the stored procedure so that we ensure this book is linked to the specified author.

Listing 7.40   InsertBook.asp continued

```
  ' Create an ADO database connection
  set dbBook = _
    server.createobject("adodb.connection")

  ' Create record set
  set rsBook = _
    server.CreateObject("adodb.recordset")

  ' Open the connection using our ODBC file DSN
  dbBook.open("filedsn=Directory")

  ' Build a SQL statement to insert a book
  sql = "execute sp_InsertBook '" & _
  replace(request("chrTitle"), "'", "''") & "', '" & _
  replace(request("chrISBN"), "'", "''") & "', " & _
  replace(request("intPrimeInterest"), "'", "''") & ", " & _
  replace(request("intSecondInterest"), "'","''") & ", '" & _
  replace(request("chrImageLink"), "'", "''") & "', '" & _
  replace(request("txtDescription"), "'", "''") & "', " & _
  request("idPublisher") & ", '" & _
  replace(request("txtTOC"), "'", "''") & "', " & _
```

```
session("idAuthor")

   ' Execute the statement and retrieve the record set
   set rsBook = dbBook.Execute(sql)

   ' Close the database connection
   dbBook.Close

%>

   Your book was succesfully added! Click
   <a href="AuthorManager.asp">here</a> to continue.

<%

end if

%>

</body>
</html>
```

The page is then closed out as appropriate with the database connection closed and a link built back to the AuthorManger.asp page. The book now appears on the AuthorManager.asp page in the list of books the author has added, and we are ready to work on updating the book data.

The UpdateBook.asp page, shown in Listings 7.41 through 7.44, is formatted similarly to the AddBook.asp page, but we need to set all of the fields to the current values in the database. The first thing we see on the page is a link to the DeleteBook.asp page. The ID of the current book is passed on the URL. This gives the author the opportunity to remove the book from the database.

Listing 7.41   UpdateBook.asp

```
<%@ Language=VBScript %>
<%Option Explicit%>
<%
'*****************************************************
'** UpdateBook.asp
'**
'** Build a pre-populated form for updating the
'** existing book data
'*****************************************************
%>
<!- #include file="checkcode.asp" ->

<HTML>
```

```
<BODY bgcolor="white">

<!- #include file="navigation.asp" ->

<!- Display a link to delete a book ->
<B>
<a href="DeleteBook.asp?idBook= ⌐
  <%=request("idBook")%>">Delete Book</a>
</b><BR><BR>

<b>Update Book:</b>

<BR><BR>

<!- Build a table to display the book data ->
<table border="0" cellpadding="5" cellspacing="5">

<%

Dim dbBook              ' Database Connection
Dim rsBook              ' Recordset
Dim SQL                 ' String
Dim txtDescription      ' String
Dim txtTOC              ' String
Dim chrImageLink        ' String
Dim dbGuestRegister     ' Database Connection
Dim rsGuestRegister     ' Recordset
Dim Selected            ' String
Dim dbPublisher         ' Database Connection
Dim rsPublisher         ' Recordset


' Create an ADO database connection
set dbBook = _
   server.createobject("adodb.connection")

' Create record set
set rsBook = _
   server.CreateObject("adodb.recordset")

' Open the connection using our ODBC file DSN
dbBook.open("filedsn=Directory")
```

After the appropriate variable declarations are added and the database connection is open, we are ready to utilize the sp_RetrieveBook stored procedure to retrieve the book data. A form is created that will post the user input to the UpdateBookData.asp page.

Following that, the form fields for the title and ISBN number are created. Note in this case that we have a hidden input field where we are storing the ID of the book that is currently displayed. This is done so that the update page can know what book to update in the database. A hidden field is utilized because the author using the page has no need to see this value.

Listing 7.42   UpdateBook.asp continued

```
' Retrieve the book data
sql = "execute sp_RetrieveBook " & request("idBook")

' Execute the statement and retrieve the record set
set rsBook = dbBook.Execute(sql)

' Retrieve record set values
txtDescription = rsBook("txtDescription")
txtTOC = rsBook("txtTOC")
chrImageLink = rsBook("chrImageLink")

%>

<!- Build a form to update the book data ->
<form method="post" action="UpdateBookData.asp">

<!- Display the book title ->
<tr>
    <td align="right">Title:</td>
    <td>
        <input type="text"
            value="<%=rsBook("chrTitle")%>"
            name="chrTitle" size="40">

        <input type="hidden"
            value="<%=request("idBook")%>"
            name="idBook">
    </td>
</tr>

<!- Display the book ISBN ->
<tr>
    <td align="right">ISBN:</td>
    <td><input type="text"
            value="<%=rsBook("chrISBN")%>"
            name="chrISBN"></td>
</tr>
```

Next we can add the topic select boxes. As before, we need to query the database to retrieve the data in the InterestTopic table, but we also need to default the select box to the current selection. This is done by checking the value stored in the Book table against the current row being displayed in the select box via the Do...Loop. When there is a match, a variable is set so that "selected" shows up in that select option and thus shows it as the selected value. The same is done for the secondary interest as well.

Listing 7.43   UpdateBook.asp continued

```asp
<!- Display the primary interest category ->
<tr>
   <td align="right">Primary Interest Category:</td>
   <td>

<%

' Create an ADO database connection
set dbGuestRegister = _
   server.createobject("adodb.connection")

' Create a record set
set rsGuestRegister = _
   server.CreateObject("adodb.recordset")

' Open the connection using our ODBC file DSN
dbGuestRegister.open("filedsn=GuestRegister")

' Retrieve the list of interest topics
sql = "execute sp_RetrieveInterestTopics"

' Execute the SQL statement
set rsGuestRegister = dbGuestRegister.execute(sql)

%>

   <!- Start the select list ->
   <select name="intPrimeInterest">

   <%

   ' Loop through the list
   do until rsGuestRegister.EOF

      ' Check to see if a previous interest topic
      ' was selected (when the user is kicked back to
      ' to an error).
      if rsBook("intPrimeInterest") = _
        rsGuestRegister("idInterestTopic") then

         ' If the current topic was selected then set
         ' the selected variable
         selected = "selected"
      else
         ' Clear the variable
```

```
                selected = ""
            end if

    %>
    <!- Build the option. Note the selected variable
        is output. When set to "selected" that option
        will be the default.   ->
    <option value="<%=rsGuestRegister("idInterestTopic")%>"↵
    <%=selected%>><%=rsGuestRegister("chrName")%>
    <%

        ' Move to the next row
        rsGuestRegister.movenext

    ' Loop back
    loop
    %>
</select>


    </td>
</tr>
<tr>
    <td align="right">Second Interest Category:</td>
    <td>

    <!- Start the select list ->
    <select name="intSecondInterest">

    <%

    rsGuestRegister.MoveFirst

    ' Loop through the list
    do until rsGuestRegister.EOF

        ' Check to see if a previous interest topic
        ' was selected (when the user is kicked back to
        ' to an error).
        if rsBook("intSecondInterest") = _
          rsGuestRegister("idInterestTopic") then

            ' If the current topic was selected then set
            ' the selected variable
            selected = "selected"
        else
            ' Clear the variable
            selected = ""
        end if

    %>
```

```
<!- Build the option. Note the selected variable
    is output. When set to "selected" that option
    will be the default.  ->
<option value="<%=rsGuestRegister("idInterestTopic")%>"⌐
<%=selected%>><%=rsGuestRegister("chrName")%>
<%

    ' Move to the next row
    rsGuestRegister.movenext

  ' Loop back
  loop

  ' Close the database connection
  dbGuestRegister.Close

  %>
</select>

  </td>
</tr>
```

The data for the image link and book description are displayed, and as with the interest topics, we retrieve the publisher data and follow the same technique to ensure the current selected publisher is the default selection.

Listing 7.44	**UpdateBook.asp continued**

```
<tr>
  <td align="right">Image Link</td>

  <!- Display the image link ->
  <td><input type="text"
      value="<%=chrImageLink%>"
      name="chrImageLink"></td>
</tr>
<tr>
  <td align="right">Description</td>
  <td>
   <!- Display the description ->
   <textarea name="txtDescription" cols="60" ⌐
   rows="5"><%=txtDescription%></textarea>
                                    </td>
</tr>
<tr>
  <td align="right">Publisher:</td>
  <td>

<%
```

```
' Create an ADO database connection
set dbPublisher = _
  server.createobject("adodb.connection")

' Create a record set
set rsPublisher = _
  server.CreateObject("adodb.recordset")

' Open the connection using our ODBC file DSN
dbPublisher.open("filedsn=Directory")

' Retrieve the list of publishers
sql = "execute sp_RetrievePublishers"

' Execute the SQL statement
set rsPublisher = dbPublisher.execute(sql)

%>

    <!- Start the select list ->
    <select name="idPublisher">

    <%

    ' Loop through the list
    do until rsPublisher.EOF

      ' Check to see if the currently selected
      ' publisher matches the current recordset
      if rsBook("idPublisher") = rsPublisher("idPublisher") ⏎
      then

        ' Set the selected variable
        selected = "selected"

      else

        ' Clear the variable
        selected = ""

      end if

    %>
    <!- Build the option. Note the selected variable
        is output. When set to "selected" that option
        will be the default.  ->
    <option value="<%=rsPublisher("idPublisher")%>"⏎
    <%=selected%>><%=rsPublisher("chrPublisher")%>

    <%
```

```
        ' Move to the next row
        rsPublisher.movenext

    ' Loop back
    loop

    ' Close the database connection
    dbPublisher.Close

    %>
 </select>

    </td>
</tr>
<tr>
    <td align="right">Table of Contents:</td>
    <td>
    <!- Display the TOC ->
    <textarea name="txtTOC" cols="60" ⏎
    rows="5"><%=txtTOC%></textarea>
                            </td>
</tr>
<tr>
    <td colspan="2">
     <input type="Submit" value="Update Book" name="Submit">
    </td>
</tr>

</form>

</table>

<%

' Close the database connection
dbBook.Close

%>

</body>

</HTML>
```

The page then closes out with the table of contents being displayed, a Submit button, and the appropriate page ending tags. We are now ready to update the book data with Update-BookData.asp. The code for UpdateBookData.asp is shown in Listings 7.45 and 7.46.

As with the insertion of the book data, we validate the title, ISBN, topics, and description. If there is an error, the user is prompted to correct it before moving on.

Listing 7.45   UpdateBookData.asp

```
<%@ Language=VBScript %>
<%Option Explicit%>
<%
'*****************************************************
'** UpdateBookData.asp
'**
'** Updates the book data entered by the user
'*****************************************************
%>
<!- #include file="checkcode.asp" ->

<HTML>
<Body>

<!- #include file="navigation.asp" ->

<%

Dim dbBook      ' Database Connection
Dim rsBook      ' Record Set
Dim sql         ' String
Dim strError    ' String

' Ensure a title was entered
if request("chrTitle") = "" then

    strError = "You did not enter in a title on the ⌐
    book.<BR>"

end if

' Ensure an ISBN number was entered
if request("chrISBN") = "" then

    strError = strError & _
    "You did not enter in an ISBN number.<BR>"

end if

' Ensure a primary interest was entered
if request("intPrimeInterest") = "" then

    strError = strError & _
    "You did not enter in a primary interest ⌐
    category.<BR>"

end if
```

```
' Ensure a secondary interest topic was entered
if request("intSecondInterest") = "" then

   strError = strError & _
    "You did not enter in a secondary interest ⏎
    category.<BR>"

end if

' Ensure a book description was entered
if request("txtDescription") = "" then

   strError = strError & _
    "You did not enter in a description.<BR>"

end if

' Check to see if an error was generated
if strError <> "" then

   ' Write out the error
   Response.Write "<i>" & strError & "</i>"

%>
<BR>
<b>Please hit your browser Back
button to update your data.</b>

<%

else

 ' Create an ADO database connection
 set dbBook = _
    server.createobject("adodb.connection")

 ' Create record set
 set rsBook = _
    server.CreateObject("adodb.recordset")

 ' Open the connection using our ODBC file DSN
 dbBook.open("filedsn=Directory")
```

Once the data has been validated and our database connection opened, we are ready to update the data. The sp_UpdateBook stored procedure is utilized with the appropriate book data passed in as parameters. Note that the ID of the book, which is retrieved from the hidden input field, is passed in as well.

Listing 7.46   UpdateBookData.asp continued

```
' Build a stored procedure to update the book
' data
sql = "execute sp_UpdateBook '" & _
replace(request("chrTitle"), "'", "''") & "', '" & _
replace(request("chrISBN"), "'", "''") & "', " & _
replace(request("intPrimeInterest"), "'", "''") & ", " & _
replace(request("intSecondInterest"), "'","''") & ", '" & _
replace(request("chrImageLink"), "'", "''") & "', '" & _
replace(request("txtDescription"), "'", "''") & "', " & _
request("idPublisher") & ", '" & _
replace(request("txtTOC"), "'", "''") & "', " & _
Request("idBook")

 ' Execute the statement and retrieve the record set
 set rsBook = dbBook.Execute(sql)

 ' Close the database connection
 dbBook.Close

   %>

   Your book was succesfully updated! Click
   <a href="AuthorManager.asp">here</a> to continue.

   <%

end if

%>

</body>
</html>
```

Finally, the SQL statement executes, the database closes, and the user is given a link back to the management page. We are now ready for our last and final function—deleting a book.

Remember that the option to delete a book was given as the top of the update book page. The ID of the book to be deleted is passed on the URL to the page. DeleteBook.asp is shown in Listing 7.47.

Listing 7.47   DeleteBook.asp

```
<%@ Language=VBScript %>
<%Option Explicit%>
<%
```

```
'*****************************************************
'** DeleteBook.asp
'**
'** Deletes the specified book from the database
'*****************************************************
%>
<!- #include file="checkcode.asp" ->

<%

Dim dbBook    ' Database Connection
Dim rsBook    ' Recordset
Dim SQL       ' String

' Create an ADO database connection
set dbBook = _
   server.createobject("adodb.connection")

' Create record set
set rsBook = _
   server.CreateObject("adodb.recordset")

' Open the connection using our ODBC file DSN
dbBook.open("filedsn=Directory")

' Build a SQL statement to delete the
' specified book
sql = "execute sp_DeleteBook " & request("idBook")

' Execute the statement and retrieve the record set
set rsBook = dbBook.Execute(sql)

' Close the database connection
dbBook.Close

' Send the user back to the author manager
Response.Redirect "AuthorManager.asp"

%>
```

A connection to the database is opened, and then the sp_DeleteBook stored procedure is utilized with the ID of the book to be deleted passes as a parameter. The SQL statement is executed, the database connection closes, and the user is redirected back to the Author-Manger.asp page.

That does it for the coding of our user contribution application that allows authors to list and manage their bio information and the books they have written. We have built all of the necessary interface pieces to allow authors to sign up and manage their bio as well as books they have written. Let's now take a look at our application in action.

Testing the Application

To test the application, we need to open a browser and enter the URL for the Web page. In this case, enter the domain name (such as localhost, if browsing on the same machine) plus the directory structure (such as community/directory/author), plus the name of the page—Default.asp. This brings up the login page, as shown in Figure 7.3. Click the "Log in as a new author!" link.

FIGURE 7.3:

Author management login form

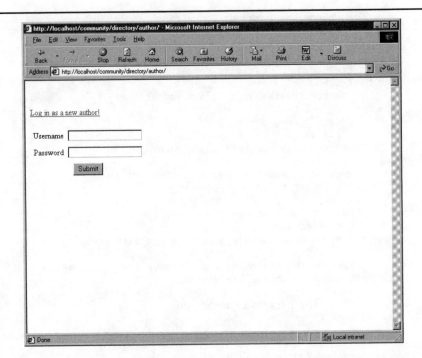

Figure 7.4 shows the new author sign up form. Sign up as a new author and be sure to remember your username and password. You might try to enter in some data that will break the validation rules to test out the logic.

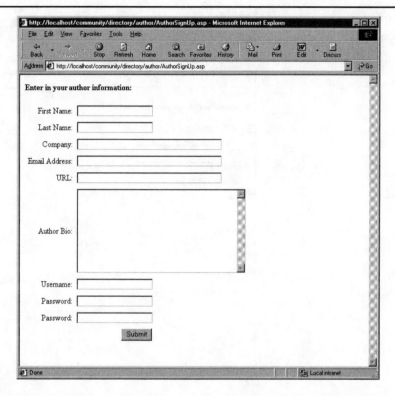

We are now ready to log in as the new author we just created. First try to log in with an incorrect username and password. You should see an error screen, as shown in Figure 7.5.

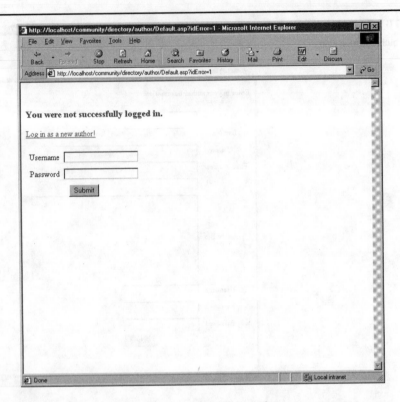

Now log in using the correct username and password. The author management center page will appear, as shown in Figure 7.6. You should see links where you can edit the author data and add a book. Two books are already shown as added for the author.

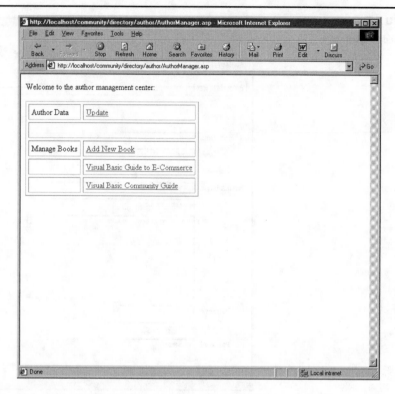

Click the Update link to display the update page, as shown in Figure 7.7. Try to break some of the validation rules to test the logic. You might want to try and enter a username and password that you know have already been put in the system by another author. By entering a username and password that are already in use, you should get an error message.

FIGURE 7.7:

Author data update page

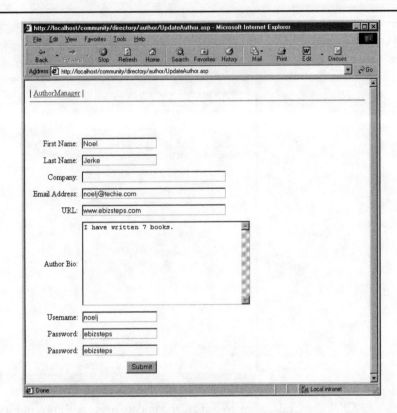

Now let's move on to book management. The first step is to add a book into the mix. Figure 7.8 shows the page where you can add the book title. Input the appropriate information. As with the other forms, try to break the validation rules to test the error checking logic.

FIGURE 7.8:

Add book page

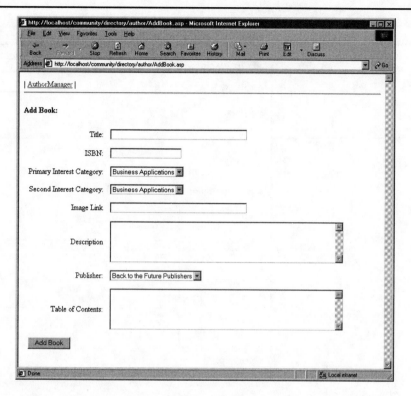

Once you have a book entered into the profile, you should be able to update the data as well as delete it. Figure 7.9 shows an updated page with new information added. Note that the Primary Interest Category and Secondary Interest Category text boxes as well as the Publisher text box are defaulted with their original values.

FIGURE 7.9:

Book update

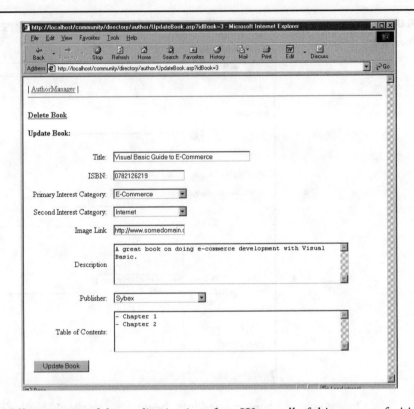

That polishes off our review of the application interface. We see all of this come to fruition in the overall community site in the next chapter. Table 7.2 outlines some enhancements you might want to consider making to the functionality presented in this chapter.

TABLE 7.2: Potential Enhancements

Enhancement	Description
Admin Approval	A site administrator may not want an author to "go live" on the main site before their content has been approved. A tracking feature could be added to the data structure to hold content before it is published live on the site. It would only go live when a site administrator approves it.
Image Upload	In the interfaces built in the manager, the author can enter in a URL link to images for the books. But, we could provide an HTTP upload feature for the image to be placed on the Web server. This is done with the HTTP file upload protocol.
Username and Password E-mail	In the scenario created in this chapter, there is no way for an author to retrieve their username and password if they have forgotten them. Many Web sites allow for the user to have the username and password e-mailed to previously input e-mail address.

Summary

The possibilities are wide open on how you can implement a way for users to contribute valuable content to your community Web site. The more focused and targeted you can make the site, the more engaging it will be for the rest of the site visitors. In this case, we have valuable input being provided by authors in which readers might be interested, especially when combined with discussion forums, polls, and other features that we explore later in this book.

In the next chapter, we are going to build the general community interface to our new author and book directory. This includes building the navigation structure, author listing, and book listing.

CHAPTER 8

Community Directory Interface

- Designing the Application

- Building the Database

- Building the User Interface

- Testing the Application

In the last chapter, we created a way for community Web site visitors to be able to contribute unique content to the site. We now need to begin the process of building the general community site interface. This chapter discusses how to build the community site home page as well as two of the community pages that display author and book information.

The pages built in this chapter are expanded in the next two chapters to include additional functionality, such as personalization, advanced searching, promotion tracking, and traffic tracking. Then in the last few chapters of the book, we will add in the bread and butter community tools of forums, polls, and a few other key applications

Designing the Application

The pages and code that you build throughout the book are purely utilitarian, and it is up to you to place a "skin" on the site that meets your community's aesthetic needs.

That being said, we now need to do a little layout and structural design of our pages. Figure 8.1 shows the basic home page layout that we are going to create.

FIGURE 8.1:

Community home page

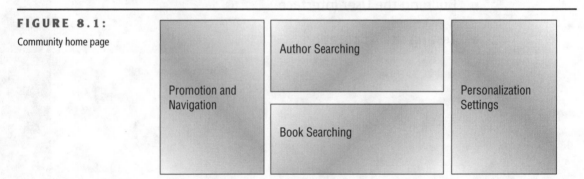

The home page is divided into four primary quadrants. Starting from the left in Figure 8.1, there is a section for navigation and promotions. This is where ads and general navigation links are shown.

Next there is a middle section that contains two parts. The top part is where we place search options for the user to find authors in our database. The bottom part is where we place search options for visitors to find books entered into the database.

On the right, we have a section that the user can personalize based on their interests. This is where we enable the site visitor to customize some of the information they see on their home page. In later chapters, we will show what kind of information can be customized.

The main structure that appears throughout the site is the promotion and navigation section. Navigation include files (similar to the author manager) are created and included on each page to set up the basic navigation structure.

In addition to setting up the home page, we round out our development from the last chapter with pages that display information about an author and on selected books. In the next chapter, we will expand the way author and book data is retrieved through the implementation of extensive search features.

Building the Database

In this chapter, we are not going to add any additional table structures to our database, but will add stored procedures to report the book and author data.

Listing 8.1 shows the SQL code used to create the sp_RetrieveAuthor stored procedure. This stored procedure is utilized to retrieve the author data specified by the author ID.

Listing 8.1   sp_RetrieveAuthor Stored Procedure

```
CREATE PROCEDURE sp_RetrieveAuthor

/* Pass in the ID of the author */
@idAuthor integer

AS

/* Retrieve the specified author ID */
select * from author
 where idAuthor = @idAuthor
GO
```

Our next stored procedure, shown in Listing 8.2, retrieves all of the books assigned to the author. This is done through a join of the book and bookauthor tables where the records match the specified author ID.

Listing 8.2   sp_RetrieveAuthorBooks Stored Procedure

```
CREATE PROCEDURE sp_RetrieveAuthorBooks

/* Pass in the ID of the author */
@idAuthor integer

AS

/* Retrieve all of the books related to the
```

```
    specified author */
select *
  from book, bookauthor
where bookauthor.idAuthor = @idAuthor and
      book.idbook = bookauthor.idbook
  GO
```

sp_RetrieveBookAuthor, the next stored procedure shown in Listing 8.3, retrieves the book and author data for a specified book ID passed in as a parameter. This is done by joining the book, author, bookauthor, and publisher tables. To display information about a book, we need to display the author name and the publisher as well as the basic book data.

Listing 8.3   sp_RetrieveBookAuthor Stored Procedure

```
CREATE PROCEDURE sp_RetrieveBookAuthor

/* Pass in the ID of the book */
@idBook integer

AS

/* Retrieve the book and author data for the
   specified book */
select author.idauthor, author.chrFirstName,
    author.chrLastName, book.idBook,
    book.chrTitle, bookauthor.idbook,
    bookauthor.idauthor, publisher.chrPublisher,
    book.txtDescription, book.txtTOC,
    book.chrImageLink, book.chrISBN,
    book.intPrimeInterest, book.intSecondInterest
  from book, author, bookauthor, publisher
where book.idbook = @idBook and
    author.idauthor = bookauthor.idauthor and
    book.idbook = bookauthor.idbook and
    book.idpublisher = publisher.idpublisher
  GO
```

NOTE   These stored procedures should be added to your existing Directory database.

That does it for database changes required to implement the functionality created in this chapter. The existing author, bookauthor, book, and publisher tables are utilized, as well as some of the Guest Register data structure.

Building the User Interface

The first step in building the user interface is designing the home page. We have already laid out the basic page structure, so now we are ready to implement it in ASP.

NOTE   On the CD, the code for these pages can be found in the "Directory2" directory. As mentioned, these pages will be updated over the next two chapters to reflect new functionality.

Listings 8.4 through 8.7 show the code for the Default.asp page. Default.asp is the home page of our community site. As we have done throughout the book, the page starts with the obligatory header information.

Listing 8.4   Default.asp

```
<%@ Language=VBScript %>
<%Option Explicit%>
<%
'*****************************************************
'** Default.asp
'**
'** Home page that provides navigation, search
'** options and personalization settings
'*****************************************************
%>
<html>
<head>
</head>
<body>
```

The page is laid out in a table structure that has three columns and nine rows. The first column is set out for the navigation and promotion section of the page and spans nine rows. We will add many more links in this section, but for now we link back to the guest register created in Chapter 6.

Listing 8.5   Default.asp continued

```
<!- Build the table to display the page ->
<table cellpadding="5" cellspacing="5" border="0">
<tr>

    <!- The first column will span 9 rows and
        show the navigation bar ->
    <td rowspan="9" valign="top">

    <!- Build the navigation. ->
```

```
<a href="/community/guestregister/GuestRegister.asp"> ⌐
Guest Register</a><br><br>

</td>
```

The next column is set out to handle the display of the author and book sections of the page. This "column" spans three columns in our table to accommodate the space needed to display the search text.

Following that we have the column for personalization settings. As with the navigation and promotion column, this one will span nine rows to provide the space needed to display the personalization settings.

Listing 8.6   Default.asp continued

```
<!- Display options to show the author ->
<td colspan="3"><font size="4"><b>
   View our list of authors:</b></font>
</td>

<!- Build the personalization column ->
<td rowspan="9" valign="top">

<ul>
<font size="4" color="blue">
   <b>Here are your personal settings:
</font><br><br></b>

<!- Display the book that matches the
   interest ->
<li>Latest book in your interest area:<br><BR>

<!- Show the latest book entered for
   the publisher ->
<li>Latest book by your selected publisher:<br>
    

<!- Display the latest book by the author ->
<li>Latest book by your selected author:<br>
    

</ul>
<br>
<center>

<!- Build a link to personalize the site ->
<i><a href="">Personalize this site!</a></i>
</center>
```

```
    </td>

  </tr>
```

Finally we need to build out the rest of the second column with rows for the author search and book search. For the search options, we have a form that posts to a page that executes the search. Right now, the form posts to nowhere but will be set up properly in the next chapter. In subsequent chapters we will also provide options for a full listing of books and authors. And, for books, we will be building out some advanced search features.

TIP
When building complex table structure, it is often helpful to set the table border tag to "1." This shows the structure of the table, which can be helpful in formatting it properly.

Listing 8.7   Default.asp continued

```html
<!- Build an option to search on the author
   name ->
<tr>
  <td> </td>
  <td align="right" valign="top">
   <b>Search Lastname:</b>
  </td>
  <td>
   <form method="post" action="">
   <input type="text" value name="SearchText">
   <input type="submit" value="Submit" name="Submit">
   <br>
   </form>
  </td>
</tr>

<!- Build an option to display a full list
   of authors ->
<tr>
  <td> </td>
  <td align="right"><b>Full List:</b></td>
  <td>
   <a href="">Display</a>
  </td>
</tr>
<tr>
  <td colspan="3"><hr></td>
</tr>
<tr>
  <td colspan="3"><font size="4">
    <b>View our list of books:</b></font>
  </td>
```

```
    </tr>

    <!- Build an option search for books by
       keyword ->
    <tr>
       <td> </td>
       <td align="right" valign="top">
        <b>Search Title:</b>
       </td>
       <td>
        <form method="post" action="">
        <input type="text" value name="SearchText">
        <input type="submit" value="Submit"
            name="Submit"><br>
        <font size="2">
        <!- Build a link to do an advanced search ->
        <a href="">Advanced Search</a>
        </font>
        </form>
       </td>
    </tr>
    <tr>
       <td> </td>
       <td align="right"><b>Full List:</b></td>
       <td>
        <!- Build a link to display a full
            list of books ->
        <a href="">Display</a>
       </td>
    </tr>

    </table>

    <br><br>
    <!- Build a link to sign up as a new
       author ->
    Want to be a new author in our list? Click
    <a href="/community/directory/author/authorsignup.asp"> ↵
      here</a>.

    </body>
    </html>
```

A link is provided at the bottom of the page for an author to sign up for the directory. Clicking this link takes them into the author management area we created in the last chapter.

We want to be able to propagate the navigation and promotion section of our home page throughout the site. This provides design consistency for visitors to always know where they can find a way to navigate the site. And, as our site grows, we want to make it easy to do a sitewide update if we add new promotion and navigation links.

To facilitate this ease of updating, we build two include files that form a table wrapper around any pages we build in our site. This wrapper contains a left section for the promotion and navigation items, and a right section for the primary page content.

Listing 8.8 shows the code for the TopNav.asp page. This code lays out the beginning of the table structure and builds in a column for the navigation and promotion links. Following that, the beginning tags for the right column in the table are started. This file will be included near the top of all the pages in our site.

Listing 8.8   TopNav.asp

```
<%
'*******************************************************
'** TopNav.asp
'**
'** Builds the top navigation table for the
'** Directory pages
'*******************************************************
%>
<!- Start the top navigation table
    for the directory ->
<table cellpadding="5" cellspacing="5" border="0">
<tr>
    <td valign="top">

    <!- Navigation Links ->
    <a href="/community/guestregister/guestregister.asp"> ↵
    Guest Register</a><br><br>

    </td>
    <td valign="top">
```

Listing 8.9 shows the code for the BottomNav.asp page. This code lays out the closing tags for the table started in TopNav.asp. This file is included near the bottom of all the pages in our site.

Listing 8.9   BottomNav.asp

```
<%
'*******************************************************
'** BottomNav.asp
'**
'** Builds the closing navigation table
'*******************************************************
```

```
%>
<!- Close out the navigation table ->
</td>
</tr>
</table>
```

We are now ready to move on to the pages that display the author and book data entered by the author members of our site. Listings 8.10 through 8.14 show the code for AuthorInfo.asp.

The page has the standard header information as well as the TopNav.asp page code. This provides the wrapper formatting for the navigation and promotion left section of the page. All of the primary contents of the page are displayed in the right column of the table.

Listing 8.10   AuthorInfo.asp

```
<%@ Language=VBScript %>
<%Option Explicit%>
<%
'****************************************************
'** AuthorInfo.asp
'**
'** Displays the selected author information
'****************************************************
%>
<HTML>

<BODY bgcolor="white">

<!- #include file="topnav.asp" ->
```

Next, we create a database connection to our author information tables. The sp_ RetrieveAuthor stored procedure retrieves the author data for the specified ID.

NOTE   To utilize this page, you need to manually add a parameter onto the URL for the ID of the author you would like to display. In the next chapter, we build the author search interface, which performs this task automatically.

Listing 8.11   AuthorInfo.asp continued

```
<%

Dim dbAuthor      ' Database Connection
Dim rsAuthor      ' Recordset
Dim SQL           ' String
```

```
Dim txtAuthorBio        ' String
DIM chrUserName         ' String
DIM chrPassword         ' String
DIM dbBook              ' Database Connection
DIM rsBook              ' Recordset

' Create an ADO database connection
set dbAuthor = _
   server.createobject("adodb.connection")

' Create record set
set rsAuthor = _
   server.CreateObject("adodb.recordset")

' Open the connection using our ODBC file DSN
dbAuthor.open("filedsn=Directory")

' Retrieve the author data
sql = "execute sp_RetrieveAuthor " & _
   request("idAuthor")

' Execute the statement and retrieve the record set
set rsAuthor = dbAuthor.Execute(sql)

' Retrieve the return values
txtAuthorBio = rsAuthor("txtAuthorBio")
chrUserName = rsAuthor("chrUserName")
chrPassword = rsAuthor("chrPassword")

%>
```

Once the author data is retrieved, we are ready to display the data and the biographical information. Note that the e-mail address is hot-linked so that the user can click it to e-mail the author. The Web page URL that the author provided is also hyperlinked for easy clicking.

When the author bio is displayed, we have to prepare the text entered by the author for display in an HTML format. In the author manager, the author can type in their bio complete with standard line breaks to format the text. Since HTML does not break lines based on the standard keyboard return characters, we need to convert those into HTML <BR> break tags. This is done with the VBScript Replace function. All carriage returns, chr(10), are replaced with <BR> tags.

Listing 8.12   AuthorInfo.asp continued

```
<b><font size="4" color="blue">Author Data:</font>
<BR><BR>
```

```
<table border="0" cellpadding="5" cellspacing="5">

<!- Display the first name ->
<tr>
   <td align="right">First Name:</td>
   <td><%=rsAuthor("chrFirstName")%></td>
</tr>

<!- Display the last name ->
<tr>
   <td align="right">Last Name:</td>
   <td><%=rsAuthor("chrLastName")%></td>
</tr>

<!- Display the company ->
<tr>
   <td align="right">Company:</td>
   <td><%=rsAuthor("chrCompany")%></td>
</tr>

<!- Display the email address ->
<tr>
   <td align="right">Email Address:</td>
   <td>
   <a href="mailto:<%=rsAuthor("chrEmail")%>"> ⏎
   <%=rsAuthor("chrEmail")%></a>
   </td>
</tr>

<!- Display the author's link ->
<tr>
   <td align="right">URL:</td>
   <td>
   <a href="<%=rsAuthor("chrUrl")%>"> ⏎
   <%=rsAuthor("chrUrl")%></a>
   </td>
</tr>

<!- Display the author's bio and ensure
   line breaks are displayed ->
<tr>
   <td align="right" valign="top">Author Bio:</td>
   <td><%=replace(txtAuthorBio, chr(10), "<BR>")%></td>
</tr>

</table>
```

Now that we have displayed the author information, we can list the books the author has entered. We need to execute another SQL query, sp_RetrieveAuthorBooks, to retrieve the books for the specified author. The ID of the author is passed into the stored procedure as passed on the URL for the page.

Listing 8.13   AuthorInfo.asp continued

```
<BR><BR>
<b><font size="4" color="blue">Books:</font>
<BR><BR>

<!- Build the table to display the books
    for the author ->
<table>

<%

' Close the database connection
dbAuthor.Close

' Create an ADO database connection
set dbBook = _
    server.createobject("adodb.connection")

' Create record set
set rsBook = _
    server.CreateObject("adodb.recordset")

' Open the connection using our ODBC file DSN
dbBook.open("filedsn=Directory")

' Retrieve the books for the author
sql = "execute sp_RetrieveAuthorBooks " & _
        request("idAuthor")

' Execute the statement and retrieve the record set
set rsBook = dbBook.Execute(sql)

' Loop through the books
do until rsBook.EOF

%>
```

We are ready to display the book information. A table row is displayed , and a link to the BookInfo.asp page is created with the ID of the book on the page. This way the site visitor can view more information on the book.

Listing 8.14   AuthorInfo.asp continued

```
<tr>
    <td> </td>
    <td>
        <!- Build a link to retrieve the
            book info ->
        <a href="BookInfo.asp?idBook= ↵
    <%=rsBook("idBook")%>"><%=rsBook("chrTitle")%></a></td>
</tr>

<%

' Move to the next row
rsBook.MoveNext

Loop

' Close the database connection
dbBook.Close

%>

</table>

<!- #include file="bottomnav.asp" ->

</body>

</HTML>
```

Finally the page is closed out with the database connection closed. We also have the BottomNav.asp include file that closes out the navigation structure for the page.

Our next page is the BookInfo.asp page which displays the information of the specified book. As with the AuthorInfo.asp page, this page requires that the ID of the book be passed on the URL in an idBook parameter. Listings 8.15 through 8.18 show the code for the BookInfo.asp page.

This page includes the TopNav.asp and BottomNav.asp include files for the navigation and promotion structure. The page starts out with a database connection being opened and the sp_RetrieveBookAuthor is executed with the book ID. This returns both the book information and the author information.

Listing 8.15   BookInfo.asp

```asp
<%@ Language=VBScript %>
<%Option Explicit%>
<%
'*******************************************************
'** BookInfo.asp
'**
'** Displays the selected book information
'*******************************************************
%>
<HTML>
<HEAD>
</HEAD>
<BODY>

<!- #include file="topnav.asp" ->

<table border="0" cellpadding="5" cellspacing="5">

<%

Dim dbBook              ' Database Connection
Dim rsBook              ' Recordset
Dim SQL                 ' String
Dim txtDescription      ' String
Dim txtTOC              ' String
Dim chrFirstName        ' String
Dim chrLastName         ' String
Dim chrImageLink        ' String
Dim dbGuestRegister     ' Database Connection
Dim rsGuestRegister     ' Recordset

' Create an ADO database connection
set dbBook = _
    server.createobject("adodb.connection")

' Create record set
set rsBook = _
    server.CreateObject("adodb.recordset")

' Open the connection using our ODBC file DSN
dbBook.open("filedsn=Directory")

' Retrieve the book and author data
sql = "execute sp_RetrieveBookAuthor " & _
    request("idBook")

' Execute the statement and retrieve the record set
set rsBook = dbBook.Execute(sql)
```

```
' Retrieve returned value
txtDescription = rsBook("txtDescription")
txtTOC = rsBook("txtTOC")
chrFirstName = rsBook("chrFirstName")
chrLastName = rsBook("chrLastName")
chrImageLink = rsBook("chrImageLink")


%>
```

We are now ready to display the book information. The table rows display the data from the table. This includes the author name that is linked to the AuthorInfo.asp page to display the full author information.

Listing 8.16	BookInfo.asp continued

```
<!- Display the title ->
<tr>
    <td align="right">Title:</td>
    <td>
        <%=rsBook("chrTitle")%>
    </td>
</tr>

<!- Display the book author ->
<tr>
    <td align="right">Author:</td>
    <td>
        <a href="AuthorInfo.asp?idAuthor= ↵
        <%=rsBook("idAuthor")%>"><%=chrLastName%>, ↵
        <%=chrFirstName%></a>
    </td>
</tr>

<!- Display the ISBN ->
<tr>
    <td align="right">ISBN:</td>
    <td><%=rsBook("chrISBN")%></td>
</tr>
<tr>
    <td align="right">Primary Interest Category:</td>
    <td>
```

Part of the information that we have to display is the topics that the book is assigned. A new database connection is created to retrieve the topic data. The ID stored in the Book record is passed to the sp_RetrieveInterestTopicByID stored procedure. Note that both the primary and secondary assigned topics are displayed.

Listing 8.17   BookInfo.asp continued

```asp
<%

    ' Create an ADO database connection
    set dbGuestRegister = _
        server.createobject("adodb.connection")

    ' Create a record set
    set rsGuestRegister = _
        server.CreateObject("adodb.recordset")

    ' Open the connection using our ODBC file DSN
    dbGuestRegister.open("filedsn=GuestRegister")

    ' Retrieve the primary interest topic
    sql = "execute sp_RetrieveInterestTopicByID " & _
        rsBook("intPrimeInterest")

    ' Execute the SQL statement
    set rsGuestRegister = dbGuestRegister.execute(sql)

%>

    <!- Show the interest topic ->
    <%=rsGuestRegister("chrName")%>

    </td>
</tr>

<tr>
    <td align="right">Second Interest Category:</td>
    <td>

    <%

    ' Retrieve the name of the interest topic
    sql = "execute sp_RetrieveInterestTopicByID " & _
        rsBook("intSecondInterest")

    ' Execute the SQL statement
    set rsGuestRegister = dbGuestRegister.execute(sql)

    %>

    <!- Show the interest name ->
    <%=rsGuestRegister("chrName")%>

    <%
```

```
    ' Close the database connection
    dbGuestRegister.Close

    %>

    </td>
  </tr>
```

The rest of the page is completed with the URL link to the book image, the description, the publisher, and the table of contents. Note that both the description and the table of contents have their carriage returned with HTML <BR> tags.

Listing 8.18   BookInfo.asp continued

```
<tr>
  <td align="right">Image Link</td>
  <td>
   <!- Show the image link ->
   <a href="<%=chrImageLink%>"><%=chrImageLink%></a>
  </td>
</tr>
<tr>
  <td align="right" valign="top">Description</td>
  <td>
    <!- Show the description. Ensure line
       breaks show up. ->
     <%=replace(txtDescription, chr(10), "<BR>")%>
  </td>
</tr>
<tr>
  <td align="right">Publisher:</td>
  <!- Show the publisher ->
  <td><%=rsBook("chrPublisher")%></td>
</tr>
<tr>
  <td align="right" valign="top">
     Table of Contents:
  </td>
  <!- Show the table of contents. Ensure line
     breaks show up. ->
  <td><%=replace(txtTOC, chr(10), "<BR>")%></td>
</tr>

<%

' Close the database connection
dbBook.Close

%>
```

```
</table>

<!- #include file="bottomnav.asp" ->

</BODY>
</HTML>
```

And with that, our coding for this section closes out. We have set the framework for our community Web site and will expand it over the next several chapters. Next, let's review these pages in action.

Testing the User Interface

Testing our Web site is fairly simple. First, call up the Default.asp page for the author directory site (/community/directory/). Figure 8.2 shows the home page. For display purposes in the book, the home page shows the table structure with the Border table tag set to 1. Note how our column and row structure appears and how the Guest Register link is in the navigation area on the left. The center of the page has the structure for the author and book searches, and we have our placeholder for the personalization of the site on the right.

NOTE   To test these pages you need to ensure that the Author and Book tables in the database have test data entered.

FIGURE 8.2:

The directory home page

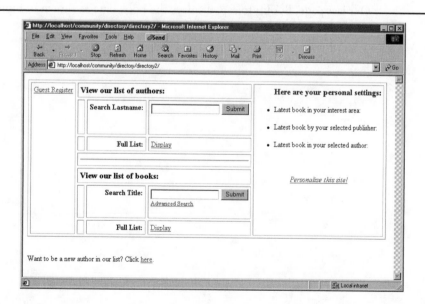

Next, let's test our Author and Book information pages. Figure 8.3 shows the AuthorInfo.asp page. Note that you will need to supply the idAuthor parameter on the page with the valid ID of an author in your database.

FIGURE 8.3:

Author listing

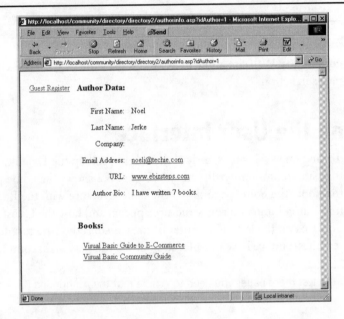

Our last page, BookInfo.asp, displays the book data as shown in Figure 8.4. Again, you will need a valid book ID on the URL with the idBook parameter.

Book information listing

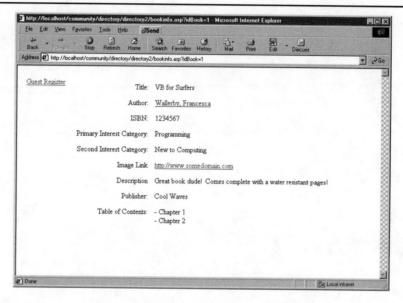

In the next chapter we will see how all of these pages will integrate together.

Summary

In this chapter we started to implement the public side of the community Web site with some integration of the data collected in the functionality we created in the last chapter. In the next two chapters, we build significant new features for our community Web site, including affiliate tracking, personalization, promotions tracking, extended search features, and a full-featured administrative interface. This sets the stage for our key interactive community features to be integrated into the site.

CHAPTER 9

Personalization and Search

- Designing the Application

- Building the Database

- Building the User Interface

- Testing the Application

We are now ready to build some additional features into our community Web site. This chapter explains how to create a search capability so the site visitor can find books and authors in the community. This provides a method for visitors to find the content they are interested in as contributed by the authors. This chapter also demonstrates how to store the search keywords as part of monitoring and analyzing our community.

In addition to the search, this chapter shows how to add personalization features to the site. By adding personalization to the site, we can provide tools for the site visitor to easily find what interests them. The goal is for our community to expand significantly and the numbers of authors and books to be more than can be easily browsed at one time. Also, we're hoping that additions and updates will be so frequent that a site visitor will not be able to keep up with them.

Designing the Application

In the last chapter, we did not "hook up" the search forms and links in the center column of the page. In this chapter, we are going to build a set of stored procedures and active server pages to implement this search functionality.

The site visitor can search by entering keywords to search for either books or authors by author name and book title. With each search, we add the keywords into a database table for further review to analyze search trends.

To implement the personalization features, we need to provide options to see books and authors by book topic area, publisher, and author. This feature is implemented with cookie technology. The site visitor can select various options and have the settings stored on their computer.

The personalization implementation provides three select boxes for personalized settings. The first will be the primary interest category to which the books are assigned. The latest book assigned to the selected topic is displayed. Next, a specific publisher can be selected and the most recent book added to the system is displayed. The final personalization setting is author specific. The most recent book added by the selected author is displayed on the home page.

Once selections have been made, the home page will reflect the visitor's personalized settings in the right column, and latest book in the selected category is displayed.

Guest Registration and Personalization

In this chapter, we are implementing personalization through the use of cookies on the client machine. As noted, these settings are not stored in the database. We could tie together the guest registration and personalization settings. In effect, we would turn the guest register into a profile of our site visitors. In that case, we would have to provide a method for the visitor to log in to update their private profile data.

Building the Database

In addition to the database structure built in Chapter 8, we make some additions in this chapter that include both stored procedures and tables. Changes are made to support primarily the search functionality and some additions to retrieve the personalization results.

Listing 9.1 shows the only table we need to add to the database. The Searches table stores the key words entered by the site visitor. There is also an intType field that stores the type of search, book, or author.

Listing 9.1   Searches Table

```
CREATE TABLE dbo.Searches (
    idSearch int IDENTITY (1, 1) NOT NULL ,
    dtSearched datetime NULL CONSTRAINT
DF_Searches_dtSearched_7__10 DEFAULT (getdate()),
    chrSearch varchar (255) NULL ,
    intType int NULL
)
GO
```

Moving onto the stored procedures, our first procedure searches the author name for the selected keywords. Listing 9.2 shows the stored procedure. The search keywords are passed in as a single parameter into the stored procedure. The SQL "like" function is utilized to find author names that contain the searched-for keywords. Note that the results are returned with the corresponding book data and ordered by the author's last name.

Listing 9.2   sp_SearchAuthorName Stored Procedure

```
CREATE PROCEDURE sp_SearchAuthorName

/* Pass in the name to be searched */
@chrName varchar(255)
```

```
AS

/* Search for authors who last name are like
   the keyword name passed in. Also return the
   book data for the specified author. */
select * from author, bookauthor, book
    where author.idauthor=bookauthor.idauthor and
        bookauthor.idbook = book.idbook and
        author.chrLastName like '%' + @chrName + '%'
    order by author.chrLastName
GO
```

Next we have a stored procedure that searches the book data for the specified keywords. Listing 9.3 displays the sp_SearchBookName stored procedure, which takes in one parameter that contains the search keywords.

As in the last stored procedure, the SQL "like" function is utilized to find book titles that contain the keywords. In this case, the author data is returned with the book information.

Listing 9.3 sp_SearchBookName Stored Procedure

```
CREATE PROCEDURE sp_SearchBookName

/* Pass in the title of the book */
@chrTitle varchar(255)

AS

/* Search for books who title are like
   the keyword title passed in. Also return
   the author data for the specified book. */
select author.idauthor, author.chrFirstName,
    author.chrLastName, book.idBook,
    book.chrTitle, bookauthor.idbook,
    bookauthor.idauthor, book.txtDescription,
    book.txtTOC, book.chrImageLink,
    book.chrISBN, book.intPrimeInterest,
    book.intSecondInterest
 from author,bookauthor,book
 where author.idauthor=bookauthor.idauthor and
    bookauthor.idbook = book.idbook and
    chrTitle like '%' + @chrTitle + '%'
 order by chrTitle
 GO
```

Now we move onto the stored procedures to return the data for the personalization settings. Our first stored procedure, sp_RetrieveBookByInterest shown in Listing 9.4, returns book information that matches the specified interest passed in as a parameter. Note that the results are ordered by the date the book was added to the database.

TIP   This stored procedure can be modified to return only the book with the latest date instead of all the books ordered by date.

Listing 9.4   sp_RetrieveBookByInterest Stored Procedure

```
CREATE PROCEDURE sp_RetrieveBookByInterest

/* Pass in the ID of the primary
   interest topic */
@intPrimeInterest integer

AS

/* Retrieve the books that are categorized
   in the specified interest */
select * from book
    where intPrimeInterest = @intPrimeInterest
    order by dtCreated
GO
```

Our next personalization stored procedure, sp_RetrieveBookByPub, is shown in Listing 9.5. This returns all of the books assigned to the specified publisher passed in the idPublisher parameter. Again, the results are ordered by date entered such that the most recent entry is returned as the first record.

Listing 9.5   sp_RetrieveBookByPub Stored Procedure

```
CREATE PROCEDURE sp_RetrieveBookByPub

/* Pass in the ID of the publisher */
@idPublisher integer

AS

/* Retrieve the books that are assigned to
   the specified publisher */
select * from book,Publisher
    where book.idPublisher = @idPublisher and
        book.idPublisher = publisher.idpublisher
    order by dtCreated
GO
```

The next stored procedure, sp_RetrieveAllAuthorsBooks shown in Listing 9.6, returns all of the authors in the database. The results are ordered by the author's last name. Note that the author's book data is also returned.

Listing 9.6   sp_RetrieveAllAuthorBooks Stored Procedure

```
CREATE PROCEDURE sp_RetrieveAllAuthorsBooks AS

/* return all authors and their related books */
select author.idauthor, author.chrFirstName,
     author.chrLastName, book.idBook,
     book.chrTitle, bookauthor.idbook,
     bookauthor.idauthor
  from book, bookauthor, author
  where bookauthor.idAuthor = Author.idAuthor and
     book.idbook = bookauthor.idbook
order by author.chrLastName
GO
```

Listing 9.7 shows the sp_RetrieveAuthors stored procedure. This stored procedure retrieves all the authors in the database and orders them by last name.

Listing 9.7   sp_RetrieveAuthors Stored Procedure

```
CREATE PROCEDURE sp_RetrieveAuthors AS

/*  Retrieve all authors and order them
     by the author's last name */
select * from author
  order by chrLastName
GO
```

The next stored procedure, sp_RetrieveAllBooksAuthor, is the mirror image of the last. This is shown in Listing 9.8. In this case, all of the books in the database are returned with the corresponding book data returned, too. The books are ordered by title.

Listing 9.8   sp_RetrieveAllBooksAuthor Stored Procedure

```
CREATE PROCEDURE sp_RetrieveAllBooksAuthor AS

/* Retrieve all books and their related authors */
 select *
  from book, bookauthor, author
  where bookauthor.idAuthor = Author.idAuthor and
     book.idbook = bookauthor.idbook
order by book.chrTitle
GO
```

Our last stored procedure, sp_InsertSearch shown in Listing 9.9, handles the insertion of the searched keywords into the Searches database. Both the keywords and the type of search are passed in to the stored procedure.

Listing 9.9 **sp_InsertSearch Stored Procedure**

```
CREATE PROCEDURE sp_InsertSearch

/* Pass in the search keywords and the
   type of search performed (author or
   book) */
@chrSearch varchar(255),
@intType integer

AS

/* Insert the search data */
insert into Searches(chrSearch, intType)
values(@chrSearch, @intType)
GO
```

That is it for the database changes. Now we are ready to build the VBscript code to implement the personalization and search features.

Building the User Interface

Our next step is to move on to the building of the user interface. We can update our home page to incorporate the new search and personalization functionality. We will also add several pages to display the search results and manage the personalization settings.

NOTE On the CD, the code for these pages can be found in the "Directory3" directory. As mentioned, these pages will be updated over the next two chapters to reflect new functionality.

Before we look at the home page, we need to look at the pages that the visitor utilizes to set their personal settings. Based on these pages, we can see how the logic for the Default.asp page will be set up.

Listings 9.10 through 9.13 show the code for Personalize.asp. As we saw in the last chapter, we have the TopNav.asp and BottomNav.asp pages included to provide our navigation structure for the page.

Listing 9.10   Personalize.asp

```
<%@ Language=VBScript %>
<%Option Explicit%>
<%
'*****************************************************
'** Personalize.asp
'**
'** Build personalization options for the user
'*****************************************************
%>
<HTML>
<HEAD>
</HEAD>

<BODY>

<!- #include file="topnav.asp" ->
```

The first thing we do on the page is read any previous personalization cookie settings. We have three cookies set—intPrimeInterest, idPublisher, and idAuthor. Each of these cookies stores the ID of the selected value. For example, the ID of the primary topic of interest for the visitor is stored in the intPrimeInterest cookies. Likewise, the selected ID of the publisher and author are stored in their respective cookies. These values are read initially so we can default the select boxes.

Listing 9.11   Personalize.asp continued

```
<b>Select your personalization options. The
latest books for each category will
be displayed on your home page:</b></BR></BR>

<%

Dim intPrimeInterest      ' Integer
Dim idPublisher           ' Integer
Dim idAuthor              ' Integer
Dim dbGuestRegister       ' Database Connection
Dim rsGuestRegister       ' Recordset
Dim SQL                   ' String
Dim Selected              ' String
Dim dbPublisher           ' Database Connection
Dim rsPublisher           ' Recordset
Dim dbAuthor              ' Database Connection
Dim rsAuthor              ' Recordset

' Retrieve the existing personalization settings
intPrimeInterest = ↵
  int(Request.Cookies("Personalize")("intPrimeInterest"))
```

```
idPublisher = ⌐
   int(Request.Cookies("Personalize")("idPublisher"))

idAuthor = int(Request.Cookies("Personalize")("idAuthor"))

%>
```

Next we build a form that posts the results of the personalization settings to the Set-Personalization.asp page. The first row built is for the Interest Topics selection. As we have done before, the GuestRegister database is queried to populate the select box. With each record reviewed, a check is done to see if the current record matches the previous personalization selection. To do this, the "selected" technique we have previously used to designate which option should be set.

Listing 9.12   Personalize.asp continued

```
<!- Build the form to post the settings ->
<form method="post" action="SetPersonalization.asp">

<!- start the table to show the select boxes ->
<table cellpadding="5" cellspacing="5">

<tr>
    <td align="right">Primary Interest Category:</td>
    <td>

<%

' Create an ADO database connection
set dbGuestRegister = _
    server.createobject("adodb.connection")

' Create a record set
set rsGuestRegister = _
    server.CreateObject("adodb.recordset")

' Open the connection using our ODBC file DSN
dbGuestRegister.open("filedsn=GuestRegister")

' Retrieve the list of interest topics
sql = "execute sp_RetrieveInterestTopics"

' Execute the SQL statement
set rsGuestRegister = dbGuestRegister.execute(sql)

%>

    <!- Start the select list ->
```

```
<select name="intPrimeInterest">

<!- Show a blank option ->
<option value="">

<%

' Loop through the list
do until rsGuestRegister.EOF

' Check to see if the current option to be
' displayed is the previous selection
if intPrimeInterest = ↵
rsGuestRegister("idInterestTopic") then

        ' Set our selected variable
        selected = "Selected"

else

        ' Clear the variable
        selected = ""

end if

%>

<!- Build the option to display
    the interest topic ->
<option value="<%=rsGuestRegister("idInterestTopic")%>" <%=selected%>>
<%=rsGuestRegister("chrName")%>
<%

        ' Move to the next row
        rsGuestRegister.movenext

    ' Loop back
    loop

    ' Close the database
    dbGuestRegister.Close
    %>
  </select>

    </td>
</tr>
```

For the publisher and author selections, the same process is followed. All of the publishers and authors are retrieved and listed in the select boxes with the previous selections defaulted.

Listing 9.13   Personalize.asp continued

```
<tr>
    <td align="right">Publisher:</td>
    <td>

<%

' Create an ADO database connection
set dbPublisher = _
    server.createobject("adodb.connection")

' Create a record set
set rsPublisher = _
    server.CreateObject("adodb.recordset")

' Open the connection using our ODBC file DSN
dbPublisher.open("filedsn=Directory")

' Retrieve the list of publishers
sql = "execute sp_RetrievePublishers"

' Execute the SQL statement
set rsPublisher = dbPublisher.execute(sql)

%>

    <!- Start the select list ->
    <select name="idPublisher">
    <option value="">

<%

' Loop through the list
do until rsPublisher.EOF

' Check to see if the current publisher is
' the one previously selected
if idPublisher = rsPublisher("idPublisher") then

    ' Set our variable to display the selection
    selected = "selected"

else

    ' Clear the variable
    selected = ""

end if
```

```
%>
<!- Build the option. Note the selected variable
    is output. When set to "selected" that option
    will be the default.  ->
<option value="<%=rsPublisher("idPublisher")%>" <%=selected%>>⌐
<%=rsPublisher("chrPublisher")%>
<%

        ' Move to the next row
        rsPublisher.movenext

    ' Loop back
    loop

    ' Close the database
    dbPublisher.Close
    %>
 </select>

    </td>
</tr>

<tr>
    <td align="right">Author:</td>
    <td>

    <select name="idAuthor">

    <!- Show a blank option ->
    <option value="">
    <%

    ' Create an ADO database connection
    set dbAuthor = _
        server.createobject("adodb.connection")

    ' Create record set
    set rsAuthor = _
        server.CreateObject("adodb.recordset")

    ' Open the connection using our ODBC file DSN
    dbAuthor.open("filedsn=Directory")

    ' Retrieve the current list of authors
    sql = "execute sp_RetrieveAuthors"

    ' Execute the statement and retrieve the record set
    set rsAuthor = dbAuthor.Execute(sql)

    ' Loop through the authors
    do until rsAuthor.EOF

    ' Check to see if the current author is
```

```asp
        ' the same as the one previously selected
        if idAuthor = int(rsAuthor("idAuthor")) then

            ' Set the selected variable
            selected = "Selected"

        else

            ' Clear the variable
            selected = ""

        end if


        %>

        <!- Build the option. Note the selected variable
            is output. When set to "selected" that option
            will be the default.  ->
        <option value="<%=rsAuthor("idAuthor")%>" <%=Selected%>>⏎
        <%=rsAuthor("chrLastName")%>, <%=rsAuthor("chrFirstName")%>

        <%

        ' Move to the next record
        rsAuthor.MoveNext

        Loop

        ' Close the database connection
        dbAuthor.Close
        %>
        </select>

        </td>
</tr>

<tr>
    <td colspan="2" align="center">
    <input type="Submit" value="Submit" name="Submit">
    </td>
</tr>

</table>

</form>

<!- #include file="bottomnav.asp" ->

</BODY>
</HTML>
```

WARNING If you have hundreds of authors or publishers, the select boxes can get extremely long. In that case consider adding a wizard interface to narrow down the list alphabetically.

After those select boxes are completed, the page is closed out. Now we are ready to look at how the settings are implemented into cookies.

The SetPersonalization.asp page reads in the settings from the personalization.asp page and stores them in client-side cookies. Listings 9.14 and 9.15 show the code for the page. Note that this page has no visible user interface, and we do not need to include the navigation include files.

Listing 9.14   SetPersonalization.asp

```
<%@ Language=VBScript %>
<%Option Explicit%>
<%
'*****************************************************
'** SetPersonalization.asp
'**
'** Processes the personalization settings by the
'** user
'*****************************************************
%>
<%

Dim intPrimeInterest    ' Integer
Dim idPublisher         ' Integer
Dim idAuthor            ' Integer
```

The values are retrieved from the form and stored into variables. If they have no value, meaning the user didn't make a selection, then the values are defaulted to –1. This ensures that a value regardless is stored in the cookies.

Next we set the cookies values. To do this, the cookies collection of the Response object is utilized. We are going to set up a cookie called "Personalize" that expires on July 31, 2005. A date has to be set to ensure the cookie is "permanent" on the client's machine. The variable values of the cookie are then set. The names of variables are the same as the database fields, intPrimeInterest, idPublisher, and idAuthor. Once the values are set, the user is then sent to the home page.

Listing 9.15   SetPersonalization.asp continued

```
' Retrieve the personalization settings
intPrimeInterest = request("intPrimeInterest")
```

```
idPublisher = request("idPublisher")
idAuthor = request("idAuthor")

' If they are blank, then store a -1 as the
' setting value
if intPrimeInterest = "" then intPrimeInterest = "-1"
if idPublisher = "" then idPublisher = "-1"
if idAuthor = "" then idAuthor = "-1"

' Write out the cookie and set the expiration
' well into the future
Response.cookies("Personalize").expires = "July 31, 2005"

' Set the values
Response.Cookies("Personalize")("intPrimeInterest") = ↵
  IntPrimeInterest

Response.Cookies("Personalize")("idPublisher") = ↵
  IdPublisher

Response.Cookies("Personalize")("idAuthor") = idAuthor

' Send the user to the home page
Response.Redirect "default.asp"

%>
```

Now we are ready to look at the updated home page. Listings 9.16 through 9.22 show the code for the updated Default.asp page. We need to add the links to the search page and build in the personalization functionality. The page starts out with the standard header and is followed by the left side navigation.

Listing 9.16   **Default.asp**

```
<%@ Language=VBScript %>
<%Option Explicit%>
<%
'********************************************************
'** Default.asp
'**
'** Home page that provides navigation, search
'** options and personalization settings
'********************************************************
%>
<html>
<head>
</head>
<body>
```

```
<%

Dim intPrimeInterest    ' Integer
Dim idPublisher         ' Integer
Dim idAuthor            ' Integer
Dim dbAuthor            ' Database Object
Dim rsAuthor            ' Record Set
Dim SQL                 ' String
%>

<!- Build the table to display the page ->
<table cellpadding="5" cellspacing="5" border="0">
<tr>

    <!- The first column will span 9 rows and
        show the navigation bar ->
    <td rowspan="9" valign="top">

    <!- Build the navigation. ->
    <a href="/community/guestregister/GuestRegister.asp"> ⏎
    Guest Register</a><br><br>

    </td>

    <!- Display options to show the author ->
    <td colspan="3"><font size="4"><b>
        View our list of authors:</b></font>
    </td>
```

The personalization section shows the books in the database that meet the visitor's settings. The first step is to read the cookies settings we established in the personalization process. The ID values in these cookies are utilized to query the database.

Listing 9.17   Default.asp continued

```
    <!- Build the personalization column ->
    <td rowspan="9" valign="top">

        <ul>
        <font size="4" color="blue">
            <b>Here are your personal settings:
        </font><br><br></b>

        <%

' Retrieve the personalization settings
intPrimeInterest = ⏎
 trim(Request.Cookies("Personalize")("intPrimeInterest"))
```

```
  idPublisher = ↵
    trim(Request.Cookies("Personalize")("idPublisher"))

  idAuthor = ↵
    trim(Request.Cookies("Personalize")("idAuthor"))
```

We need to query the database with each setting. For the interest topics, the sp_retrieve-BookByInterest stored procedure is utilized. The ID read from the cookie is passed in as a parameter.

We first check to see if there is a value in the cookie, because there is a chance that a cookie has not been set. If the cookie has been set, then the query is executed and a check is done to see if a record is returned. It is possible that the user selected no default. If a result was returned, the first record is displayed for the user. The book is linked to the BookInfo.asp page.

Listing 9.18   Default.asp continued

```
        ' Create an ADO database connection
        set dbAuthor = _
            server.createobject("adodb.connection")

        ' Create record set
        set rsAuthor = _
            server.CreateObject("adodb.recordset")

        ' Open the connection using our ODBC file DSN
        dbAuthor.open("filedsn=Directory")

        ' See if a primary interest topic setting
        ' is set
        if intPrimeInterest <> "" then

        ' Retrieve the books that meet the interest
        ' setting
        sql = "execute sp_RetrieveBookByInterest " & _
            intPrimeInterest

        ' Execute the statement and retrieve the record set
        set rsAuthor = dbAuthor.Execute(sql)

        ' Ensure a record was returned
        if not rsAuthor.EOF then

        %>

        <!- Display the book that matches the
```

```
    interest ->
<li>Latest book in your interest area:<br>
    
<a href="bookinfo.asp?idBook=↵
<%=rsAuthor("idBook")%>"> ↵
<%=rsAuthor("chrTitle")%></a>
<br><br>

<%

end if

end if
```

Next we handle the publisher search. The sp_RetrieveBookByPub stored procedure is utilized, as long as a value is set in the cookie. If a record is returned, the latest book entered by the publisher is displayed. The book is linked to the BookInfo.asp page.

Listing 9.19   Default.asp continued

```
' Check and see if a preferred publisher
' was entered.
if idPublisher <> "" then

' Execute the stored procedure to retrieve books
' for the publisher
sql = "execute sp_RetrieveBookByPub " & _
      idPublisher

' Execute the statement and retrieve the record set
set rsAuthor = dbAuthor.Execute(sql)

' Ensure a record was returned
if not rsAuthor.EOF then

%>

<!- Show the latest book entered for
    the publisher ->
<li>Latest book by your selected publisher:<br>
    
<a href="bookinfo.asp?idBook= ↵
<%=rsAuthor("idBook")%>"> ↵
<%=rsAuthor("chrTitle")%></a>
<br><br>

<%

end if
end if
```

The author setting is handled in the same fashion. The sp_RetrieveBookByAuthor stored procedure is called. The book last posted by the author is displayed and linked to the BookInfo.asp page.

Listing 9.20   Default.asp continued

```
' See if a preferred author was entered
if idAuthor <> "" then

' Execute the stored procedure to retrieve the
' latest books by the author
sql = "execute sp_RetrieveBookByAuthor " & _
      idAuthor

' Execute the statement and retrieve the record set
set rsAuthor = dbAuthor.Execute(sql)

' Ensure a record set was returned
if not rsAuthor.EOF then

%>

<!- Display the latest book by the author ->
<li>Latest book in your selected author:<br>
    
<a href="bookinfo.asp?idBook= ↵
<%=rsAuthor("idBook")%>"> ↵
<%=rsAuthor("chrTitle")%></a>
<br><br>

<%
end if
end if

' Close the database connection
dbAuthor.Close
%>
</ul>
<br>
<center>

<!- Build a link to personalize the site ->
<i><a href="personalize.asp"> ↵
Personalize this site!</a></i>
</center>
</td>

</tr>
```

The database connection for the personalization is closed out and a link is built to the Personalize.asp page for updating the settings.

We are now ready to update the search section of the page. The primary action we need to take is to update the form posts and the links to the full listing display.

In the first section for the author name, we update the search form to post to the SearchAuthors.asp page. Next, the full list display link is updated to link to the same page, but we pass a parameter on the URL called "type" that indicates a full listing is to be performed versus a search listing.

Listing 9.21   Default.asp continued

```
<!- Build an option to search on the author
   name ->
<tr>
    <td> </td>
    <td align="right" valign="top">
     <b>Search Lastname:</b>
    </td>
    <td>
     <form method="post" action="SearchAuthors.asp">
     <input type="text" value name="SearchText">
     <input type="submit" value="Submit" name="Submit">
     <br>
     </form>
    </td>
</tr>

<!- Build an option to display a full list
   of author ->
<tr>
    <td> </td>
    <td align="right"><b>Full List:</b></td>
    <td>
     <a href="SearchAuthors.asp?type=full">Display</a>
    </td>
</tr>
<tr>
    <td colspan="3"><hr></td>
</tr>
<tr>
    <td colspan="3"><font size="4">
        <b>View our list of books:</b></font>
    </td>
</tr>
```

The last section that is updated is the search form for the book search. The post is set to the SearchBooks.asp page. For the books, we also provide an advance search option for the user. This is linked to the AdvBookSearch.asp page, and the full book listing option links to SearchBooks.asp. We also pass a parameter, in this case to indicate a full search.

Listing 9.22   Default.asp continued

```
<!- Build an option search for books by
    keyword ->
<tr>
    <td> </td>
    <td align="right" valign="top">
     <b>Search Title:</b>
    </td>
    <td>
     <form method="post" action="SearchBooks.asp">
     <input type="text" value name="SearchText">
     <input type="submit" value="Submit"
         name="Submit"><br>
     <font size="2">
     <!- Build a link to do an advanced search ->
     <a href="AdvBookSearch.asp?type=advanced"> ⏎
     Advanced Search</a>
     </font>
     </form>
    </td>
</tr>
<tr>
    <td> </td>
    <td align="right"><b>Full List:</b></td>
    <td>
     <!- Build a link to display a full
         list of books ->
     <a href="SearchBooks.asp?type=full">Display</a>
    </td>
</tr>

</table>

<br><br>
<!- Build a link to sign up as a new
    author ->
Want to be a new author in our list? Click
<a href="/community/directory/author/authorsignup.asp"> ⏎
  here</a>.

</body>
</html>
```

That does it for the Default.asp page. The personalization settings should now appear, and we are ready to program the search pages. It's time to update the TopNav pages.

Listing 9.23 shows the updated TopNav.asp page. The only thing we have added to the page is a link back to the default.asp page so the user can get back home easily. The Bottom-Nav.asp page has not been changed at all.

Listing 9.23   TopNav.asp

```
<%
'******************************************************
'** TopNav.asp
'**
'** Builds the tob navigation table for the
'** Directory pages
'******************************************************
%>
<!- Start the top navigation table
    for the directory ->
<table cellpadding="5" cellspacing="5" border="0">
<tr>
    <td valign="top">

    <!- Navigation Links ->
    <a href="default.asp">Home</a><br><br>
    <a href="/community/guestregister/guestregister.asp"> ⏎
    Guest Register</a><br><br>

    </td>
    <td valign="top">
```

We are now ready to begin our search logic for the site. The SearchAuthors.asp page, shown in Listings 9.24 though 9.27, takes in parameters from two different methods. The first method is the posting of a form with search keywords, and the second is a parameter on the URL.

The page starts out by checking if either method was utilized in calling the page. If neither method was utilized, we send the user back to the home page.

Listing 9.24   SearchAuthors.asp

```
<%@ Language=VBScript %>
<%Option Explicit%>
<%
'******************************************************
'** SearchAuthors.asp
'**
'** Build search options for the author data
'******************************************************
```

```
%>
<%

    ' Ensure a keyword was entered for search
    if request("type") = "" and _
      request("SearchText") = "" then

        ' If not send the user back
        Response.Redirect("default.asp")

    end if
%>
<HTML>
<HEAD>
</HEAD>
<BODY>

<!- #include file="topnav.asp" ->

<%

    Dim dbAuthor          ' Database Connection
    Dim rsAuthor          ' Recordset
    Dim SQL               ' String
    Dim idLastAuthor      ' Integer
    Dim chrFirstName      ' String
    Dim chrLastName       ' String
    Dim idBook            ' Integer
    Dim idAuthor          ' Integer
    Dim chrTitle          ' String
```

The first thing we do in the search logic is open a database connection, and then check to see if the "type" parameter was passed and is set to "full." This indicates that we want to do a full listing of all the authors in the directory.

If the type parameter is not set, we know we are doing a keyword search. In that case, we want to invoke our search tracking by calling the sp_InsertSearch stored procedure. The keywords are passed as a parameter as well as a value indicating the type of search. In this case we are passing a 1.

NOTE   We are not explicitly tracking the full list search, but we could do this and store the keyword "full" or something similar in the Searches table.

In that case, the sp_SearchAuthorName stored procedure is called with the keywords passed as a parameter. The query is then executed.

Listing 9.25   SearchAuthors.asp continued

```
' Create an ADO database connection
set dbAuthor = _
    server.createobject("adodb.connection")

' Create record set
set rsAuthor = _
    server.CreateObject("adodb.recordset")

' Open the connection using our ODBC file DSN
dbAuthor.open("filedsn=Directory")

' Check to see if we are doing a full listing
if request("type") = "full" then

    ' Execute the stored procedure to retrieve
    ' all authors and books
    sql = "execute sp_RetrieveAllAuthorsBooks"

end if

' Check to see if we are doing a keyword search
if request("SearchText") <> "" then

    ' Build a SQL statement to insert the keyword(s)
    ' into the database
    sql = "sp_InsertSearch '" & _
        replace(request("SearchText"), "'", "''") & "', 1"

    ' Execute the statement and retrieve the record set
    set rsAuthor = dbAuthor.Execute(sql)

    ' Now build the SQL statement to execute the
    ' search
    sql = "execute sp_SearchAuthorName '" & _
        replace(request("SearchText"), "'", "''") & "'"

end if

' Execute the statement and retrieve the record set
set rsAuthor = dbAuthor.Execute(sql)
```

Once the query is executed, we are ready to begin displaying the data. Our goal is to display each author and then each book published by the author. Keep in mind that our result set from the query contains a row for each book with the author data included and sorted by author.

The first thing we need to do is ensure that something was returned by the query. If so, then we grab the first author's data so we can display it in our table, and begin looping through the records.

Listing 9.26   SearchAuthors.asp continued

```
' Check to ensure a match was made
if not rsAuthor.EOF then

' Retrieve values
idLastAuthor = rsAuthor("idAuthor")
chrFirstName = rsAuthor("chrFirstName")
chrLastName = rsAuthor("chrLastName")

%>
<ul>

<table cellpadding="5" cellspacing="5">

    <tr>
        <td align="center">
            <font size="4" color="blue">Author</font>
        </td>
        <td align="center">
            <font size="4" color="blue">Books</font>
        </td>
    </tr>

    <!- Display the first author ->
    <tr>
        <td>
        <!- Display the author data ->
        <a href="authorinfo.asp?idAuthor= ⏎
        <%=rsAuthor("idAuthor")%>"><b> ⏎
        <%=rsAuthor("chrLastName")%>, ⏎
        <%=rsAuthor("chrFirstName")%></b></a>
        </td>
        <td> </td>
    </tr>
```

As we loop through each record, we have to check to see if our author has changed before we show the new author data. We want to display each book after the author, but we don't want to display the author with each book because that would look too cluttered on the page and be repetitive.

Thus, we are storing the last author ID and comparing it with each iteration to the next author ID. When they no longer match, we know we have a new author and should display

their data. Note that we are linking each author and each book to link to the information
pages.

Listing 9.27   SearchAuthors.asp continued

```asp
<%

' Loop through record set
do until rsAuthor.EOF

' Get author and book ids
idAuthor = rsAuthor("idAuthor")
idBook = rsAuthor("idBook")

' Check to see if we have moved to the next author
if (idAuthor <> idLastAuthor) then

' Set the last author id for tracking
idLastAuthor = idAuthor

%>

    <tr>
        <td>
        <!- Display the author data ->
        <a href="authorinfo.asp?idAuthor= ↵
        <%=rsAuthor("idAuthor")%>"><b> ↵
        <%=rsAuthor("chrLastName")%>, ↵
        <%=rsAuthor("chrFirstName")%></b></a>
        </td>
        <td> </td>
    </tr>

<%
end if

%>

<tr>
    <td> </td>
    <td>
    <!- Display the book data ->
    <li><a href="bookinfo.asp?idBook= ↵
    <%=idBook%>"><%=rsAuthor("chrTitle")%></a></li>
    </td>
</tr>

<%

' Move to the next record
```

```
rsAuthor.MoveNext

Loop

else

%>

No matches were found.

<%

end if

' Close the database
dbAuthor.Close

%>

</table>
</ul>

<!- #include file="bottomnav.asp" ->

</BODY>
</HTML>
```

If no authors are returned from the query, then we simply indicate that to the user. Then the page closes out.

TIP

As mentioned earlier, if there are hundreds or thousands of authors in the database, then displaying a large result set can be problematic. Some sort of paging could be built into the result set, or the user could be asked to narrow their search.

Our next page is SearchBooks.asp, shown in Listings 9.28 through 9.30. It operates similarly to the SearchAuthors.asp page. As we saw before, a check is done to ensure that either the form was posted to the page or there is a parameter on the URL. Then the bulk of the page begins.

Listing 9.28   SearchBooks.asp

```
<%@ Language=VBScript %>
<%Option Explicit%>
<%
'*********************************************************
'** SearchBooks.asp
'**
'** Build search options for the book data
'*********************************************************
```

```
%>
<%

' Check to see if search text was entered
if request("type") = "" and _
  request("SearchText") = "" then

    ' If not send the user back to the
    ' home page
    Response.Redirect("default.asp")

end if

%>
<HTML>
<HEAD>
</HEAD>
<BODY>

<!- #include file="topnav.asp" ->

<%

Dim dbAuthor      ' Database Connection
Dim rsAuthor      ' Recordset
Dim SQL           ' String
Dim idBook        ' Integer
Dim idAuthor      ' Integer
Dim chrFirstname  ' String
Dim chrLastname   ' String
```

We next check to see if we are doing a keyword search or a full listing. If the "type" parameter on the URL is set to "full," then we execute the sp_RetrieveAllBooksAuthor stored procedure. Otherwise, we perform a keyword search.

As on the author search page, we insert the search keywords into the database using the sp_InsertSearch stored procedure. In this case we pass in a "2" to indicate that this is a book search. Then the sp_SearchBookName stored procedure is called to search for books with the keywords.

Listing 9.29   SearchBooks.asp continued

```
' Create an ADO database connection
set dbAuthor = _
    server.createobject("adodb.connection")

' Create record set
set rsAuthor = _
    server.CreateObject("adodb.recordset")
```

```
' Open the connection using our ODBC file DSN
dbAuthor.open("filedsn=Directory")

' Check to see if we are doing a full listing
if request("type") = "full" then

    ' Retrieve all books
    sql = "execute sp_RetrieveAllBooksAuthor"

end if

' Check to see if we are doing a keyword
' search
if request("SearchText") <> "" then

    ' Insert the keyword(s) searched on
    sql = "execute sp_InsertSearch '" & _
        replace(request("SearchText"), "'", "''") & "', 2"

    ' Execute the statement and retrieve the record set
    set rsAuthor = dbAuthor.Execute(sql)

    ' Now build a SQL statement to search books
    ' for that keyword
    sql = "execute sp_SearchBookName '" & _
        replace(request("SearchText"), "'", "''") & "'"

end if

' Execute the statement and retrieve the record set
set rsAuthor = dbAuthor.Execute(sql)

%>
```

Unlike the authors, we only need to display one book with each author since there is a one-to-one relationship in our database. The result set is looped through and each record's book and author data is displayed.

NOTE If two authors co-write a book, they could each have a listing and the book would show up twice, given the current functionality. We have not built in a provision in the database for authors to check if their book is listed already and to select it instead of entering a new entry. This, however, could be done.

Listing 9.30   **SearchBooks.asp continued**

```
<!- Start the table to display the
    book and corresponding author ->
<table cellpadding="5" cellspacing="5">
```

```
        <tr>
            <td align="center">
                <font size="4" color="blue">Book</font>
            </td>
            <td align="center">
                <font size="4" color="blue">Author</font>
            </td>
        </tr>

<%

' Loop through the record set
do until rsAuthor.EOF

' Retrieve book values
idBook = rsAuthor("idBook")
idAuthor = rsAuthor("idAuthor")
chrFirstName = rsAuthor("chrFirstName")
chrLastName = rsAuthor("chrLastName")

%>

<tr>
    <td>
    <!- Display the book title ->
    <a href="BookInfo.asp?idBook= ↵
    <%=idBook%>"><%=rsAuthor("chrTitle")%></a>
    </td>
    <td>
    <!- Display the author name ->
    <a href="AuthorInfo.asp?idAuthor= ↵
    <%=idAuthor%>"><%=rsAuthor("chrLastName")%>, ↵
    <%=rsAuthor("chrFirstName")%></a>
    </td>
</tr>

<%

' Move to the next record
rsAuthor.MoveNext

Loop

' Close the database
dbAuthor.Close

%>

</table>

<!- #include file="bottomnav.asp" ->
```

```
</BODY>
</HTML>
```

The page closes out with the database closing and the ending tags. That does it for displaying the results of a book search.

TIP

As with our earlier comments, if the list of books starts to get lengthy, consider giving options for the user to pare down the resulting list.

We are now ready to move on to our advanced book search features. The code for AdvBookSearch.asp is shown in Listings 9.31 through 9.34. In this case, we want to provide the user with options to search for books based on ISBN, first assigned interest topic, second assigned interest topic, publisher, keyword in the description, table of contents, or any combination thereof. We also want the user to be able to sort by publisher or last name of the author. The page starts out by building a table and form to display the search options and to post the results to the DispAdvSrchBooks.asp page.

Listing 9.31   AdvBookSearch.asp

```
<%@ Language=VBScript %>
<%Option Explicit%>
<%
'********************************************************
'** AdvBookSearch.asp
'**
'** Build advanced search options for the book data
'********************************************************
%>
<HTML>
<HEAD>
</HEAD>
<BODY>

<!- #include file="topnav.asp" ->

<!- Build a table to display the search options ->
<table cellpadding="5" cellspacing="5">

<form method="post" action="DispAdvSrchBooks.asp">
```

The first input field is a text box for the user to type in an ISBN that they would like to match in the search. We then have the two select boxes for the interest topics. These are built by pulling the options from the guest register database, as we have seen in previous examples.

Listing 9.32   AdvBookSearch.asp continued

```
<!- Option to search by ISBN ->
<tr>
    <td align="right">ISBN:</td>
    <td>
     <input type="text" value="" name="chrISBN">
    </td>
</tr>

<tr>
    <td align="right">
        Primary Interest Category:
    </td>
    <td>

<%

Dim dbGuestRegister    ' Database Connection
Dim rsGuestRegister    ' Recordset
Dim SQL                ' String
Dim Selected           ' String
Dim dbPublisher        ' Database Connection
Dim rsPublisher        ' Recordset

' Create an ADO database connection
set dbGuestRegister = _
    server.createobject("adodb.connection")

' Create a record set
set rsGuestRegister = _
    server.CreateObject("adodb.recordset")

' Open the connection using our ODBC file DSN
dbGuestRegister.open("filedsn=GuestRegister")

' Retrieve the list of interest topics
sql = "execute sp_RetrieveInterestTopics"

' Execute the SQL statement
set rsGuestRegister = dbGuestRegister.execute(sql)

%>

    <!- Start the select list ->
    <select name="intPrimeInterest">

    <!- Display a blank search option ->
    <option value="">
    <%
```

```
                ' Loop through the list
                do until rsGuestRegister.EOF

            %>
            <!- Build the option. Note the selected variable
            is output. When set to "selected" that option
            will be the default.  ->
            <option value="<%=rsGuestRegister("idInterestTopic")%>"↵
            <%=selected%>><%=rsGuestRegister("chrName")%>
            <%

                    ' Move to the next row
                    rsGuestRegister.movenext

                ' Loop back
                loop
                %>
        </select>


            </td>
    </tr>
    <tr>
        <td align="right">Second Interest Category:</td>
        <td>

            <!- Start the select list ->
            <select name="intSecondInterest">

            <!- Show a blank search option ->
            <option value="">
            <%

            ' Move to the next row
            rsGuestRegister.MoveFirst

            ' Loop through the list
            do until rsGuestRegister.EOF

            %>
            <!- Build the option. Note the selected variable
                is output. When set to "selected" that option
                will be the default.  ->
            <option value="<%=rsGuestRegister("idInterestTopic")%>"↵
                <%=selected%>><%=rsGuestRegister("chrName")%>
            <%

                    ' Move to the next row
                    rsGuestRegister.movenext

            ' Loop back
```

```
        loop

        ' Close the database connection
        dbGuestRegister.Close
        %>
    </select>

        </td>
    </tr>
```

For the publisher option, we need to build a select box that displays all of the publishers in the database. The sp_RetrievePublishers stored procedure is utilized to retrieve the listing.

Listing 9.33   AdvBookSearch.asp continued

```
    <tr>
        <td align="right">Publisher:</td>
        <td>

<%

' Create an ADO database connection
set dbPublisher = _
    server.createobject("adodb.connection")

' Create a record set
set rsPublisher = _
    server.CreateObject("adodb.recordset")

' Open the connection using our ODBC file DSN
dbPublisher.open("filedsn=Directory")

' Retrieve the list of publishers
sql = "execute sp_RetrievePublishers"

' Execute the SQL statement
set rsPublisher = dbPublisher.execute(sql)

%>

        <!- Start the select list ->
        <select name="idPublisher">

        <!- Show a blank search option ->
        <option value="">

        <%

        ' Loop through the list
        do until rsPublisher.EOF
```

```
    %>
    <!- Build the option. Note the selected variable
        is output. When set to "selected" that option
        will be the default.  ->
    <option value="<%=rsPublisher("idPublisher")%>" <%=selected%>>⏎
    <%=rsPublisher("chrPublisher")%>
    <%

            ' Move to the next row
            rsPublisher.movenext

        ' Loop back
        loop

        ' Close the database connection
        dbPublisher.close

        %>
    </select>

        </td>
    </tr>
```

Finally, we close the page with a text box for the user to type in keywords by which to search, followed by two checkboxes to order the results by publisher or author.

Listing 9.34   AdvBookSearch.asp continued

```
<!- Option to search on the description and TOC
    for a specific key word ->
<tr>
    <td align="right">Description/TOC:</td>
    <td><input type="text" value="" name="chrText"></td>
</tr>

<!- Show two options to sort by publisher and
    last name ->
<tr>
    <td align="right">Sort By:</td>
    <td>
        <input type="checkbox" value="1"
            name="chrPublisher">Publisher
        <input type="checkbox" value="1"
            name="chrLastName">Author Last Name

    </td>
</tr>

<tr>
    <td colspan="2" align="center">
```

```
            <input type="submit" value="Submit" name="Submit">
        </td>
    </tr>

    </table>

</form>

<!- #include file="bottomnav.asp" ->

</BODY>
</HTML>
```

Now comes the heavy lifting in our VBScript code. Listings 9.35 through 9.40 show the code for DispAdvSrchBooks.asp. To do the advanced search, we have to build a query on the fly that reflects the parameters set by the user. To get started, the values are all retrieved from the request variables.

Listing 9.35   DispAdvSrchBooks.asp

```
<%@ Language=VBScript %>
<%Option Explicit%>
<%
'***************************************************
'** DispAdvSrchBooks.asp
'**
'** displays results of the advanced search
'***************************************************
%>
<HTML>
<HEAD>
</HEAD>
<BODY>

<!- #include file="topnav.asp" ->

<%

Dim dbSearch                ' Database Connection
Dim rsSearch                ' Recordset
Dim SQL                     ' String
Dim chrISBN                 ' String
Dim intPrimeInterest        ' Integer
Dim intSecondInterest       ' Integer
Dim chrText                 ' String
Dim chrPublisher            ' String
Dim chrFirstName            ' String
Dim chrLastName             ' String
Dim idPublisher             ' Integer
```

```
Dim idAuthor          ' Integer
Dim Flag              ' String

' Retrieve values
chrISBN = request("chrISBN")
intPrimeInterest = request("intPrimeInterest")
intSecondInterest = request("intSecondInterest")
chrText = replace(request("chrText"), "'", "''")
chrPublisher = replace(request("chrPublisher"), "'", "''")
chrLastname = replace(request("chrLastName"), "'", "''")
idPublisher = request("idPublisher")
```

To start building our query, we first build the join statement that brings all of the appropriate tables together in our query. We begin with the publisher. If the user enters in a publisher selection, we add the ID of the publisher to our SQL statement.

Next, we add the ISBN to the search. Note that we are doing an exact match and not a SQL "like" function that would search for a subtext match. As with all of the parameters selected, the checks are joined together with an "and" clause, not an "or" clause. This means that all of the user entries must be matched for a result.

Listing 9.36   **DispAdvSrchBooks.asp continued**

```
' Build the first part of the SQL statement to
' retrieve joined author, bookauthor, book and publisher
' data.
sql = "select * from author,bookauthor,book, publisher" & _
      " where author.idauthor=bookauthor.idauthor and " & _
      "bookauthor.idbook = book.idbook and " & _
      "book.idpublisher = publisher.idpublisher"

' Check to see if the user selected a publisher
' to be searched.
if idPublisher <> "" then

    ' Add the SQL lanaguage to search for the
    ' publisher
    sql = sql & " and book.idPublisher = " & _
        request("idPublisher")

end if

' Check to see if the user entered an ISBN #
' to be searched.
if chrISBN <> "" then

    ' Add the SQL lanaguage to search for the
    ' ISBN
    sql = sql & " and chrISBN = '" & _
```

```
                        request("chrISBN") & "'"

end if
```

The interest topics are then searched. We add the query checks of intPrimeInterest and intSecondInterest to our SQL statement that checks for the selected IDs. Then the text and table of contents are searched for the entered keywords. In this case we are using the SQL "like" function to check the keywords. Note that we need the keywords to show up in either the description or the table of contents.

Listing 9.37   **DispAdvSrchBooks.asp continued**

```
' Check to see if the user entered a primary
' interest to be searched.
if intPrimeInterest <> "" then

    ' Add the SQL lanaguage to search for the
    ' interest topic
    sql = sql & " and intPrimeInterest = " & _
        request("intPrimeInterest")

end if

' Check to see if the user entered a secondary
' interest to be searched.
if intSecondInterest <> "" then

    ' Add the SQL lanaguage to search for the
    ' interest topic
    sql = sql & " and intSecondInterest = " & _
        request("intSecondInterest")

end if

' Check to see if search text was entered for
' searching the description and TOC
if chrText <> "" then

    ' Add the SQL lanaguage to search for the
    ' keyword match
    sql = sql & " and (txtDescription like '%' + '" & _
        chrText & "' + '%' or txtTOC like '%' + '" & _
        chrText & "' + '%')"

end if
```

Finally, we are ready to define how the results should be ordered. If the user selected neither the last name nor the publisher, we will default the ordering to be done by book title; otherwise, we add the selections. Note the use of the flag to indicate whether an "and" needs to be added into the query.

Listing 9.38   DispAdvSrchBooks.asp continued

```
' Add the order by text to the search
sql = sql & " order by"

' If the user didn't select the list to
' be ordered by last name or publisher then
' default to the book title
if chrLastName = "" and chrPublisher="" then

        ' Add the SQL lanaguage to sort by the
        ' book title
        sql = sql & " chrTitle"

end if

' If the user selected the last name sort option
if chrLastName <> "" then

        ' Add the SQL language to order by the author's
        ' last name
        sql = sql & " chrLastName"

        ' Set a flag indicating we add this option to
        ' the order by clause
        flag = 1

end if

' Check to see if the user wants to sort by the
' publisher
if chrPublisher <> "" then

        ' Check to see if the author last name
        ' was already added to the SQL statement
        if flag = 1 then

                ' If so then add the SQL language to
                ' include a comma between the two
                ' sort options
                sql = sql & ", chrPublisher"

        else

                ' If not then just append the publisher
```

```
              ' sort option.
              sql = sql & " chrPublisher"

      end if

  end if
```

We are now ready to execute our query. We open a database connection and the query is executed. As with the book search results, we need to list individual books with the author data in the right column.

Listing 9.39   DispAdvSrchBooks.asp continued

```
' Create an ADO database connection
set dbSearch = _
    server.createobject("adodb.connection")

' Create a record set
set rsSearch = _
    server.CreateObject("adodb.recordset")

' Open the connection using our ODBC file DSN
dbSearch.open("filedsn=Directory")

' Execute the SQL statement
set rsSearch = dbSearch.execute(sql)

%>

<!- Build a table to display the search
    results. ->
<table cellpadding="5" cellspacing="5">

    <tr>
        <td align="center">
            <font size="4" color="blue">Book</font>
        </td>
        <td align="center">
            <font size="4" color="blue">Author</font>
        </td>
        <td align="center">
            <font size="4" color="blue">Publisher</font>
        </td>
    </tr>
```

The results are then looped through with the book and author data being displayed. In both the author and the book display, we link them to the appropriate information page.

Listing 9.40   DispAdvSrchBooks.asp continued

```asp
<%

do until rsSearch.EOF

' Retrieve results value
idAuthor = rsSearch("idAuthor")
chrFirstName = rsSearch("chrFirstName")
chrLastName = rsSearch("chrLastName")

%>

<tr>
    <td>
    <!- Display the book title and link to see
        the full book data ->
    <a href="bookinfo.asp?idBook= ↵
    <%=rsSearch("idBook")%>"> ↵
    <%=rsSearch("chrTitle")%></a>
    </td>
    <td>
    <!- Display the author and link to see
        the full author data ->
    <a href="authorinfo.asp?idAuthor= ↵
<%=idAuthor%>"><%=rsSearch("chrLastName")%>, ↵
<%=rsSearch("chrFirstName")%></a>
    </td>
    <!- Display the publisher ->
    <td><%=rsSearch("chrPublisher")%></td>
</tr>

<%

' Move to the next row
rsSearch.MoveNext

Loop

' Close the database connection
dbSearch.Close

%>

</table>

<!- #include file="bottomnav.asp" ->

</BODY>
</HTML>
```

That finishes the advanced search capabilities. This type of searching will be especially effective when the database of books and authors begins to grow in length. This allows the visitor to pinpoint books in which they are interested.

Testing the User Interface

Now we are ready to see our coding in action. We first need to start by pulling up the new Default.asp page (/community/directory/default.asp), as shown in Figure 9.1.

FIGURE 9.1:

Updated default.asp page

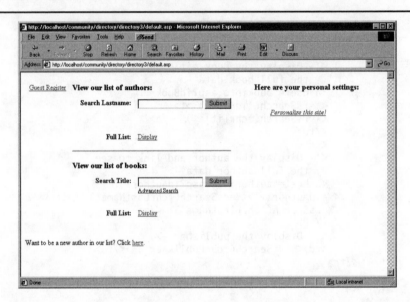

The page doesn't look much different than before, except that there is a link to personalize the site on the right. We will see more there in a minute when we personalize the site.

First test the author searching capabilities by performing a simple search on the keyword "a." In the examples entered by the author, only one match has a last name with an "a" in it. The results are shown in Figure 9.2.

FIGURE 9.2:

Author search results

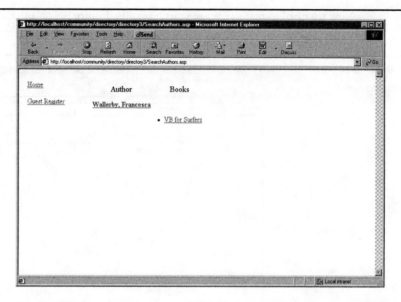

We next need to test the full author listing. Simply click on the link for the full author listing. The full listing is displayed as shown in Figure 9.3. Note that the "type" parameter with a value of "full" is on the URL.

FIGURE 9.3:

Full author listing

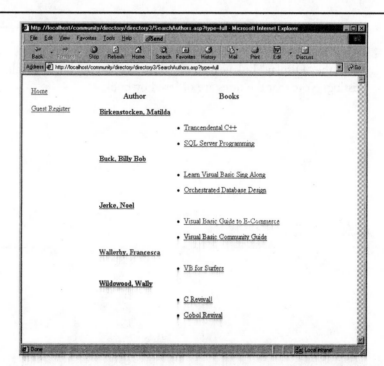

Now we need to test the book search results. Figure 9.4 shows the search results on the keyword "Visual". In this case, three books are returned that meet the match.

FIGURE 9.4:

Book search results

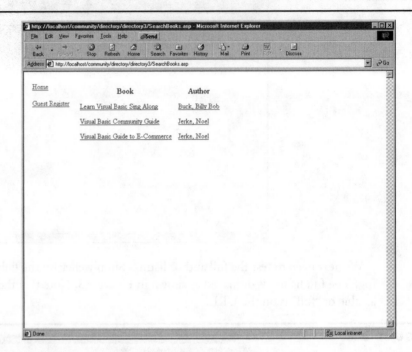

FIGURE 9.4:

Book search results

Finally we can show the full listing of all entries on the book search. On the default page, click the "Display" link next to the "Full List" in the book search. Figure 9.5 shows the full listing. Note that the titles are ordered by book.

FIGURE 9.5:

Full book listing

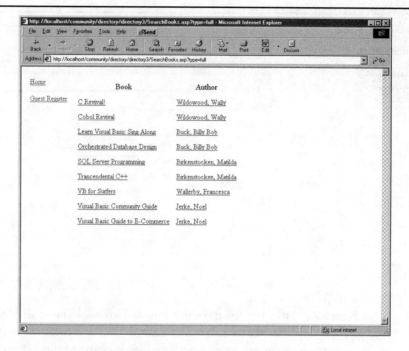

We can now test the advanced book search. Figure 9.6 shows the advanced search page. We can do a search by selecting "programming" as the Primary Interest category. Enter "Visual" in the title and table of contents search text boxes. Finally, check the "Publisher" and "Author Last Name" check boxes.

FIGURE 9.6:

Advanced search page

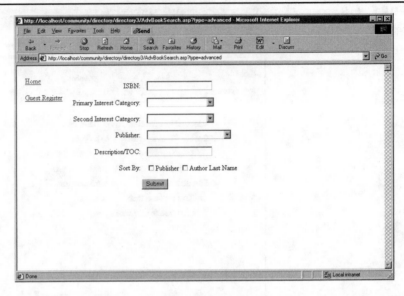

Figure 9.7 shows the results of the search. Two books meet all of the criteria we entered. Note that the titles are sorted by publisher in the right column. You can test different options to work through the advanced search and see how the results are returned.

TIP It might be helpful to see the SQL query generation in action by displaying the SQL statement generated. That way, you can review the full statement.

FIGURE 9.7:

Advanced search results

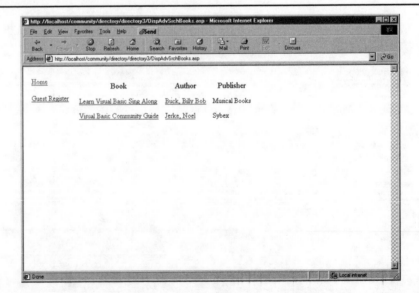

We can now move to the personalization settings. Click the "Personalize this site!" link on the home page. Figure 9.8 shows the page where the personalization is set by the user. Note that each option provides a "no selection" option if the user is not interested in making a personalization choice.

FIGURE 9.8:

Personalization settings

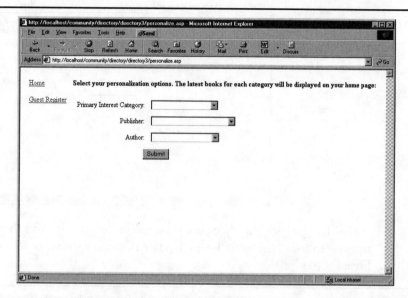

Select settings for each option. For this example, the Primary Interest Category option is set to "E-Commerce." The Publisher option is set to "Back to the Future Publishers," and the Author option is set to "Birkenstock, Matilda." Figure 9.9 shows the customized home page with a book shown under each personalization selection. For the "E-Commerce" interest area, the "Visual Basic Guide to E-Commerce" is displayed.

Under the books by our "Back to the Future Publishers", the "C Revival!" book is displayed. Finally, Matilda Birkenstock's book, "Transendental C++" is displayed as her latest book.

FIGURE 9.9:

Customized home page

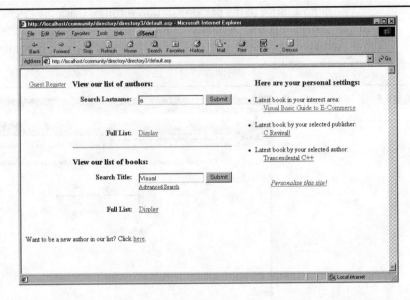

Now let's go back and check our personalization settings. You should see your current settings defaulted in the select boxes. Update them now with new selections as shown in Figure 9.10.

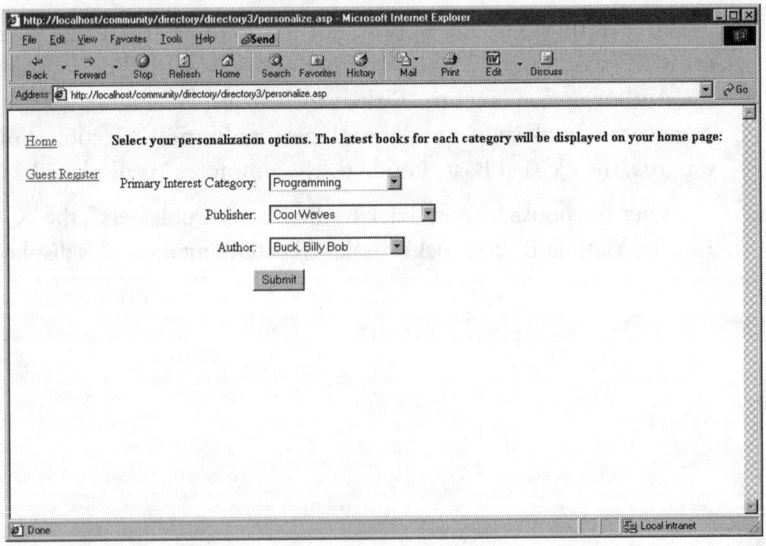

FIGURE 9.10:

Personalization settings

With your latest changes, the home page is updated to display the new settings, as shown in Figure 9.11.

FIGURE 9.11:

Updated personalization settings

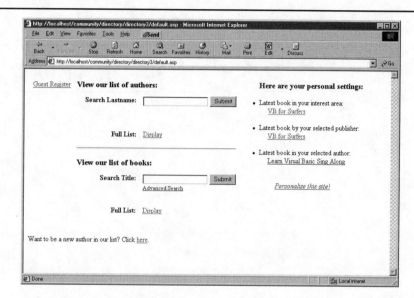

We have now successfully added personalization capabilities to our site as well as extended search features. With our search tools, we provide multiple levels of search as well as tracking keywords site visitors are searching on.

Summary

We were able in this chapter to take the next step and add in search and personalization functionality to our community site foundation. This helps to make the author-contributed content more useful and relevant to the site visitors.

We have one more set of functionality to add to the user side of the equation before we take a look at the management tools for all of these features. In the next chapter, we add more key features to our community site, which include tracking, affiliate links, and promotion tracking.

Following in Chapter 11, we will look at all of the management tools needed for the site administrator to manage all of the features we have been building in these chapters.

CHAPTER 10

Promotion and Traffic Tracking

- Designing the Application

- Building the Database

- Building the User Interface

- Testing the Application

A community Web site would not be complete without promotions and the capability to track traffic. This chapter shows how to implement features that can be used to track what Web sites our visitors are linking to our community site from, as well as track the utilization of various tools on our Web site.

Designing the Application

The first feature we build into our community site is the capability to track affiliates who have built links to our site. An affiliate in this example might be a publisher or an author who would want to drive traffic to our community because it might ultimately lead to sales of their book. In our site we will track affiliate links on the home page.

The next feature we add into our site is the capability of promotion tracking. In essence, any feature that is promoted on the site will be tracked when a site visitor clicks it. For example, we might track all of the clicks into our discussion forums.

In addition, if the visitor has personalized their site, we can store their profile settings with each promotion link to get a feel for what types of visitors are visiting which sections of the site.

Building the Database

We need to add two tables to our data structure. The first table is utilized for tracking affiliates of our Web site. Listing 10.1 shows the SQL code to generate the table.

Listing 10.1	Affiliates Table

```
CREATE TABLE dbo.Affiliates (
    idAffiliate int IDENTITY (1, 1) NOT NULL ,
    chrName varchar (255) NULL ,
    dtCreated datetime NULL CONSTRAINT
  DF_Affiliates_dtCreated_4__10 DEFAULT (getdate())
)
GO
```

Each affiliate is given a unique identifier, a name, and a date they were created in the system. This table will have a one-to-many relationship with the AffiliateLinks table shown in Listing 10.2.

Listing 10.2   AffiliateLinks Table

```
CREATE TABLE dbo.AffiliateLinks (
    idLink int IDENTITY (1, 1) NOT NULL ,
    dtLinked datetime NOT NULL CONSTRAINT
DF_AffiliateL_dtLinked_5__10 DEFAULT (getdate()),
    chrReferrer varchar (255) NULL ,
    idAffiliate int NULL
)
GO
```

Every time a visitor links to our site from an affiliate site, we can store that action in our table. A unique record is given to each row, the date the link was made, and the referring URL. By storing the referring URL, we can tell from what pages on the affiliate site the user is linking. It might not always be the same page if the affiliate links in multiple ways.

NOTE   If we have a high volume traffic site, inserting individual records into the AffiliateLinks table may cause the site to slow down as the number of rows increase. In that case, consider doing a rollup of data on a time basis, such as hourly.

Next, we build a similar table structure for tracking promotions on our Web site. Each promotion will have a link ID, description, and URL, as shown in Listing 10.3.

Listing 10.3   LinkTrack Table

```
CREATE TABLE dbo.LinkTrack (
    idLink int IDENTITY (1, 1) NOT NULL ,
    chrDescription varchar (255) NULL ,
    chrURL varchar (255) NULL
)
GO
```

As with the affiliates, we have a one-to-many relationship with a table to track the actual promotion links. Listing 10.4 stores the ID of the link click and the date the click was made, followed by the personalization settings for the user including the primary interest, the publisher, and the author. This is followed by the browser the user is utilizing and finally the ID of the link.

Listing 10.4   LinkClick Table

```
CREATE TABLE dbo.LinkClick (
    idClick int IDENTITY (1, 1) NOT NULL ,
    dtClicked datetime NULL ,
```

```
        intPerPrimeInterest int NULL ,
        idPerPublisher int NULL ,
        idPerAuthor int NULL ,
        chrBrowser varchar (255) NULL ,
        idLink int NULL
)
GO
```

Now we need to create our stored procedures. The first is sp_InsertAffiliateLink, shown in Listing 10.5, which handles inserting the affiliate link into the AffiliateLinks table.

Listing 10.5   sp_InsertAffiliateLink Stored Procedure

```
CREATE PROCEDURE sp_InsertAffiliateLink

/* Pass in the id of the affiliate and
   the referring URL */
@idAffiliate integer,
@chrReferrer varchar(255)

AS

/* Insert the affiliate link into the database */
insert into AffiliateLinks(idAffiliate, chrReferrer)
 values(@idAffiliate, @chrReferrer)
GO
```

Next we need to create the stored procedure that retrieves a specific link from the database, as shown in Listing 10.6. The ID of the link is passed as an argument.

Listing 10.6   sp_RetrieveLink Stored Procedure

```
CREATE PROCEDURE sp_RetrieveLink

/* Pass in the id of the link */
@idLink integer

AS

/* Retrieve the link data for the
   specified link */
select * from LinkTrack
 where idLink = @idLink
GO
```

Finally we need to create our stored procedure to insert promotions clicks into the database. The ID of the link, the browser, and the personalization settings are passed in as arguments, and then the data is inserted into the table. The SQL code for the sp_InsertLinkClick stored procedure is shown in Listing 10.7.

Listing 10.7   sp_InsertLinkClick Stored Procedure

```
CREATE PROCEDURE sp_InsertLinkClick

/* Pass in the data for the link click.
  And, the ID of the link to tie the
  click to. */
@idLink integer,
@chrBrowser varchar(255),
@intPrimeInterest integer,
@idPublisher integer,
@idAuthor integer


AS

/* Insert the link into the database */
insert into LinkClick(idLink, chrBrowser,
          intPerPrimeInterest, idPerPublisher,
          idPerAuthor)
        values(@idLink, @chrBrowser,
          @intPrimeInterest, @idPublisher,
          @idAuthor)
  GO
```

In the next chapter we build the management interface to manage the affiliates and promotions in the database, but we need data to test this chapter. Table 10.1 shows the seed entries for the LinkTrack table. Ensure that the community URLs match the locations of the specified functions on your Web server. For the moment, the poll and forums will not actually link to these pages until we build them in later chapters.

TABLE 10.1: LinkTrack Table Entries

ID	Name	URL
1	Poll/Survey Engine - Poll ID 1	/community/poll/Poll1.asp?idPoll=5
2	Discussion Forums	/community/forums/
3	Example data	none
4	Guest Register	/community/guestregister/guestregister.asp
5	Ad One	http://www.somedomain.com
6	Ad Two	http://www.somedomain.com
7	Personalize	/community/directory/personalize.asp
8	Author Sign Up	/community/directory/author/authorsignup.asp

Finally, we need affiliates for testing. Table 10.2 shows the seed values for this table.

TABLE 10.2: Affiliates Table Entries

ID	Name
1	Affiliate One
2	Example data
3	Affiliate Two
4	Affiliate Three

That does it for setting up our data structures and preparing our tables for utilization. Next, we build the user interface to implement the affiliate tracking and promotions.

Building the User Interface

To implement the user interface, we modify the default page, the navigation page, and add a new page for handling the promotion tracking.

The first page we modify is the Default.asp page to implement the affiliate link tracking. The page starts out with the standard header and variable declarations. Listings 10.8 through 10.12 show the code for Default.asp.

Listing 10.8   **Default.asp**

```
<%@ Language=VBScript %>
<%Option Explicit%>
<%
'*****************************************************
'** Default.asp
'**
'** Home page that provides navigation, search
'** options and personalization settings
'*****************************************************
%>
<html>
<head>
</head>
<body>

<%

Dim intPrimeInterest   ' Integer
Dim idPublisher        ' Integer
```

```
Dim idAuthor        ' Integer
Dim dbAuthor        ' Database Object
Dim rsAuthor        ' Record Set
Dim SQL             ' String
```

The affiliate tracking is implemented by checking to see if our default page was called with an ID parameter on it called "idAffiliate." If that parameter exists, we are ready to process the affiliate link.

The database is opened and we insert the affiliate link. The sp_InsertAffiliateLink stored procedure is called with the ID of the affiliate and the referrer passed in. The referrer is retrieved from the HTTP header by using the ServerVariables collection of the Request object. The database object is then closed and we are done with our affiliate tracking.

Listing 10.9   Default.asp continued

```
' Check to see if an affiliate ID was passed
' on the URL
if request("idAffiliate") <> "" then

   ' Create an ADO database connection
   set dbAffiliate = _
      server.createobject("adodb.connection")

   ' Create record set
   set rsAffiliate = _
      server.CreateObject("adodb.recordset")

   ' Open the connection using our ODBC file DSN
   dbAffiliate.open("filedsn=Directory")

   ' Insert the affiliate data including the
   ' referring URL into the database for tracking
   sql = "execute sp_InsertAffiliateLink " & _
      request("idAffiliate") & ", '" & _
      Request.ServerVariables("HTTP_REFERER") & _
      "'"

   ' Execute the statement and retrieve the record set
   set rsAffiliate = dbAffiliate.Execute(sql)

   ' Close the database connection
   dbAffiliate.Close

end if

%>
```

Now we are ready to implement our link tracking. We change the links we want to track from direct links to the URL to links to Track.asp, which will be created later in the chapter.

On each link to Track.asp, we pass the ID of the promotion. The ID of the promotion is passed on the URL to Track.asp as the "idLink" parameter. Our navigation menu on the left is updated to include some new links. We add in two promotions on the top and bottom of our nav bar. These can link anywhere, and clicks will be tracked similarly to ads.

In addition, we update the links to our guest register, discussion forums, and so on to link to track.asp, too. The IDs that are on the URL come from our sample Table 10.1.

The rest of the page continues as built earlier in this chapter. The next link that is updated is to set the personalization settings.

Listing 10.10   Default.asp continued

```
<!- Build the table to display the page ->
<table cellpadding="5" cellspacing="5" border="0">
<tr>

    <!- The first column will span 9 rows and
        show the navigation bar ->
    <td rowspan="9" valign="top">

    <!- Build the navigation. Note the links
        will be tracked. ->
    <a href="track.asp?idLink=5"> ↵
    <img src="images/adone.jpg" ↵
    WIDTH="87" HEIGHT="85"></a><br><br>

    <a href="track.asp?idLink=1">Take our Poll</a><br><br>
    <a href="track.asp?idLink=2"> ↵
    Visit our Forums</a><br><br>

    <a href="track.asp?idLink=4">Guest Register</a><br><br>

    <a href="track.asp?idLink=6"> ↵
    <img src="images/adtwo.jpg" WIDTH="87" ↵
        HEIGHT="85"></a><br><br>

    </td>

    <!- Display options to show the author ->
    <td colspan="3"><font size="4"><b>
        View our list of authors:</b></font>
    </td>

    <!- Build the personalization column ->
    <td rowspan="9" valign="top">
```

```
<ul>
<font size="4" color="blue">
   <b>Here are your personal settings:
</font><br><br></b>

<%

' Retrieve the personalization settings
intPrimeInterest = ↵
trim(Request.Cookies("Personalize") ↵
("intPrimeInterest"))

idPublisher = ↵
trim(Request.Cookies("Personalize") ↵
("idPublisher"))

idAuthor = ↵
trim(Request.Cookies("Personalize") ↵
("idAuthor"))

' Create an ADO database connection
set dbAuthor = _
   server.createobject("adodb.connection")

' Create record set
set rsAuthor = _
   server.CreateObject("adodb.recordset")

' Open the connection using our ODBC file DSN
dbAuthor.open("filedsn=Directory")

' See if a primary interest topic setting
' is set
if intPrimeInterest <> "" then

' Retrieve the books that meet the interest
' setting
sql = "execute sp_RetrieveBookByInterest " & _
   intPrimeInterest

' Execute the statement and retrieve the record set
set rsAuthor = dbAuthor.Execute(sql)

' Ensure a record was returned
if not rsAuthor.EOF then

%>

<!- Display the book that matches the
   interest ->
```

```
<li>Latest book in your interest area:<br>
    
<a href="bookinfo.asp?idBook= ↵
<%=rsAuthor("idBook")%>"> ↵
<%=rsAuthor("chrTitle")%></a>
<br><br>

<%

end if

end if

' Check and see if a preferred publisher
' was entered.
if idPublisher <> "" then

' Execute the stored procedure to retrieve books
' for the publisher
sql = "execute sp_RetrieveBookByPub " & _
    idPublisher

' Execute the statement and retrieve the record set
set rsAuthor = dbAuthor.Execute(sql)

' Ensure a record was returned
if not rsAuthor.EOF then

%>

<!- Show the latest book entered for
    the publisher ->
<li>Latest book by your selected publisher:<br>
    
<a href="bookinfo.asp?idBook= ↵
<%=rsAuthor("idBook")%>"> ↵
<%=rsAuthor("chrTitle")%></a>
<br><br>

<%

end if
end if

' See if a preferred author was entered
if idAuthor <> "" then

' Execute the stored procedure to retrieve the
' latest books by the author
sql = "execute sp_RetrieveBookByAuthor " & _
    idAuthor
```

```
' Execute the statement and retrieve the record set
set rsAuthor = dbAuthor.Execute(sql)

' Ensure a record set was returned
if not rsAuthor.EOF then

%>

<!- Display the latest book by the author ->
<li>Latest book in your selected author:<br>
    
<a href="bookinfo.asp?idBook= ↵
<%=rsAuthor("idBook")%>"> ↵
<%=rsAuthor("chrTitle")%></a>
<br><br>

<%
end if
end if

' Close the database connection
dbAuthor.Close
%>
</ul>
<br>
<center>
```

The link to set the personalization setting is also useful to track the utilization of this feature. In Listing 10.12, we update the link to go to Track.asp with an ID of 7 from Table 10.1.

Listing 10.12   Default.asp continued

```
<!- Build a link to personalize the site ->
<i><a href="track.asp?idLink=7"> ↵
Personalize this site!</a></i>
</center>
</td>

</tr>

<!- Build an option to search on the author
  name ->
<tr>
<td> </td>
<td align="right" valign="top">
<b>Search Lastname:</b>
</td>
<td>
<form method="post" action="SearchAuthors.asp">
```

```
        <input type="text" value name="SearchText">
        <input type="submit" value="Submit" name="Submit">
        <br>
        </form>
      </td>
  </tr>

  <!- Build an option to display a full list
     of author ->
  <tr>
      <td> </td>
      <td align="right"><b>Full List:</b></td>
      <td>
       <a href="SearchAuthors.asp?type=full">Display</a>
      </td>
  </tr>
  <tr>
      <td colspan="3"><hr></td>
  </tr>
  <tr>
      <td colspan="3"><font size="4">
         <b>View our list of books:</b></font>
      </td>
  </tr>

  <!- Build an option search for books by
     keyword ->
  <tr>
      <td> </td>
      <td align="right" valign="top">
       <b>Search Title:</b>
      </td>
      <td>
       <form method="post" action="SearchBooks.asp">
       <input type="text" value name="SearchText">
       <input type="submit" value="Submit"
          name="Submit"><br>
       <font size="2">
       <!- Build a link to do an advanced search ->
       <a href="AdvBookSearch.asp?type=advanced"> ⏎
       Advanced Search</a>
       </font>
       </form>
      </td>
  </tr>
  <tr>
      <td> </td>
      <td align="right"><b>Full List:</b></td>
      <td>
       <!- Build a link to display a full
          list of books ->
```

```
        <a href="SearchBooks.asp?type=full">Display</a>
      </td>
  </tr>

  </table>

  <br><br>
  <!- Build a link to sign up as a new
      author ->
  Want to be a new author in our list? Click
  <a href="track.asp?idLink=8">here</a>.

  </body>
  </html>
```

The rest of the page continues on as created in earlier chapters. Finally, we update the new author sign up link. We also want to track the utilization of the new author sign up form.

We perform the same treatment on our TopNav.asp include file, which is shown in Listing 10.13. We add in the top and bottom promotion graphics for tracking, just as we did on the default page.

All of the links are then updated as we did on the default page. The appropriate IDs are set on the idLink argument to Track.asp. By implementing these changes on this page, we can track click-throughs to all of these pages throughout our site.

Listing 10.13   TopNav.asp

```
<%
'****************************************************
'** TopNav.asp
'**
'** Builds the tob navigation table for the
'** Directory pages
'****************************************************
%>
<!- Start the top navigation table
    for the directory ->
<table cellpadding="5" cellspacing="5" border="0">
<tr>
  <td valign="top">

  <!- Navigation Links - Note all are
      tracked in our link tracker ->
  <a href="track.asp?idLink=5"> ↵
  <img src="images/adone.jpg" WIDTH="87" ↵
  HEIGHT="85"></a><br><br>

  <a href="default.asp">Home</a><br><br>
```

```html
<a href="track.asp?idLink=1">Take our Poll</a><br><br>

<a href="track.asp?idLink=2"> ↵
Visit our Forums</a><br><br>

<a href="track.asp?idLink=4">Guest Register</a><br><br>

<a href="track.asp?idLink=6"> ↵
<img src="images/adtwo.jpg" WIDTH="87" ↵
HEIGHT="85"></a><br><br>

</td>
<td valign="top">
```

We are now ready to build our page that handles the processing of the clicked links that we want to track. Listings 10.14 through 10.18 show the code for Track.asp. As we saw with building the links, this page is called for any link that we want to track, and the ID of the link is passed as an argument to the page.

Listing 10.14   Track.asp

```asp
<%@ Language=VBScript %>
<%Option Explicit%>
<%
'*******************************************************
'** Track.asp
'**
'** Processes the tracking request from the
'** referencing link.
'*******************************************************
%>
<%

Dim URL              ' String
Dim dbLink           ' Database Connection
Dim rsLink           ' Recordset
Dim SQL              ' String
Dim RedURL           ' String
Dim Browser          ' String
Dim intPrimeInterest ' Integer
Dim idPublisher      ' Integer
Dim idAuthor         ' Integer
```

The first thing we do in the page is check to ensure that an ID has been passed on the URL. If not, we send the user back to the page they came from. That page is determined by once again using the ServerVariables collection of the request object to retrieve the referrer.

Listing 10.15   Track.asp continued

```
' Get the URL the user came from
URL = Request.ServerVariables("HTTP_REFERER")

' Ensure a link id was passed in
if request("idLink") = "" then

    ' Send them back
    Response.Redirect URL

end if

' Create an ADO database connection
set dbLink = _
    server.createobject("adodb.connection")

' Create record set
set rsLink = _
    server.CreateObject("adodb.recordset")

' Open the connection using our ODBC file DSN
dbLink.open("filedsn=Directory")
```

We also need to ensure that the ID passed on the URL is valid. With our open database connection, we query the database with the sp_RetrieveLink stored procedure to validate the ID. If no record is returned, then we know the ID is invalid and we return the user to the page they came from.

Listing 10.16   Track.asp continued

```
' Retrieve the link information
sql = "execute sp_RetrieveLink " & request("idLink")

' Execute the statement and retrieve the record set
set rsLink = dbLink.Execute(sql)

' Ensure there is a valid entry
if rsLink.EOF then

    ' If not close the DB and send them back
    dbLink.Close

    Response.Redirect URL

else
```

If we are set with a valid ID, then we are ready to process the click. The first thing we do is retrieve the URL from our record so we know what page to send the user to once the data has been processed.

We then retrieve the browser information by once again using the ServerVariables collection. This time we use the HTTP_USER_AGENT parameter to retrieve the browser data in the HTTP header.

Following that, we are ready to begin retrieving the personalization data. As was demonstrated in the last chapter, we utilize the Cookies collection of the Request object to retrieve the personalization settings. If nothing is returned from the cookie retrieval, we set the values to "–1" to indicate no setting.

Listing 10.17   Track.asp continued

```
' Get the redirect URL to send the user to
RedURL = rsLink("chrURL")

' Retrieve the type of browser they are
' using
Browser = Request.ServerVariables("HTTP_USER_AGENT")

' Retrieve the personalization settings to
' store in the tracking DB
intPrimeInterest = ↲
   trim(Request.Cookies("Personalize") ↲
   ("intPrimeInterest"))

idPublisher = ↲
 trim(Request.Cookies("Personalize") ↲
 ("idPublisher"))

idAuthor = trim(Request.Cookies("Personalize")("idAuthor"))

' Check to see the cookies are set, if not then
' set -1 values
if intPrimeInterest = "" then intPrimeInterest = "-1"
if idPublisher = "" then idPublisher = "-1"
if idAuthor = "" then idAuthor = "-1"
```

We finally execute the sp_InsertLinkClick stored procedure to store the data. The appropriate parameters are set to store the data, then the database is closed and we redirect the user to the appropriate page for the link.

Listing 10.18   Track.asp continued

```
' Execute the stored procedure to
' insert the link click
sql = "execute sp_InsertLinkClick " & _
    request("idLink") & ", '" & _
    Browser & "', " & _
    intPrimeInterest & ", " & _
    idPublisher & ", " & _
    idAuthor

' Execute the statement and retrieve the record set
set rsLink = dbLink.Execute(sql)

' Close the database connection
dbLink.Close

' Send the user to the target URL
Response.Redirect RedURL

end if

%>
```

There are some additional features you might want to add to the functionality demonstrated here. One of the valuable features you can provide an affiliate would be a custom branded home page if a visitor links from their site. For example, you might highlight a publisher's books on the home page if the visitor linked from the publisher's Web site.

In addition, affiliates may not want to just link to the home page of your community site. They might want to link to specific books. The affiliate tracking code could be added to the TopNav.asp page as well to track affiliate links to any page in the Web site.

That does it for implementing the affiliate and promotion tracking. Now we are ready to test the tracking.

Testing the User Interface

With this particular functionality, there isn't much to see for the implementation. Figure 10.1 shows the updated home page with our two promotions added on the navigation bar on the left.

FIGURE 10.1:

Updated Default.asp page

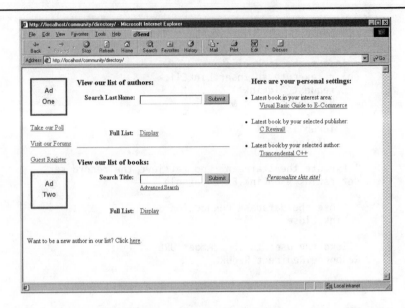

If you scroll your cursor over the links, you will see in the link bar on the bottom of your browser that the links are now going to Track.asp with the appropriate parameters. Clicking the links will store the click in the LinkTrack table, which you can then query to see the activity.

To test the affiliate tracking, you need to set up a link on another site to have a valid referrer. The best way to do this is to set up a test page on your server that links to the Default.asp page with the appropriate affiliate ID on the URL. When you click that link, it triggers off the affiliate tracking.

NOTE   If you simply type in "Default.asp?idAffiliate=1" on the URL, there is actually no referral from another site to track.

Summary

In this chapter, we examined additional features to add promotion and traffic tracking. This is really the tip of the iceberg regarding what kind of data can be tracked in our community Web site.

We are now ready to delve into the management interface needed for not only the affiliate and promotion tracking demonstrated in this page, but all of the other functionality we have created in our community Web site. We will then be ready to add in the poll and survey functionality alluded to in the tracking links of this chapter.

Community Site Administration

- Designing the Application

- Building the Database

- Building the Management Interface

- Testing the Application

The last several chapters have discussed building the user interface of our community Web site. Now we need to build the tools for the site administrator to use to manage the Web site. In many ways these tools are as important, if not more important, than the tools the site visitor utilizes.

Designing the Application

We build a number of administrative tools in this chapter that are all grouped and organized in the same management interface. Table 11.1 outlines the functionality we will be building in the administrative tools.

TABLE 11.1: Management Interface Functionality

Function	Description
Affiliate Management	Managing affiliate traffic data
Author & Book Management	Managing author logins and their book data
Search Management	Search reporting and management
Link Tracking Management	Managing link traffic data

Each tool will have appropriate functional features built in to manage it. Figure 11.1 shows the lay out of the functional tools we build.

FIGURE 11.1:

Administrative interface functionality

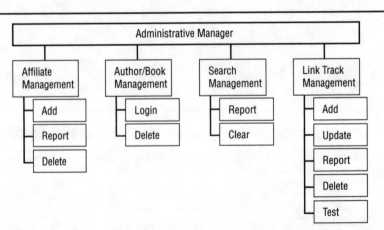

One thing we will not build in this example is a security interface for these administrative tools. This could be similar to what was done in Chapter 7 to secure the author management interface, and would be easy to implement. In that example we built a username and password database and allowed users to log in to see their author profile.

In this case, we might want to assign administrators to the different functional management interfaces and then have some "super" administrators who can manage any of the tools. All this will be determined by your desire to control security access to the management interface, but the techniques demonstrated in Chapter 7 could be utilized to build the security.

Building the Database

We don't add to our community data structure in this chapter. What we do add, however, are a series of stored procedures that provide additional functionality in our database interface to support the adding, deleting, updating, and reporting of data.

First we work on the stored procedures for the affiliate management. Listing 11.1 shows the sp_RetrieveAffiliates stored procedure that returns all of the affiliates in the database.

Listing 11.1   sp_RetrieveAffiliates Stored Procedure

```
CREATE PROCEDURE sp_RetrieveAffiliates AS

/* Retrieves all affiliates in the database */
select * from affiliates
GO
```

Next we have the sp_GetDateAffiliateTraffic stored procedure, as shown in Listing 11.2. This procedure takes in three parameters that include the ID of the affiliate, the start date, and the end date of the range to be reported. These parameters are utilized to query the affiliatelinks table to get the total number of links made for the specified affiliate in the specified date range. Note that the SQL count function is utilized to return the count of rows in that range.

Listing 11.2   sp_GetDateAffiliateTraffic Stored Procedure

```
CREATE PROCEDURE sp_GetDateAffiliateTraffic

/* The ID of the affiliate and the start
   and end date are passed in */
@idAffiliate integer,
@StartDate datetime,
@EndDate datetime

AS
```

```
/* Retrieve the total number of entries for
   the specified affiliate in the specified
   date range. */
select TotalCount=count(*) from AffiliateLinks
where idAffiliate = @idAffiliate and
      dtLinked >= @StartDate and
      dtLinked <= @EndDate
GO
```

Our next stored procedure, sp_GetTotalAffiliateTraffic, returns all of the affiliate traffic for the specified affiliate. The code is shown in Listing 11.3. This is similar to the last stored procedure, but we are not specifying a data range to search.

Listing 11.3   sp_GetTotalAffiliateTraffic Stored Procedure

```
CREATE PROCEDURE sp_GetTotalAffiliateTraffic

/* Pass in the ID of the affiliate */
@idAffiliate integer

AS

/* Get the total count of link entries for
   the specified affiliate */
select TotalCount=count(*) from AffiliateLinks
 where idAffiliate = @idAffiliate
GO
```

Next we have our stored procedure that allows us to delete an affiliate from the database. The SQL code is shown in Listing 11.4.

Listing 11.4   sp_DeleteAffiliate Stored Procedure

```
CREATE PROCEDURE sp_DeleteAffiliate

/* Pass in the ID of the affiliate */
@idAffiliate integer

AS

/* Deletes the specified affiliate */
delete from Affiliates
 where idAffiliate = @idAffiliate
GO
```

Finally, for our affiliate stored procedures, we have sp_InsertAffiliate, as shown in Listing 11.5. This stored procedure inserts a new affiliate into the database, and the name of the affiliate is passed as a parameter.

Listing 11.5   **sp_InsertAffiliate Stored Procedure**

```
CREATE PROCEDURE sp_InsertAffiliate

/* Pass in the name of the new
   affiliate */
@chrName varchar(255)

AS

/* Insert the new affiliate into the
   database */
insert into Affiliates(chrName) values(@chrName)
GO
```

We need to add one stored procedure for our author management capabilities. In our administrative interface, we rely on most of the functionality built in Chapter 7 to manage the author and book data.

Listing 11.6 shows the sp_DeleteAuthor stored procedure that allows the site administrator to remove an author from the database. The ID of the author is passed into the stored procedure.

Listing 11.6   **sp_DeleteAuthor Stored Procedure**

```
CREATE PROCEDURE sp_DeleteAuthor

/* Pass in the ID of the author */
@idAuthor integer

AS

/* Delete the specified author */
delete from Author
 where idAuthor = @idAuthor

GO
```

Next we have our search functionality. We add two stored procedures to administer the search data. The first, sp_RetrieveSearches, shown in Listing 11.7, retrieves all of the search data in the database. To make the output easier to manage, the search keywords will be ordered alphabetically.

Listing 11.7   sp_RetrieveSearches Stored Procedure

```
CREATE PROCEDURE sp_RetrieveSearches AS

/* Retrieve the keyword search data and
   order by the keywords */
select * from searches
 order by chrSearch
GO
```

Next we build a stored procedure to clear out the search data. Listing 11.8 shows the SQL code to delete the search data.

Listing 11.8   sp_DeleteSearches Stored Procedure

```
CREATE PROCEDURE sp_DeleteSearches AS

/* Delete all searches from
   the database */
delete from searches
GO
```

We are now ready to move on to our stored procedures to manage the link data. We build several stored procedures to provide rich reporting functionality for the administrator and to manage the link data.

Listing 11.9 shows the SQL code for our sp_RetrieveLinks stored procedure. This returns all of the links in the database.

Listing 11.9   sp_RetrieveLinks Stored Procedure

```
CREATE PROCEDURE sp_RetrieveLinks AS

/* Retrieve the link data and order
   by the description */
select * from linktrack
 order by chrDescription
GO
```

Next we have the code that manages inserting a new tracking link into the table. sp_InsertLink, shown in Listing 11.10, takes in the name of the tracking link and the URL it links to, and then inserts the data into the LinkTrack table.

Listing 11.10   sp_InsertLink Stored Procedure

```
CREATE PROCEDURE sp_InsertLink

/* Pass in the description and URL
   for the new link */
@chrDescription varchar(255),
@chrURL varchar(255)

AS

/* Insert the tracking link */
insert into LinkTrack(chrDescription, chrURL)
values(@chrDescription, @chrURL)
GO
```

Listing 11.11 shows the SQL code for the sp_RetrieveLink stored procedure. The ID of the link is passed in and the data for the link is returned.

Listing 11.11   sp_RetrieveLink Stored Procedure

```
CREATE PROCEDURE sp_RetrieveLink

/* Pass in the ID of the link */
@idLink integer

AS

/* Retrieve the link data for the
   specified link */
select * from LinkTrack
 where idLink = @idLink
GO
```

We now build a stored procedure that allows us to update link data. Listing 11.12 shows the SQL code for the sp_UpdateLink stored procedure which takes in three parameters. The first is the ID of the link, the second the description, and the third is the URL. The data for the specified link is then updated.

Listing 11.12   sp_UpdateLink Stored Procedure

```
CREATE PROCEDURE sp_UpdateLink

/* Pass in the link data to be updated */
@idLink integer,
@chrDescription varchar(255),
```

```
@chrURL varchar(255)

AS

/* Update the LinkTrack entry */
update LinkTrack set
    chrDescription = @chrDescription,
    chrURL = @chrURL
 where idLink = @idLink
GO
```

Next is the stored procedure, sp_DeleteLink, shown in Listing 11.13, which removes a link from the database. The ID of the link is passed in and the SQL delete function is utilized to remove it from the table.

Listing 11.13   sp_DeleteLink Stored Procedure

```
CREATE PROCEDURE sp_DeleteLink

/* Pass in the ID of the link */
@idLink integer

AS

/* Delete the specified link */
delete from LinkTrack
 where idLink = @idLink
GO
```

Our final administrative stored procedure, before we jump into the reporting stored procedures, handles the clearing of link clicks from the database. The sp_DeleteLinkClicks stored procedure, as shown in Listing 11.14, removes all of the click rows for the specified link.

Listing 11.14   sp_DeleteLinkClicks Stored Procedure

```
CREATE PROCEDURE sp_DeleteLinkClicks

/* Pass in the ID of the link */
@idLink integer

AS

/* Delete the specified link */
delete from linkclick
 where idLink = @idLink
GO
```

Next we move to the stored procedures we utilize for reporting on the link data. Collectively, these provide data mining techniques that we can put to good use in tracking the link activity.

Listing 11.15 shows the sp_RepLinkCount stored procedure that is utilized to report on the number of times the particular link was clicked. Again we use the SQL Count function to return the total count instead of all the matching rows in the table.

Listing 11.15   sp_RepLinkCount Stored Procedure

```
/* Returns the total link count
   for the specified link */
CREATE PROCEDURE sp_RepLinkCount

/* The ID of the link is passed in */
@idLink integer

AS

/* Return the total count */
select totalcount = count(*) from linkclick
where idlink = @idLink
GO
```

Our next stored procedure, sp_RepLinkPublisher, shown in Listing 11.16, reports on the visitor publisher personalized preferences of the specified link. To retrieve this data, we have to build a complex SQL query that retrieves the total count by publisher.

The SQL Group By functionality is utilized to group the data returned by publisher so we don't get every click of that link and the specified publisher. We also have to join the linkclick, linktrack, and publisher tables to get all of the relational data we need. Finally, we again use the Count function to total the number of rows. This all results in a set of rows returned, by publisher, with a specified click count.

Listing 11.16   sp_RepLinkPublisher Stored Procedure

```
/* Returns data on the personalized publisher
   preferences of the users who clicked on
   the specified link */
CREATE PROCEDURE sp_RepLinkPublisher

/* Pass in the ID of the link */
@idLink integer

AS
```

```
/* Return the total count grouped by publisher
   for the specified link */
select totalcount = count(idPerPublisher), chrPublisher
 from linkclick, linkTrack, publisher
 where linkclick.idlink = linktrack.idlink and
     linktrack.idlink = @idLink and
     linkclick.idPerPublisher = publisher.idPublisher
group by idPerPublisher, chrPublisher
GO
```

Next we have the sp_RepLinkAuthor stored procedure as shown in Listing 11.17. This is similar to the last stored procedure, but it returns the number of link clicks correlated to the specific author preference of the site visitor.

In this case we group the returned data by the author, and we return the count data along with each author's name. The linkclick, linktrack, and author tables are joined together to return the correct relational data.

Listing 11.17   sp_RepLinkAuthor Stored Procedure

```
/* Returns data on the personalized author
   preferences of the users who clicked on
   the specified link */
CREATE PROCEDURE sp_RepLinkAuthor

/* Pass in the ID of the link */
@idLink integer

AS

/* Get the count grouped by author. Return the first
   and last name of each author */
select totalcount = count(idPerAuthor), chrFirstName,
        chrLastName
      from linkclick, linkTrack, author
      where linkclick.idlink = linktrack.idlink
        and linktrack.idlink = @idLink
        and linkclick.idPerPublisher =
          author.idauthor
      group by idPerAuthor, chrFirstName,
        chrLastName
GO
```

Remember that in our click tracking, we are also storing the browser the visitor is utilizing. Listing 11.18 contains the sp_RepLinkBrowser stored procedure that returns the number of clicks made by browser.

In this case, we are grouping by browser type. The total count is then returned by browser with the linkclick and linktrack tables being joined.

Listing 11.18   sp_RepLinkBrowser Stored Procedure

```
/* Returns data on the browser preferences
   of the users who clicked on the specified
   link */
CREATE PROCEDURE sp_RepLinkBrowser

/* Pass in the ID of the link */
@idLink integer

AS

/* Retrieve the total count grouped by the
   type of browser */
select totalcount = count(chrBrowser), chrBrowser
  from linkclick, linkTrack
 where linkclick.idlink = linktrack.idlink and
     linktrack.idlink = @idLink
  group by chrBrowser
GO
```

Finally we need to report on the interest topic preferences of the user. The sp_RepLink-Interest stored procedure, shown in Listing 11.19, returns the total count based on the interest setting of the user. The data is grouped by interest.

Listing 11.19   sp_RepLinkInterest Stored Procedure

```
/* Returns data on the personalized topic
   interest preferences of the users who
   clicked on the specified link */
CREATE PROCEDURE sp_RepLinkInterest

/* Pass in the ID of the link */
@idLink integer

AS

/* Retrieve the total count grouped by the ID
   of the interest for the specified link */
select totalcount = count(intPerPrimeInterest), intPerPrimeInterest
  from linkclick, linkTrack
 where linkclick.idlink = linktrack.idlink and
     linktrack.idlink = @idLink and
     intPerPrimeInterest <> -1
  group by intPerPrimeInterest
GO
```

That does it for the database additions we need to make. Now we need to put all of these stored procedures to use in building our management interface functionality.

Building the Management Interface

We can now move to building out the management interface with the functionality outlined in Table 11.1. We explore each functionality separately, but they are all tied together by the management home page and navigation include file.

Home and Navigation

The management interface starts with a general default page that provides simple navigation to the different functional features We also build a general navigation include, as we have incorporated in previous chapters.

Listing 11.20 shows the default page. It starts with the standard header and is followed by a bulleted list of links to the different management pages for each of our functions.

Listing 11.20   Default.asp

```
<%@ Language=VBScript %>
<%Option Explicit%>
<%
'****************************************************
'** Default.asp
'**
'** Provides the entry navigation for the
'** administrator
'****************************************************
%>
<HTML>
<HEAD>
</HEAD>
<BODY>

<!- Build links to the main management tools ->
<UL>
<li><a href="ManageAffiliates.asp">Affiliate Managemet</a></li>
<li><a href="ManageAuthors.asp">Author/Book Management</a></li>
<li><a href="ShowSearches.asp">Search Management</a></li>
<li><a href="ManageLinkTrack.asp">Link Track Management</a></li>
</UL>

</BODY>
</HTML>
```

The standard navigation provides quick access to all of the management functions we build and includes all of the pages on the management section.

Listing 11.21 shows the code for Navigation.asp. A bar is built across the top of the page that has links to the primary page for each management tool.

Listing 11.21   Navigation.asp

```
<%
'*****************************************************
'** Navigation.asp
'**
'** Builds a navigation bar for the administrator
'*****************************************************
%>
<!- Build the navigation for the manager ->
| <a href="ManageAffiliates.asp">Affiliate Management</a> |
<a href="ManageAuthors.asp">Author/Book Management</a> |
<a href="ShowSearches.asp">Search Management</a> |
<a href="ManageLinkTrack.asp">Link Track Management</a> |
<HR><BR>
```

Affiliate Management

The first functionality we explore is the affiliate management. We build the capability to add and delete affiliates, as well as report on affiliate traffic.

The first page, shown in Listings 11.22 through 11.25, is the management interface for our affiliate tools. We provide the link to add a new affiliate on this page as well as list current affiliates for deleting and reporting. Note that the page begins with the Navigation.asp include.

Listing 11.22   ManageAffiliates.asp

```
<%@ Language=VBScript %>
<%Option Explicit%>
<%
'*****************************************************
'** ManageAffiliates.asp
'**
'** Provides management options for the affiliates
'** manager
'*****************************************************
%>
<HTML>
<HEAD>
</HEAD>
```

```
<BODY>

<!- #include file="navigation.asp" ->

<%

Dim dbAffiliate      ' Database Connection
Dim rsAffiliate      ' Recordset
Dim SQL              ' String

' Create an ADO database connection
set dbAffiliate = _
   server.createobject("adodb.connection")

' Create record set
set rsAffiliate = _
   server.CreateObject("adodb.recordset")

' Open the connection using our ODBC file DSN
dbAffiliate.open("filedsn=Directory")
```

Next, the sp_RetrieveAffiliates stored procedure is executed to retrieve all of the current affiliates in the database. The table structure is then started for showing the affiliate data.

Listing 11.23   ManageAffiliates.asp continued

```
' Build a SQL statement to retrieve the
' affiliates in the database
sql = "execute sp_RetrieveAffiliates"

' Execute the statement and retrieve the record set
set rsAffiliate = dbAffiliate.Execute(sql)

%>

<!- Build a table to manage the affiliates ->
<table cellpadding="5" cellspacing="5" border="1">
<tr>
   <th>Name</th>
   <th>Date Created</th>
   <th>Traffic</th>
   <th>Delete</th>
</tr>
```

Now a row is added to our table that provides the option to add a new affiliate to the database. The link goes to the AddNewAffiliate.asp page. Following that, we start the loop through the existing affiliates.

Listing 11.24   ManageAffiliates.asp continued

```
<!- Build a link to add a new affiliate ->
<tr>
  <td colspan="4" align="center">
   <a href="AddNewAffiliate.asp">Add New</a>
  </td>
</tr>

<%

' Loop through the affiliates
do until rsAffiliate.EOF

%>
```

The name for each affiliate is displayed. That is followed by the date the affiliate was created in the database. Next, a link is built to the AffiliateTraffic.asp page to report on the traffic for that affiliate. The ID of the affiliate is passed on the URL. Finally, we build a link to
the DeleteAffiliate.asp page to delete the affiliate. The ID is also passed on this URL.

Listing 11.25   ManageAffiliates.asp continued

```
<tr>
    <!- Display the affiliate name ->
    <td><%=rsAffiliate("chrName")%></td>

    <!- Display the date created ->
    <td><%=rsAffiliate("dtCreated")%></td>

    <!- Build a link to view the traffic ->
    <td>
     <a href="AffiliateTraffic.asp? ⏎
     IdAffiliate=<%=rsAffiliate("idAffiliate")%>"> ⏎
     View Traffic Report</a>
    </td>

    <!- Build a link to delete the affiliate ->
    <td>
     <a href="DeleteAffiliate.asp?idAffiliate= ⏎
     <%=rsAffiliate("idAffiliate")%>">Delete</a>
    </td>
</tr>

<%

' Move to the next row
rsAffiliate.MoveNext
```

```
Loop

' Close the database
dbAffiliate.Close

%>

</table>

</BODY>
</HTML>
```

The AddNewAffiliate.asp page, shown in Listings 11.26 and 11.27, provides the capability to insert a new affiliate into the database. Again, our page starts out with the navigation.asp include so that we can easily navigate to any functionality in our manager. A form is then started that posts the entered data to the InsertAffiliate.asp page for processing.

Listing 11.26   AddNewAffiliate.asp

```
<%@ Language=VBScript %>
<%Option Explicit%>
<%
'*****************************************************
'** AddNewAffiliate.asp
'**
'** Provides a form for adding a new affiliate
'** to the database
'*****************************************************
%>
<HTML>
<HEAD>
</HEAD>
<BODY>

<!- #include file="navigation.asp" ->

<!- Build a table to add a new affiliate ->
<table border="0" cellpadding="5" cellspacing="5">

<!- Build a form for entering the data ->
<form method="post" action="InsertAffiliate.asp">
```

Our form contains just one field for entering the affiliate name. The Submit button is then placed on the page and the page is closed out.

Listing 11.27 AddNewAffiliate.asp continued

```
<!- Build a field for the affiliate name ->
<tr>
   <td align="right">Affiliate Name:</td>
   <td>
   <input type="text" value="" name="chrName">
   </td>
</tr>

<tr>
   <td colspan="2" align="center">
   <input type="Submit"
      value="Submit" name="Submit">
   </td>
</tr>

</form>

</table>

</BODY>
</HTML>
```

The next page, InsertAffiliate.asp shown in Listings 11.28 through 11.30, handles the insertion of the new affiliate into the database. It handles validating as well as inserting the data. Because this page has a user interface (versus just ASP processing), we show the navigation include on the page.

Listing 11.28 InsertAffiliate.asp

```
<%@ Language=VBScript %>
<%Option Explicit%>
<%
'*****************************************************
'** InsertAffiliate.asp
'**
'** Inserts a new affiliate into the database
'*****************************************************
%>
<HTML>
<Body>

<!- #include file="navigation.asp" ->

<%
```

```
Dim dbAffiliate    ' Database Connection
Dim rsAffiliate    ' Record Set
Dim sql            ' String
Dim strError       ' String
```

A check is done to see if a name was entered. If not, then we build an error message and display it. We then indicate to the user that they need to correct their entry before continuing.

Listing 11.29   InsertAffiliate.asp continued

```
' Check to ensure an affiliate name was entered
if request("chrName") = "" then

    strError = "You did not enter in an affiliate name.<BR>"

end if

' See if an error was generated
if strError <> "" then

    ' Show the error
    Response.Write "<i>" & strError & "</i>"

%>
<BR>
<b>Please hit your browser back button
    to update your data.</b>

<%

else
```

If the name was entered properly, then we are ready to process the entry and insert it into the database. The sp_InsertAffiliate stored procedure is utilized to insert the data. Note that we ensure single quotes are doubled up for insertion.

Listing 11.30   InsertAffiliate.asp continued

```
' Create an ADO database connection
set dbAffiliate = _
    server.createobject("adodb.connection")

' Create record set
set rsAffiliate = _
    server.CreateObject("adodb.recordset")

' Open the connection using our ODBC file DSN
dbAffiliate.open("filedsn=Directory")
```

```
' Build a SQL statement to insert the affiliate
sql = "execute sp_InsertAffiliate '" & _
    replace(request("chrName"), "'", "''") & "'"

' Execute the statement and retrieve the record set
set rsAffiliate = dbAffiliate.Execute(sql)

' Close the database connection
dbAffiliate.Close

%>

Your affiliate was succesfully added!
Click <a href="ManageAffiliates.asp">here</a>
to continue.

<%

end if

%>

</body>
</html>
```

The page then closes out with a link back to the affiliate manager page. The database is closed and the page is closed out.

We are now ready to look at the traffic reporting page, AffiliateTraffic.asp as shown in Listings 11.31 through 11.33. This page takes two approaches to displaying data. We display the full count of affiliate links, and we also provide an option for reporting on the number clicks generated in a certain date range.

Listing 11.31   AffiliateTraffic.asp

```
<%@ Language=VBScript %>
<%Option Explicit%>
<%
'*******************************************************
'** AffiliateTraffic.asp
'**
'** Displays affiliate traffic count for the
'** specified affiliate and provides options
'** to get a count based on a date range
'*******************************************************
%>
<HTML>
<HEAD>
</HEAD>
```

```
<BODY>

<!- #include file="navigation.asp" ->

<%

Dim dbAffiliate      ' Database Connection
Dim rsAffiliate      ' Recordset
Dim SQL              ' String

%>
```

The form that posts the reported data range is displayed first on the page. Note that the form posts back to this page. The form contains two fields: one for the start date and one for the end date. Note also that a hidden field is added to the form that stores the ID of the affiliate on which we are reporting.

Listing 11.32   AffiliateTraffic.asp continued

```
<b>Enter in a Date Range to Report:</b><BR><BR>

<!- Build a form for posting a date search on
    the affiliate traffic. ->
<form action="AffiliateTraffic.asp" method="post">

<table>
<tr>
   <td align="right">Start Date:</td>
   <td>
      <!- Start date and ID of the affiliate ->
      <input type="Text" value="" name="StartDate">
      <input type="hidden"
         value="<%=request("idAffiliate")%>"
         name="idAffiliate">
   </td>
</tr>

<!- Build a field for entering the end date ->
<tr>
   <td align="right">End Date:</td>
   <td><input type="Text" value="" name="EndDate"></td>
</tr>

<tr>
   <td colspan="2" align="center">
   <input type="Submit" value="Submit" name="Submit">
   </td>
</tr>
```

```
</table>

<BR><BR>
```

Next we are ready to query the database. We generate two different SQL queries based on whether we are reporting all of the clicks or a date range. To see if a date range is being reported, we check to see if a start date was reported. The sp_GetDateAffiliateTraffic stored procedure is utilized for a date range. The sp_GetTotalAffiliateTraffic stored procedure is used for a full reporting.

Listing 11.33   AffiliateTraffic.asp continued

```
<%

' Create an ADO database connection
set dbAffiliate = _
   server.createobject("adodb.connection")

' Create record set
set rsAffiliate = _
   server.CreateObject("adodb.recordset")

' Open the connection using our ODBC file DSN
dbAffiliate.open("filedsn=Directory")

' Check to see if a start date was entered
if request("StartDate") <> "" then

   ' Build a SQL statement to retrieve the
   ' affiliate traffic in the data range
   sql = "execute sp_GetDateAffiliateTraffic " & _
      request("idAffiliate") & ", '" & _
      request("StartDate") & "', '" & _
      request("EndDate") & "'"

else

   ' Build a SQL statement to retrieve the
   ' total traffic for the affiliate
   sql = "execute sp_GetTotalAffiliateTraffic " & _
      request("idAffiliate")

end if

' Execute the statement and retrieve the record set
set rsAffiliate = dbAffiliate.Execute(sql)

%>
```

```
<!- Show the traffic count ->
Traffic Count: <%=rsAffiliate("TotalCount")%>

<%
' Close the database connection
dbAffiliate.Close
%>

</BODY>
</HTML>
```

Finally, the count is displayed and page is closed out. We are now ready to build the logic to delete an affiliate. Remember that the ID of the affiliate needs to be passed on the URL to the page. The code for DeleteAffiliate.asp is shown in Listing 11.34.

Listing 11.34   DeleteAffiliate.asp

```
<%@ Language=VBScript %>
<%Option Explicit%>
<%
'******************************************************
'** DeleteAffiliate.asp
'**
'** Deletes the specified affiliate from the
'** database
'******************************************************
%>
<%

Dim dbAffiliate        ' Database Connection
Dim rsAffiliate        ' Recordset
Dim SQL                ' String

' Create an ADO database connection
set dbAffiliate = _
    server.createobject("adodb.connection")

' Create record set
set rsAffiliate = _
    server.CreateObject("adodb.recordset")

' Open the connection using our ODBC file DSN
dbAffiliate.open("filedsn=Directory")

' Build a SQL statement do delete the specified
' affiliate
sql = "execute sp_DeleteAffiliate " & _
    request("idAffiliate")
```

```
' Execute the statement and retrieve the record set
set rsAffiliate = dbAffiliate.Execute(sql)

' Close the database connection
dbAffiliate.Close

' Send the user back to the affiliates manager
Response.Redirect "ManageAffiliates.asp"

%>
```

The sp_DeleteAffiliate stored procedure is utilized to delete the affiliate. The stored procedure is then executed and the user is sent back to the ManageAffiliates.asp page. That closes out the functionality for the affiliate management.

Author Management

We now move on to the author management interface. This one is fairly simple because we rely on the tools we already built for the authors themselves to manage their author data and books. We simply facilitate the login by the site administrator.

Our first page, ManageAuthors.asp shown in Listings 11.35 through 11.37, handles listing the authors in the database. Note that once again we include the Navigation.asp file to provide overall site management links.

NOTE   If there are hundreds or thousands of authors, simply listing them on this page will not work. You might want to consider building a search function up front to return matching results instead of the full list.

Listing 11.35   ManageAuthors.asp

```
<%@ Language=VBScript %>
<%Option Explicit%>
<%
'*******************************************************
'** ManageAuthors.asp
'**
'** Provides management options for the authors
'** manager
'*******************************************************
%>
<HTML>
<HEAD>
</HEAD>
<BODY>
```

```
<!- #include file="navigation.asp" ->

<%

Dim dbAuthor    ' Database Connection
Dim rsAuthor    ' Recordset
Dim SQL         ' String

' Create an ADO database connection
set dbAuthor = _
    server.createobject("adodb.connection")

' Create record set
set rsAuthor = _
    server.CreateObject("adodb.recordset")

' Open the connection using our ODBC file DSN
dbAuthor.open("filedsn=Directory")
```

The sp_RetrieveAuthors stored procedure is utilized to return the authors from the database, and then a table is built that displays the data. Note that we build a link to the author sign up page that allows the site administrator to enter a new author.

Listing 11.36   ManageAuthors.asp continued

```
' Retrieve the authors list
sql = "execute sp_RetrieveAuthors"

' Execute the statement and retrieve the record set
set rsAuthor = dbAuthor.Execute(sql)

%>

<!- Build a table to list the authors ->
<table cellpadding="5" cellspacing="5" border="1">
<tr>
    <th>Name</th>
    <th>Login in as Author</th>
    <th>Delete</th>
</tr>

<tr>
    <td colspan="3" align="center">
    <!- Link to the author sign up form to add a
        new form. Note the page opens in a
        new browser. ->
    <a href="../author/authorsignup.asp" target="new"> ↵
    Add New</a>
    </td>
</tr>
```

Next we build the table by looping through the authors. We display the author name, followed by a link to the author management tools login page. Note that on the URL, the username, and password are passed as parameters. This allows the Login.asp page to successfully process the administrator and port them to the management tools for the author. Remember that the Login.asp page is the one that checks the validation of the user's login request.

A link is also built to the DeleteAuthor.asp page with the ID of the author passed as a parameter. This allows the administrator to delete the author from the system.

Listing 11.37   ManageAuthors.asp continued

```asp
<%

' Loop through the record set
do until rsAuthor.EOF

%>

<tr>
   <td>
    <!- Display the author ->
    <%=rsAuthor("chrLastName")%>, <%=rsAuthor("chrFirstName")%>
   </td>
   <td>
   <!- Link to the login validation page of the manager
      and pass the username and password ->
    <a href="../author/login.asp?chrUserName= ⏎
    <%=rsAuthor("chrUserName")%>&chrPassword= ⏎
    <%=rsAuthor("chrPassword")%>" target="new">Login</a>
   </td>
   <td>
    <!- Build a link to delete the author ->
    <a href="DeleteAuthor.asp?idAuthor= ⏎
    <%=rsAuthor("idAuthor")%>">Delete</a>
   </td>
</tr>

<%

' Move to the next author
rsAuthor.MoveNext

Loop

' Close the database connection
dbAuthor.Close

%>
```

```
</table>

</BODY>
</HTML>
```

The page then closes out with the closing table and page tags and the database being closed. Next we have the DeleteAuthor.asp page, as referenced in the previous table. The code for the page is shown in Listings 11.38. The ID of the author is passed on the URL.

Listing 11.38 DeleteAuthor.asp

```
<%@ Language=VBScript %>
<%Option Explicit%>
<%
'*******************************************************
'** DeleteAuthor.asp
'**
'** Deletes the specified author from the database
'*******************************************************
%>
<%

Dim dbAuthor      ' Database Connection
Dim rsAuthor      ' Recordset
Dim SQL           ' String

' Create an ADO database connection
set dbAuthor = _
    server.createobject("adodb.connection")

' Create record set
set rsAuthor = _
    server.CreateObject("adodb.recordset")

' Open the connection using our ODBC file DSN
dbAuthor.open("filedsn=Directory")

' Build a SQL statement to delete the specified
' author
sql = "execute sp_DeleteAuthor " & _
    request("idAuthor")

' Execute the statement and retrieve the record set
set rsAuthor = dbAuthor.Execute(sql)

' Close the database connection
dbAuthor.Close

' Send the user to authors manager
```

```
Response.Redirect "ManageAuthors.asp"

%>
```

The sp_DeleteAuthor stored procedure is utilized to delete the author. Once the author is deleted, the administrator is sent back to the ManageAuthors.asp page.

That does it for our additional author management functionality. Next we are ready to explore the search reporting capabilities.

Search Management

For the search functionality, we build a report that shows all of the searches performed since the report data was last cleared. ShowSearches.asp, shown in Listings 11.39 through 11.41, implements this functionality.

Listing 11.39   ShowSearches.asp

```
<%@ Language=VBScript %>
<%Option Explicit%>
<%
'*****************************************************
'** ShowSearches.asp
'**
'** Displays the list of key word searches
'*****************************************************
%>
<HTML>
<HEAD>
</HEAD>
<BODY>

<!- #include file="navigation.asp" ->

<%

Dim dbSearch    ' Database Connection
Dim rsSearch    ' Recordset
Dim SQL         ' String


' Create an ADO database connection
set dbSearch = _
   server.createobject("adodb.connection")

' Create record set
set rsSearch = _
   server.CreateObject("adodb.recordset")
```

```
' Open the connection using our ODBC file DSN
dbSearch.open("filedsn=Directory")
```

The sp_RetrieveSearches stored procedure is called to return the search data. Note that it returns the search data in alphabetical order. The first link on the page is built to the ClearSearches.asp page to remove the current list of searches and begin tracking again. The table header is then started where we display the search type (Author or Book), search keyword, and date the keyword was entered.

Listing 11.40   ShowSearches.asp continued

```
' Build a SQL query to retrieve the search
' entries
sql = "execute sp_RetrieveSearches"

' Execute the statement and retrieve the record set
set rsSearch = dbSearch.Execute(sql)

%>

<!- Build a link to clear the search entries ->
<a href="ClearSearches.asp">Clear Search List</a>
<BR><BR>

<!- Build a table to show the searches ->
<table cellpadding="5" cellspacing="5">
<tr>
    <th>Search Type</th>
    <th>Search</th>
    <th>Date</th>
</tr>
```

We now loop through the results to display the search data. We first check the search type to see if it is a 1 or a 2. The number 1 signifies that an author search was performed, and the number 2 signifies a book search. The search keywords and the date the keywords were entered are then displayed.

Listing 11.41   ShowSearches.asp continued

```
<%

' Loop through the search results
do until rsSearch.EOF

%>
```

```
<tr>
   <td>

   <%

   ' Indicate the type of search based on the
   ' ID
   if rsSearch("intType") = 1 then
   %>
   Author
   <%
   else
   %>
   Book
   <%
   end if

   %>
   </td>

   <!- Show the search keyword(s) ->
   <td><%=rsSearch("chrSearch")%></td>

   <!- Show the date searched ->
   <td><%=rsSearch("dtSearched")%></td>

</tr>

<%

' Move to the next record
rsSearch.MoveNext

loop

' Close the database connection
dbSearch.Close

%>

</table>

</BODY>
</HTML>
```

Our next page handles clearing the searches from the database. It is straightforward because no parameters are passed to the page. The sp_DeleteSearches stored procedure is called, which clears the keywords. ClearSearches.asp is shown in Listing 11.42.

Listing 11.42   ClearSearches.asp

```asp
<%@ Language=VBScript %>
<%Option Explicit%>
<%
'*****************************************************
'** ClearSearches.asp
'**
'** Clears the keyword search entries from the
'** database
'*****************************************************
%>
<%

Dim dbSearch    ' Database Connection
Dim rsSearch    ' Recordset
Dim SQL         ' String

' Create an ADO database connection
set dbSearch = _
   server.createobject("adodb.connection")

' Create record set
set rsSearch = _
   server.CreateObject("adodb.recordset")

' Open the connection using our ODBC file DSN
dbSearch.open("filedsn=Directory")

' Build the SQL statement to clear the searches
sql = "execute sp_DeleteSearches"

' Execute the statement and retrieve the record set
set rsSearch = dbSearch.Execute(sql)

' Close the database connection
dbSearch.Close

' Send the user back to the show searches page
Response.Redirect "ShowSearches.asp"

%>
```

That does it for our simple search reporting. This section could be expanded greatly to include more data mining features, but it serves to provide the basic idea of search reporting. In particular, if we find that visitors are searching extensively on different book topics, we might want to try and include more books that meet their requirements.

Link Tracking Management

Finally we are going to build the link tracking management pages. We build extensive functionality in this area and are able to add, update, delete, and data mine our link tracking data.

The first page we build is our home page for the link tracking. ManageLinkTrack.asp is shown in Listings 11.43 through 11.45. This presents all the options in a single page for managing our link tracking data. Note that we again utilize the navigation.asp include for our overall menu management.

Listing 11.43   ManageLinkTrack.asp

```
<%@ Language=VBScript %>
<%Option Explicit%>
<%
'*****************************************************
'** ManageLinkTrack.asp
'**
'** Provides management options for the link track
'** manager
'*****************************************************
%>
<HTML>
<HEAD>
</HEAD>
<BODY>

<!- #include file="navigation.asp" ->
```

A table is then build that provides the structure for our link data, followed by a row that provides a link to add a new entry in the link tracking database.

Listing 11.44   ManageLinkTrack.asp continued

```
<!- Build a table for the link track management ->
<table cellspacing="5" cellpadding="5" border="1">
<tr>
    <th>Link ID</th>
    <th>Description</th>
    <th>Reports</th>
    <th>Delete</th>
    <th>URL</th>
</tr>

<!- Build an option to add a new link ->
<tr>
    <td colspan="5" align="center">
    <a href="AddLink.asp">Add New Link</a>
```

```
        </td>
    </tr>

<%

Dim dbLink        ' Database Connection
Dim rsLink        ' Recordset
Dim SQL           ' String

' Create an ADO database connection
set dbLink = _
    server.createobject("adodb.connection")

' Create record set
set rsLink = _
    server.CreateObject("adodb.recordset")

' Open the connection using our ODBC file DSN
dbLink.open("filedsn=Directory")
```

The sp_RetrieveLinks stored procedure is utilized to return the current links in the database. The database is then looped through to display the data. The ID of the link tracker is displayed and linked to EditLink.asp for editing the basic link information.

The description is displayed next, followed by a link that we build to the LinkTraffic-Report.asp with the ID of the link on the URL. We then build a link to the DeleteLink.asp page with the ID of the link on the URL. Finally, we build a link to the URL associated with the link we are tracking.

Listing 11.45   ManageLinkTrack.asp continued

```
' Build a SQL query to retrieve the current
' links in the database
sql = "execute sp_RetrieveLinks"

' Execute the statement and retrieve the record set
set rsLink = dbLink.Execute(sql)

' Loop through the links
do until rsLink.eof

%>

<tr>
    <td>
    <!- Build an option to edit the link ->
    <a href="EditLink.asp?idLink= ⌐
    <%=rsLink("idLink")%>"><%=rsLink("idLink")%></a>
    </td>
```

```
                      <!- Show the link description ->
                      <td><%=rsLink("chrDescription")%></td>
                      <td>
                       <!- Build an option to get a traffic report
                           on the link ->
                       <a href="LinkTrafficReport.asp?idLink= ↵
                       <%=rsLink("idLink")%>">Traffic Report</a>
                      </td>
                      <td>
                       <!- Build an option to delete the link ->
                       <a href="DeleteLink.asp?idLink= ↵
                       <%=rsLink("idLink")%>">Delete</a>
                      </td>
                      <td>
                       <!- Build the link URL for testing ->
                       <a href="<%=rsLink("chrURL")%>"> ↵
                       <%=rsLink("chrURL")%></a>
                      </td>
                 </tr>

                 <%

                 ' Move to the next record
                 rsLink.MoveNext

                 Loop

                 ' Close the database connection
                 dbLink.Close

                 %>
                 </table>

                 </BODY>
                 </HTML>
```

Now we can step through the functionality. The first step is the adding of a link to the database. In this process, we add the description and the URL. The full code is shown in Listing 11.46.

Listing 11.46   AddLink.asp

```
<%@ Language=VBScript %>
<%Option Explicit%>
<%
'****************************************************
'** AddLink.asp
'**
'** Builds a form for adding a new link into the
'** database
'****************************************************
```

```
%>
<HTML>
<HEAD>
</HEAD>
<BODY>

<!- #include file="navigation.asp" ->

<!- Build a form to insert the link into
    the database ->
<form method="post" action="InsertLink.asp">

<!- Build a table to enter the link data ->
<table cellpadding="5" cellspacing="5">

<!- Build a field for the description ->
<tr>
    <td>Description</td>
    <td><input type="text" value=""
        name="chrDescription" size="60">
    </td>
</tr>

<!- Build a field for the URL ->
<tr>
    <td>URL</td>
    <td><input type="text" value=""
        name="chrURL" size="60">
    </td>
</tr>
<tr>
    <td colspan="2">
    <input type="Submit" value="Submit" name="Submit">
    </td>
</table>

</form>

</BODY>
</HTML>
```

It is important to ensure that the URL you enter is accessible from the pages where you place the link on your community Web site. You might want to put in the full URL (with the HTTP) rather than a relative URL. The form posts to the InsertLink.asp page, which processes the data.

Listings 11.47 and 11.48 show the code for the InsertLink.asp page. The data that was entered needs to be validated. Both a description and a URL need to be entered. If they are not successfully entered, we indicate that the user needs to correct the data.

Listing 11.47   InsertLink.asp

```asp
<%@ Language=VBScript %>
<%Option Explicit%>
<%
'*****************************************************
'** InsertLink.asp
'**
'** Inserts a new link into the database
'*****************************************************
%>
<HTML>
<Body>

<!- #include file="navigation.asp" ->

<%

Dim dbLink       ' Database Connection
Dim rsLink       ' Record Set
Dim sql          ' String
Dim strError     ' String

' Check to see if a link description was entered
if request("chrDescription") = "" then

   strError = "You did not enter in a description.<BR>"

end if

' Check to see if a URL for the link was entered
if request("chrURL") = "" then

   strError = "You did not enter in a URL.<BR>"

end if

' Check to see if an error was generated
if strError <> "" then

   ' Write out the error
   Response.Write "<i>" & strError & "</i>"

%>
<BR>
<b>Please hit your browser back button
   to update your data.</b>

<%

else
```

If the data was validated, then we insert the information into the database. The sp_InsertLink stored procedure is called and the data is inserted. Note that the Description field is checked to double any single quotes. We do not have to do the same with the URL because they cannot contain single quotes.

Listing 11.48   InsertLink.asp continued

```
' Create an ADO database connection
set dbLink = _
    server.createobject("adodb.connection")

' Create record set
set rsLink = _
    server.CreateObject("adodb.recordset")

' Open the connection using our ODBC file DSN
dbLink.open("filedsn=Directory")

' Build a SQL statement to insert the link
' into the database
sql = "execute sp_InsertLink '" & _
    replace(request("chrDescription"), "'", "''") & _
    "', '" & request("chrURL") & "'"

' Execute the statement and retrieve the record set
set rsLink = dbLink.Execute(sql)

' Close the database connection
dbLink.Close

%>

Your link was succesfully added!
Click <a href="ManageLinkTrack.asp">here</a>
to continue.

<%

end if

%>

</body>
</html>
```

Once the data is successfully inserted, we indicate that the operation is complete and provide a link to the user to return to the link tracking management page.

Next we work on editing existing link data. The code for EditLink.asp is shown in Listings 11.49 and 11.50. This allows the user to edit the description and the URL.

Listing 11.49   EditLink.asp

```
<%@ Language=VBScript %>
<%Option Explicit%>
<%
'****************************************************
'** EditLink.asp
'**
'** Builds a form for editing a link
'****************************************************
%>
<HTML>
<HEAD>
</HEAD>
<BODY>

<!- #include file="navigation.asp" ->

<%

Dim dbLink    ' Database Connection
Dim rsLink    ' Recordset
Dim SQL       ' String

' Create an ADO database connection
set dbLink = _
   server.createobject("adodb.connection")

' Create record set
set rsLink = _
   server.CreateObject("adodb.recordset")

' Open the connection using our ODBC file DSN
dbLink.open("filedsn=Directory")
```

The sp_RetrieveLink stored procedure is utilized to retrieve the link data. Note that the ID of the link is passed on the URL and is passed as a parameter to the stored procedure. Our form is then built to post the data to the UpdateLink.asp page.

Listing 11.50   EditLink.asp continued

```
' Build a SQL statement to retrieve the specified
' link
sql = "execute sp_RetrieveLink " & request("idLink")
```

```
' Execute the statement and retrieve the record set
set rsLink = dbLink.Execute(sql)

%>

<!- Build a form to update the link data ->
<form method="post" action="UpdateLink.asp">

<!- Build a table to show the link data ->
<table cellpadding="5" cellspacing="5">
<tr>
    <td>Description</td>
    <td>
    <!- Build field forms for the link description
        and a hidden field for the link ID ->
    <input type="text"
        value="<%=rsLink("chrDescription")%>"
        name="chrDescription" size="60">
    <input type="hidden"
        value="<%=rsLink("idLink")%>"
        name="idLink">
    </td>
</tr>
<tr>
    <td>URL</td>
    <td>
    <!- Build a field for the link URL ->
    <input type="text"
        value="<%=rsLink("chrURL")%>"
        name="chrURL" size="60">
    </td>
</tr>
<tr>
    <td colspan="2">
    <input type="Submit" value="Submit" name="Submit">
    </td>
</table>

</form>

<%

' Close the database connection
dbLink.Close

%>

</BODY>
</HTML>
```

The rows of the form contain the fields for the description and the URL. Note that we have to build a hidden field that contains the ID of the link that we want to update. This is used in the UpdateLink.asp page. The page is then closed out appropriately.

We now move to the UpdateLink.asp page, as shown in Listings 11.51 and 11.52. As we did when entering a new link, we need to validate the description and the URL. A check is done to ensure that the data has been entered properly, and if not, the user is asked to correct their data.

Listing 11.51   UpdateLink.asp

```
<%@ Language=VBScript %>
<%Option Explicit%>
<%
'*****************************************************
'** UpdateLink.asp
'**
'** Updates the link data
'*****************************************************
%>
<HTML>
<Body>

<!- #include file="navigation.asp" ->

<%

Dim dbLink        ' Database Connection
Dim rsLink        ' Record Set
Dim sql           ' String
Dim strError      ' String

' Check to see if a description was entered
if request("chrDescription") = "" then

    strError = "You did not enter in a description.<BR>"

end if

' Check to see if a URL was entered
if request("chrURL") = "" then

    strError = "You did not enter in a URL.<BR>"

end if

' Check to see if an error was generated
if strError <> "" then
```

```
' Write out the error
Response.Write "<i>" & strError & "</i>"

%>
<BR>
<b>Please hit your browser back button
   to update your data.</b>

<%
```

else

If the data was entered correctly, then we are ready to update the entry. The sp_UpdateLink stored procedure is utilized with the ID of the link, the description, and the URL passed as parameters. The ID is read from the hidden field.

Listing 11.52   UpdateLink.asp continued

```
' Create an ADO database connection
set dbLink = _
   server.createobject("adodb.connection")

' Create record set
set rsLink = _
   server.CreateObject("adodb.recordset")

' Open the connection using our ODBC file DSN
dbLink.open("filedsn=Directory")

' Build SQL statement to update the link
' data
sql = "execute sp_UpdateLink " & _
   request("idLink") & ", '" & _
   replace(request("chrDescription"), "'", "''") & _
   "', '" & _
   request("chrURL") & "'"

' Execute the statement and retrieve the record set
set rsLink = dbLink.Execute(sql)

' Close the database connection
dbLink.Close

%>

Your link was succesfully added! Click
<a href="ManageLinkTrack.asp">here</a> to continue.

<%
```

```
   end if

%>

</body>
</html>
```

Now we are ready to move on to the reporting of our link traffic data. Remember that we store data based on the user profile settings they may have set and the browser they are utilizing. LinkTrafficReport.asp is shown in Listings 11.53 through 11.57.

Listing 11.53   LinkTrafficReport.asp

```vbscript
<%@ Language=VBScript %>
<%Option Explicit%>
<%
'*****************************************************
'** LinkTrafficReport.asp
'**
'** Provides a report on the link traffic for the
'** specified link
'*****************************************************
%>
<HTML>
<HEAD>
</HEAD>
<BODY>

<!- #include file="navigation.asp" ->

<%

Dim dbLink              ' Database Connection
Dim rsLink              ' Recordset
Dim SQL                 ' String
Dim dbGuestRegister     ' Database Connection
Dim rsGuestRegister     ' Recordset

' Create an ADO database connection
set dbLink = _
   server.createobject("adodb.connection")

' Create record set
set rsLink = _
   server.CreateObject("adodb.recordset")

' Open the connection using our ODBC file DSN
dbLink.open("filedsn=Directory")
```

First we retrieve the data for the link with the sp_RetrieveLink stored procedure. The description is written at the top of the page and then we build a link to the ClearLink-Clicks.asp page where the user can clear the current link data.

Listing 11.54   LinkTrafficReport.asp continued

```
' Build a SQL statement to retrieve the link
sql = "sp_RetrieveLink " & request("idLink")

' Execute the statement and retrieve the record set
set rsLink = dbLink.Execute(sql)

' Write out the description
response.write "<B>" & rsLink("chrDescription") & _
        "<HR><BR></b>"

%>

<!- Build a link to clear the link data ->
<a href="ClearLinkClicks.asp?idLink= ⏎
   <%=request("idLink")%>">Clear report</a>
<BR><BR>
```

Now we are ready to begin using our data mining stored procedures we built earlier in the chapter. We start with the sp_RepLinkCount that indicates the total number of clicks on the link, followed by the sp_RepLinkPublisher stored procedure that reports all the link clicks for each possible publisher profile setting. Each publisher with a count is looped through and displayed.

Listing 11.55   LinkTrafficReport.asp continued

```
<%

' Build a SQL statement to get the total link count
sql = "sp_RepLinkCount " & request("idLink")

' Execute the statement and retrieve the record set
set rsLink = dbLink.Execute(sql)

%>

<!- Write out the traffic count ->
<b>Total Traffic Count = <%=rsLink("totalcount")%>
<BR><BR></b>

<%
```

```
' Build a SQL statement to get the count of
' people who visited this page and what their
' publisher personalized settings are.
sql = "execute sp_RepLinkPublisher " & _
    request("idLink")

' Execute the statement and retrieve the record set
set rsLink = dbLink.Execute(sql)

%>

<table cellpadding="5" cellspacing="5" border="1">
<tr>
    <th width="400">Publisher Profile</th>
    <th>Count</th>
</tr>
<%

' Loop through the publishers
do until rsLink.eof

%>

<!- Show the publisher and total count ->
<tr>
    <td><%=rsLink("chrPublisher")%></td>
    <td><%=rsLink("totalcount")%></td>
</tr>

<%

' Move to the next row
rsLink.movenext

loop

%>

</table>
```

Next we have the author settings reporting. The sp_RepLinkAuthor stored procedure is utilized and, as with the publisher, we loop through the results to display the author name and the number of clicks.

The browser data follows, and the sp_RepLinkBrowser stored procedure is utilized to retrieve the data. The data is then displayed in a formatted table structure.

Listing 11.56   LinkTrafficReport.asp continued

```
<%

' Build a SQL statement to get the count of
' people who visited this page and what their
' preferred author personalized settings are.
sql = "execute sp_RepLinkAuthor " & request("idLink")

' Execute the statement and retrieve the record set
set rsLink = dbLink.Execute(sql)

%>

<table cellpadding="5" cellspacing="5" border="1">
<tr>
    <th width="400">Author</th>
    <th>Count</th>
</tr>
<%

' Loop through the authors
do until rsLink.eof

%>

<!- Show the author name and count ->
<tr>
    <td><%=rsLink("chrLastName")%>,
      <%=rsLink("chrFirstName")%></td>
    <td><%=rsLink("totalcount")%></td>
</tr>

<%

' Move to the next row
rsLink.movenext

loop

%>

</table>

<%

' Build a SQL statement to get the count of
' people who visited this page and what browser
' they are utilizing.
sql = "execute sp_RepLinkBrowser " & request("idLink")
```

```
' Execute the statement and retrieve the record set
set rsLink = dbLink.Execute(sql)

%>

<table cellpadding="5" cellspacing="5" border="1">
<tr>
   <th width="400">Browser</th>
   <th>Count</th>
</tr>
<%

' Loop through the browsers
do until rsLink.eof

%>

<!- Show the browser and the count ->
<tr>
   <td><%=rsLink("chrBrowser")%></td>
   <td><%=rsLink("totalcount")%></td>
</tr>

<%

' Move to the next row
rsLink.movenext

loop

%>

</table>
```

Finally we have the interest topics selected by the user. The sp_RepLinkInterest stored procedure is utilized. We again loop through and display the clicks by interest topic. This time, though, we have to look up the topic name because only the ID is returned by the stored procedure.

Listing 11.57   LinkTrafficReport.asp continued

```
<%

' Build a SQL statement to get the count of
' people who visited this page and what their
' primary interest topic personalized settings are.
sql = "execute sp_RepLinkInterest " & _
   request("idLink")
```

```
' Execute the statement and retrieve the record set
set rsLink = dbLink.Execute(sql)

%>

<table cellpadding="5" cellspacing="5" border="1">
<tr>
   <th width="400">Interest Topic</th>
   <th>Count</th>
</tr>
<%

' Loop through the topics
do until rsLink.eof

   ' Create an ADO database connection
   set dbGuestRegister = _
     server.createobject("adodb.connection")

   ' Create record set
   set rsGuestRegister = _
     server.CreateObject("adodb.recordset")

   ' Open the connection using our ODBC file DSN
   dbGuestRegister.open("filedsn=GuestRegister")

   ' Look up the name of the interest topic
   sql = "sp_RetrieveInterestTopicByID " & _
     rsLink("intPerPrimeInterest")

   ' Execute the statement and retrieve the record set
   set rsGuestRegister = dbGuestRegister.Execute(sql)

%>

<!- Show the name and the total count ->
<tr>
   <td><%=rsGuestRegister("chrName")%></td>
   <td><%=rsLink("totalcount")%></td>
</tr>

<%

' Move to the next row
rsLink.movenext

loop

' Close the database connection
dbLink.Close
```

```
%>

</table>

</BODY>
</HTML>
```

Our next page, ClearLinkClicks.asp as shown in Listing 11.58, handles clearing the link click data for a given link. This is utilized when the administrator wants to clear out link data after a period of time.

Listing 11.58   ClearLinkClicks.asp

```
<%@ Language=VBScript %>
<%Option Explicit%>
<%
'*****************************************************
'** ClearLinkClicks.asp
'**
'** Clears the link clicks from the database for
'** the specified link
'*****************************************************
%>
<%

Dim dbLink         ' Database Connection
Dim rsLink         ' Recordset
Dim SQL            ' String

' Create an ADO database connection
set dbLink = _
    server.createobject("adodb.connection")

' Create record set
set rsLink = _
    server.CreateObject("adodb.recordset")

' Open the connection using our ODBC file DSN
dbLink.open("filedsn=Directory")

' Build a SQL statement to delete link
' clicks for the specified link
sql = "execute sp_DeleteLinkClicks " & _
    request("idLink")

' Execute the statement and retrieve the record set
set rsLink = dbLink.Execute(sql)

' Close the database connection
```

```
dbLink.close

' Send the user to the link track manager
Response.Redirect "ManageLinkTrack.asp"

%>
```

The last page in our administrative tool set is DeleteLink.asp. This removes a link from the database. Listing 11.59 shows the code for the page.

Listing 11.59   DeleteLink.asp

```
<%@ Language=VBScript %>
<%Option Explicit%>
<%
'****************************************************
'** DeleteLink.asp
'**
'** Deletes the specified link from the database
'****************************************************
%>
<%

Dim dbLink        ' Database Connection
Dim rsLink        ' Recordset
Dim SQL           ' String

' Create an ADO database connection
set dbLink = _
   server.createobject("adodb.connection")

' Create record set
set rsLink = _
   server.CreateObject("adodb.recordset")

' Open the connection using our ODBC file DSN
dbLink.open("filedsn=Directory")

' Build a SQL statement to delete the
' specified link
sql = "execute sp_DeleteLink " & request("idLink")

' Execute the statement and retrieve the record set
set rsLink = dbLink.Execute(sql)

' Close the database connection
dbLink.close
```

```
' Send the user to the link track manager
Response.Redirect "ManageLinkTrack.asp"

%>
```

The ID of the link to delete is passed on the URL to the page. The sp_DeleteLink stored procedure is called with the link ID passed as a parameter. Once the link is removed, the user is given a link back to the link track manager.

Testing the User Interface

Now we are ready to see our coding in action. Start by opening the new Default.asp page, (/community/directory/admin/default.asp), as shown in Figure 11.2.

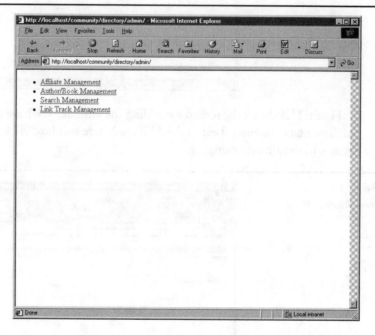

We start with the affiliate manager. Click on the first link of the default page and you arrive at the affiliate manager. Note that our standard administrative navigation menu appears at the top of the page.

The page then provides a link for adding a new affiliate. The page also lists the current affiliates as well as reporting options, and offers the capability to delete an affiliate. Figure 11.3 shows the manager page.

FIGURE 11.3:

Affiliate manager
home page

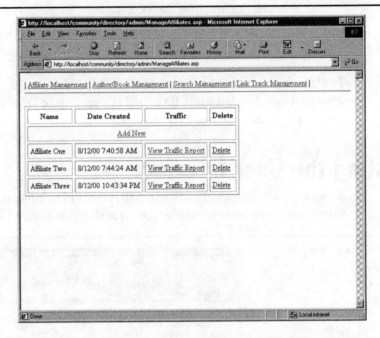

Figure 11.4 shows the screen for adding the affiliate. We have one field for entering in the affiliate name, so enter **Test** in the Affiliate Name text box, click the Submit button, and then return to the affiliate manager.

FIGURE 11.4:

Adding new affiliate

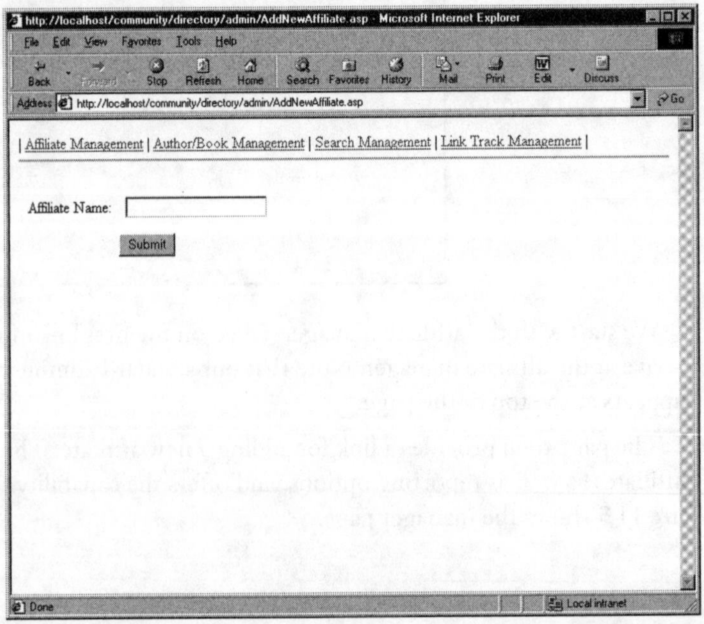

Figure 11.5 shows the updated affiliate manager with our test record. We can now provide the option for an affiliate to start linking to our site. Use the Delete function to remove our test affiliate.

FIGURE 11.5:

New affiliate added

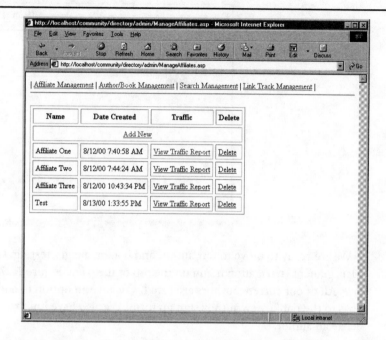

FIGURE 11.5:

New affiliate added

Now test the reporting. You have to ensure that you have some test data for reporting. Figure 11.6 shows a sample report. Try searching on different data ranges as well.

FIGURE 11.6:

Affiliate traffic report

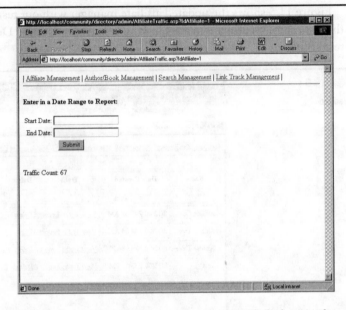

FIGURE 11.6:

Affiliate traffic report

We are ready to move to our author and book manager testing. Click the "Author/Book Management" navigation menu on the top of the page. Figure 11.7 shows the manager interface. All of our current authors are listed. We have an option to add a new author, which links to the public new author sign up form. We also have links to log in as the author and to delete an author.

FIGURE 11.7:

Author and book manager

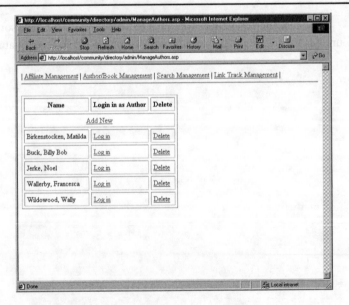

If you roll your mouse over the author login links, you see the link to login.asp in the browser status bar with the username and password on the URL. This will effectively log in the administrator as the author. Click on a link to display the pop-up screen shown in Figure 11.8 that has the administrator logged in.

FIGURE 11.8:

Automatic author login

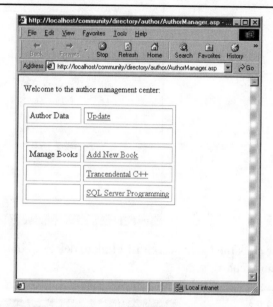

That completes the author management, because we are primarily utilizing the existing author management pages. Now we are ready to utilize the keyword search reporting.

Figure 11.9 shows a sample report that is straightforward and shows the keywords ordered alphabetically. The search type is indicated as well as the date the searches were made.

FIGURE 11.9:

Searches report

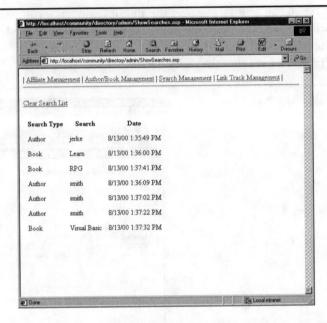

Now click the Clear Search List link to delete all of the search data. Figure 11.10 shows the blank report.

FIGURE 11.10:

Searches report cleared

Finally, let's test the link tracking. Click the "Link Track Management" link on the menu bar. Figure 11.11 shows the manager for the link tracker with several options, including adding a new link, updating an existing link, reporting, deleting, and testing.

FIGURE 11.11:

Link tracking manager

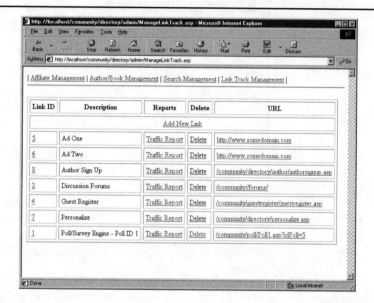

Now let's test the adding of a new link as shown in Figure 11.12. Fill in the Description and URL text boxes, and then click the Submit button to submit the form. Your new link shows up on the management page. Now test the update as well as the delete options with the test link.

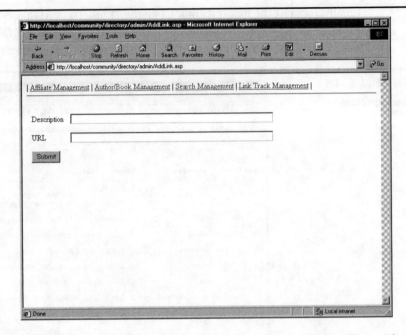

Finally, let's look at our link traffic report. Make sure that you have sufficient data with different personalization profiles to really test the functionality. It will also be helpful to test with different browsers. Figure 11.13 shows a sample report.

FIGURE 11.13:

Link traffic report

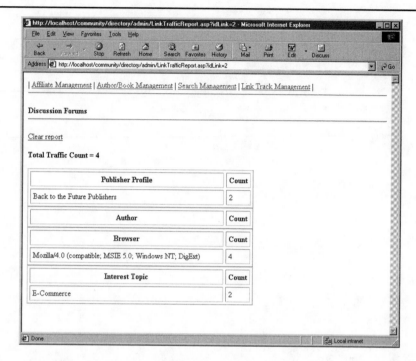

We have now completed testing our user interface. All of the functionality is designed to demonstrate what can be done, however additional tools can be added, including a security interface, extended reporting functions, and so much more. It is important to work with the people who utilize the tools to ensure that the workflow, functionality, and navigation fit with their day-to-day needs as site managers.

Summary

In this chapter we completed the functionality circle of our community functions by adding in the appropriate administrative functionality. We have completed the demonstration functionality for our community foundation. Not only can specific users and authors build custom content, but site visitors can search the content and make personalization settings. We can also track their utilization of the site.

In the next two chapters, we explore two of the more popular community tools: discussion forums and polls.

CHAPTER 12

Discussion Forums

- Designing the Application

- Building the Database

- Building the User Interface

- Building the Management Interface

- Testing the Application

This chapter tackles the kingpin of the community tools—discussion forums. Forums can be the lifeblood of a community Web site as they provide a central meeting place for site members to discuss the content of the site, issues, interests, news, and much more.

The basic principle of discussion topics and messages are at the core of any good forum solution, but there are any number of features and formats that the forums can include. In this chapter, we build the fundamental tools that comprise a forum solution and that include the administrative tools as well.

Designing the Application

The structure of the forums follows the "conversation" process. The forum administrator firsts starts out by setting up discussion sections. These can be thought of as buckets that the community administrator creates to lend focus to conversations.

Within those section buckets, the site visitor can create conversation threads. The threads ideally are topics related to the section topic set up by the administrator. Of course, the site visitor can title the thread anything they want.

Finally, within the thread, site visitors can post messages. These messages constitute the primary conversational tool of the forums with the sections and threads. Figure 12.1 depicts the structural flow of the forums we are designing.

FIGURE 12.1:

Discussion forums structure

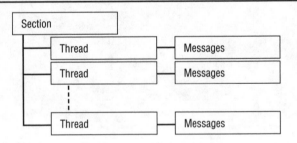

With active forums, you need a solid administrative interface to keep up with your site visitors. The tool we build allows for the management of sections, threads, and messages. If you don't like what someone posts, you can edit or delete the message. If a visitor creates a thread that is not germane to the section, you can delete it.

Building the Database

Not surprisingly, our database structure is going to reflect the discussion structure outlined above. We have a slew of stored procedures that we use to manage the messaging database.

Tables

There are three tables as part of our forum data structure. Figure 12.2 shows the relationships between the Section, Thread, and Message tables.

FIGURE 12.2:

Forums database structure

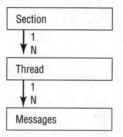

We create a table to hold the section data. This table is related to the thread table, which has a one-to-many relationship. Messages in the message table will have a one-to-many relationship with the thread table.

Listing 12.1 shows the SQL code to generate the Section table. Note that we store the date when the section was created. In addition, we store the last modification date to the section. Modification in this case means when any message is updated for that section. This enables the user to know when a new message has been posted for a quick look before browsing.

Listing 12.1   Section Table

```
CREATE TABLE dbo.Section (
    idSection int IDENTITY (1, 1) NOT NULL ,
    chrName varchar (255) NULL ,
    dtCreated datetime NOT NULL CONSTRAINT
    DF_Section_dtCreated_2__12 DEFAULT (getdate()),
    dtLastMod datetime NULL CONSTRAINT
    DF_Section_dtLastMod_1__12 DEFAULT (getdate())
)
GO
```

Listing 12.2 shows the SQL code to generate the Thread table. The ID of the section is stored in the table to identify to which section the thread is related. The name, date created, owner, and, of course, the date last modified are also stored. The owner is identified when they log in to the forums.

Listing 12.2   Thread Table

```
CREATE TABLE dbo.Thread (
    idThread int IDENTITY (1, 1) NOT NULL ,
    idSection int NOT NULL ,
    chrName varchar (255) NULL ,
    dtCreated datetime NOT NULL CONSTRAINT
    DF_Thread_dtCreated_1__12 DEFAULT (getdate()),
    chrOwner varchar (255) NULL ,
    dtLastMod datetime NULL CONSTRAINT
    DF_Thread_dtLastMod_1__12 DEFAULT (getdate())
)
GO
```

Our final table, Message, stores the messages of the forums. The ID of the thread is stored to make the relationship. The date the message was created, the text of the message, the owner, and the subject are also stored. Listing 12.3 shows the SQL Script code to create the table.

Listing 12.3   Message Table

```
CREATE TABLE dbo.Message (
    idMessage int IDENTITY (1, 1) NOT NULL ,
    dtCreated datetime NOT NULL CONSTRAINT
    DF_Message_dtCreated_3__12 DEFAULT (getdate()),
    txtMessage text NULL ,
    idThread int NOT NULL ,
    chrOwner varchar (255) NULL ,
    chrSubject varchar (255) NULL
)
GO
```

Stored Procedures

Next we create the stored procedures to manage all of the forum data. Let's first look at the stored procedures related to the section

First for the section data we have the sp_AddSection stored procedure, as shown in Listing 12.4. This stored procedure handles inserting a new section into the database. The name of the section is passed in as a parameter.

Listing 12.4   sp_AddSection Table

```
CREATE PROCEDURE sp_AddSection

/* Pass in the section name */
@chrName varchar(255)

AS

/* Insert the section into the table */
insert into section(chrName) values(@chrName)
GO
```

If we add a section, we will of course want to be able to delete it. Listing 12.5 shows the code to create the sp_DeleteSection stored procedure. The ID of the section is passed in and the SQL Delete function is utilized.

Listing 12.5   sp_DeleteSection Table

```
CREATE PROCEDURE sp_DeleteSection

/* Pass the ID of the section */
@idSection int

AS

/* Delete the section from the database */
delete from section where idSection = @idSection
GO
```

The next stored procedure, sp_UpdateSectionName shown in Listing 12.6, manages updating the name of a section. The ID of the section and the new name is passed in as a parameter. The SQL Update function is utilized to update the data.

Listing 12.6   sp_UpdateSectionName Table

```
CREATE PROCEDURE sp_UpdateSectionName

/* Pass in the ID of the section and the
   name of the section */
@idSection int,
@chrName varchar(255)

AS

/* Update the name of the section for the
```

```
          specified section ID */
update section set chrName =
     @chrName where idSection = @idSection
GO
```

When we display the sections to the user, not only do we want to let them know when the last message update was done, but we also want to tell them how many messages are in the section. Listing 12.7 shows the sp_RetrieveSectionPostCount stored procedure that will retrieve the message count for the specified section.

To get the count for the section, we have to join the Message and Thread tables. Remember that the ID of the section is stored in the Thread table, thus we don't need to actually query the Section table directly.

Listing 12.7   **sp_RetrieveSectionPostCount Table**

```
CREATE PROCEDURE sp_RetrieveSectionPostCount

/* Pass in the ID of the section */
@idSection int

AS

/* Retrieve the number of messages posted
   for all threads in the section */
select count(*) from message, thread
where thread.idSection = @idSection and
     message.idThread = thread.idthread
GO
```

Our final stored procedure retrieves all of the sections in the database. Listing 12.8 shows the code to create the sp_RetrieveSections stored procedure.

Listing 12.8   **sp_RetrieveSections Table**

```
CREATE PROCEDURE sp_RetrieveSections AS

/* Retrieve all the forum sections */
select * from section order by chrName
GO
```

Now we are ready to move on to the thread management stored procedures. These are similar to the section stored procedures.

Not unsurprisingly our first stored procedure handles inserting a new thread into the database. The ID of the section related to the thread, the name of the thread, and the owner are passed in as parameters. The SQL script code used to create the stored procedure is shown in Listing 12.9.

Listing 12.9   sp_InsertThread Table

```
CREATE PROCEDURE sp_InsertThread

/* Pass in the ID of the section,
   the name of the thread and the
   owner of the thread */
@idSection int,
@chrName varchar(255),
@chrOwner varchar(255)

AS

/* Insert the new thread into the database */
insert into Thread(idSection, chrName, chrOwner)
values(@idSection, @chrName, @chrOwner)
GO
```

Listing 12.10 shows the SQL code to create the sp_DeleteThread stored procedure. The ID of the thread is passed in and the SQL Delete function is utilized to delete the thread.

Listing 12.10   sp_DeleteThread Table

```
CREATE PROCEDURE sp_DeleteThread

/* Pass in the ID of the thread */
@idThread int

AS

/* Delete the thread from the database */
delete from thread where idThread = @idThread
GO
```

Listing 12.11 shows the SQL code that handles updating a thread name and owner. The ID of the thread is passed in and the name and the owner are updated.

Listing 12.11   sp_UpdateThread Table

```
CREATE PROCEDURE sp_UpdateThread

/* Pass in the ID of the thread,
   the name of the thread and
   the owner */
```

```
@idThread int,
@chrName varchar(255),
@chrOwner varchar(255)

AS

/* Update the thread name and owner for the
   specified thread */
update thread set chrName = @chrName,
        chrOwner = @chrOwner
where idThread = @idThread
GO
```

As with the sections, we want to indicate to the site visitor how many posts there are per thread. The sp_RetrieveThreadPostCount stored procedure, shown in Listing 12.12, takes in the ID of the thread and return the count per thread. To get the count, we have to query the message table by thread ID.

Listing 12.12   **sp_RetrieveThreadPostCount Table**

```
CREATE PROCEDURE sp_RetrieveThreadPostCount

/* Pass in the ID of the thread */
@idThread int

AS

/* Retrieve a count of all the messages
   posted for this thread */
select count(*) from message
where message.idThread = @idthread
GO
```

Finally, we have our stored procedure that returns all of the threads for a specified section. The ID of the section is passed into the stored procedure and the related thread data is returned. sp_RetrieveThreads is shown in Listing 12.13.

Listing 12.13   **sp_RetrieveThreads Table**

```
CREATE PROCEDURE sp_RetrieveThreads

/* Pass in the ID of the section */
@idSection int

AS

/* Retrieve all of the thread for the
```

```
    specified section */
select * from thread where
    idSection = @idSection order by dtCreated
GO
```

Last but not least, we have our stored procedures to manage the message data. We have a similar set of functional stored procedures as we have seen for sections and threads, but in addition, we need to add additional stored procedures for managing paging through message data.

The first stored procedure, sp_InsertMessage, we build inserts a new message into the table as shown in Listing 12.14. We have a number of actions that have to take place aside from inserting the new message. We also have to update the corresponding thread and section data to indicate when the last update was completed.

Within this transaction we update the section data to set the date last modified. And the thread data is updated to also indicate the last modification.

Listing 12.14   sp_InsertMessage Table

```
CREATE PROCEDURE sp_InsertMessage

/* Pass in the ID of the section,
   the ID of the thread, the subject
   of the message and the owner of
   the message */
@idSection int,
@idThread int,
@chrSubject varchar(255),
@txtMessage text,
@chrOwner varchar(255)

AS

/* Insert the message into the database */
insert into Message(idThread, chrSubject, txtMessage, chrOwner)
values(@idThread, @chrSubject, @txtMessage, @chrOwner)

/* Update the date the section was last
   modified with a new message. */
update section set dtLastMod =
   getdate() where idSection = @idSection

/* Update the date the thread was last
   modified by adding the new message */
update thread set dtLastMod =
   getdate() where idThread = @idThread
GO
```

Next we have the sp_UpdateMessage stored procedure, shown in Listing 12.15, that updates the message data. The ID of the message, the subject, owner, and message are passed in as parameters.

Listing 12.15   sp_UpdateMessage Table

```
CREATE PROCEDURE sp_UpdateMessage

/* Pass in the ID of the message,
   the subject of the message,
   the owner of the message and
   the text of the message */
@idMessage int,
@chrSubject varchar(255),
@chrOwner varchar(255),
@txtMessage text

AS

/* Update the message data for the specified
   message */
update Message set chrSubject = @chrSubject,
        chrOwner = @chrOwner,
        txtMessage = @txtMessage
    where idMessage = @idMessage
GO
```

We also have the obligatory stored procedure to delete a message from the database. Listing 12.16 shows the code for the stored procedure. The ID of the message is passed in and the SQL Delete function is utilized to remove the message from the database.

Listing 12.16   sp_DeleteMessage Table

```
CREATE PROCEDURE sp_DeleteMessage

/* Pass in the ID of the message */
@idMessage int

AS

/* Delete the message from the database */
Delete from message where idMessage = @idMessage
GO
```

Listing 12.17 shows the SQL code to generate the sp_GetMessageCountByThread stored procedure. The ID of the thread is passed in and the number of messages related to that thread is returned.

Listing 12.17 sp_GetMessageCountByThread Table

```
CREATE PROCEDURE sp_GetMessageCountbyThread

/*  Pass in the ID of the thread */
@idThread int

AS

/*  Get the total number of messages posted
    for the specified thread */
select total=count(*) from Message
   where idThread = @idThread
GO
```

Listing 12.18 shows the SQL code to generate the sp_RetrieveMessage stored procedure. The ID of the message is passed in and the data is returned for the specific message.

Listing 12.18 sp_RetrieveMessage Table

```
CREATE PROCEDURE sp_RetrieveMessage

/* Pass in the ID of the message */
@idMessage int

AS

/* Retrieve the message data for
   the specified message */
select * from message where idMessage = @idMessage
GO
```

The next stored procedure, sp_RetrieveMessages, retrieves the all of the messages related to the specified thread. The SQL script code to generate the stored procedure is shown in Listing 12.19.

Listing 12.19 sp_RetrieveMessages Table

```
CREATE PROCEDURE sp_RetrieveMessages

/* Pass in the ID of the thread */
@idThread int
```

```
AS

/* Retrieve the messages for the thread */
select * from message where idThread = @idThread
GO
```

Our last two stored procedures are related to retrieving messages looking forward or backward from a specific message. Because we have the potential for hundreds of messages per thread, we want to display those in reasonable increments for the user to view the data.

The first stored procedure, sp_RetrieveNextMessages, handles retrieving the set of messages after the specified message passed into the stored procedure for the specified thread. To execute the query, we want all messages with IDs greater than the ID passed in and where the thread ID matches the current thread being viewed. The SQL script code to generate the stored procedure is shown in Listing 12.20.

Listing 12.20   sp_RetrieveNextMessages Table

```
CREATE PROCEDURE sp_RetrieveNextMessages

/* The ID of the thread and the ID
   of the last message displayed */
@idThread int,
@idMessage int


AS

/* Retrieve the next set of messages in list
   for the specified thread */
select * from Message where
   idMessage >= @idMessage and
   idThread = @idThread
   order by dtCreated
GO
```

Our last stored procedure, shown in Listing 12.21, handles retrieving messages that were posted previous to the specified messages. Again we are retrieving messages that relate to the specified thread and, in this case, were posted prior to the current message.

Listing 12.21   sp_RetrievePreviousMessages Table

```
CREATE PROCEDURE sp_RetrievePreviousMessages

/* Pass in the ID of the thread and the
   last message displayed */
```

```
@idThread int,
@idMessage int

AS

/* Retrieve all messages for the thread
   in the list before the specified
   message */
select * from Message where
   idMessage < @idMessage and
   idThread = @idThread
   order by dtCreated
GO
```

That does it for our database programming for the forums. Now are we ready to put the database to work with our script code. First we need to take a look at the user interface code, and then examine the administrative interface.

Building the User Interface

The user interface follows a logical flow of leading the user through login, section selection, thread selection, and then message browsing.

The first page, Default.asp, handles having the forums user log in with a handle. They don't have to use the same login handle with each visit, nor do they have to remember a password. This is done as a way for users to identify each other and build conversations. Listings 12.22 and 12.23 show the code for the page.

Listing 12.22   Default.asp

```
<%@ Language=VBScript %>
<%
'****************************************************
'** Default.asp
'**
'** Provides a login form for the forum user
'****************************************************
%>
<HTML>
<HEAD>
</HEAD>
<BODY>

<center>
<font color="blue" size="4">
<B>Welcome to our Message Boards!</b>
</font>
```

A simple form is created to post the form data to Section.asp, and an input field is created that is utilized by the user to enter their handle.

Listing 12.23 Default.asp continued

```
<BR><BR>
Please log in with a handle:

<!- Form to enter in a handle for being
    identified in the forums. ->
<form method="post" action="Section.asp">
<input type="text" value="" name="Handle">
<input type="submit" value="Submit" name="Submit">
</form>

</center>
<P> </P>

</BODY>
</HTML>
```

Next we have the Section.asp page, as shown in Listings 12.24 through 12.26. This page handles displaying the sections available in the forums. As we have done throughout the book, the page begins with our standard documentation header.

Listing 12.24 Section.asp

```
<%@ Language=VBScript %>
<% Option Explicit %>
<%
'*****************************************************
'** Section.asp
'**
'** Displays the forums sections
'*****************************************************
%>
<HTML>
<HEAD>
</HEAD>
<BODY>

<font color="blue" size="4">Select a topic area below:
<BR><BR></font>
```

Now we create our database connection and execute the sp_RetrieveSections stored procedure. This returns all of the current sections in the database.

The first thing that the page does is retrieve the handle entered by the user. We do not enforce any validation, so the user can remain anonymous, if they so choose. The handle is stored in a session variable for easy access throughout the rest of the pages.

Listing 12.25   Section.asp continued

```asp
<%

Dim dbForums      ' database connection
Dim rsForums      ' record set
Dim rsPostCount   ' record set
Dim SQL           ' string

' Get the handle of the message owner.
' We go ahead and double up an single quotes
' for on insertion into the database.
session("Handle") = replace(request("Handle"), "'", "''")

' Create an ADO database connection
set dbForums = _
   server.createobject("adodb.connection")

' Create record set
set rsForums = _
   server.CreateObject("adodb.recordset")

' Create record set
set rsPostCount = _
   server.CreateObject("adodb.recordset")

' Open the connection using our ODBC file DSN
dbForums.open("filedsn=Forums")

' Retrieve the sections for the forums
sql = "execute sp_RetrieveSections"

' Execute the statement and retrieve the record set
set rsForums = dbForums.Execute(sql)
%>

<!- Build a table to display the sections ->
<Table border=1 cellpadding="5" cellspacing="5">
<TR>
   <TH>Forum</TH>
   <TH># of Posts</TH>
   <TH>Last Post</TH>
</TR>
```

The section data is displayed in a table that includes the section name, number of message posts, and the date of the last message post. As we loop through the data returned from our first query, we execute the sp_RetrieveSectionPostCount stored procedure for each section. That returns the number of messages posted for that section. Note that the section name is linked to the Thread.asp page and the ID of the section is passed on the URL.

Listing 12.26   Section.asp continued

```asp
<%

' Loop through the forums
do until rsForums.EOF

' Get the a count of the number of messages posted
' for the current section.
sql = "execute sp_RetrieveSectionPostCount " & _
   rsForums("idSection")

' Get the count
set rsPostCount = dbForums.Execute(SQL)

%>

<TR>
   <td>
   <!- Build a link to the thread listing ->
   <a href="thread.asp?idSection= ↵
   <%=rsForums("idSection")%>"> ↵
   <%=rsForums("chrName")%></a>
   </td>
   <TD>
      <!- Display the number of messages ->
      <% = rsPostCount(0) %>
   </td>
   <td>
      <!- Show the date the message was
         last modified. ->
      <%=rsForums("dtLastMod")%>
   </td>
</tr>

<%

   ' Loop to the next row
   rsForums.MoveNext

loop

' Close the database
```

```
dbForums.Close

%>

</table>

</BODY>
</HTML>
```

The page is then closed out with the proper ending table tags, closed database connection, and end page tags. We next have the Thread.asp page, as shown in Listings 12.27 through 12.30. This page handles displaying the threads related to the section ID passed on the URL.

The first thing we do on the page is check if the referring page was Section.asp. If so, then we store the current section in a session variable for each access through out the thread and message pages. This is a bit easier than storing it on the URL throughout the entire process. The Thread.asp page can be accessed from other pages besides Section.asp, so we need to always know what section the user has currently selected so we can display the appropriate threads.

Listing 12.27   Thread.asp

```
<%@ Language=VBScript %>
<% Option Explicit %>
<%
'******************************************************
'** Thread.asp
'**
'** Displays all the threads for a section
'******************************************************
%>
<%

' Check to ensure we came from the section.asp page
' to display a list of threads.
if instr(1, _
        lcase(Request.ServerVariables("HTTP_REFERER")), _
        "section.asp") then

    ' Get the ID of the section.
    session("CurrentSection") = request("idSection")

end if
```

We now need to ensure that the CurrentSection session variable is not empty. If it is, we need to send the user back to the section page so a section can be selected.

Next we build a simple navigation header for the thread page. This gives the user the option of returning to the section page or creating a new thread. Note that we are not using navigation includes because each page has unique navigation options based on where the user is at in the message drill down process.

Listing 12.28   Thread.asp continued

```
' Ensure we have a section ID so we can display
' threads
if session("CurrentSection") = "" then _
    Response.Redirect("section.asp")

%>
<HTML>
<HEAD>
</HEAD>
<BODY>

<!- Build the forums navigation ->
| <a href="section.asp">Forums List<a> |

<HR>
<BR>

<!- Build a link to create a new thread ->
| <a href="CreateThread.asp">Create New Thread</a> |

<BR><BR>
```

We are ready to display the list of threads related to the selected section. The sp_Retrieve-Threads stored procedure is utilized to query the database for all threads related to the section.

Listing 12.29   Thread.asp continued

```
<%

Dim dbForums      ' Database Connection
Dim rsForums      ' Record Set
Dim rsPosts       ' Record Set
Dim sql           ' String

' Create an ADO database connection
set dbForums = _
    server.createobject("adodb.connection")

' Create record set
set rsForums = _
```

```
      server.CreateObject("adodb.recordset")

  ' Create record set
  set rsPosts = _
      server.CreateObject("adodb.recordset")

  ' Open the connection using our ODBC file DSN
  dbForums.open("filedsn=Forums")

  ' Build a SQL statement to retrieve threads
  ' for the specified section
  sql = "execute sp_RetrieveThreads " & _
      session("CurrentSection")

  ' Execute the statement and retrieve the record set
  set rsForums = dbForums.Execute(sql)

%>

<!- Build a table to display the threads ->
<table border="1" cellpadding="5" cellspacing="5">

<TR>
    <TH>Topic</TH>
    <TH># of Posts</TH>
    <TH>Last Post</TH>
    <TH>Started By</TH>
</TR>
```

As with the section data, a table is set up to display the thread listing, including the topic name, number of messages posts, last message post date, and who the owner (handle) is. With each iteration of the record set loop, the sp_RetrieveThreadPostCount stored procedure is called to return the number of message posts for each thread. Note that the thread topic is linked to the Messages.asp page with the ID of the thread passed on the URL.

Listing 12.30 Thread.asp continued

```
<%

' Loop through the threads
do until rsForums.EOF

' Execute the SQL statement to retrieve the
' number of messages posted for the specified
' thread.
sql = "execute sp_RetrieveThreadPostCount " & _
    rsForums("idThread")

' Get the message count
```

```
set rsPosts = dbForums.execute(sql)

%>

<TR>
   <TD>
   <!- Link to display the messages for thread ->
   <a href="Messages.asp?idThread= ↵
   <%=rsForums("idThread")%>"> ↵
   <%=rsForums("chrName")%></a>
   </td>
   <td>
      <!- Show the number of messages posted
         for the thread ->
      <%=rsPosts(0)%>
   </td>
   <td>
      <!- Show when the last messages was
         posted ->
      <%=rsForums("dtLastMod")%>
   </td>
   <td>
      <!- Show the thread owner ->
      <%=rsForums("chrOwner")%>
   </td>
</tr>

<%

' Move to the next row
rsForums.MoveNext

loop

' Close the databases
dbForums.Close

%>

</table>

<BR>

<HR>

<!- Show the forms navigation ->
| <a href="section.asp">Forums List<a> |

</BODY>
</HTML>
```

Finally the page is closed out as appropriate. In addition to the navigation links on the top of the page, we include a navigation link at the bottom of the page to take the user back to the Section.asp page.

Next we have our page, CreateThread.asp, that is utilized by the user to create a new thread in the section. A check is done up front to ensure that the user has selected a section to post the thread to. If not, the user is sent back to the Section.asp page. The navigation to take the user back to the section page is included as well. The code for the page is shown in Listings 12.31 through 12.33.

Listing 12.31   CreateThread.asp

```
<%@ Language=VBScript %>
<% Option Explicit %>
<%
'*******************************************************
'** CreateThread.asp
'**
'** Creates a new thread in the database
'*******************************************************
%>
<%
' Check to ensure that we have a section ID to
' assign this new thread to.
if session("CurrentSection") = "" then _
    Response.Redirect("section.asp")
%>

<HTML>
<HEAD>
</HEAD>
<BODY>

<!- Build the forums navigation ->
| <a href="section.asp">Forums List<a> |

<HR>
<BR>
```

If the user does not enter their data correctly, there will be a parameter on the URL called idError with a value of 1. If it is set, we indicate to the user that there is an error.

Listing 12.32   CreateThread.asp continued

```
<%

' See if there was an error in trying to insert
' a new thread.
```

```
if request("idError") = 1 then

%>

<font color="red">
You did not enter in a thread name.</font>
<BR><BR>

<%

end if

%>
```

A form is created to post to InsertThread.asp. The only field we ask the user to enter is for the Thread name. The page is then closed out with a closing navigation link.

Listing 12.33   CreateThread.asp continued

```
<!- Form to insert a new thread. ->
<form method="post" action="InsertThread.asp">
<TABLE cellpadding="4">
<TR>
    <TD colspan=2>Enter in your Thread Information</td>
</tr>

<tr>
   <td align="right">Name:</td>
  <td>
  <!- Input field for the thread name ->
  <input type="text" value="" name="chrName">
  </td>
</tr>

<TR>
    <TD colspan=2 align="center">
    <input type="submit" value="Submit" name="submit">
    </td>
</tr>

</TABLE>

</form>

<HR>

<!- Show the forms navigation ->
| <a href="section.asp">Forums List<a> |

</BODY>
</HTML>
```

The InsertThread.asp page, as shown in Listing 12.34, handles inserting the new thread into the database. A check is done on this page to ensure that we have a section ID to associate with the new thread.

Listing 12.34   InsertThread.asp

```
<%@ Language=VBScript %>
<%Option Explicit%>
<%
'***************************************************
'** InsertThread.asp
'**
'** Inserts a new thread into the database
'***************************************************
%>
<%

Dim dbForums    ' Database Connection
Dim rsForums    ' Record Set
Dim sql         ' String

' Check to ensure we have a current section ID
' to assign the thread to.
if session("CurrentSection") = "" then _
   Response.Redirect("section.asp")

' Ensure that a thread name was entered
if request("chrName") = "" then

   ' If not send the user back to the
   ' create thread page
   Response.Redirect "CreateThread.asp?idError=1"

end if

' Create an ADO database connection
set dbForums = _
   server.createobject("adodb.connection")

' Create record set
set rsForums = _
   server.CreateObject("adodb.recordset")

' Open the connection using our ODBC file DSN
dbForums.open("filedsn=Forums")

' Execute the sp_InsertThread stored procedure to
' insert the new thread
sql = "execute sp_InsertThread " & _
 session("CurrentSection") & ", '" & _
```

```
      replace(request("chrName"), "'", "''") & "', '" & _
      session("Handle") & "'"

 ' Execute the statement and retrieve the record set
 set rsForums = dbForums.Execute(sql)

 ' Close the database
 dbForums.Close

 ' Send the user back to the thread page
 Response.Redirect "thread.asp"

%>
```

Next we are ready to work on displaying messages. Messages.asp, shown in Listings 12.35 through 12.46, handles displaying a series of messages and providing page navigation through the messages. It is also the page that handles displaying a single message. When a single message is displayed, the list of messages is still displayed below it. This keeps the amount of back and forth navigation to a minimum.

A check is done to ensure that we have a thread ID set by linking to this page from Thread.asp or by checking the CurrentThread session variable.

Listing 12.35   Messages.asp

```
<%@ Language=VBScript %>
<% Option Explicit %>
<%
'********************************************************
'** Messages.asp
'**
'** Shows all messages for a thread
'********************************************************
%>
<%

 ' Ensure we arrived at this page after selecting a
 ' thread on the thread.asp page.
 if instr(1, _
       lcase(Request.ServerVariables("HTTP_REFERER")), _
       "thread.asp") then

     ' Get the current thread ID
     session("CurrentThread") = request("idThread")

 end if

 ' If there is no thread ID then send the user back
 ' to the thread selection page
```

```
  if session("CurrentThread") = "" then _
    Response.Redirect("Thread.asp")

  Dim dbForums        ' Database Connection
  Dim rsForums        ' Record Set
  Dim connForums
  Dim cmdForums
  Dim sql             ' String
  Dim MessageCount    ' Integer
  Dim Count           ' Integer
  Dim Direction       ' string
  Dim NumDisplay      ' Integer
  Dim dbMessage       ' Database Connection
  Dim rsMessage       ' Record Set
  Dim txtMessage      ' string
  Dim chrOwner        ' string
  Dim N               ' integer

  ' Static Variables
  Dim adCmdText
  Dim adCmdTable
  Dim adCmdStoredProc
  Dim adCmdUnknown
  Dim adOpenForwardOnly
  Dim adOpenKeyset
  Dim adOpenDynamic
  Dim adOpenStatic
  Dim adLockReadOnly
  Dim adLockPessimistic
  Dim adLockOptimistic
  Dim adLockBatchOptimistic

%>
<HTML>
<HEAD>
</HEAD>
<BODY>
```

We have two tiers of navigation on our message page. The first gives the user the option to link back to the section and thread pages, followed by our message navigation.

The message navigation puts a parameter on the URL that indicates if the user would like to move to the first, last, next, or previous messages. We display a maximum of 10 messages onscreen at one time.

Listing 12.36   Messages.asp continued

```
<!- Top level navigation ->
| <a href="section.asp">Forums List<a>
```

```
| <a href="Thread.asp">Discussion Thread List<a> |

<HR>

<BR>

<!- Messages navigation ->
| <a href="Messages.asp?dir=First">First</a>
| <a href="Messages.asp?dir=Next">Next</a>
| <a href="Messages.asp?dir=Previous">Previous</a>
| <a href="Messages.asp?dir=Last">Last</a>
| <a href="CreateMessage.asp">Create New Message</a> |

<BR><BR>
```

If, there is a message ID on the URL, we know that we need to display the actual text of the message before we display the message list. A link is displayed to reply to the message that links to CreateMessage.asp.

Listing 12.37   Messages.asp continued

```
<%

' Check to see if a request was made to display
' the contents of a message
if request("idMessage") <> "" then

%>

<!- Show the option to reply to the message ->
<a href="CreateMessage.asp">Reply to Message</a>
<BR><BR>

<%

' Create an ADO database connection
set dbMessage = _
    server.createobject("adodb.connection")

' Create record set
set rsMessage = _
    server.CreateObject("adodb.recordset")

' Open the connection using our ODBC file DSN
dbMessage.open("filedsn=Forums")
```

The sp_RetrieveMessage stored procedure is called with the ID of the message passed as a parameter. The subject, owner, and date posted are all displayed in a table format.

Listing 12.38   Messages.asp continued

```
' Retrieve the message based on the ID
sql = "execute sp_RetrieveMessage " & _
    Request("idMessage")

' Execute the statement and retrieve the record set
set rsMessage = dbMessage.Execute(sql)

txtMessage = rsMessage("txtMessage")
chrOwner = rsMessage("chrOwner")

%>

<!- Build a table to display the message ->
<table border="1" cellpadding="5" cellspacing="5">
<tr>
    <td align="right"><b>Subject:</b></td>
    <td><%=rsMessage("chrSubject")%></td>
</tr>

<tr>
    <td align="right"><b>Created By:</b></td>
    <td><%=chrOwner%></td>
</tr>

<tr>
    <td align="right"><b>Date Posted:</b></td>
    <td><%=rsMessage("dtCreated")%></td>
</tr>

<tr>
    <td align="right"><b>Message:</b></td>
    <td><%=txtMessage%></td>
</tr>

</table>

<%

' Close the subject
dbMessage.Close

end if
```

We are now ready to display the list of messages. We can change the number of messages displayed at one viewing by changing the NumDisplay variable. We also have a series of constants that are used in our database query.

Listing 12.39   Messages.asp continued

```
' Set the number of messages to display
NumDisplay = 10

REM - ADO command types
adCmdText     = 1
adCmdTable    = 2
adCmdStoredProc = 4
adCmdUnknown  = 8

REM - ADO cursor types
adOpenForwardOnly = 0 '# (Default)
adOpenKeyset   = 1
adOpenDynamic  = 2
adOpenStatic   = 3

REM - ADO lock types
adLockReadOnly     = 1
adLockPessimistic  = 2
adLockOptimistic   = 3
adLockBatchOptimistic = 4

' Create our database connection object
Set connForums = _
   Server.CreateObject("ADODB.Connection")

' Open the database connection
connForums.Open "FileDsn=Forums"

' Create a ADA command object
Set cmdForums = _
   Server.CreateObject("ADODB.Command")
```

We have a different twist in how we use ADO to query the database. Because we have to be able to move forward *and* backward to support the previous/next browsing functionality, we have to create an ADO command that supports moving to previous records. This is done with a record set that is returned from our command object. When that command object is called, the adOpenStatic and adLockReadOnly parameters are utilized. These indicate that the data returned to the record set is static, meaning it will not change, and is locked for read-only. That way, we can page through the record set in either direction.

Listing 12.40   Messages.asp continued

```
' Set the command type to 1 to evaluate the command
' as text. Also, the time out is set to 0.
```

```
cmdForums.CommandType = adCmdText
cmdForums.CommandTimeout = 0

' Set the command object connection
Set cmdForums.ActiveConnection = connForums

' Create a record set
Set rsForums = _
    Server.CreateObject("ADODB.Recordset")

' Execute the sp_GetMessageCountByThread message
' to get the number of messages in this thread
sql = "execute sp_GetMessageCountByThread " & _
    session("CurrentThread")

' Set the SQL Command
cmdForums.CommandText = sql

' Open the record set and use the adOpenStatic
' and adLockReadOnly paramters. adOpenStatic
' creates a static cursor in the record set.
' adLockReadOnly makes the record set read only.
rsForums.Open cmdForums, ,_
    adOpenStatic,adLockReadOnly
```

Next we check to see which direction the user wants to navigate in the messages. Based on the direction, we call sp_RetrieveNextMessages or sp_RetrievePreviousMessages stored procedures. In each case the current thread ID and the last message ID are passed in to return the appropriate result set.

Listing 12.41   Messages.asp continued

```
' Get the message count
MessageCount = rsForums("total")

' Set the direction
Direction = request("Dir")

' Check to see if we know the last message ID
' displayed. If not set it at 1.
if Session("idLastMessage") = "" then _
    Session("idLastMessage") = 1

' If there is no direction for the messages to be
' displayed then set it as "First"
if Direction = "" then Direction = "First"

' Build the SQL statement based on the navigational
```

```
' direction
select case Direction

    ' First of the list
    case "First"
        ' Execute the sp_RetrieveNextMessages stored
        ' procedure to get the next set of messages in
        ' the list, but we set flags to start at the
        ' first message.
        sql = "execute sp_RetrieveNextMessages " & _
            session("CurrentThread") & ", 1"
            session("idLastMessage") = 1


    ' Retrieve the next set in the list
    case "Next"
        ' Execute the sp_RetrieveNextMessages stored
        ' procedure to get the next set of messages in
        ' the list.
        sql = "execute sp_RetrieveNextMessages " & _
            session("CurrentThread") & ", " & _
            session("idLastMessage")


    ' Get the previous set of messages
    case "Previous"
        ' Execute the sp_RetrievePreviousMessages stored
        ' procedure to get the previous set of messages
        ' in the list.
        sql = "execute sp_RetrievePreviousMessages " & _
            session("CurrentThread") & ", " & _
            session("idLastMessage")


    ' Get the last set of messages in the list
    case "Last"
        ' Execute the sp_RetrievePreviousMessages stored
        ' procedure to get the last set of messages
        ' in the list. In this case we start at the very
        ' end of the list by passing a 1,000,000 message ID
        ' parameter
        sql = "execute sp_RetrievePreviousMessages " & _
            session("CurrentThread") & ", 1,000,000"


    ' Get the current list of messages being displayed
    case "Current"
        ' Execute the sp_RetrieveNextMessages stored
        ' procedure to get the next set of messages
        ' in the list. Note that the idLastMessage
        ' parameter will not have changed if the
        ' current set of messages is to be displayed.
        sql = "execute sp_RetrieveNextMessages " & _
            session("CurrentThread") & ", " & _
            session("idLastMessage")
```

```
end select

' Close the recrod set
rsForums.Close
```

Finally the stored procedure is executed. Again, the appropriate parameters are utilized to return a result set that we can traverse forward and backward. We also check to see if any results are returned. If not, we simply start at the first message.

Listing 12.42 Messages.asp continued

```
' Set the SQL command
cmdForums.CommandText = sql

' Open the record set with the appropriate
' parameters
rsForums.Open cmdForums, ,adOpenStatic,adLockReadOnly

' Check to see if we are at the end of the
' record set
if rsForums.EOF then

    ' Retrieve the next set of message starting
    ' at the first message
    sql = "execute sp_RetrieveNextMessages " & _
        session("CurrentThread") & ", 1"
        session("idLastMessage") = 1

    ' Set the direction to next
    Direction = "Next"

    ' Set the SQL statement
    cmdForums.CommandText = sql

    ' Close the record set
    rsForums.close

    ' Open the record set
    rsForums.Open cmdForums, ,_
        adOpenStatic,adLockReadOnly

end if
```

Now we are ready to begin the display of the messages. We set a Count variable so we can track how many rows have been displayed; then the table is started. The message subject, date posted, and owner are displayed.

Listing 12.43   Messages.asp continued

```
' Start our loop counter at 1
Count = 1

%>

<BR>

<!- Start the table to display the messages ->
<table border=1 cellpadding="5" cellspacing="5">
<tr>
    <th>Subject</th>
    <th>Date Posted</th>
    <th>Owner</th>
</tr>
```

Next we have our logic to handle moving backward in the record set. We have to do some fancy footwork to ensure that we don't hit the beginning of the record set. If so, we have to end the loop. With each iteration, we store the last ID of the message so we can execute the next query when the user is ready to navigate to the next set of messages. In the end, we will have looped back to the first of the 10 messages we are going to display.

Listing 12.44   Messages.asp continued

```
<%

' Check to see if the direction is moving backward
if Direction = "Last" or Direction = "Previous" then

    ' Move to the last message in the record set
    rsForums.MoveLast

    ' Loop back
    for N = 1 to NumDisplay - 2

        ' Move back a row
        rsForums.MovePrevious

        ' See if we are at the beginning of the
        ' record set
        if rsForums.bOF then

            ' Exit the for loop
            exit for
```

```
        end if

        ' Set the last message displayed
        session("idLastMessage") = _
            rsForums("idMessage")

    next


end if
```

We do a quick check to ensure that we are not at the end or beginning of the record set. If so, we need to reset to the first record. Then we begin looping through the messages and the data is displayed. The message subject is linked back to the messages.asp page with the ID of the message on the URL.

Listing 12.45   Messages.asp continued

```
' Check to see if we are at the beginning or the
' end of the file.
if rsForums.BOF and not rsForums.eof then

    ' Move to the first row
    rsForums.movefirst

end if

' Loop through the messages
do until rsForums.EOF

%>

<tr>
    <td>
        <!- Build a link to display the
            message ->
        <a href="Messages.asp?dir=Current&idMessage= ↵
        <%=rsForums("idMessage")%>"> ↵
        <%=rsForums("chrSubject")%></a>
    </td>
    <td>
        <!- Show the data created ->
        <%=rsForums("dtCreated")%>
    </td>
    <td>
        <!- Show the message owner ->
        <%=rsForums("chrOwner")%>
    </td>
</tr>
```

We then have the record set advanced to the next record, followed by a check to see if we are at the end of the record set. If the direction was originally set to move forward, we store the ID of the last message for handling the next message direction move by the user. Our counter is then incremented, and if we have reached the number to display, the Do Loop is exited.

Listing 12.46   Messages.asp continued

```asp
<%

    ' Move to the next row
    rsForums.MoveNext

    ' Check to see if we are not at the end of
    ' the record set and if the direction is
    ' moving forward.
    if not rsForums.eof and _
        (Direction = "Next" or Direction = "First") _
        then

        ' Get the ID of the message to store as the
        ' last message displayed
        session("idLastMessage") = rsForums("idMessage")

    end if

    ' Increase the counter
    Count = Count + 1

    ' See if our counter meets the number
    ' displayed
    if Count = NumDisplay then exit do

loop

' Close the database connection
connForums.Close

%>

</table>

<font size="2" color="blue">
    <!- Display the message count ->
    There are <%=MessageCount%> messages in this thread.
</font>

<BR><BR>

<HR>
```

```
<!- Show the navigation for the forums ->
| <a href="section.asp">Forums List<a>
| <a href="Thread.asp">Discussion Thread List<a> |

</BODY>
</HTML>
```

Finally, the page is closed out with a display of the number of messages in the thread and navigation links to the section and thread page.

This ends a very complex page that manages to provide forward and backward paging through the messages, displaying a message, and all the tracking it takes to manage the state of the user.

Next we have the CreateMessage.asp page, as shown in Listings 12.47 through 12.49. We first check to see if we have a thread ID to associate with the new message; then we have our navigation header.

Listing 12.47   CreateMessage.asp

```
<%@ Language=VBScript %>
<% Option Explicit %>
<%
'*****************************************************
'** CreateMessage.asp
'**
'** Creates a new message in the database
'*****************************************************
%>
<%

' Check to ensure a thread selection has been
' made
if session("CurrentThread") = "" then _
    Response.Redirect("Thread.asp")
%>

<HTML>
<HEAD>
</HEAD>
<BODY>

| <a href="section.asp">Forums List<a>
| <a href="Thread.asp">Discussion Thread List<a> |

<HR>

<BR>
```

As when adding a new thread, we check the URL to see if an error parameter is set. If so, we indicate to the user that they didn't fill out the new message form properly.

Listing 12.48   CreateMessage.asp continued

```
<%

' Check to see if there is an error.
if request("idError") = 1 then

%>

<!- Display the error message ->
<font color="red">You did not enter in a message.
</font><BR><BR>

<%

end if

%>
```

The form is set up to post to the InsertMessage.asp page. We have two fields on the form. The first field is an input box for the message subject. The second field is a text box for the body of the message.

TIP   You might want to consider defaulting the Subject to the subject of the message that is being replied to. This will require some additional tracking to pull the subject on this page.

Listing 12.49   CreateMessage.asp continued

```
<!- Form to pass the data so the message can be
   inserted. ->
<form method="post" action="InsertMessage.asp">

<TABLE cellpadding="4">

<TR><TD colspan="2">Enter in your Message</td></tr>
<tr>
   <td align="right">Subject:</td>
   <td>
   <!- Field to enter in the message subject. ->
   <input type="text" value="" name="chrSubject">
   </td>
</tr>
```

```
<tr>
  <td align="right">Message:</td>
  <td>
  <!- Text area to enter in the text of
      the message ->
  <textarea name="txtMessage" cols="60" rows="10"></textarea>
  </td>
</tr>
<TR>
  <TD align="center">
  <input type="submit" value="Submit" name="submit">
  </td>
</tr>

</TABLE>

</form>


<HR>

<!- Navigation bar ->
| <a href="section.asp">Forums List<a>
| <a href="Thread.asp">Discussion Thread List<a> |


</BODY>
</HTML>
```

Finally the page is closed out and the navigation links provided. Next we have the page InsertMessage.asp that processes the new message request. The code is shown in Listing 12.50. We do a check to ensure that we have a thread ID; if not, we send the user to the Thread.asp page.

We also check to ensure that the user has entered a subject and a message. If they have not, then the user is sent back to the CreateMessage.asp page with the error value set.

TIP   When we send the user back because of an error on this page as well as the CreateThread.asp page, consider defaulting the fields with what they did enter. This would require the use of session variables to store and read the data.

Listing 12.50   InsertMessage.asp

```
<%@ Language=VBScript %>
<%Option Explicit%>
<%
```

```asp
'****************************************************
'** InsertMessage.asp
'**
'** Inserts a new message into the database
'****************************************************
%>
<%

Dim dbForums     ' Database Connection
Dim rsForums     ' Record Set
Dim sql          ' String

' Make sure we have a thread ID so we know what
' thread to assign the message to.
if session("CurrentThread") = "" then _
   Response.Redirect("thread.asp")

' Ensue message text and a subject have been
' entered.
if request("txtMessage") = "" or _
   request("chrSubject") = "" then

   ' If not send back to the createmessage.asp
   ' page
   Response.Redirect "CreateMessage.asp?idError=1"

end if

' Create an ADO database connection
set dbForums = _
   server.createobject("adodb.connection")

' Create record set
set rsForums = _
   server.CreateObject("adodb.recordset")

' Open the connection using our ODBC file DSN
dbForums.open("filedsn=Forums")

' SQL statement to insert the new message into the
' database. Note that the relationship of the message
' is set by identifying the ID of the section and the
' ID of the thread.
sql = "execute sp_InsertMessage " & _
session("CurrentSection") & ", " & _
session("CurrentThread") & ", '" & _
replace(request("chrSubject"), "'", "''") & "', '" & _
replace(request("txtMessage"), "'", "''") & "', '" & _
session("Handle") & "'"

' Execute the statement and retrieve the record set
```

```
set rsForums = dbForums.Execute(sql)

' Close the database connection
dbForums.Close

' Send the user back to the message listing page
Response.Redirect "messages.asp"

%>
```

If all of the values are in good order, the sp_InsertMessage stored procedure is utilized to add the message to the database. Note that the ID of the section, ID of the thread, the message subject, message text, and message owner are passed to the stored procedure. The user is then directed back to the Messages.asp page.

This concludes the user interface side of our forums application. As we have seen throughout the book, the "design" isn't that pretty, but it can be gussied up to look very professional. The basic code here can be tweaked and improved upon to work smoothly in your environment.

Building the Management Interface

Next we move to the management interface for our forums. It stands to reason that the administrator will browse through the forums much in the way a site visitor would. Thus, the flow of our administrative interface is going to closely parallel the user interface, but we insert in the proper tools to add, update, and delete sections, threads, and messages.

WARNING   Our management interface works in real time (as have all the examples in this book). If you are performing edits, additions, or deletions, visitors on the site will see this happen in real time.

Our first page is AdminSections.asp, shown in Listings 12.51 through 12.53. One change from the user interface is that we do not need to have a handle to login. If you want to implement a security interface (and you should), follow the security interface design for the author/book management interface.

The first thing we do on this page is execute the sp_RetrieveSections to retrieve the current active sections. We then build a table to display the sections.

Listing 12.51   AdminSections.asp

```
<%@ Language=VBScript %>
<% Option Explicit %>
<%
```

```
'****************************************************
'** AdminSections.asp
'**
'** List sections
'****************************************************
%>
<HTML>
<HEAD>
</HEAD>
<BODY>

<%

Dim dbForums      ' database connection
Dim rsForums      ' record set
Dim SQL           ' string

' Create an ADO database connection
set dbForums = _
   server.createobject("adodb.connection")

' Create record set
set rsForums = _
   server.CreateObject("adodb.recordset")

' Open the connection using our ODBC file DSN
dbForums.open("filedsn=Forums")

' Execute the stored procedure to retrieve the
' sections
sql = "execute sp_RetrieveSections"

' Execute the statement and retrieve the record set
set rsForums = dbForums.Execute(sql)
%>

<!- Start the table to display the sections. ->
<table cellpadding="5" cellspacing="5" border="1">
<tr>
   <th>Edit Section</th>
   <th>New Name</th>
   <th>Delete</th>
</tr>
```

The first row in our table is built to add a new section to the list. The page posts to AddSection.asp for processing. We only have one field that the administrator utilizes to enter in the section name.

The current sections are now displayed. The section name is linked to AdminThread.asp with the ID of the section passed on the URL.

Listing 12.52 AdminSections.asp continued

```
<tr>
   <td>Add a New Section</td>
   <td>

   <!- A form is created to insert a new
       section. ->
   <form method="post" action="AddSection.asp">
   <input type="text" value="" name="chrName">
   <input type="Submit" value="Add New" name="Submit">
   </form>
   </td>
   <td> </td>
</tr>

<%

' Loop through the sections
do until rsForums.EOF

%>
<tr>
   <td>
   <!- Link to the threads for the section. ->
   <a href="adminthread.asp?idSection= ↵
<%=rsForums("idSection")%>"> ↵
<%=rsForums("chrName")%></a>
   </td>
```

With the display of each section, we also need to build in an option to edit the section name. Another form is created that, in this case, posts to UpdateSectionName.asp. The current name is defaulted in the name field. Also, a hidden field is created with the ID of the section to be updated.

Listing 12.53 AdminSections.asp continued

```
<td>
   <!- A form is created for each section to the
      name can be updated. ->
   <form method="post" action="UpdateSectionName.asp">

   <!- The current name value is displayed. ->
   <input type="text"
          value="<%=rsForums("chrName")%>"
          name="chrName">

   <!- A hidden field stored the form ID so we
```

```
        know what form to update. ->
    <input type="hidden"
        value="<%=rsForums("idSection")%>"
        name="idSection">

    <input type="Submit" value="Update" name="Submit">
    </form>
    </td>
    <td>
    <!- Link to delete the section. ->
    <a href="deletesection.asp?idSection= ↵
    <%=rsForums("idSection")%>">Delete</a>
    </td>
</tr>

<%

    ' Move to the next row
    rsForums.MoveNext

loop

' Close the database connection.
dbForums.Close

%>

</table>

</BODY>
</HTML>
```

Following the section update form, we have a link to delete the section with the ID of the section to be deleted passed on the URL. Finally, the page closes out with the appropriate closing tags. Next we have the AddSection.asp page, as shown in Listing 12.54, that processes the addition of a new section. The new section name is posted to this page from AdminSections.asp.

Listing 12.54   AddSection.asp

```
<%@ Language=VBScript %>
<%Option Explicit%>
<%
'*****************************************************
'** AddSection.asp
'**
'** Adds a new section to the database
'*****************************************************
%>
```

```
<%

Dim dbForums    ' Database Connection
Dim rsForums    ' Record Set
Dim sql         ' String

' Create an ADO database connection
set dbForums = _
   server.createobject("adodb.connection")

' Create record set
set rsForums = _
   server.CreateObject("adodb.recordset")

' Open the connection using our ODBC file DSN
dbForums.open("filedsn=Forums")

' Execute the sp_AddSection stored procedure to
' insert the new section into the database.
sql = "execute sp_AddSection '" & _
  replace(request("chrName"), "'", "''") & "'"

' Execute the statement and retrieve the record set
set rsForums = dbForums.Execute(sql)

' Close the database connection
dbForums.Close

' Redirect the user back to the section admin
Response.Redirect "adminsections.asp"

%>
```

The sp_AddSection stored procedure is utilized to insert the new section into the database. Once the insert is complete, the user is sent back to the section administration.

We next have the page that processes the updating of a section name. The code for UpdateSectionName.asp is shown in Listing 12.55. This page is also posted to from the AdminSections.asp page with the new name.

Listing 12.55   UpdateSectionName.asp

```
<%@ Language=VBScript %>
<%Option Explicit%>
<%
'****************************************************
'** UpdateSectionName.asp
'**
'** Updates the section name
'****************************************************
```

```
%>
<%

Dim dbForums    ' Database Connection
Dim rsForums    ' Record Set
Dim sql         ' String

' Create an ADO database connection
set dbForums = _
    server.createobject("adodb.connection")

' Create record set
set rsForums = _
    server.CreateObject("adodb.recordset")

' Open the connection using our ODBC file DSN
dbForums.open("filedsn=Forums")

' Executes the sp_UpdateSectionName stored
' procedure to update the name of the specified
' Section
sql = "execute sp_UpdateSectionName " & _
 request("idSection") & ", '" & _
 replace(request("chrName"), "'", "''") & "'"

' Execute the statement and retrieve the record set
set rsForums = dbForums.Execute(sql)

' Close the database connection
dbForums.Close

' Send the user back to the sections administration
Response.Redirect "adminsections.asp"

%>
```

The sp_UpdateSectionName stored procedure is utilized to update the section name for the specified section ID that is read from the hidden variable. The user is then sent back to the section administration.

Our last section administration page allows us to delete the specified section. The ID of the section is passed to the page. The sp_DeleteSection stored procedure is utilized to remove the section from the database. The user is then sent back to the sections administration. The code for the DeleteSection.asp page is shown in Listing 12.56.

Listing 12.56   DeleteSection.asp

```
<%@ Language=VBScript %>
<%Option Explicit%>
<%
```

```
'****************************************************
'** DeleteSection.asp
'**
'** Deletes a section from the database
'****************************************************
%>
<%

Dim dbForums    ' Database Connection
Dim rsForums    ' Record Set
Dim sql         ' String

' Create an ADO database connection
set dbForums = _
   server.createobject("adodb.connection")

' Create record set
set rsForums = _
   server.CreateObject("adodb.recordset")

' Open the connection using our ODBC file DSN
dbForums.open("filedsn=Forums")

sql = "execute sp_DeleteSection " & _
    request("idSection")

' Execute the statement and retrieve the record set
set rsForums = dbForums.Execute(sql)

dbForums.close

Response.Redirect "adminsections.asp"

%>
```

We now move to the thread administration. The functionality is similar to the sections administration and supports adding, editing, and deleting threads. The AdminThread.asp page is shown in Listings 12.57 through 12.60.

The first part of the page checks to see if we came from the adminsections.asp page. If so, we store the ID of the section in a session variable for easy administrative access throughout the thread and message pages. This is similar to the technique utilized in the user interface. If there is no section ID, we send the user back to the section administration.

Listing 12.57   AdminThread.asp

```
<%@ Language=VBScript %>
<% Option Explicit %>
<%
```

```
'***************************************************
'** AdminThread.asp
'**
'** Lists threads
'***************************************************
%>
<%

' Check to ensure that the linking page is the admin
' sections page.
if instr(1, _
        lcase(Request.ServerVariables("HTTP_REFERER")), _
        "adminsections.asp") then

    ' Set the current section ID we are working on
    session("AdminCurrentSection") = request("idSection")

end if

' If there is no section ID then we can't display
' threads.
if session("AdminCurrentSection") = "" then _
    Response.Redirect("adminsections.asp")

%>
<HTML>
<HEAD>
</HEAD>
<BODY>
```

We also include navigation on each page, as we did in the user interface. The sp_Retrieve-Threads stored procedure is utilized to retrieve the threads for the specified section.

Listing 12.58   AdminThread.asp continued

```
<!- Navigation ->
| <a href="adminsections.asp">Forums List<a> |

<HR>
<BR>

<%

Dim dbForums      ' Database Connection
Dim rsForums      ' Record Set
Dim sql           ' String

' Create an ADO database connection
set dbForums = _
    server.createobject("adodb.connection")
```

```
' Create record set
set rsForums = _
   server.CreateObject("adodb.recordset")

' Open the connection using our ODBC file DSN
dbForums.open("filedsn=Forums")

' Retrieve the threads for the current section.
sql = "execute sp_RetrieveThreads " & _
    session("AdminCurrentSection")

' Execute the statement and retrieve the record set
set rsForums = dbForums.Execute(sql)

%>
```

The first thing we display in our table is a form to add a new thread to the section. The form posts to AddThread.asp, the new name is passed in the form, and then we list the thread name. The name is linked to the message display for the thread.

Listing 12.59   AdminThread.asp continued

```
<!- Start the table to display the threads. ->
<table cellpadding="5" cellspacing="5" border="1">
<tr>
   <th>Edit Thread</th>
   <th>New Name/Owner</th>
   <th>Delete</th>
</tr>

<tr>
   <td>Add a New Thread</td>
   <td>
   <!- Form to create a new thread. ->
   <form method="post" action="AddThread.asp">
   <input type="text" value="" name="chrName">
   <input type="Submit" value="Add New"
        name="Submit">
   </form>
   </td>
   <td> </td>
</tr>


   <%
```

```
' Loop through the threads
do until rsForums.EOF

%>

<TR>
   <td>
   <a href="AdminMessages.asp?idThread= ↵
   <%=rsForums("idThread")%>"> ↵
   <%=rsForums("chrName")%></a>
   </td>
```

We also build a form for updating the thread name and the thread owner. The form posts to the UpdateThread.asp page. The ID of the thread is also passed in a hidden form variable.

Listing 12.60   AdminThread.asp continued

```
<td>
  <!- Form to update the thread data. ->
  <form method="post" action="UpdateThread.asp">
  <!- Input field for the name. Defaulted to the
     current name. ->
  <input type="text"
       value="<%=rsForums("chrName")%>"
       name="chrName">

  <!- Input field for the owner. Defaulted to the
     current owner. ->
  <input type="text"
       value="<%=rsForums("chrOwner")%>"
       name="chrOwner">

  <!- Hidden field for the thread ID so we can
     update the right thread. ->
  <input type="hidden"
       value="<%=rsForums("idThread")%>"
       name="idThread">

  <input type="Submit" value="Update"
       name="Submit">
  </form>

</td>
<td>
   <!- Link to delete the thread. ->
   <a href="deleteThread.asp?idThread= ↵
   <%=rsForums("idThread")%>">Delete</a>
</td>
</tr>
```

```
<%

' Move to the next row
rsForums.MoveNext

loop

' Close the database
dbForums.Close

%>

</table>

<BR>

<HR>

<!- Navigation bar ->
| <a href="adminsections.asp">Forums List<a> |

</BODY>
</HTML>
```

A link is also built to the DeleteThread.asp page with the ID of the thread on the URL. The page is then closed out with the appropriate tags and with a navigation link back to the section administration.

Next, we have our page that handles adding a new thread to the database. The code for AddThread.asp is shown in Listing 12.61. The name of the thread and the owner (which is defaulted to Admin) is posted to the page. The sp_InsertThread stored procedure is utilized to insert the thread. Note that the section the thread is related to is read from the Admin-CurrentSection session variable. The user is then redirected back to the thread administration.

Listing 12.61   AddThread.asp

```
<%@ Language=VBScript %>
<%Option Explicit%>
<%
'****************************************************
'** AddThread.asp
'**
'** Adds a new thread to the database
'****************************************************
%>
<%
```

```
Dim dbForums    ' Database Connection
Dim rsForums    ' Record Set
Dim sql         ' String

' Create an ADO database connection
set dbForums = _
    server.createobject("adodb.connection")

' Create record set
set rsForums = _
    server.CreateObject("adodb.recordset")

' Open the connection using our ODBC file DSN
dbForums.open("filedsn=Forums")

' Execute the sp_InsertThread stored procedure
' to insert the new thread into the section.
sql = "execute sp_InsertThread " & _
  session("AdminCurrentSection") & ", '" & _
  replace(request("chrName"), "'", "''") & _
  "', 'Admin'"

' Execute the statement and retrieve the record set
set rsForums = dbForums.Execute(sql)

' Close the database connection
dbForums.Close

' Redirect the user to the thread admin
Response.Redirect "adminthread.asp"

%>
```

We now have the UpdateThread.asp page that handles updating the thread name and owner. The code is shown in Listing 12.62. The sp_UpdateThread stored procedure is utilized, which passes the thread ID that is read from a hidden variable, the thread name, and the owner. Once the update is done, the user is redirected to the thread administration page.

Listing 12.62   UpdateThread.asp

```
<%@ Language=VBScript %>
<%Option Explicit%>
<%
'*******************************************************
'** UpdateThread.asp
'**
'** Updates the thread name
'*******************************************************
%>
<%
```

```
Dim dbForums    ' Database Connection
Dim rsForums    ' Record Set
Dim sql         ' String

' Create an ADO database connection
set dbForums = _
    server.createobject("adodb.connection")

' Create record set
set rsForums = _
    server.CreateObject("adodb.recordset")

' Open the connection using our ODBC file DSN
dbForums.open("filedsn=Forums")

' Execute the sp_UpdateThread stored procedure that
' will update the thread name and owner
sql = "execute sp_UpdateThread " & _
  request("idThread") & ", '" & _
  replace(request("chrName"), "'", "''") & "', '" & _
  replace(request("chrOwner"), "'", "''") & "'"

' Execute the statement and retrieve the record set
set rsForums = dbForums.Execute(sql)

' Close the database connection
dbForums.Close

' Send back to the administration threads
Response.Redirect "adminthread.asp"

%>
```

Finally, for the thread administration, we have the DeleteThread.asp page as shown in Listing 12.63. The ID of the thread to delete is passed on the URL to the page. The sp_DeleteThread stored procedure is utilized to delete the thread. The user is sent back to the thread administration page once the SQL statement has been executed.

Listing 12.63   DeleteThread.asp

```
<%@ Language=VBScript %>
<%Option Explicit%>
<%
'*****************************************************
'** DeleteThread.asp
'**
'** Deletes a thread from the database
'*****************************************************
```

```
%>
<%

Dim dbForums    ' Database Connection
Dim rsForums    ' Record Set
Dim sql         ' String

' Create an ADO database connection
set dbForums = _
   server.createobject("adodb.connection")

' Create record set
set rsForums = _
   server.CreateObject("adodb.recordset")

' Open the connection using our ODBC file DSN
dbForums.open("filedsn=Forums")

sql = "execute sp_DeleteThread " & _
    request("idThread")

' Execute the statement and retrieve the record set
set rsForums = dbForums.Execute(sql)

dbForums.Close

Response.Redirect "adminThread.asp"

%>
```

The first thing we display in our table is a form to add a new thread to the section. The form posts to AddThread.asp, the new name is passed in the form, and then we list the thread name. The name is linked to the message display for the thread.

Next we are ready to move onto the message administration. The messages flow in the same fashion as they did in the user interface, but we have the option of deleting and updating the messages.

Listings 12.64 through 12.66 show the code for the AdminMessages.asp page. We do not explore all the intricacies of the code; instead, we highlight the changes to support the administration.

Listing 12.64   AdminMessages.asp

```
<%@ Language=VBScript %>
<% Option Explicit %>
<%
'****************************************************
'** AdminMessages.asp
'**
'** Lists messages for a thread
'****************************************************
```

```
%>
<%

' Declare the variables
Dim dbForums          ' Database Connection
Dim rsForums          ' Record Set
Dim connForums        ' Database Connection
Dim cmdForums         ' ADO Command Object
Dim sql               ' String
Dim MessageCount      ' Integer
Dim Count             ' Integer
Dim Direction         ' string
Dim NumDisplay        ' Integer
Dim dbMessage         ' Database Connection
Dim rsMessage         ' Record Set
Dim txtMessage        ' character variable
Dim chrOwner          ' string
Dim N                 ' Integer

' ADO Static Variables
Dim adCmdText
Dim adCmdTable
Dim adCmdStoredProc
Dim adCmdUnknown
Dim adOpenForwardOnly
Dim adOpenKeyset
Dim adOpenDynamic
Dim adOpenStatic
Dim adLockReadOnly
Dim adLockPessimistic
Dim adLockOptimistic
Dim adLockBatchOptimistic

' Check to ensure the referrer is adminthread.asp.
if instr(1, _
      lcase(Request.ServerVariables("HTTP_REFERRER")), _
      "adminthread.asp") then

   ' Set the ID of the thread
   session("AdminCurrentThread") = request("idThread")

end if

' If the value for the thread blank then send
' them back.
if session("AdminCurrentThread") = "" then _
   Response.Redirect("AdminThread.asp")

%>
<HTML>
<HEAD>
```

```
</HEAD>
<BODY>

<!- Build the navigation ->
| <a href="adminsections.asp">Forums List<a>
| <a href="adminThread.asp">Discussion Thread List<a> |

<HR><BR>

| <a href="adminMessages.asp?dir=First">First</a>
| <a href="adminMessages.asp?dir=Next">Next</a>
| <a href="adminMessages.asp?dir=Previous">Previous</a>
| <a href="adminMessages.asp?dir=Last">Last</a>
| <a href="NewMessage.asp">Create New Message</a> |

<BR><BR>

<%

' Check to see if there is an ID of a message to
' display
if request("idMessage") <> "" then

%>

<!- Link to reply to the message ->
<a href="NewMessage.asp">Reply to Message</a>
<BR><BR>

<%

' Create an ADO database connection
set dbMessage = _
    server.createobject("adodb.connection")

' Create record set
set rsMessage = _
    server.CreateObject("adodb.recordset")

' Open the connection using our ODBC file DSN
dbMessage.open("filedsn=Forums")

' Execute the sp_RetrieveMessage stored
' procedure to get the data for the
' specific message
sql = "execute sp_RetrieveMessage " & _
    Request("idMessage")

' Execute the statement and retrieve the
' record set
set rsMessage = dbMessage.Execute(sql)
```

```
' Retrieve the text of the message and the
' owner
txtMessage = rsMessage("txtMessage")
chrOwner = rsMessage("chrOwner")

%>
```

The section of our page that handles displaying a selected message now provides the administrator with the ability to edit the message. A form is created that posts to the UpdateMessage.asp page. Each field of the form is defaulted to the current values. The ID of the message is also passed as a hidden variable.

Listing 12.65   AdminMessages.asp continued

```
<!- The form will post to UpdateMessage.asp to
    update the message data. ->
<form method="post" action="UpdateMessage.asp">

<!- Start the table to display the message ->
<TABLE cellpadding="4">

<TR><TD colspan="2">Edit Message</td></tr>

<!- Show the owner. The ID of the message is
    stored in a hidden variable so the right
    message data can be updated. ->
<tr>
   <td align="right">Owner:</td>
   <td>
   <input type="hidden"
       value="<%=rsMessage("idMessage")%>"
       name="idMessage">
   <input type="text" value="<%=chrOwner%>"
       name="chrOwner">
   </td>
</tr>

<!- Show the subject of the message. ->
<tr>
   <td align="right">Subject:</td>
   <td>
   <input type="text"
       value="<%=rsMessage("chrSubject")%>"
       name="chrSubject">
   </td>
</tr>

<!- Show the text of the message. ->
<tr>
```

```
        <td align="right">Message:</td>
        <td>
        <textarea name="txtMessage" cols="60" rows="10"><%=txtMessage%></textarea>
        </td>
</tr>

<!- Submit button ->
<TR>
    <TD align="center">
    <input type="submit" value="Submit" name="submit">
    </td>
</tr>

</TABLE>

</form>

<%

' Close the database connection
dbMessage.Close

end if

' Variable that sets how many messages are shown
' in the list.
NumDisplay = 10

REM - ADO command types
adCmdText     = 1
adCmdTable    = 2
adCmdStoredProc = 4
adCmdUnknown  = 8

REM - ADO cursor types
adOpenForwardOnly = 0 '# (Default)
adOpenKeyset   = 1
adOpenDynamic  = 2
adOpenStatic   = 3

REM - ADO lock types
adLockReadOnly     = 1
adLockPessimistic  = 2
adLockOptimistic   = 3
adLockBatchOptimistic = 4

' Create the database connection
Set connForums = _
    Server.CreateObject("ADODB.Connection")

' Open the database connection
```

```
connForums.Open "FileDsn=Forums"

' Create an ADO command object
Set cmdForums = _
    Server.CreateObject("ADODB.Command")

' Set the command type to 1 to evaluate the command
' as text. Also, the time out is set to 0.
cmdForums.CommandType = adCmdText
cmdForums.CommandTimeout = 0

' Set the command object connection to the
' forums connection
Set cmdForums.ActiveConnection = connForums

' Create a record set
Set rsForums = _
    Server.CreateObject("ADODB.Recordset")

' SQL statement to retrieve message count
' for the thread.
sql = "execute sp_GetMessageCountByThread " & _
    session("AdminCurrentThread")

' Set the command text
cmdForums.CommandText = sql

' Open the record set and use the adOpenStatic
' and adLockReadOnly paramters. adOpenStatic
' creates a static cursor in the record set.
' adLockReadOnly makes the record set read only.
rsForums.Open cmdForums, ,_
    adOpenStatic,adLockReadOnly

' Get the message count for display.
MessageCount = rsForums("total")

' Retrieve the direction of the navigation
Direction = request("Dir")

' If there is no last message set, then start at 1.
if Session("idLastMessage") = "" then _
    Session("idLastMessage") = 1

' If there is no direction, then start at the
' beginning of the list.
if Direction = "" then Direction = "First"

' Build the SQL statement based on the navigational
' direction
select case Direction
```

```
' First of the list
case "First"
   ' Execute the sp_RetrieveNextMessages stored
   ' procedure to get the next set of messages in
   ' the list, but we set flags to start at the
   ' first message.
   sql = "execute sp_RetrieveNextMessages " & _
      session("AdminCurrentThread") & ", 1"
      session("idLastMessage") = 1

' Retrieve the next set in the list
case "Next"
   ' Execute the sp_RetrieveNextMessages stored
   ' procedure to get the next set of messages in
   ' the list.
   sql = "execute sp_RetrieveNextMessages " & _
      session("AdminCurrentThread") & ", " & _
      session("idLastMessage")

' Get the previous set of messages
case "Previous"
   ' Execute the sp_RetrievePreviousMessages stored
   ' procedure to get the previous set of messages
   ' in the list.
   sql = "execute sp_RetrievePreviousMessages " & _
      session("AdminCurrentThread") & ", " & _
      session("idLastMessage")

' Get the last set of messages in the list
case "Last"
   ' Execute the sp_RetrievePreviousMessages stored
   ' procedure to get the last set of messages
   ' in the list. In this case we start at the very
   ' end of the list by passing a 1,000,000 message ID
   ' parameter
   sql = "execute sp_RetrievePreviousMessages " & _
      session("AdminCurrentThread") & ", 1,000,000"

' Get the current list of messages being displayed
case "Current"
   ' Execute the sp_RetrieveNextMessages stored
   ' procedure to get the next set of messages
   ' in the list. Note that the idLastMessage
   ' parameter will not have changed if the
   ' current set of messages is to be displayed.
   sql = "execute sp_RetrieveNextMessages " & _
      session("AdminCurrentThread") & ", " & _
      session("idLastMessage")

end select
```

```
' Close the record set connection
rsForums.Close

' Set the SQL command to be executed
cmdForums.CommandText = sql

' Open the record set with the appropriate parameters
rsForums.Open cmdForums, ,adOpenStatic,adLockReadOnly

' Check to see if we are at the end of the list
if rsForums.EOF then

   ' Move to the first of the list if there are no
   ' results returned
   sql = "execute sp_RetrieveNextMessages " & _
      session("AdminCurrentThread") & ", 1"
      session("idLastMessage") = 1

   ' Set the direction
   Direction = "Next"

   ' Set the SQL command
   cmdForums.CommandText = sql

   ' Close the forums connection
   rsForums.close

   ' Retrieve the new record set of messages
   rsForums.Open cmdForums, ,_
      adOpenStatic,adLockReadOnly

end if

' Start the loop count at 1
Count = 1

%>

<BR>

<!- Create the table to display the
    messages list ->
<table border=1 cellpadding="5" cellspacing="5">

<!- Build the table header ->
<tr>
   <th>Subject</th>
   <th>Date Posted</th>
   <th>Owner</th>
   <th>Delete</th>
</tr>
```

```
<%

' Check to see if the direct is either the last set
' or the previous set. In both cases we are moving
' back in a record set of lists.
if Direction = "Last" or Direction = "Previous" then

    ' Move to the last row in the returned record set
    rsForums.MoveLast

    ' Loop through the messages in the list
    for N = 1 to NumDisplay - 2

        ' Move back a row
        rsForums.MovePrevious

        ' Check to see if we are at the beginning
        ' of the record set
        if rsForums.BOF then

            ' Exit the FOR loop
            exit for

        end if

        ' Set the last message
        session("idLastMessage") = _
            rsForums("idMessage")

    next

end if

' Check to see if we are at the beginning
' or the end of the record set
if rsForums.BOF and not rsForums.eof then

    ' Move to the first record
    rsForums.movefirst

end if

' Loop through the record set
do until rsForums.EOF

%>

<!- Build the row to show the message subject,
    date created and message owner. ->
<tr>
    <td>
```

```
      <a href="adminMessages.asp?dir=Current&idMessage= ↵
      <%=rsForums("idMessage")%>"> ↵
      <%=rsForums("chrSubject")%></a>
   </td>
   <td>
      <%=rsForums("dtCreated")%>
   </td>
   <td>
      <%=rsForums("chrOwner")%>
   </td>
```

An additional column is built in our messages table to provide a link to delete the message. The ID of the message is passed on the URL to the DeleteMessage.asp page.

Listing 12.66   **AdminMessages.asp continued**

```
      <td><a href="DeleteMessage.asp?idMessage= ↵
      <%=rsForums("idMessage")%>"> ↵
      Delete</a></td>
   </tr>

   <%

      ' Move to the next row
      rsForums.MoveNext

      ' Check to see we are at the end of the record set
      '   and we are moving in a forward direction.
      if not rsForums.eof and _
          (Direction = "Next" or Direction = "First") _
          then

          ' Set the last message
          session("idLastMessage") = rsForums("idMessage")

      end if

      ' Increment our counter
      Count = Count + 1

      ' See if we have reached the maximum number of
      ' messages to display
      if Count = NumDisplay then exit do

   loop

   ' Close the database connection
   connForums.Close

   %>
```

```
</table>

<!- Show the message count ->
<font size="2" color="blue">
   There are <%=MessageCount%> messages in this thread.
</font>

<BR><BR>

<!- Close out the navigation ->
<HR>

| <a href="adminsections.asp">Forums List<a>
| <a href="adminThread.asp">Discussion Thread List<a> |

</BODY>
</HTML>
```

As with the user interface, we also have a page to create a new message. This page uses a process similar to the one on the user interface. The code has been updated to reflect the administrative navigation. Listing 12.67 shows the code for NewMessage.asp.

Listing 12.67   NewMessage.asp

```
<%@ Language=VBScript %>
<% Option Explicit %>
<%
'******************************************************
'** NewMessage.asp
'**
'** Adds a new message to the database
'******************************************************
%>
<%
' Ensure we came from a thread page to ensure we have a
' thread selected
if session("AdminCurrentThread") = "" then _
   Response.Redirect("AdminThread.asp")
%>

<HTML>
<HEAD>
</HEAD>
<BODY>

<!- Build the navigation ->
| <a href="adminsections.asp">Forums List<a>
| <a href="adminThread.asp">Discussion Thread List<a> |
```

```html
<HR><BR>

<!- Form to add a message to the thread list. ->
<form method="post" action="AddMessage.asp">

<TABLE cellpadding="4">

<TR><TD colspan="2">Enter in your Message</td></tr>
<tr>
   <td align="right">Owner:</td>
   <td>
   <!- Field to set the owner ->
   <input type="text" value="" name="chrOwner">
   </td>
</tr>
<tr>
   <td align="right">Subject:</td>
   <td>
   <!- Field to create a subject ->
   <input type="text" value="" name="chrSubject">
   </td>
</tr>
<tr>
   <td align="right">Message:</td>
   <td>
   <!- Text area to input the message ->
   <textarea name="txtMessage" cols="60" rows="10"></textarea>
   </td>
</tr>
<TR>
   <TD align="center">
   <input type="submit" value="Submit" name="submit">
   </td>
</tr>

</TABLE>

</form>


<!- Close out the navigation ->
<HR>

| <a href="adminsections.asp">Forums List<a>
| <a href="adminThread.asp">Discussion Thread List<a> |

</BODY>
</HTML>
```

The AddMessge.asp page, shown in Listing 12.68, handles adding the new message to the database. This page is also similar to the page on the user interface, but has been updated to reflect the administrative navigation and page structure.

Listing 12.68   AddMessage.asp

```
<%@ Language=VBScript %>
<%Option Explicit%>
<%
'*******************************************************
'** AddMessage.asp
'**
'** Adds a new message to the thread list
'*******************************************************
%>
<%

Dim dbForums    ' Database Connection
Dim rsForums    ' Record Set
Dim sql         ' String

' Check to see if a thread has been selected
' If not send the user to the thread selection
' page
if session("AdminCurrentThread") = "" then _
    Response.Redirect("Adminthread.asp")

' Create an ADO database connection
set dbForums = _
    server.createobject("adodb.connection")

' Create record set
set rsForums = _
    server.CreateObject("adodb.recordset")

' Open the connection using our ODBC file DSN
dbForums.open("filedsn=Forums")

' Execute the sp_InsertMessage stored
' procedure to make the new message.
sql = "execute sp_InsertMessage " & _
session("AdminCurrentSection") & ", " & _
session("AdminCurrentThread") & ", '" & _
replace(request("chrSubject"), "'", "''") & "', '" & _
replace(request("txtMessage"), "'", "''") & "', '" & _
replace(Request("chrOwner"), "'", "''") & "'"

' Execute the statement and retrieve the record set
set rsForums = dbForums.Execute(sql)
```

```
' Close the connection
dbForums.Close

' Send the user to the message admin page
Response.Redirect "adminmessages.asp"

%>
```

Our next page, shown in Listing 12.69, handles updating the message with changes made by the administrator. The sp_UpdateMessage stored procedure is utilized to update the message. Once the update is done, the user is redirected back to the AdminMessages.asp page.

Listing 12.69   UpdateMessage.asp

```
<%@ Language=VBScript %>
<%Option Explicit%>
<%
'*****************************************************
'** UpdateMessage.asp
'**
'** Updates the data in an existing message
'*****************************************************
%>
<%

Dim dbForums    ' Database Connection
Dim rsForums    ' Record Set
Dim sql         ' String

' Create an ADO database connection
set dbForums = _
   server.createobject("adodb.connection")

' Create record set
set rsForums = _
   server.CreateObject("adodb.recordset")

' Open the connection using our ODBC file DSN
dbForums.open("filedsn=Forums")

' Executes the sp_UpdateMessage stored procedure
' to update from the data entered
sql = "execute sp_UpdateMessage " & _
 request("idMessage") & ", '" & _
 replace(request("chrSubject"), "'", "''") & "', '" & _
 replace(request("chrOwner"), "'", "''") & "', '" & _
 replace(request("txtMessage"), "'", "''") & "'"

' Execute the statement and retrieve the record set
```

```
set rsForums = dbForums.Execute(sql)

' Close the database
dbForums.Close

'. Return to the messages administration
Response.Redirect "adminmessages.asp"

%>
```

Our final forum page handles deleting messages as shown in Listing 12.70. If you don't like the content of something posted by one of your site visitors, then ZAP! You can kill it. The ID of the message is passed on the URL. The sp_DeleteMessage stored procedure is utilized to delete the message. Once it is deleted, the user is redirected back to the messages page.

Listing 12.70   DeleteMessage.asp

```
<%@ Language=VBScript %>
<%Option Explicit%>
<%
'****************************************************
'** DeleteMessage.asp
'**
'** Deletes a message from the database
'****************************************************
%>
<%

Dim dbForums    ' Database Connection
Dim rsForums    ' Record Set
Dim sql         ' String

' Create an ADO database connection
set dbForums = _
    server.createobject("adodb.connection")

' Create record set
set rsForums = _
    server.CreateObject("adodb.recordset")

' Open the connection using our ODBC file DSN
dbForums.open("filedsn=Forums")

' SQL statement to delete a message
sql = "execute sp_DeleteMessage " & _
    request("idMessage")

' Execute the statement and retrieve the record set
set rsForums = dbForums.Execute(sql)
```

```
' Close the database
dbForums.Close

' Redirect to the messages administration
Response.Redirect "adminmessages.asp"

%>
```

That does it for our example forums code. The foundation has been laid for building a robust forum solution. Careful consideration of how frequently your forums will be utilized and what administrative tools are needed, as well as how these tools will be utilized can greatly affect the final implementation.

Some additional feature to consider include profiling, user editing of their messages, message searching, user moderation, and much more. One site to look at for successful forum implementation is www.Delphi.com.

Testing the User Interface

We are now ready to see our coding in action. First we browse through the user interface code. You want to ensure that you have two sections—"SQL Server Books" and "Visual Basic Books"—added to the database through the administrator or by directly inserting them in SQL Enterprise manager. We walk through the process of browsing and adding threads and messages

Start by opening the login page, Default.asp (/community/forums/default.asp), as shown in Figure 12.3.

FIGURE 12.3:

Forums login page

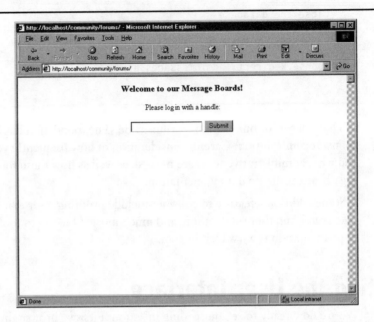

Enter in a handle of your choosing and click the Submit button. The sections page appears with our two sections listed, as shown in Figure 12.4.

FIGURE 12.4:

Sections listing page

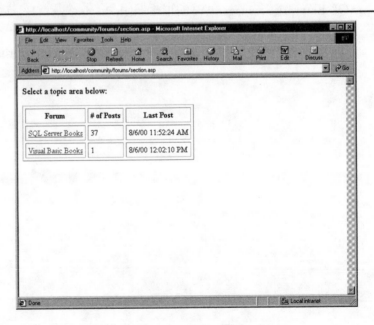

Now select the "Visual Basic Books" sections to start thread management. Any existing threads will display. An example is shown in Figure 12.5 with a thread listed. Note the last post date and the owner.

FIGURE 12.5:

Thread listing page

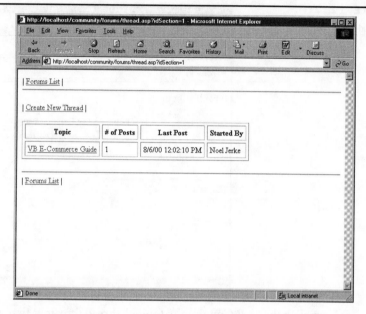

Now create a new thread. Click the "Create New Thread" link that takes you to the new thread creation page, as shown in Figure 12.6.

FIGURE 12.6:

New thread creation

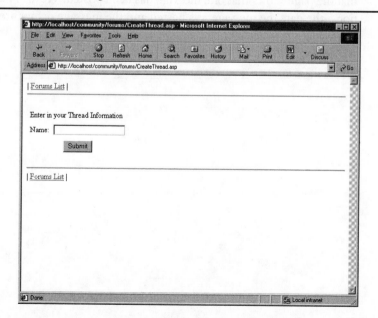

You should get an error if you don't enter a thread name. Now enter in a new thread titled "VB Community Guide." Figure 12.7 shows the new thread added onto the thread listing.

FIGURE 12.7:

New thread listed

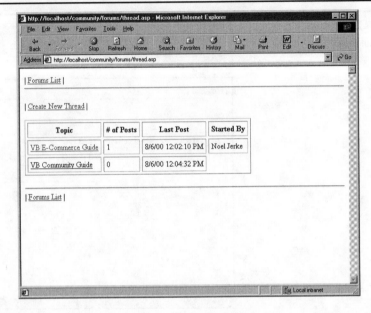

Next click the "VB Community Guide" thread (create it first, if you don't have it). This takes you to the message-listing page. You see a sample message listed in Figure 12.8. Note that the page shows that one message has been posted. We also have our two levels of navigation—the date the message was posted and the message owner are displayed as well.

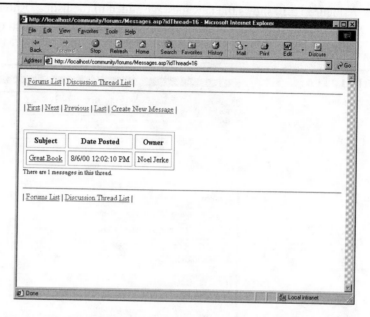

Next create a new message by clicking the "Create New Message" link. The new message page is shown in Figure 12.9. Try posting some invalid data before entering a new message, then enter a valid message.

FIGURE 12.9:

New message
creation page

Figure 12.10 shows the new message added to the listing. Enter a number of messages so that there are more than can be displayed on a single page, then test the navigation functionality as well.

FIGURE 12.10:

New message added

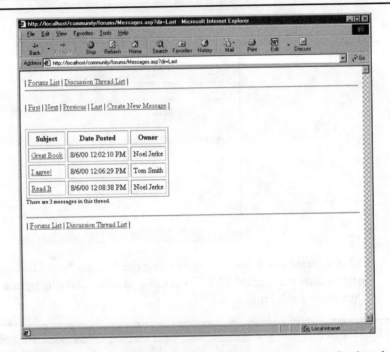

Finally, select one of the messages to display. The details of the message are displayed as well as the following listing of messages. Figure 12.11 shows a sample message view.

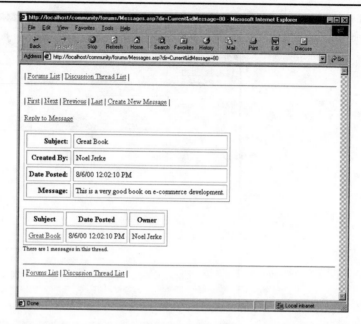

Now we are ready to move to the site administrator. To access the section administration, go to the adminsections.asp page (/community/forums/admin/adminsections.asp). Figure 12.12 shows the section administration where you should see your two sections listed. You will also note the addition of a row to add a new section, fields to update the existing section names, and links to delete the existing sections.

FIGURE 12.12:

Section administration

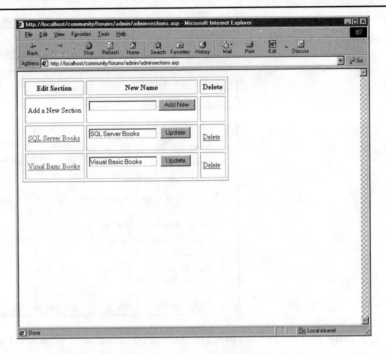

Now let's add a new section called "Test," as shown in Figure 12.13.

FIGURE 12.13:

New section added

We can delete the section we just added by clicking the Delete link. Figure 12.14 shows the section now deleted.

FIGURE 12.14:

Section deleted

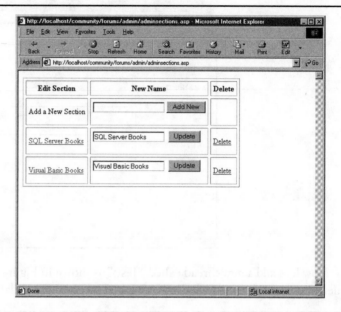

We are now ready to move to the thread administration. Click the "Visual Basic Books" section. Figure 12.15 shows the thread administration page. As with the section page, there is a row to add a new thread, fields to update existing threads, and links to delete existing threads.

FIGURE 12.15:

Thread administration

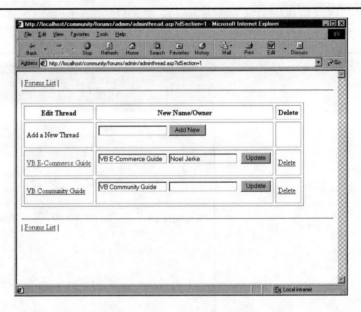

Now let's add a new thread called "Test," as shown in Figure 12.16. Note that the owner is defaulted to "Admin." That can be changed by using the update features.

FIGURE 12.16:

New thread added

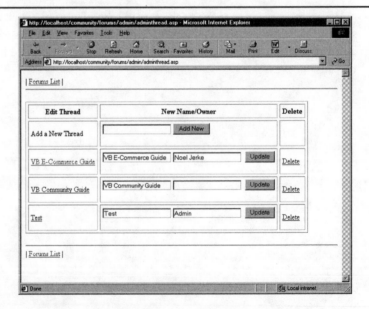

Before moving on to the message administration, let's delete the Test thread that was just created. Click the Delete link and the thread is removed, as shown in Figure 12.17.

FIGURE 12.17:

Thread deleted

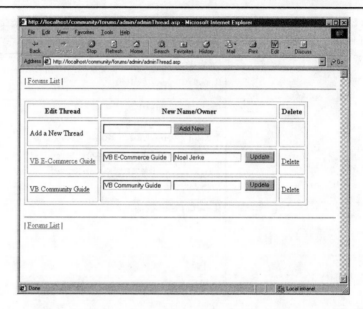

We are finally ready to test the message administration, as shown in Figure 12.18. Note the addition of the Delete links next to each message.

FIGURE 12.18:

Message administration

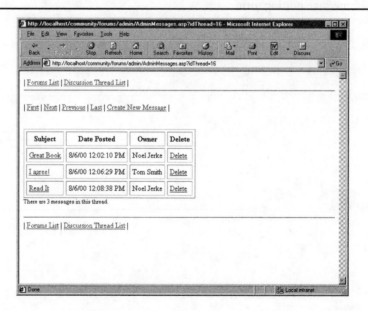

We can test the delete functionality by removing one of the messages from the list. Figure 12.19 shows the updated message list after the delete.

FIGURE 12.19:

Message deleted

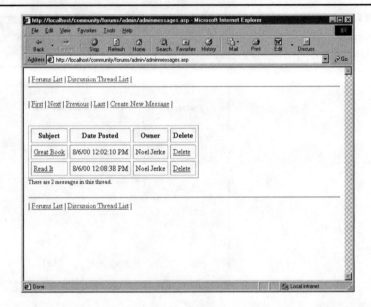

Finally, click one of the messages in the list. The message contents are displayed within a form that allows the administrator to update the message contents. Figure 12.20 shows the message editing form.

FIGURE 12.20:

Message editing

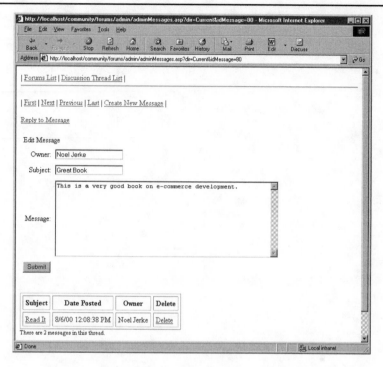

That does it for browsing through our user and management interfaces. Continue to explore and utilize the interface. If you are prepping a solution for a wide audience, have focus group users use the interface to provide feedback for the success of the interface.

Summary

Our community Web site is coming to its completion. With the addition of the crown jewel of community Web sites—discussion forums—our site visitors have both valuable content as well as a way to discuss it. Our forums provide a multi-tiered conversation threading that facilitates member-to-member communication, and our administrative interface allows the site administrator to maintain control over the content of the forums.

In the next chapter we build a poll-taking tool to provide another avenue for our site visitors to give input to the site and provide valuable information and insight to other site visitors.

CHAPTER 13

Polls and Surveys

- Designing the Application

- Building the Database

- Building the Management Interface

- Building the User Interface

- Testing the Application

This chapter deals with the last set of functionality we need to build. These functionalities revolve around our ability to build polls for the community Web site. We have all seen those quick polls on different sites that allow users to give input to some current, hot topic. In this chapter we build the basic foundation for managing and displaying polls.

Designing the Application

The basic structure of the polling application is fairly simple, consisting of poll questions and poll responses. The poll responses consist of both the different response options as well as the specific selections made by the poll takers.

One of the considerations we have to make is how the poll will be displayed. Certainly the poll questions can be displayed in a targeted format on a page, but where will the results be displayed when the poll is taken? Many sites display the poll and the results on the same page and don't allow the poll to be taken again. We explore these options as we build the user interface.

Building the Database

Our database is fairly straightforward for the poll application. We have two tables that build the relational structure, and several stored procedures for managing the poll data.

Table Structure

As mentioned, we have two tables for managing the poll data. The SQL code for creating our first table, Polls, is shown in Listing 13.1. The table is fairly simple and contains fields for the title, the date the poll was created, and a primary key column.

Listing 13.1   Polls Table

```
CREATE TABLE dbo.Polls (
    idPoll int IDENTITY (1, 1) NOT NULL ,
    chrTitle varchar (255) NULL ,
    dtCreated datetime NULL CONSTRAINT
      DF_Poll_dtCreated_3__10 DEFAULT (getdate()))
GO
```

Responses, our second table shown in Listing 13.2, stores the question response options as well as the response count for that specific poll response. The idPoll field defines which poll this question is an option for. We also store the date the response was created as well as a primary key for the table.

```
CREATE TABLE dbo.Responses (
    idResponse int IDENTITY (1, 1) NOT NULL ,
    chrResponse varchar (255) NULL ,
    dtCreated datetime NULL CONSTRAINT
    DF_Questions_dtCreated_2__10 DEFAULT (getdate()),
    idPoll int NULL ,
    intRespCount int NULL
)
GO
```

The intRespCount column is used as a counter to increment every time the specified response is selected as the user's choice for the poll. In earlier chapters we talked about the possible issues of inserting rows for every potential insert into a database instead of rolling up the data. In this case we are simply going to roll the data up on the fly by counting the responses instead of inserting a response answer in a separate table and storing all of those rows.

There are some cases where you might want to insert the response individually. For example, if you want to track responses and correlate them to a user profile, you might store the user's profile/personalization ID along with the response. You could then do some data mining to correlate poll responses to profile settings.

Stored Procedures

Next we have our stored procedures that manage the poll data. The stored procedures are loosely segregated into stored procedures to manage the poll table and stored procedures to manage the responses data. Of course, there are reporting stored procedures as well for the display of poll data.

Our first stored procedure, sp_RetreivePolls, is shown in Listing 13.3. It handles retrieving all of the current polls in the database.

```
CREATE PROCEDURE sp_RetrievePolls AS

/* Retrieve all of the polls from the database */
select * from polls
GO
```

Next we have the sp_RetrievePoll stored procedure that handles retrieving a specific poll set of data, as shown in Listing 13.4. The ID of the poll to retrieve is passed into the stored procedure as a parameter.

Listing 13.4   sp_RetrievePoll Table

```
CREATE PROCEDURE sp_RetrievePoll

/* Pass in the ID of the poll to be retrieved */
@idPoll integer

AS

/* retrieve the poll */
select * from polls where idPoll = @idPoll
GO
```

Next we have our stored procedure that handles inserting a new poll into the database, as shown in Listing 13.5. A parameter is passed in that contains the title of the poll as an argument.

Listing 13.5   sp_InsertNewPoll Table

```
CREATE PROCEDURE sp_InsertNewPoll

/* Pass in the title of the poll to create the
   new poll */
@chrTitle varchar(255)

AS

/* Insert the poll into the database */
insert into polls(chrTitle) values(@chrTitle)
GO
```

Next we have the stored procedure, sp_DeletePoll shown in Listing 13.6, to delete a poll from the database. The ID of the poll is passed in as a parameter. This stored procedure handles deleting the poll data as well as any associated responses to the poll.

Listing 13.6   sp_DeletePoll Table

```
CREATE PROCEDURE sp_DeletePoll

/* The ID of the poll is passed into to delete */
@idPoll integer
```

```
AS

/* We have to delete the responses for the poll first */
delete from responses where idPoll = @idPoll

/* Then we delete the poll record */
delete from polls where idPoll = @idPoll
GO
```

Our last poll management stored procedure handles updating a poll title. Listing 13.7 shows the SQL code to create the sp_UpdatePoll stored procedure. Both the ID of the poll and the new poll title are passed in as parameters.

Listing 13.7   sp_UpdatePoll Table

```
CREATE PROCEDURE sp_UpdatePoll

/* Pass in the ID of the poll and the title */
@idPoll integer,
@chrTitle varchar(255)

AS

/* Update the poll title for the specified poll */
update polls set chrTitle = @chrTitle
where idPoll = @idPoll
GO
```

We can now move to the stored procedures to manage the poll responses. Our first stored procedure, sp_RetrievePollResponses shown in Listing 13.8, handles retrieving the responses for a specific poll. The ID of the poll is passed as a parameter and all of the responses are returned.

Listing 13.8   sp_RetrievePollResponses Table

```
CREATE PROCEDURE sp_RetrievePollResponses

/* Pass in the ID of the poll */
@idPoll integer

AS

/* Retrieve the response questions for the specified
   poll */
select * from responses where
idPoll = @idPoll
GO
```

The next stored procedure handles returning the total response count for a specific poll. Listing 13.9 shows the code to create the SQL stored procedure. The SQL Sum function is utilized to sum up the count total for all of the responses to the specific poll.

Listing 13.9   sp_GetTotalRespCount Table

```
CREATE PROCEDURE sp_GetTotalRespCount

/* Pass in the ID of the poll */
@idPoll integer

AS

/* Use the sum function to tally the responses to the poll
   for each response */
select totalcount=sum(intRespCount) from responses where idPoll = @idPoll
GO
```

Our next stored procedure, shown in Listing 13.10, handles inserting a new response into the database. The ID of the poll that the response is related to is passed as an argument. The name of the response is also passed.

Listing 13.10   sp_AddResponse Table

```
CREATE PROCEDURE sp_AddResponse

/* Pass in the text for the response
   and the poll it is assigned to. */
@chrResponse varchar(255),
@idPoll Integer

AS

/* Insert the response into the responses
   table and relate it to the appropriate
   poll. */
insert into responses(chrResponse, idPoll)
values(@chrResponse, @idPoll)
GO
```

Next we have our stored procedure to update the response count for a specific response. The code for sp_UpdateRespCount is shown in Listing 13.11. We have to go through a couple of steps to make the update. The ID of the response is passed in as an argument.

First we need to get the current count and then increment it by one. All of this must be done within a single SQL transaction so that we do not overwrite an update by another user.

The current count is then retrieved for the specified response. That count is stored in a variable, intRespCount. The intRespCount variable is then incremented by one, and we update the table with the new count.

Listing 13.11   sp_UpdateRespCount Table

```
CREATE PROCEDURE sp_UpdateRespCount

/* Pass in the ID of the response */
@idResponse integer

AS

/* Begin the transaction so we ensure that
   updates are not overwriting each other */
begin transaction

/* Declare a variable to get the current count */
declare @intRespCount integer

/* Get the current count and store it in the variable */
select @IntRespCount = intRespCount from Responses
 where idResponse = @idResponse

/* Increment the count by one */
select @intRespCount = @intRespCount + 1

/* Update the count */
update Responses set intRespCount = @intRespCount
 where idResponse = @idResponse

commit transaction
GO
```

Next we have our stored procedure, sp_UpdateResponse as shown in Listing 13.12, to update a response. The ID of the response and the new response name are passed in as arguments. The SQL Update function is utilized to update the response.

Listing 13.12   sp_UpdateResponse Table

```
CREATE PROCEDURE sp_UpdateResponse

/* Pass in the ID of the response and the text
   of the question */
@idResponse integer,
@chrResponse varchar(255)

AS
```

```
/* Update the question */
update responses set chrResponse = @chrResponse,
            dtCreated = getdate()
where idResponse = @idResponse
GO
```

Our last stored procedure handles deleting a response from the database. Listing 13.13 shows the SQL code to create the sp_DeleteResponse stored procedure. The ID of the response is passed as a parameter and the SQL Delete function is utilized to remove the response.

Listing 13.13   sp_DeleteResponse Table

```
CREATE PROCEDURE sp_DeleteResponse

/* The ID of the response to be deleted is
   passed in */
@idResponse integer

AS

/* Delete the response from the table */
delete from responses
where idResponse = @idResponse
GO
```

That does it for the data structure for the poll engine. We are now ready to dive into the management interface for the poll engine.

Building the Management Interface

In this section, we start out with the management interface instead of the user interface. Building this functionality will walk us through the poll structure, which makes it easier to build the user interface.

NOTE   Once again we are not building the code to protect the management interface. The techniques utilized to protect the author management interface can be utilized here as well.

Our first page, PollList.asp, handles listing the polls in the database. The code for the page is shown in Listings 13.14 through 13.17. The page starts with the usual headers, and in this case, the database connection is opened to query the database.

Listing 13.14   PollList.asp

```
<%@ Language=VBScript %>
<% Option Explicit %>
<%
'*****************************************************
'** PollList.asp
'**
'** List all current polls
'*****************************************************
%>
<HTML>
<HEAD>
</HEAD>
<BODY>

<%

Dim dbPolls        ' database connection
Dim rsPolls        ' record set
Dim SQL            ' string

' Create an ADO database connection
set dbPolls = _
   server.createobject("adodb.connection")

' Create record set
set rsPolls = _
   server.CreateObject("adodb.recordset")

' Open the connection using our ODBC file DSN
dbPolls.open("filedsn=Polls")
```

The sp_RetrievePolls stored is utilized to retrieve all of the polls from the stored procedure. We then start a table structure for displaying the poll data. We provide several options to the user, including editing the poll data, updating the poll name, showing the date the poll was created, providing a poll preview option, and deleting the poll.

Listing 13.15   PollList.asp continued

```
' Execute the stored procedure to retrieve any
' active polls
sql = "execute sp_RetrievePolls"

' Execute the statement and retrieve the record set
set rsPolls = dbPolls.Execute(sql)
%>
```

```
<!- Start the table to display the polls. ->
<table cellpadding="5" cellspacing="5" border="1">
<tr>
   <th>Edit Poll</th>
   <th>New Title</th>
   <th>Date Created</th>
   <th>Preview</th>
   <th>Delete</th>
</tr>
```

The first row in our table provides an option for the administrator to add a new poll to the database. A form is created that posts to the AddPoll.asp page. A field is provided for the user to enter in the title of the poll.

We then loop through the existing poll data. To administrate the poll, a link is built with the poll name to the AdminPoll.asp page with the ID of the poll passed on the URL. A form is then created to post updates to the poll name. The form posts to the UpdatePoll.asp page. Note that a hidden variable stores the ID of the poll to be updated.

Listing 13.16   PollList.asp continued

```
<tr>
   <td>Add a New Poll</td>
   <td>

   <!- A form is created to insert a new
       poll. ->
   <form method="post" action="AddPoll.asp">
   <input type="text" value="" name="chrTitle">
   <input type="Submit" value="Add New"
       name="Submit">
   </form>
   </td>
   <td> </td>
   <td> </td>
   <td> </td>
</tr>

<%

' Loop through the polls
do until rsPolls.EOF

%>
<tr>
   <td>
   <!- Link to the responses for the poll. ->
   <a href="adminPoll.asp?idPoll= ↵
   <%=rsPolls("idPoll")%>"> ↵
```

```
        <%=rsPolls("chrTitle")%></a>
      </td>
      <td>
        <!- A form is created for each poll so the
           title can be updated. ->
        <form method="post" action="UpdatePoll.asp">

        <!- The current title value is displayed. ->
        <input type="text"
               value="<%=rsPolls("chrTitle")%>"
               name="chrTitle">

        <!- A hidden field stored the poll ID so we
           know what form to update. ->
        <input type="hidden"
               value="<%=rsPolls("idPoll")%>"
               name="idPoll">

        <!- Submit button ->
        <input type="Submit" value="Update" name="Submit">
        </form>
      </td>
```

The date that the poll was created is displayed next. A poll preview option is provided by linking to the PreviewPoll.asp page with the ID of the poll on the URL. Finally a link is built to the DeletePoll.asp page with the ID of the poll on the URL as well.

Listing 13.17	PollList.asp continued

```
      <td>
          <!- Show the date the poll was created ->
          <%=rsPolls("dtCreated")%>
      </td>
      <td>
      <!- Link to a preview of the poll ->
      <a href="PreviewPoll.asp?idPoll= ┘
      <%=rsPolls("idPoll")%>">Preview</a>
      </td>
      <td>
      <!- Link to delete the poll ->
      <a href="deletepoll.asp?idpoll= ┘
      <%=rsPolls("idPoll")%>">Delete</a>
      </td>
    </tr>

  <%

    ' Move to the next row
    rsPolls.MoveNext
```

```
loop

' Close the database connection.
dbPolls.Close

%>

</table>

</BODY>
</HTML>
```

That closes out the page to display the current polls in the database. Next we have the page that handles adding a new poll into the database. AddPoll.asp is shown in Listings 13.18. The first thing that we do is a check to ensure that the administrator has entered a title. If a title has not been entered, the user is sent back to the PollList.asp page.

Listing 13.18   AddPoll.asp

```
<%@ Language=VBScript %>
<% Option Explicit %>
<%
'****************************************************
'** AddPoll.asp
'**
'** Inserts a new poll into the database
'****************************************************
%>
<%

Dim dbPolls        ' database connection
Dim rsPolls        ' record set
Dim SQL            ' string

' Check to ensure a title was entered
if request("chrTitle") = "" then
   Response.Redirect "PollList.asp"
end if

' Create an ADO database connection
set dbPolls = _
   server.createobject("adodb.connection")

' Create record set
set rsPolls = _
   server.CreateObject("adodb.recordset")

' Open the connection using our ODBC file DSN
dbPolls.open("filedsn=Polls")
```

```
' Execute the stored procedure to insert the new
' poll into the database
sql = "execute sp_InsertNewPoll '" & _
   replace(request("chrTitle"), "'", "''") & "'"

' Execute the statement and retrieve the record set
set rsPolls = dbPolls.Execute(sql)

' Close the database connection
dbPolls.Close

' Redirect to the poll listing
Response.Redirect "PollList.asp"

%>
```

We now have the page that handles the updating of the poll data. UpdatePoll.asp is shown in Listing 13.19. Remember that the ID of the poll to be updated is passed as a hidden variable to the page. A check is first done on the page to ensure that the user has entered a title, and that a poll ID has been found.

Listing 13.19   UpdatePoll.asp

```
<%@ Language=VBScript %>
<% Option Explicit %>
<%
'********************************************************
'** UpdatePoll.asp
'**
'** Updates the title of an existing poll
'********************************************************
%>
<%

Dim dbPolls       ' database connection
Dim rsPolls       ' record set
Dim SQL           ' string

' Check the title and the ID of the poll to ensure
' we have both to update the poll
if request("chrTitle") = "" or _
   request("idPoll") = "" then
     Response.Redirect "PollList.asp"
end if

' Create an ADO database connection
set dbPolls = _
   server.createobject("adodb.connection")
```

```
' Create record set
set rsPolls = _
   server.CreateObject("adodb.recordset")

' Open the connection using our ODBC file DSN
dbPolls.open("filedsn=Polls")

' Execute the stored procedure to update the
' poll data
sql = "execute sp_UpdatePoll " & request("idPoll") & _
      ", '" & replace(request("chrTitle"),"'","''") & "'"

' Execute the statement and retrieve the record set
set rsPolls = dbPolls.Execute(sql)

' Close the database connection
dbPolls.Close

' Send the user back to the poll list
Response.Redirect "PollList.asp"

%>
```

Finally we have the page to delete the poll from the database. DeletePoll.asp is shown in Listing 13.20. Keep in mind that this deletes all of the related responses along with the poll. A check is done to see if a poll ID has been passed to the page. If not, the user is returned to the PollList.asp page.

Listing 13.20   DeletePoll.asp

```
<%@ Language=VBScript %>
<% Option Explicit %>
<%
'*****************************************************
'** DeletePoll.asp
'**
'** Deletes an existing poll and responses
'*****************************************************
%>
<%

Dim dbPolls      ' database connection
Dim rsPolls      ' record set
Dim SQL          ' string

' Check to ensure that a poll has been selected
if request("idPoll") = "" then
    Response.Redirect "PollList.asp"
end if
```

```
' Create an ADO database connection
set dbPolls = _
   server.createobject("adodb.connection")

' Create record set
set rsPolls = _
   server.CreateObject("adodb.recordset")

' Open the connection using our ODBC file DSN
dbPolls.open("filedsn=Polls")

' Execute the stored procedure to retrieve any
' active polls
sql = "execute sp_DeletePoll " & request("idPoll")

' Execute the statement and retrieve the record set
set rsPolls = dbPolls.Execute(sql)

' Close the database connection
dbPolls.Close

' Send the user back to the poll list
Response.Redirect "PollList.asp"

%>
```

The sp_DeletePoll stored procedure removes the poll from the database and the page is closed out.

We are now ready to move on to the poll response management. Our first page, Admin-Poll.asp as shown in Listings 13.21 through 13.23, handles a number of functions for us. It allows us to add new poll responses, update existing responses, display the current poll response count, and of course gives us the option to delete a response.

The first thing we do is check to see if the page was linked from the PollList.asp page by checking the HTTP_REFERER HTTP header with the ServerVariables collection of the Response object. If so, we then retrieve the poll ID with which we will be working and store it in a session variable.

Listing 13.21   AdminPoll.asp

```
<%@ Language=VBScript %>
<% Option Explicit %>
<%
'*****************************************************
'** AdminPoll.asp
'**
'** List all questions for the selected poll
'*****************************************************
```

```
%>
<%

' Ensure we arrived at this page after selecting a
' poll on the polllist.asp page.
if instr(1, _
      lcase(Request.ServerVariables("HTTP_REFERER")), _
      "polllist.asp") then

   ' Get the current thread ID
   session("idPoll") = request("idPoll")

end if

' Ensure a poll ID has been entered or previously
' selected
if request("idPoll") = "" and _
   session("idPoll") = "" then
   Response.Redirect "PollList.asp"
end if
%>
<html>
<head>
</head>
<body>

<%

Dim dbPolls      ' database connection
Dim rsPolls      ' record set
Dim SQL          ' string

' Create an ADO database connection
set dbPolls = _
   server.createobject("adodb.connection")

' Create record set
set rsPolls = _
   server.CreateObject("adodb.recordset")

' Open the connection using our ODBC file DSN
dbPolls.open("filedsn=Polls")
```

Next we execute the sp_RetrievePollResponses to retrieve all of the responses for the specified poll. We also provide a navigation link at the top of the page back to the poll listing.

Listing 13.22   AdminPoll.asp continued

```
' Execute the stored procedure to retrieve the
' poll responses
sql = "execute sp_RetrievePollResponses " & _
```

```
        session("idPoll")

' Execute the statement and retrieve the record set
set rsPolls = dbPolls.Execute(sql)
%>

<!- Build a link back to the poll list ->
<a href="polllist.asp">Return to Poll List</a>

<HR>

<BR>

<!- Start the table to display the responses. ->
<table cellpadding="5" cellspacing="5" border="1">
<tr>
    <th>Edit Response</th>
    <th>Date Created/Updated</th>
    <th>Response Count</th>
    <th>Delete</th>
</tr>
```

The first row in our table provides an option for adding a new response to the database. A form is created that posts to the AddResponse.asp page. The user enters in the response name.

We then loop through the current responses. The first column displays the response name and encapsulates it in a form for updating the name. The form posts to the UpdateResponse .asp page. Note that a hidden variable is utilized to store the ID of the response to update. The date the response was created or updated is then displayed along with the current user response count, followed by a link to DeleteResponse.asp.

Listing 13.23   AdminPoll.asp continued

```
<tr>
    <td>Add a New Question</td>
    <td>

    <!- A form is created to insert a new
        response. ->
    <form method="post" action="AddResponse.asp">
    <input type="text" value name="chrResponse">
    <input type="Submit" value="Add New" name="Submit">
    </form>
    </td>
    <td> </td>
    <td> </td>
</tr>
```

```
<%

' Loop through the responses
do until rsPolls.EOF

%>
<tr>
   <td>
     <!- A form is created for each response so the
        question can be updated. ->
     <form method="post" action="UpdateResponse.asp">

     <!- The current question is displayed. ->
     <input type="text"
         value="<%=rsPolls("chrResponse")%>"
          name="chrResponse">

     <!- A hidden field stored the response ID so we
        know what form to update. ->
     <input type="hidden"
         value="<%=rsPolls("idResponse")%>"
          name="idResponse">

     <!- Submit button to post the form ->
     <input type="Submit" value="Update" name="Submit">
     </form>
   </td>
   <td>
      <!- Show the date the response was created ->
      <%=rsPolls("dtCreated")%>
   </td>
   <td>
      <!- Show the current count ->
      <%=rsPolls("intRespCount")%>
   </td>
   <td>
   <!- Link to delete the response. ->
   <a href="deleteResponse.asp?idresponse= ↵
<%=rsPolls("idResponse")%>">Delete</a>
   </td>
</tr>

<%

   ' Move to the next row
   rsPolls.MoveNext

loop

' Close the database connection.
dbPolls.Close
```

```
%>

</table>

</body>
</html>
```

We now have the AddResponse.asp page that handles adding a response to the poll. Listings 13.24 and 13.25 show the code for the page. As appropriate, the response field is checked to ensure that the user enters in a response name. If not, the user is sent back to the AdminPoll.asp page.

Listing 13.24   AddResponse.asp

```
<%@ Language=VBScript %>
<% Option Explicit %>
<%
'*****************************************************
'** AddResponse.asp
'**
'** Adds a response into the database for the
'** specified poll
'*****************************************************
%>
<%

Dim dbPolls        ' database connection
Dim rsPolls        ' record set
Dim SQL            ' string

' Check to ensure a response was entered
if request("chrResponse") = "" then
   Response.Redirect "AdminPoll.asp"
end if

' Create an ADO database connection
set dbPolls = _
   server.createobject("adodb.connection")

' Create record set
set rsPolls = _
   server.CreateObject("adodb.recordset")

' Open the connection using our ODBC file DSN
dbPolls.open("filedsn=Polls")
```

The sp_AddResponse stored procedure is utilized to add the response. The response name entered is updated to double up any single quotes. Once the page is complete, the user is returned to the AdminPoll.asp page.

Listing 13.25   AddResponse.asp continued

```
' Execute the stored procedure to add the
' response to the database
sql = "execute sp_AddResponse '" & _
   replace(request("chrResponse"), "'", "''") & _
   "', " & session("idPoll")

' Execute the statement and retrieve the record set
set rsPolls = dbPolls.Execute(sql)

' Close the database connection
dbPolls.Close

' Redirect to the poll administration page
Response.Redirect "AdminPoll.asp"

%>
```

Next we have the page to update the response name. UpdateResponse.asp is shown in Listings 13.26 and 13.27. A check is done up front to ensure a response, and a response ID is passed to the page. If there is no response, the user is redirected back to the AdminPoll .asp page.

Listing 13.26   UpdateResponse.asp

```
<%@ Language=VBScript %>
<% Option Explicit %>
<%
'********************************************************
'** UpdateResponse.asp
'**
'** Updates the response of an existing poll
'********************************************************
%>
<%

Dim dbPolls      ' database connection
Dim rsPolls      ' record set
Dim SQL          ' string

' Check to see if a response and an ID of the
' response have been entered
if request("chrResponse") = "" or _
```

```
    request("idResponse") = "" then

      ' Send the user back to the poll
      ' administration
      Response.Redirect "AdminPoll.asp"

   end if

   ' Create an ADO database connection
   set dbPolls = _
      server.createobject("adodb.connection")

   ' Create record set
   set rsPolls = _
      server.CreateObject("adodb.recordset")

   ' Open the connection using our ODBC file DSN
   dbPolls.open("filedsn=Polls")
```

The sp_UpdateResponse stored procedure handles making the update. Once the update is completed, the user is redirected back to the AdminPoll.asp page.

Listing 13.27   UpdateResponse.asp continued

```
' Execute the stored procedure to update the
' poll response
sql = "execute sp_UpdateResponse " & _
    request("idResponse") & ", '" & _
    replace(request("chrResponse"), "'", "''") & "'"

' Execute the statement and retrieve the
' record set
set rsPolls = dbPolls.Execute(sql)

' Close the database connection
dbPolls.Close

' Send the user back to the poll admin
Response.Redirect "AdminPoll.asp"

%>
```

The final page we have for managing the responses handles deleting a response. Delete-Response.asp is shown in Listing 13.28. As with the other pages, a check is done to see if a poll ID was passed to the page. If not, the user is redirected back to the AdminPoll.asp page.

Listing 13.28   DeleteResponse.asp

```
<%@ Language=VBScript %>
<% Option Explicit %>
<%
'*******************************************************
'** DeleteResponse.asp
'**
'** Deletes a response for an existing poll
'*******************************************************
%>
<%

Dim dbPolls        ' database connection
Dim rsPolls        ' record set
Dim SQL            ' string

' Check to see if a response was selected and if
' not then send the user back to the poll admin
if request("idResponse") = "" then
    Response.Redirect "AdminPoll.asp"
end if

' Create an ADO database connection
set dbPolls = _
    server.createobject("adodb.connection")

' Create record set
set rsPolls = _
    server.CreateObject("adodb.recordset")

' Open the connection using our ODBC file DSN
dbPolls.open("filedsn=Polls")

' Execute the stored procedure to delete the poll
sql = "execute sp_DeleteResponse " & _
      request("idResponse")

' Execute the statement and retrieve the record set
set rsPolls = dbPolls.Execute(sql)

' Close the database connection
dbPolls.Close

' Send the user back to the poll admin page
Response.Redirect "AdminPoll.asp"

%>
```

The sp_DeleteResponse stored procedure handles removing the response from the database. This will kill all of the counted user responses for that specific response answer. When the delete is complete, the user is redirected back to the AdminPoll.asp page.

That does it for the response management. One tool we did not provide that could be easily added is an option to clear the counts and effectively reset the poll.

Finally we have an option to preview our poll from the administrative interface. PreviewPoll.asp is shown in Listings 13.29 through 13.31. This page provides a means for the administrator to see the poll in action before linking it up in the community site.

Listing 13.29   PreviewPoll.asp

```asp
<%@ Language=VBScript %>
<% Option Explicit %>
<%
'*****************************************************
'** PreviewPoll.asp
'**
'** Previews the poll for easy administration
'*****************************************************
%>
<HTML>
<HEAD>
</HEAD>
<BODY>

<a href="polllist.asp">Return to Poll List</a>

<HR>

<BR>

<%

Dim dbPolls        ' database connection
Dim rsPolls        ' record set
Dim SQL            ' string

' Create an ADO database connection
set dbPolls = _
   server.createobject("adodb.connection")

' Create record set
set rsPolls = _
   server.CreateObject("adodb.recordset")

' Open the connection using our ODBC file DSN
dbPolls.open("filedsn=Polls")
```

First we utilize the sp_RetrievePoll stored procedure to retrieve the specified poll data. A form is then created to post the poll response back to the PollList.asp page. Note that there will be no response processing since we don't want to arbitrarily throw invalid counts into the mix. The poll name is displayed at the top of the page.

Listing 13.30   PreviewPoll.asp continued

```
' Execute the stored procedure to retrieve any
' active polls
sql = "execute sp_RetrievePoll " & request("idPoll")

' Execute the statement and retrieve the record set
set rsPolls = dbPolls.Execute(sql)
%>

<!- A form is created to simply post back to
    the poll list since this is a preview ->
<form method="post" action="polllist.asp">

<center>

<!- Build a table to display the poll ->
<table cellpadding="5">
<tr>
    <td colspan="2">
    <!- Show the title ->
    <b><%=rsPolls("chrTitle")%></b>
    <BR><BR>
    </td>
</tr>
```

Next we execute the sp_RetrievePollResponses stored procedure to display the response options to the poll. The ID of the poll is passed to the stored procedure.

The responses are looped through and a radio option button is built to select a response. The value of the radio option is set to the ID of the response.

Listing 13.31   PreviewPoll.asp continued

```
<%
' Execute the stored procedure to retrieve the
' poll responses for the specified poll
sql = "execute sp_RetrievePollResponses " & _
    request("idPoll")

' Execute the statement and retrieve the record set
set rsPolls = dbPolls.Execute(sql)
```

```
' Loop through the responses
do until rsPolls.EOF
%>

<tr>
    <td align="right">
    <!- Display the question ->
    <%=rsPolls("chrResponse")%>
    </td>
    <td>
    <!- Display the selection box ->
    <input type="radio"
        value="<%=rsPolls("idResponse")%>"
        name="idPoll">
    </td>
</tr>

<%

' Move to the next poll
rsPolls.MoveNext

loop

%>

<tr>
<td colspan="2">
<BR><BR>

<!- Submit button for the form ->
<input type="submit" value="submit" name="Submit">

</td>
</tr>

</table>
</center>

</form>

</BODY>
</HTML>
```

This ends the management interface of the poll engine that provides the basic tools to build quick, single-response polls. Now we move on to the user interface techniques to add the poll to our community Web site.

Building the User Interface

We are ready to start building the user interface. We build a couple of demonstration pages to display the polls and process the responses.

Our first page, SelectPoll.asp as shown in Listing 13.32, lists the current polls. We provide two options for displaying the poll, and the sp_RetrievePolls stored procedure is utilized again to list the poll data.

Listing 13.32   SelectPoll.asp

```
<%@ Language=VBScript %>
<% Option Explicit %>
<%
'****************************************************
'** SelectPoll.asp
'**
'** List all current polls and give options to
'** take the poll
'****************************************************
%>
<HTML>
<HEAD>
</HEAD>
<BODY>

<%

Dim dbPolls      ' database connection
Dim rsPolls      ' record set
Dim SQL          ' string

' Create an ADO database connection
set dbPolls = _
   server.createobject("adodb.connection")

' Create record set
set rsPolls = _
   server.CreateObject("adodb.recordset")

' Open the connection using our ODBC file DSN
dbPolls.open("filedsn=Polls")

' Execute the stored procedure to retrieve any
' active polls
sql = "execute sp_RetrievePolls"

' Execute the statement and retrieve the record set
set rsPolls = dbPolls.Execute(sql)
```

```asp
%>

<!- Start the table to display the sections. ->
<table cellpadding="5" cellspacing="5" border="1">
<tr>
    <th>Title</th>
    <th>Display 1</th>
    <th>Display 2</th>
</tr>

<%

' Loop through the sections
do until rsPolls.EOF

%>
<tr>
    <td>
    <!- Show the poll title ->
    <%=rsPolls("chrTitle")%>
    </td>
    <td>
    <!- Link to the first option to take the poll ->
    <a href="Poll1.asp?idPoll= ↵
    <%=rsPolls("idPoll")%>">View</a>
    </td>
    <td>
    <!- Link to the section option to take the poll ->
    <a href="Poll2.asp?idPoll= ↵
    <%=rsPolls("idPoll")%>">View</a>
    </td>
</tr>

<%

    ' Move to the next row
    rsPolls.MoveNext

loop

' Close the database connection.
dbPolls.Close

%>

</table>

</BODY>
</HTML>
```

As we loop through each poll, a link is provided to Poll1.asp to view one option, and another link is to Poll2.asp for the second option. We see the differences in these two options in the next set of pages.

Our first option shows the poll and response options on one page with the results displayed on a second page. Poll1.asp, as shown in Listing 13.33, handles displaying the poll and responses. This page follows nearly the same logic as PreviewPoll.asp, but the form posts to ProcessPoll1.asp.

Listing 13.33   Poll1.asp

```
<%@ Language=VBScript %>
<% Option Explicit %>
<%
'*******************************************************
'** Poll1.asp
'**
'** Displays the poll and posts to a seperate page
'*******************************************************
%>
<HTML>
<HEAD>
</HEAD>
<BODY>

<%

Dim dbPolls      ' database connection
Dim rsPolls      ' record set
Dim SQL          ' string

' Create an ADO database connection
set dbPolls = _
   server.createobject("adodb.connection")

' Create record set
set rsPolls = _
   server.CreateObject("adodb.recordset")

' Open the connection using our ODBC file DSN
dbPolls.open("filedsn=Polls")

' Execute the stored procedure to retrieve any
' active polls
sql = "execute sp_RetrievePoll " & request("idPoll")

' Execute the statement and retrieve the record set
set rsPolls = dbPolls.Execute(sql)
```

```
%>

<!- Create a form to post the poll response ->
<form method="post" action="ProcessPoll1.asp">
<center>

<!- Build a table to display the poll ->
<table cellpadding="5">
<tr>
   <td colspan="2">
   <b><%=rsPolls("chrTitle")%></b>
   <input type="hidden"
    value="<%=rsPolls("idPoll")%>" name="idPoll">
   <BR><BR>
   </td>
</tr>

<%
' Execute the stored procedure to retrieve the poll
' questions
sql = "execute sp_RetrievePollResponses " & _
    request("idPoll")

' Execute the statement and retrieve the record set
set rsPolls = dbPolls.Execute(sql)

' Loop through the questions
do until rsPolls.EOF
%>

<tr>
   <td align="right">
   <!- Show the question ->
   <%=rsPolls("chrResponse")%>
   </td>

   <td>
   <!- Build a radio button with the ID
      of the response. ->
   <input type="radio"
       value="<%=rsPolls("idResponse")%>"
       name="idResponse">
   </td>
</tr>

<%

' Move to the next poll
rsPolls.MoveNext

loop
```

```
%>

<tr>
<td colspan="2">
<BR><BR>
<center>
<!- Show the submit button ->
<input type="submit" value="Submit" name="Submit">
</center>
</td>
</tr>

</table>
</center>

</form>

</BODY>
</HTML>
```

ProcessPoll1.asp, as shown in Listings 13.34 through 13.36, handles storing the selection by the user in the database, and then displaying the current results. The first thing that is done on the page is updating the count by calling the sp_UpdateRespCount stored procedure that increments the specified response count by one.

Listing 13.34   ProcessPoll1.asp

```
<%@ Language=VBScript %>
<% Option Explicit %>
<%
'****************************************************
'** ProcessPoll1.asp
'**
'** Posts a poll responses and shows current
'** responses
'****************************************************
%>
<HTML>
<HEAD>
</HEAD>
<BODY>

<%

Dim dbPolls      ' database connection
Dim rsPolls      ' record set
Dim SQL          ' string
Dim TotalCount   ' integer
```

```
' Create an ADO database connection
set dbPolls = _
    server.createobject("adodb.connection")

' Create record set
set rsPolls = _
    server.CreateObject("adodb.recordset")

' Open the connection using our ODBC file DSN
dbPolls.open("filedsn=Polls")

' Get the counts on the responses
sql = "execute sp_UpdateRespCount " & _
      request("idResponse")

' Execute the statement
set rsPolls = dbPolls.Execute(sql)
```

We now utilize the sp_GetTotalRespCount stored procedure on the page to get the total count of responses to the poll. This is utilized to calculate the percentage of user responses by response option. The sp_RetrievePoll stored procedure then retrieves the title of the poll.

Listing 13.35 **ProcessPoll1.asp continued**

```
' Get the total number of responses
sql = "execute sp_GetTotalRespCount " & _
      request("idPoll")

' Execute the statement and retrieve the record set
set rsPolls = dbPolls.Execute(sql)

' Get the total number of responses
TotalCount = rsPolls(0)

' Execute the stored procedure to retrieve the
' questions and responses for the poll
sql = "execute sp_RetrievePoll " & request("idPoll")

' Execute the statement and retrieve the record set
set rsPolls = dbPolls.Execute(sql)

%>

<!- Build a table to display the poll ->
<center>
<table cellpadding="5">
<tr>
    <td colspan="3" align="center">
    <font size="4">
```

```
   <!- Show the poll title ->
   <b><%=rsPolls("chrTitle")%></b>
   </font>
   <BR><BR>
   </td>
</tr>

<tr>
   <th>Question</th>
   <th colspan="2">Responses</th>
</tr>
```

Next the sp_RetrievePollResponses stored procedure retrieves the responses for the poll so we can display them and the corresponding counts for each. The responses are looped through and displayed. With each count, we divide by the total count to calculate a percentage response. Note that the number is multiplied by 100, formatted to two decimal points, and then the integer is taken to get a whole percentage number for display.

Listing 13.36 **ProcessPoll1.asp continued**

```
<%
' Execute the stored procedure to retrieve the
' poll responses
sql = "execute sp_RetrievePollResponses " & _
    request("idPoll")

' Execute the statement and retrieve the
' record set
set rsPolls = dbPolls.Execute(sql)

' Loop through polls
do until rsPolls.EOF
%>

<tr>
   <td align="right">
      <!- Show the question ->
      <%=rsPolls("chrResponse")%>
   </td>
   <td align="center">
      <!- Show the # of responses for
          the question ->
      <%=rsPolls("intRespCount")%>
   </td>
   <td align="center">
      <!- Show the % of responses for
          this question ->
      <%=int(formatnumber ↵
(rsPolls("intRespCount")/totalcount*100, 2))%>%
```

```
        </td>
    </tr>

<%

' Move to the next response
rsPolls.MoveNext

loop

%>
</table>
</center>

</BODY>
</HTML>
```

Our next page displays the poll question as well as the response data. The structure of the page closely follows ProcessPoll1.asp, but we have a couple of checkpoints to handle the different actions. Poll2.asp is shown in Listings 13.37 through 13.41.

Listing 13.37	Poll2.asp

```
<%@ Language=VBScript %>
<% Option Explicit %>
<%
'****************************************************
'** Poll2.asp
'**
'** Handles posting and displaying results in
'** one page
'****************************************************
%>
<HTML>
<HEAD>
</HEAD>
<BODY>

<%

Dim dbPolls        ' database connection
Dim rsPolls        ' record set
Dim SQL            ' string
Dim TotalCount     ' integer

' Create an ADO database connection
set dbPolls = _
    server.createobject("adodb.connection")
```

```
' Create record set
set rsPolls = _
    server.CreateObject("adodb.recordset")

' Open the connection using our ODBC file DSN
dbPolls.open("filedsn=Polls")
```

We put a check in place to see if we are processing a response. If we are, we execute the logic to increment the counter for the response. Note that the idResponse URL parameter is set later in the page.

Listing 13.38   Poll2.asp continued

```
' Check to see if we are posting results
if request("idResponse") <> "" then

    ' Update the count for the specified response
    sql = "execute sp_UpdateRespCount " & _
        request("idResponse")

    ' Execute the statement and retrieve the record set
    set rsPolls = dbPolls.Execute(sql)

    ' Execute the stored procedure to get the
    ' total number of responses for the poll
    sql = "execute sp_GetTotalRespCount " & _
        request("idPoll")

    ' Execute the statement and retrieve the
    ' record set
    set rsPolls = dbPolls.Execute(sql)

    ' Get the total count
    TotalCount = rsPolls(0)

end if


' Execute the stored procedure to retrieve any
' active polls
sql = "execute sp_RetrievePoll " & request("idPoll")

' Execute the statement and retrieve the record set
set rsPolls = dbPolls.Execute(sql)

%>

<!- Build a form to post back to this page to
    display the results. ->
```

```
<form method="post" action="Poll2.asp">
<center>

<!- Build a table to display the poll/results ->
<table cellpadding="5">
<tr>
   <td colspan="2">
   <!- Show the poll title ->
   <b><%=rsPolls("chrTitle")%></b>
     <input type="hidden"
     value="<%=rsPolls("idPoll")%>" name="idPoll">
   <BR><BR>
   </td>
```

We have an extra column if we want to show poll percentages as well as poll counts, so we build the column in the header for the display.

Listing 13.39   Poll2.asp continued

```
   <!- Check to see if a response was posted
      to this page. ->
   <% if request("idResponse") = "" then %>

   <!- Build in an extra column for the % ->
   <td></td>

   <% end if %>

</tr>

<%
' Execute the stored procedure to retrieve the
' poll questions
sql = "execute sp_RetrievePollResponses " & _
    request("idPoll")

' Execute the statement and retrieve the record set
set rsPolls = dbPolls.Execute(sql)

' Loop through the questions
do until rsPolls.EOF
%>

<tr>
   <td align="right">
   <!- Show the question ->
   <%=rsPolls("chrResponse")%>
   </td>
   <td>
```

Our next check is for building the display table. We decide whether to display radio option buttons, or counts and percentages. The If...Else statement handles building the two options.

Listing 13.40   Poll2.asp continued

```
<!- Check to see if we are showing radio buttons
    or results ->
<% if request("idResponse") = "" then %>

    <!- Show the radio button selection ->
    <input type="radio"
        value="<%=rsPolls("idResponse")%>"
        name="idResponse">

</td>

<% else %>

    <!- Show the count of the responses ->
    <%=rsPolls("intRespCount")%>

</td>

<!- Calculate the % responses for each question.
    The response is rounded to an integer value. ->
<td align="center">
    <%=int(formatnumber(rsPolls ↵
 ("intRespCount")/totalcount*100, 2))%>%
</td>

<% end if %>

</tr>

<%

' Move to the next question
rsPolls.MoveNext

loop

%>
<td>
```

Our last check is whether or not to display the Submit button. If we are providing the radio options buttons, we need to provide the Submit button.

Listing 13.41   Poll2.asp continued

```
    <!- Only show the submit button if we are not
        displaying response data. ->
    <% if request("idResponse") = "" then %>
    <input type="submit" value="Submit" name="Submit">
    <% end if %>
</td>
</table>
</center>

</form>

</BODY>
</HTML>
```

This demonstrates just a couple of ways to show the poll data in your community Web site. You can build on these techniques to place these polls in just the right spots to entice your community to participate.

Testing the User Interface

Now we are ready to see our coding in action. Let's first work on the poll administration so we have something to test in the user interface. We need to start by opening the PollList.asp page (/community/poll/admin/polllist.asp), as shown in Figure13.1.

FIGURE 13.1:

Poll administration page

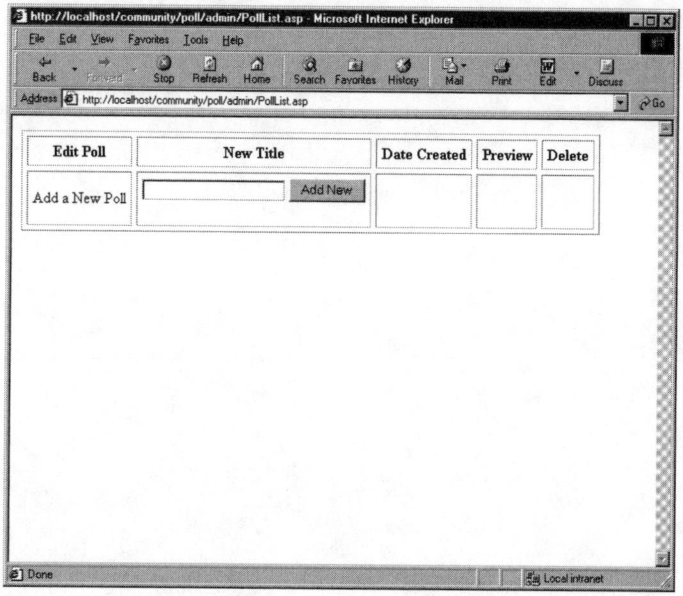

Now let's add a poll titled "What is your favorite programming language?" to the system. Enter the text in the New Title text box, then click the Add New button to add it to the database. Figure 13.2 shows the results.

FIGURE 13.2:

New poll added

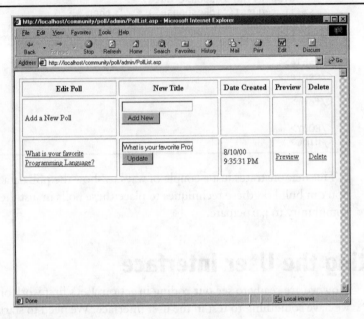

We can now test the rest of the functionality. Add another poll, update it, and then delete it. Now click the Poll link so we can manage the questions and responses. Figure 13.3 shows the page.

FIGURE 13.3:

Poll deleted

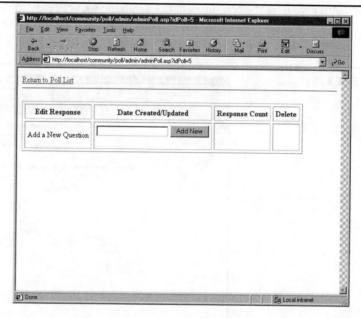

Figure 13.4 shows the entry screen with several responses. Enter in the same response options for testing.

FIGURE 13.4:

Response administration

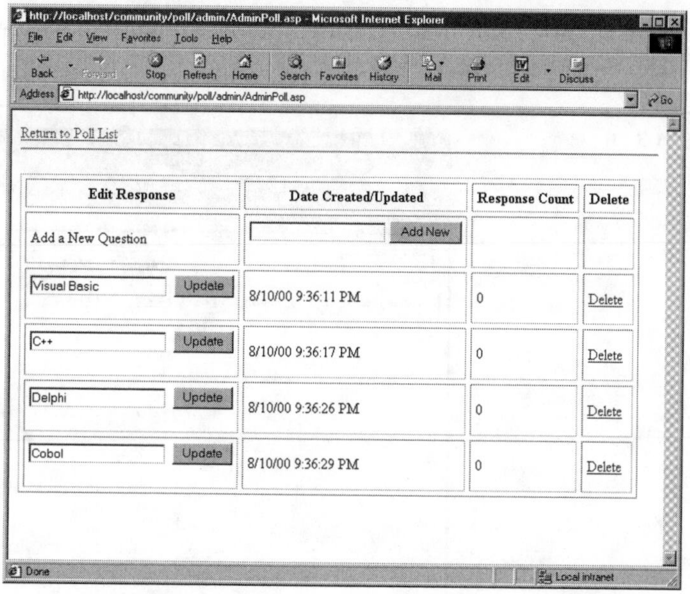

After we have the responses in the database, we are ready to preview our poll. Click the navigation link at the top of the response administration page to go back to the poll listing, and then click the preview link to see the poll displayed. Figure 13.5 shows the sample poll.

FIGURE 13.5:

Poll preview

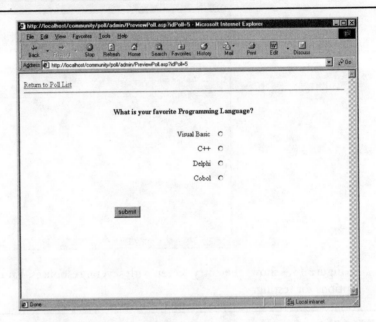

We are now ready to test the user interface. Figure 13.6 shows the poll link page that provides the different preview options.

FIGURE 13.6:

Poll link page

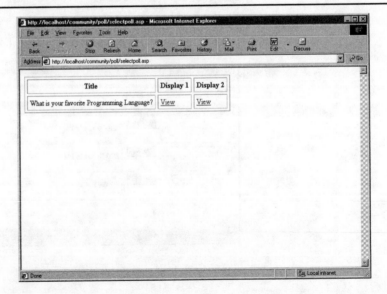

We can now test the first preview option. Figure 13.7 shows the page with the poll and response options displayed.

FIGURE 13.7:

Poll format display option one

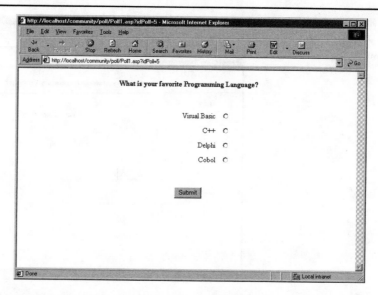

Now select one of the responses and click the Submit button. Figure 13.8 shows the response page. Be sure and check the URL closely to ensure that a different page was displayed. If you utilized this method and placed a poll on a page, visitors would be taken to a new page that shows the current poll responses.

FIGURE 13.8:

Poll response page

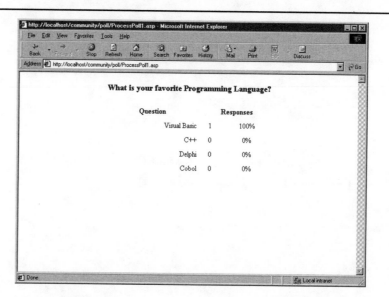

Now return to the poll link page and check out the second option, as shown in Figure 13.9. The initial poll and responses display similarly to our first option.

FIGURE 13.9:

Poll format display
option two

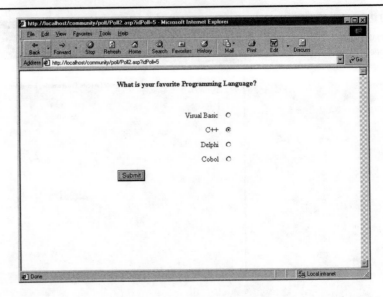

Select on a response and click the Submit button. Figure 13.10 shows the results. Note that the same page is being displayed in the URL, so you could display the poll on the content page, have the user select a response, and then return back to the same page.

FIGURE 13.10:

Poll response on
same page

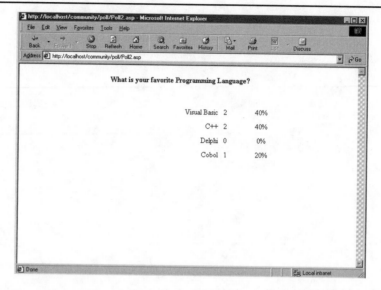

That does it for demonstrating our polling interface. There is a wide range of options that could be added to make the engine more robust and customized. You might consider providing different question types, including multiple answer, comments text boxes, and so on. You might want to provide an option for not displaying the results if you are going for more of a survey-type capability. You might also want to ask multiple questions.

Summary

In this chapter we built a simple polling engine that provides options for the site visitors to express their opinions on various topics. And, more importantly, they can see what the rest of the community thinks on the topic as well.

Thus ends the coding examples for our book. The next chapter explores some of the issues surrounding performance tuning your community Web site. This can be a welcome problem because it can indicate that your site is successful and generating lots of traffic.

CHAPTER 14

Best Practices and Scalability

- Database Best Practices

- IIS Best Practices

- Programming

- Additional Resources

Throughout this book we have built a series of code examples to map out the building of a community Web site. But it is important to understand that in a very dynamic Web environment with potential for incredible traffic peaks and difficult loading issues, use of best practices for scalability and performance is critical.

This chapter explores all of the key elements that make up community Web site. For each key, we address plans for handling traffic load to ensure reliability and a solid user experience.

NOTE   Note that the last section of the chapter provides links to further resources regarding these topics.

System Architecture

In Chapter 4, "System Configuration," we covered the basics of planning for the system architecture. With respect to best practices and scalability, several key factors come into play.

System Hardware

The first critical piece of the system architecture is the underlying hardware. For Web servers, IIS is going to be more CPU bound than disk I/O or memory bound. Planning for servers with single, dual, or quad processors will have a significant impact on performance.

With regard to reliability, a RAID 5 system gives the most redundancy and fail over capability. On a database server with heavy write transactions, however, the RAID 5 architecture can have a significant overhead cost to write out the data to the different drives. RAID 1 can enhance database performance, but additional steps need to be taken to ensure backup reliability.

Load Balancing

Load balancing across multiple servers can be critical, as mentioned in Chapter 4. If traffic exceeds what a single Web server can handle, then the load needs to be spread across multiple servers. There are some critical items to consider in a load-balanced environment to make it successful.

Let's play out a scenario as follows:

1. There are four Web servers sitting in front of a single database server.

2. Each Web server can handle up to 500 concurrent users.

3. Current traffic spikes have up to 450 concurrent users load-balanced to each server for a total of 1,800 users.

4. One of the Web servers goes down.

When the Web server goes down, we now have 600 users on each Web server. As specified, though, each Web server can handle only 500 users. This means our site is either down or giving very slow response.

Basically, our server farm of N (4) servers was able to handle the peak capacity, but we did not have $N + X$ capacity where X would allow for reliability in the event some of the servers were not available.

Three-Tier Architecture

In addition to load balancing, we can utilize other techniques to spread out the processing load. Specifically, we can model our architecture to use a third tier in addition to the Web server tier and the database tier.

The third tier is used to handle business code processing. All of the code in our book was written in ASP scripting, but we have the option of porting any of it to the full version Visual Basic and compiling it into COM objects. The code could then be moved off of the Web server and put into a second tier of servers for faster processing. Figure 14.1 shows the architectural diagram for adding the third tier.

FIGURE 14.1:

Diagram of three-tier architecture

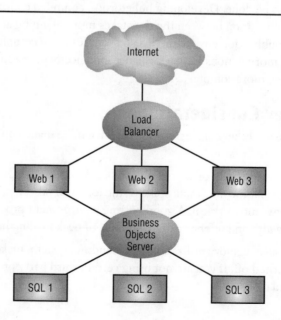

By adding the third tier, we accomplish several key scalability benefits, as outlined in Table 14.1.

TABLE 14.1: Three-Tier Architecture Benefits

Benefit	Description
Segmentation	By moving more of the code to secondary processing servers, we segment more of the logic to multiple points instead of single points of failure.
Processor load spreading	The front-end Web servers in this model are primarily involved in serving static content, calling our second tier objects, and retrieving responses.
Redundancy	We can have backups to our second tier architecture for specific redundancy.
Database abstraction	It is easier to scale our databases by not directly affecting the front line Web servers. If one of the database servers is no longer available, our second tier objects should intelligently *know* what to do. The Web servers continue to process user requests regardless.
Code compilation	By moving code into a compiled environment instead of a scripted, interpreted environment, we gain a significant performance increase.
Server optimization	By breaking out databases, Web servers, and business logic, we can tune each server to provide best performance for the specified functionality. We are also loading less services and overhead onto each server.

By adding the second tier—make no mistake about it—there is more work and more planning to be done. Developing bulletproof, compiled code takes more doing. Architecting the communication between the tiers takes more planning and staging. The development and code publication environment also becomes more complex, and while adding this tier gives many more options for performance enhancement, estimating load and making decisions become more complex.

Other Considerations

There are other considerations that have to be made concerning the scalability and reliability of the server farm.

Bandwidth will, of course, always be a key. A challenge in determining bandwidth is to know what the maximum spike traffic load will be. That is when maximum bandwidth becomes most critical. A good hosting environment provides a guaranteed average load of bandwidth and offers a certain amount of peak loading beyond the average.

To save memory utilization in a Windows system, make sure that any unnecessary services are turned off. If you are not using certain third party product services, ensure that they are turned off as well.

Other factors, such as the basic network architecture for switches, hubs, backup software, and so on, have an impact on performance and reliability. For example, in certain instances, having a network card for each processor on a machine makes a difference in performance and processor utilization.

Database Best Practices

One of the biggest challenges in highly active sites with extensive database integration is managing database load. If there are database calls on nearly every page the user is requesting, the number of transactions can become significant.

Often these types of environments include ad server tracking, where multiple ads may show up on every page of a Web site. As we have seen in this book, community sites tend to be heavily database driven with extensive visitor tracking, data retrieval, and so on.

Configuring and Utilizing SQL Server

In sites that have heavy database utilization, it is critical to ensure that SQL Server is tuned appropriately. Proper configuration settings for user connections, open connections, open databases, and other key values are crucial. Additional information on making and setting these changes appropriately can be found on Microsoft TechNet and Microsoft Developer Network (MSDN).

A second important practice is the use of stored procedures (as was done throughout the book). Stored procedures are compiled code and can be executed quickly on the database server. Any time that columns can be specified in a «Xtags error: No such font: tag f»select query instead of * for all columns, the query also returns faster results.

Finally, the careful use of Microsoft Transaction Server (and the COM+ Application Services in Windows 2000) can help you get the most out of the precious database resources that are available. MTS/COM+ allows for load balancing of components across multiple servers, with the least-heavily-loaded application server at any given time handling component-based services.

In addition, database connections can be pooled, allowing multiple threads of an application to use the database without each having to physically open and close a connection to that database.

Redundancy and Reliability

Another key practice for reliability is the use of some kind of fail over for the SQL servers. If the database goes down for whatever reason, including maintenance, we need to ensure our Web site stays up.

W can have a warm backup utilizing methods such as replication. Another fail over method would be to implement clustering in which a shared file storage system is utilized with two sets of servers. One server is on real-time fail over backup in the event the second server goes down. Technologies are available that will do a double commit on all database write transactions to servers on the same server farm, or even to servers in different servers farms in different facilities.

In the sample code built in the book, we used the *sa* username with no password. In a live system, we would not want to use these settings; instead, we would want to choose an appropriate login name and password, and then limit the rights of that account so that general SQL Server administration cannot be done. Ideally, the password should change on a regular basis.

Database Design

There are many basic database design options available to improve performance. In the basic implementation, we can strategically utilize indexes to speed up queries on databases that are heavily read-oriented.

Even with all of the techniques outlined in this chapter, we may ultimately hit a point on superscaled sites where one SQL server for a specified function (such as a commerce store) will not be able to independently handle all of the transactions. We then have to look at splitting functions to multiple servers for scalability purposes.

In the case of the community site, a first step could be to split the functionality. For example, we might want to put the profile data on one system and the forums on another. This would make one of the servers heavily read-oriented (profile) and the other much more read/write-oriented (forums). This successfully splits the transactions across two servers.

If that isn't enough, we need to consider strategies for minimizing the number of transactions hitting the database at one time. We have alluded to several of these strategies throughout the book.

Let's look at one example: the poll engine. In the example, we rolled up the counts instead of inserting a new row in another table for each response to the poll. This definitely is faster than executing a database write in an ever-growing table every time a response is made; however, we could still run into slow-downs as the number of responses per second goes up on a busy Web site.

The fix? One technique is to cache count data in application variables on the Web server and write the data every so often to the database. In other words, an application variable counter is incremented when a visitor responds to the poll. The database call is made on a set interval to increment the poll data in the database. There is work to be done when the IIS application starts to load the application variables for the first time with the latest counts, and when building in the timer to write the data. There is always the chance the server could lock up and you could lose a few poll responses, but this technique can drastically lower the overhead on the database server on an extremely busy site.

Many of the application built in this book are simple and easy to understand; however, if you are going to utilize these applications in a live environment, consider performance issues and ensure that your site is ready for the expected traffic.

IIS Best Practices

Performance-tuning Internet Information Server (IIS) can be a bit of an art form. It is not that there are so many options that can be tuned, but setting the options correctly depends on a large number of factors.

> **NOTE**   Most of the techniques described in this section apply to Windows NT. Windows 2000 does a much better job of dynamically managing CPU and memory utilization.

Queued requests and threads are two key factors in tuning IIS. Internet Information Server tunes the number of threads in its process dynamically. The dynamic values are usually optimal. In extreme cases of very active or underused processors, you might want to adjust the maximum number of threads in the Inetinfo process. If you do change the maximum number of threads, you should continue careful testing to ensure that the change has improved performance. The difference is usually quite subtle.

Tuning the IIS threads has to do with effective computer use. Allowing more threads generally encourages more CPU use, and fewer threads suggest low processor use. For example, if you have a busy site, the queue length never goes up, and the actual processor use is low, then you probably have more computer capacity than required. On the other hand, if the queue length goes up and down, and the CPU use is still low, the threads should be increased because you have unused processor capacity.

Configuring the IIS queue is important because a high-transaction volume defines busy Web sites. Ideally, each transaction has a short life cycle. Under a high load, significant slowdowns (blocking) can occur when a component gets called at a greater rate than the number of transactions per second the component can satisfy. When this occurs, incoming requests are placed in a queue for later first in/first out processing. If the blocking only occurs for several seconds, the queue smooths out and the request is handled in a timely fashion. However, when the blocking lasts for a longer period of time, an effect called *queue saturation* may occur. Queue saturation happens when the number of queued services exceeds the maximum number allowed (RequestQueueMax) and IIS returns a *Server Too Busy* message.

No matter what, there is a limit to what one Web server can handle in terms of the number of threads and items in the queue. Carefully monitoring the use of each will have a significant impact on the performance of the site, and may allow you to squeeze out bigger and better performance.

Another option is to reduce logging on the Web server to an absolute minimum, if not eliminate it completely. This reduces the requirement to log every transaction request on the Web site, but will have an effect on tracking Web statistics.

In general, you can improve performance and reduce the processor workload with IIS by substituting static Web pages for dynamic pages and eliminating large, bitmapped images. For more information on these topics and the specifics of how to manage each, see the Microsoft IIS documentation.

Programming

As a developer, you have a great amount of impact on how the Web site performs. You also have the most options available for improving performance and scalability, as outlined in Table 14.2.

Not only does the code handle how database connections are made, it also handles the kind of loading on the server that takes place. That is what ultimately implements a three-tier architecture.

TABLE 14.2: Code Performance Techniques

Technique	Description
Caching	Performance will be enhanced when commonly used data can be cached. This way, the data is not constantly being manipulated, and potentially written or read from a database frequently. It is also possible to use techniques, such as disconnected record sets and caching, to manage database data on the Web server or business objects servers. These kinds of techniques are commonly used for data that is heavily read-oriented, such as a product database in a store, or heavily write-oriented, such as impressions and clicks of ads.
Database connections	Throughout the sample code in this book, most of the database connections were opened immediately before the data was utilized. It is important to keep that connection open for as short a time as possible. In high traffic sites, it is also good practice to close the connection immediately by using the *close* connection.

Continued on next page

TABLE 14.2 CONTINUED: Code Performance Techniques

Technique	Description
Error handling	No matter how perfect the system is architected or how well the code is done, something will inevitably happen. Good error handling for a graceful recovery from high peak loads, database downtime, and so on, can help save ugly errors by not showing them to the user and displaying something more user friendly.
Session variables	Adding the overhead of managing session data for each user of a Web site can add significant overhead onto the server. Session variables can be replaced with URL parameters, but requires significant work and tracking compared to session variables.
Option Explicit	Using Option Explicit at the start of each module or class in your code can ferret out any potentially unused variables that can be removed.
Application variables	Commonly used data that all users access will be far more efficient when stored in an application-level variable instead of in many session variables.
Code compilation	Moving script code into compiled Visual Basic or Visual C++ code will improve performance significantly, as mentioned in the three-tier discussion.
Stored procedures	Always use stored procedures to store the SQL code in compiled fashion on the SQL server.
Static pages	Make pages static whenever possible. If data needs to be passed between pages, use the URL parameters.
Code blocking	Place as much ASP code in the same block as possible. This will help to reduce context switching between HTML and Scripting.
Object tag	Use the <OBJECT> tag instead of Server.CreateObject. Server.CreateObject creates the object immediately. The <OBJECT> tag creates it only when needed.
Local versus global variables	Use local variables whenever possible. These are commonly created in subroutines and functions, but can be locally created by using the Set statement.

Of course, good programming practices serve to build a better application. In the world of the Internet and superscaled sites, every little bit counts.

 TIP   You have additional options with Windows 2000, .NET, and ASP to build compiled script code as well as object-based script code. If you are working in this environment, consider taking advantage of these new tools.

Additional Resources

There are many resources available for additional information on how to tune a Web server farm. Table 14.3 lists Web links to various resources you can turn to for additional information and support.

TABLE 14.3: Resource Links

Link	Description
TechNet	www.microsoft.com/technet/
MSDN	http://msdn.microsoft.com/default.asp
ASP Conventions	http://msdn.microsoft.com/workshop/server/asp/aspconv.asp
IIS 4.0 Tuning	http://msdn.microsoft.com/workshop/server/feature/tune.asp
Creating a highly available Web site	www.microsoft.com/technet/winnt/winntas/technote/crhasite.asp
25+ ASP programming tips	http://msdn.microsoft.com/workshop/server/asp/asptips.asp
SQL Server	www.microsoft.com/sql/
IIS 4—Web Services	www.microsoft.com/ntserver/Web/default.asp
IIS 5	www.microsoft.com/windows2000/library/howitworks/iis/iis5techoverview.asp
IIS 5—What's New	http://support.microsoft.com/support/kb/articles/Q222/4/87.ASP
Windows NT 4	www.microsoft.com/ntserver/nts/default.asp
Windows 2000	www.microsoft.com/windows/server/default.asp
Windows Web Platform	www.microsoft.com/business/products/Webplatform/

Microsoft has done a significant amount of performance tuning for their various .com sites. They have done a fairly good job of documenting performance expectations, tuning recommendations, and best practices. Use the search feature on the site to find what you are looking for and have at it.

Summary

This chapter touched on many of the issues you will face in performance tuning your Web site. Performance tuning a Web server farm for scalability and reliability is a critical task. Each element of the overall system must be planned for, examined, and carefully tweaked, but nothing can beat the thorough monitoring of server and database resources during peak loading times.

Database Tables and Stored Procedures

This appendix provides an alphabetical listing of all the tables and stored procedures used in our community site.

Tables

```
CREATE TABLE dbo.AffiliateLinks (
idLink int IDENTITY (1, 1) NOT NULL ,
dtLinked datetime NOT NULL
CONSTRAINT DF_AffiliateL_dtLinked_5__10 DEFAULT (getdate()),
chrReferrer varchar (255) NULL ,
idAffiliate int NULL
)
GO

CREATE TABLE dbo.Affiliates (
idAffiliate int IDENTITY (1, 1) NOT NULL ,
chrName varchar (255) NULL ,
dtCreated datetime NULL
CONSTRAINT DF_Affiliates_dtCreated_4__10 DEFAULT (getdate())
)
GO

CREATE TABLE dbo.Author (
idAuthor int IDENTITY (1, 1) NOT NULL ,
chrFirstName varchar (100) NULL ,
chrLastName varchar (100) NULL ,
chrEmail varchar (50) NULL ,
chrImageLink varchar (150) NULL ,
chrURL varchar (150) NULL ,
txtAuthorBio text NULL ,
chrUserName varchar (50) NULL ,
chrPassword varchar (50) NULL ,
chrCompany varchar (150) NULL
)
GO

CREATE TABLE dbo.Book (
idBook int IDENTITY (1, 1) NOT NULL ,
chrISBN varchar (150) NULL ,
intPrimeInterest int NULL ,
intSecondInterest int NULL ,
chrTitle varchar (255) NULL ,
txtDescription text NULL ,
chrPublisherold varchar (150) NULL ,
txtTOC text NULL ,
chrImageLink varchar (150) NULL ,
dtCreated datetime NULL
CONSTRAINT DF_Book_dtCreated_3__10 DEFAULT (getdate()),
```

```
    idPublisher int NULL
)
GO

CREATE TABLE dbo.BookAuthor (
    idAuthor int NOT NULL ,
    idBook int NOT NULL ,
    idAuthorBook int IDENTITY (1, 1) NOT NULL
)
GO

    GO



CREATE TABLE dbo.LinkClick (
    idClick int IDENTITY (1, 1) NOT NULL ,
    dtClicked datetime NULL
    CONSTRAINT DF_LinkClick_dtClicked_3__14 DEFAULT (getdate()),
    intPerPrimeInterest int NULL ,
    idPerPublisher int NULL ,
    idPerAuthor int NULL ,
    chrBrowser varchar (255) NULL ,
    idLink int NULL
)
GO

CREATE TABLE dbo.LinkTrack (
    idLink int IDENTITY (1, 1) NOT NULL ,
    chrDescription varchar (255) NULL ,
    chrURL varchar (255) NULL
)
GO



CREATE TABLE dbo.Publisher (
    idPublisher int IDENTITY (1, 1) NOT NULL ,
    chrPublisher varchar (255) NULL
)
GO


CREATE TABLE dbo.Searches (
    idSearch int IDENTITY (1, 1) NOT NULL ,
    dtSearched datetime NULL
    CONSTRAINT DF_Searches_dtSearched_7__10 DEFAULT (getdate()),
    chrSearch varchar (255) NULL ,
    intType int NULL
)
GO
```

Stored Procedures

```
CREATE PROCEDURE sp_AddResponse

/* Pass in the text for the response
   and the poll it is assigned to. */
@chrResponse varchar(255),
@idPoll Integer

AS

/* Insert the response into the responses
   table and relate it to the appropriate
   poll. */
insert into responses(chrResponse, idPoll)
values(@chrResponse, @idPoll)
GO

CREATE PROCEDURE sp_AddSection

/* Pass in the section name */
@chrName varchar(255)

AS

/* Insert the section into the table */
insert into section(chrName) values(@chrName)
GO

CREATE PROCEDURE sp_CheckAuthentication

/* Pass in the username, password, and
   the ID of the author */
@chrUsername varchar(255),
@chrPassword varchar(255),
@idAuthor integer

AS


/* Search for a record that matches the specified
   username and password but isn't the record of
   the specified user */
select * from author
 where chrUsername = @chrUsername and
     chrPassword = @chrPassword and
     idAuthor <> @idAuthor
GO

CREATE PROCEDURE sp_DeleteAffiliate

/* Pass in the ID of the affiliate */
```

```
@idAffiliate integer

AS

/* Deletes the specified affiliate */
delete from Affiliates
 where idAffiliate = @idAffiliate
GO

CREATE PROCEDURE sp_DeleteAuthor

/* Pass in the ID of the author */
@idAuthor integer

AS

/* Delete the specified author */
delete from Author
 where idAuthor = @idAuthor
GO

CREATE PROCEDURE sp_DeleteBook

/* Pass in the ID of the book */
@idBook integer

AS

/* Delete the specified book */
delete from book where idBook = @idBook
GO

CREATE PROCEDURE sp_DeleteLink

/* Pass in the ID of the link */
@idLink integer

AS

/* Delete the specified link */
delete from LinkTrack
 where idLink = @idLink
GO

CREATE PROCEDURE sp_DeleteLinkClicks

/* Pass in the ID of the link */
@idLink integer

AS
```

```
/* Delete the specified link */
delete from linkclick
 where idLink = @idLink
GO

CREATE PROCEDURE sp_DeleteMessage

/* Pass in the ID of the message */
@idMessage int

AS

/* Delete the message from the database */
Delete from message where idMessage = @idMessage
GO

CREATE PROCEDURE sp_DeletePoll

/* The ID of the poll is passed into to delete */
@idPoll integer

AS

/* We have to delete the responses for the poll first */
delete from responses where idPoll = @idPoll

/* Then we delete the poll record */
delete from polls where idPoll = @idPoll
GO

CREATE PROCEDURE sp_DeleteResponse

/* The ID of the response to be deleted is
   passed in */
@idResponse integer

AS

/* Delete the response from the table */
delete from responses
where idResponse = @idResponse
GO

CREATE PROCEDURE sp_DeleteSearches AS

/* Delete all searches from
   the database */
delete from searches
GO

CREATE PROCEDURE sp_DeleteSection
```

```
/* Pass the ID of the section */
@idSection int

AS

/* Delete the section from the database */
delete from section where idSection = @idSection
GO

CREATE PROCEDURE sp_DeleteThread

/* Pass in the ID of the thread */
@idThread int

AS

/* Delete the thread from the database */
delete from thread where idThread = @idThread
GO

CREATE PROCEDURE sp_GetDateAffiliateTraffic

/* The ID of the affiliate and the start
   and end date are passed in */
@idAffiliate integer,
@StartDate datetime,
@EndDate datetime

AS

/* Retrieve the total number of entries for
   the specified affiliate in the specified
   date rante. */
select TotalCount=count(*) from AffiliateLinks
where idAffiliate = @idAffiliate and
    dtLinked >= @StartDate and
    dtLinked <= @EndDate
GO

/* Stored procedure to retrieve feedback
   entries */
CREATE PROCEDURE sp_GetFeedback AS

/* Select statement */
select * from feedback
GO

CREATE PROCEDURE sp_GetMessageCountbyThread

/* Pass in the ID of the thread */
@idThread int
```

```
AS

/* Get the total number of messages posted
   for the specified thread */
select total=count(*) from Message
    where idThread = @idThread
GO

CREATE PROCEDURE sp_GetTotalAffiliateTraffic

/* Pass in the ID of the affiliate */
@idAffiliate integer

AS

/* Get the total count of link entries for
   the specified affiliate */
select TotalCount=count(*) from AffiliateLinks
 where idAffiliate = @idAffiliate
GO

CREATE PROCEDURE sp_GetTotalRespCount

/* Pass in the ID of the poll */
@idPoll integer

AS

/* Use the sum function to tally the responses to the poll
   for each response */
select totalcount=sum(intRespCount) from responses where idPoll = @idPoll
GO

CREATE PROCEDURE sp_InsertAffiliate

/* Pass in the name of the new
   affiliate */
@chrName varchar(255)

AS

/* Insert the new affiliate into the
   database */
insert into Affiliates(chrName) values(@chrName)
GO

CREATE PROCEDURE sp_InsertAffiliateLink

/* Pass in the ID of the affiliate and
   the referring URL */
@idAffiliate integer,
```

```
@chrReferrer varchar(255)

AS

/* Insert the affiliate link into the database */
insert into AffiliateLinks(idAffiliate, chrReferrer)
 values(@idAffiliate, @chrReferrer)
GO

CREATE PROCEDURE sp_InsertAuthor

/* Pass in all of the data for a new
   author */
@chrFirstName varchar(255),
@chrLastName varchar(255),
@chrCompany varchar(255),
@chrEmail varchar(255),
@chrURL varchar(255),
@txtAuthorBio text,
@chrUserName varchar(255),
@chrPassword varchar(255)

AS

/* Insert the author data into the table */
insert into Author(chrFirstName, chrLastName,
         chrCompany, chrEmail,
         chrURL, txtAuthorBio,
         chrUserName, chrPassword)
     values(@chrFirstName, @chrLastName,
         @chrCompany, @chrEmail,
         @chrURL, @txtAuthorBio,
         @chrUserName, @chrPassword)
GO

CREATE PROCEDURE sp_InsertBook

/* Pass in all of the data for the
   new book. Also pass in the ID
   of the author to link the book
   to. */
@chrTitle varchar(255),
@chrISBN varchar(255),
@intPrimeInterest integer,
@intSecondInterest integer,
@chrImageLink varchar(255),
@txtDescription text,
@idPublisher integer,
@txtTOC text,
@idAuthor integer
```

```
AS

/* Declare a variable for storing
   the new book ID from our insert */
declare @idBook integer

/* Insert the book into the database */
insert into book(chrTitle, chrISBN,
        intPrimeInterest, intSecondInterest,
        chrImageLink, txtDescription,
        idPublisher, txtTOC)
    values(@chrTitle, @chrISBN,
        @intPrimeInterest, @intSecondInterest,
        @chrImageLink, @txtDescription,
        @idPublisher, @txtTOC)

/* Retrieve the ID of the book just inserted */
select @idBook = @@identity

/* Build the relationship of the book to the
   author */
insert into BookAuthor(idBook, idAuthor)
        values(@idBook, @idAuthor)
GO

/* Stored procedure to insert feedback
   entries into the database */
CREATE PROCEDURE sp_InsertFeedback

/* Variables containing the feedback
   data */
@chrName     varchar(255),
@chrEmail    varchar(255),
@chrRecipient   varchar(255),
@chrSubject   varchar(255),
@txtMessage    text

AS

/* Insert statement for the feedback data */
insert into feedback(chrName, chrEmail, chrRecipient, chrSubject, txtMessage)
     values(@chrName, @chrEmail, @chrRecipient, @chrSubject, @txtMessage)
GO

CREATE PROCEDURE sp_InsertGuestRegister

/* Declare the parameters to be
   passed into the stored procedure */
@chrFirstName varchar(255),
@chrLastname varchar(255),
@chrAddress varchar(255),
```

```
    @chrCity varchar(255),
    @chrState varchar(255),
    @chrProvince varchar(255),
    @chrZipPostal varchar(255),
    @chrPhone varchar(255),

    @chrEmail varchar(255),
    @intPrimeInterest int,
    @intSecondInterest int,
    @txtComments text

AS

/* Build the SQL Insert statement
   to add the new data */
insert into guestregister(
    chrFirstName, chrLastname, chrAddress,
    chrCity, chrState, chrProvince,
    chrZipPostal, chrPhone, chrEmail,
    intPrimeInterest, intSecondInterest,
     txtComments)
values (
    @chrFirstName, @chrLastName, @chrAddress,
    @chrCity, @chrState, @chrProvince,
    @chrZipPostal, @chrPhone, @chrEmail,
    @intPrimeInterest, @intSecondInterest,
     @txtComments)
GO


CREATE PROCEDURE sp_InsertLink

/* Pass in the description and URL
   for the new link */
@chrDescription varchar(255),
@chrURL varchar(255)

AS

/* Insert the tracking link */
insert into LinkTrack(chrDescription, chrURL)
values(@chrDescription, @chrURL)
GO

CREATE PROCEDURE sp_InsertLinkClick

/* Pass in the data for the link click.
   And, the ID of the link to tie the
   click to. */
@idLink integer,
@chrBrowser varchar(255),
```

```
@intPrimeInterest integer,
@idPublisher integer,
@idAuthor integer


AS

/* Insert the link into the database */
insert into LinkClick(idLink, chrBrowser,
          intPerPrimeInterest, idPerPublisher,
          idPerAuthor)
      values(@idLink, @chrBrowser,
          @intPrimeInterest, @idPublisher,
          @idAuthor)
GO

CREATE PROCEDURE sp_InsertMessage

/* Pass in the ID of the section,
   the ID of the thread, the subject
   of the message and the owner of
   the message */
@idSection int,
@idThread int,
@chrSubject varchar(255),
@txtMessage text,
@chrOwner varchar(255)

AS

/* Insert the message into the database */
insert into Message(idThread, chrSubject, txtMessage, chrOwner)
values(@idThread, @chrSubject, @txtMessage, @chrOwner)

/* Update the date the section was last
   modified with a new message. */
update section set dtLastMod =
   getdate() where idSection = @idSection

/* Update the date the thread was last
   modified by adding the new message */
update thread set dtLastMod =
   getdate() where idThread = @idThread
GO

CREATE PROCEDURE sp_InsertNewPoll

/* Pass in the title of the poll to create the
   new poll */
@chrTitle varchar(255)
```

```
AS

/* Insert the poll into the database */
insert into polls(chrTitle) values(@chrTitle)
GO

CREATE PROCEDURE sp_InsertSearch

/* Pass in the search keywords and the
   type of search performed (author or
   book) */
@chrSearch varchar(255),
@intType integer

AS

/* Insert the search data */
insert into Searches(chrSearch, intType)
values(@chrSearch, @intType)
GO

CREATE PROCEDURE sp_InsertThread

/* Pass in the ID of the section,
   the name of the thread and the
   owner of the thread */
@idSection int,
@chrName varchar(255),
@chrOwner varchar(255)

AS

/* Insert the new thread into the database */
insert into Thread(idSection, chrName, chrOwner)
values(@idSection, @chrName, @chrOwner)
GO

CREATE PROCEDURE sp_ProcessRegistrations

/* Declare our parameters */
@idRegistration int

AS

/* Build an update statement to update the
   bitProcessed parameter to 1 based on the
   ID of the registration. Note that ALL
   registration IDs smaller than the one
   passed in will be set to 1. */
update guestregister set bitProcessed = 1
where idGuestRegister <= @idRegistration
```

```
GO


/* Returns data on the personalized author
   preferences of the users who clicked on
   the specified link */
CREATE PROCEDURE sp_RepLinkAuthor

/* Pass in the ID of the link */
@idLink integer

AS

/* Get the count grouped by author. Return the first
   and last name of each author */
select totalcount = count(idPerAuthor), chrFirstName,
         chrLastName
      from linkclick, linkTrack, author
      where linkclick.idlink = linktrack.idlink


         and linktrack.idlink = @idLink and
         linkclick.idPerPublisher = author.idauthor
      group by idPerAuthor, chrFirstName, chrLastName
GO

/* Returns data on the browser preferences
   of the users who clicked on the specified
   link */
CREATE PROCEDURE sp_RepLinkBrowser

/* Pass in the ID of the link */
@idLink integer

AS

/* Retrieve the total count grouped by the
   type of browser */
select totalcount = count(chrBrowser), chrBrowser
   from linkclick, linkTrack
  where linkclick.idlink = linktrack.idlink and
     linktrack.idlink = @idLink
   group by chrBrowser
GO

/* Returns the total link count
   for the specified link */
CREATE PROCEDURE sp_RepLinkCount

/* The ID of the link is passed in */
@idLink integer
```

```
AS

/* Return the total count */
select totalcount = count(*) from linkclick
where idlink = @idLink
GO

/* Returns data on the personalized topic
   interest preferences of the users who
   clicked on the specified link */
CREATE PROCEDURE sp_RepLinkInterest

/* Pass in the ID of the link */
@idLink integer

AS

/* Retrieve the total count grouped by the ID
   of the interest for the specified link */
select totalcount = count(intPerPrimeInterest), intPerPrimeInterest
 from linkclick, linkTrack
 where linkclick.idlink = linktrack.idlink and
     linktrack.idlink = @idLink and intPerPrimeInterest <> -1
 group by intPerPrimeInterest
GO

/* Returns data on the personalized publisher
   preferences of the users who clicked on
   the specified link */
CREATE PROCEDURE sp_RepLinkPublisher

/* Pass in the ID of the link */
@idLink integer

AS

/* Return the total count grouped by publisher
   for the specified link */
select totalcount = count(idPerPublisher), chrPublisher
 from linkclick, linkTrack, publisher
 where linkclick.idlink = linktrack.idlink and
     linktrack.idlink = @idLink and
     linkclick.idPerPublisher = publisher.idPublisher
group by idPerPublisher, chrPublisher
GO

CREATE PROCEDURE sp_RetrieveAffiliates AS

/* Retrieves all affiliates in the database */
select * from affiliates
GO
```

```
CREATE PROCEDURE sp_RetrieveAllRegistrations AS

/* Retrieve all registrations */
select * from GuestRegister
GO

CREATE PROCEDURE sp_RetrieveAllAuthorsBooks AS

/* return all authors and their related books */
select author.idauthor, author.chrFirstName,
     author.chrLastName, book.idBook,
     book.chrTitle, bookauthor.idbook,
     bookauthor.idauthor
  from book, bookauthor, author
  where bookauthor.idAuthor = Author.idAuthor and
     book.idbook = bookauthor.idbook
order by author.chrLastName
GO

CREATE PROCEDURE sp_RetrieveAllBooksAuthor AS

/* Retrieve all books and their related authors */
 select *
  from book, bookauthor, author
  where bookauthor.idAuthor = Author.idAuthor and
     book.idbook = bookauthor.idbook
order by book.chrTitle
GO

CREATE PROCEDURE sp_RetrieveAuthentication

/* The username and password are passed in */
@chrUsername varchar(255),
@chrPassword varchar(255)

AS

/* Retrieves all author profiles that
   have a matching username and password */
select * from author
 where chrUsername = @chrUsername and
    chrPassword = @chrPassword
GO

CREATE PROCEDURE sp_RetrieveAuthor

/* Pass in the ID of the author */
@idAuthor integer

AS
```

```
/* Retrieve the specified author ID */
select * from author
 where idAuthor = @idAuthor
GO

CREATE PROCEDURE sp_RetrieveAuthorBooks

/* Pass in the ID of the author */
@idAuthor integer

AS

/* Retrieve all of the books related to the
   specified author */
select *
 from book, bookauthor
where bookauthor.idAuthor = @idAuthor and
   book.idbook = bookauthor.idbook
GO

CREATE PROCEDURE sp_RetrieveAuthors AS

/* Retrieve all authors and order them
   by the author's last name */
select * from author
 order by chrLastName
GO

CREATE PROCEDURE sp_RetrieveBook

/* Pass in the ID of the book */
@idBook integer

AS

/* Retrieve the book data for the
   specified book */
select * from book
 where idBook = @idBook
GO

CREATE PROCEDURE sp_RetrieveBookAuthor

/* Pass in the ID of the book */
@idBook integer

AS

/* Retrieve the book and author data for the
   specified book */
select author.idauthor, author.chrFirstName,
```

```
        author.chrLastName, book.idBook,
        book.chrTitle, bookauthor.idbook,
        bookauthor.idauthor, publisher.chrPublisher,
        book.txtDescription, book.txtTOC,
        book.chrImageLink, book.chrISBN,
        book.intPrimeInterest, book.intSecondInterest
    from book, author, bookauthor, publisher
    where book.idbook = @idBook and
        author.idauthor = bookauthor.idauthor and
        book.idbook = bookauthor.idbook and

        book.idpublisher = publisher.idpublisher
GO

CREATE PROCEDURE sp_RetrieveBookByAuthor

/* Pass in the ID of the author */
@idAuthor integer

AS

/* Retrieve the author and book data for the
   specified author */
select *
  from book, author, bookauthor
where author.idAuthor = @idAuthor and
    book.idBook = bookauthor.idbook and
    bookauthor.idauthor = author.idauthor
order by dtCreated
GO

CREATE PROCEDURE sp_RetrieveBookByInterest

/* Pass in the ID of the primary
   interest topic */
@intPrimeInterest integer

AS

/* Retrieve the books that are categorized
   in the specified interest */
select * from book
    where intPrimeInterest = @intPrimeInterest
    order by dtCreated
GO

CREATE PROCEDURE sp_RetrieveBookByPub

/* Pass in the ID of the publisher */
@idPublisher integer
```

```
AS

/* Retrieve the books that are assigned to
   the specified publisher */
select * from book,Publisher
    where book.idPublisher = @idPublisher and
        book.idPublisher = publisher.idpublisher
    order by dtCreated
GO

CREATE PROCEDURE sp_RetrieveInterestTopicByID

/* Declare the parameters for the
   stored procedure */
@idInterestTopic int

AS

/* SQL statement to retrieve the interest topic
   based on the ID passed in. */
select * from InterestTopic

where idInterestTopic = @idInterestTopic
GO

CREATE PROCEDURE sp_RetrieveInterestTopics AS

/* Retrieve all interest topics in the table
   and order them by name */
select * from InterestTopic order by chrName
GO

CREATE PROCEDURE sp_RetrieveLink

/* Pass in the ID of the link */
@idLink integer

AS

/* Retrieve the link data for the
   specified link */
select * from LinkTrack
 where idLink = @idLink
GO

CREATE PROCEDURE sp_RetrieveLinks AS

/* Retrieve the link data and order
   by the description */
select * from linktrack
 order by chrDescription
```

```
GO

CREATE PROCEDURE sp_RetrieveMessage

/* Pass in the ID of the message */
@idMessage int

AS

/* Retrieve the message data for
   the specified message */
select * from message where idMessage = @idMessage
GO


CREATE PROCEDURE sp_RetrieveMessages

/* Pass in the ID of the thread */
@idThread int

AS

/* Retrieve the messages for the thread */
select * from message where idThread = @idThread
GO

CREATE PROCEDURE sp_RetrieveNextMessages

/* The ID of the thread and the ID
   of the last message displayed */
@idThread int,
@idMessage int


AS

/* Retrieve the next set of messages in list
   for the specified thread */
select * from Message where
   idMessage >= @idMessage and
   idThread = @idThread
   order by dtCreated
GO

CREATE PROCEDURE sp_RetrievePoll

/* Pass in the ID of the poll to be retrieved */
@idPoll integer

AS
```

```
/* retrieve the poll */
select * from polls where idPoll = @idPoll
GO

CREATE PROCEDURE sp_RetrievePollResponses

/* Pass in the ID of the poll */
@idPoll integer

AS

/* Retrieve the response questions for the specified
   poll */
select * from responses where
idPoll = @idPoll
GO

CREATE PROCEDURE sp_RetrievePolls AS

/* Retrieve all of the polls from the database */
select * from polls
GO

CREATE PROCEDURE sp_RetrievePreviousMessages

/* Pass in the ID of the thread and the
   last message displayed */
@idThread int,
@idMessage int


AS

/* Retrieve all messages for the thread
   in the list before the specified
   message */
select * from Message where
    idMessage < @idMessage and
    idThread = @idThread
    order by dtCreated
GO

CREATE PROCEDURE sp_RetrievePublishers AS

/* Retrieve the publisher data and
   order by publisher name */
select * from publisher
 order by chrPublisher
GO

CREATE PROCEDURE sp_RetrieveSearches AS
```

```
/* Retrieve the keyword search data and
   order by the keywords */
select * from searches
 order by chrSearch
GO

CREATE PROCEDURE sp_RetrieveUnProcRegistrations AS

/* Retrieve all registrations that are un
   processed by checking the bitProcessed
   field */
select * from guestregister where bitProcessed = 0
GO

CREATE PROCEDURE sp_SearchAuthorName

/* Pass in the name to be searched */
@chrName varchar(255)

AS

/* Search for authors who last name are like
   the keyword name passed in. Also return the
   book data for the specified author. */
select * from author,bookauthor,book
    where author.idauthor=bookauthor.idauthor and
        bookauthor.idbook = book.idbook and
        author.chrLastName like '%' + @chrName + '%'
    order by author.chrLastName
GO

CREATE PROCEDURE sp_SearchBookName

/* Pass in the title of the book */
@chrTitle varchar(255)

AS

/* Search for books who title are like
   the keyword title passed in. Also return
   the author data for the specified book. */
select author.idauthor, author.chrFirstName,
    author.chrLastName, book.idBook,
    book.chrTitle, bookauthor.idbook,
    bookauthor.idauthor, book.txtDescription,
    book.txtTOC, book.chrImageLink,
    book.chrISBN, book.intPrimeInterest,
    book.intSecondInterest
  from author,bookauthor,book
 where author.idauthor=bookauthor.idauthor and
    bookauthor.idbook = book.idbook and
```

```
     chrTitle like '%' + @chrTitle + '%'
order by chrTitle
GO

CREATE PROCEDURE sp_RetrieveSectionPostCount

/* Pass in the ID of the section */
@idSection int

AS

/* Retrieve the number of messages posted
   for all threads in the section */
select count(*) from message, thread
where thread.idSection = @idSection and
   message.idThread = thread.idthread
GO

CREATE PROCEDURE sp_RetrieveSections AS

/* Retrieve all the forum sections */
select * from section order by chrName
GO

CREATE PROCEDURE sp_RetrieveThreadPostCount

/* Pass in the ID of the thread */
@idThread int

AS

/* Retrieve a count of all the messages
   posted for this thread */
select count(*) from message
where message.idThread = @idthread
GO

CREATE PROCEDURE sp_RetrieveThreads

/* Pass in the ID of the section */
@idSection int

AS

/* Retrieve all of the thread for the
   specified section */
select * from thread where
   idSection = @idSection order by dtCreated
GO

CREATE PROCEDURE sp_SearchByDateRange
```

```
/* Declare our parameters for the stored
   procedure */
@begindate datetime,
@enddate datetime

AS

/* Build a SQL statement to retrieve all the
   registrations in the given date range. */
select * from guestregister
where dtEntered >= @begindate and
   dtEntered <= @enddate
GO

CREATE PROCEDURE sp_SearchByEmail

/* Declare the parameters to be passed in */
@email varchar

AS

/* Retrieve the registration where the email
   contains the parameter passed in. */
select * from guestregister
where chrEmail like '%' + @email + '%'
GO

CREATE PROCEDURE sp_SearchByInterestTopic

/* Declare the parameters to be passed in */
@idInterest int

AS

/* Build a SQL statement that checks for registrations
   that have as either the primary or secondary
   interest the ID passed in. */
select * from guestregister
where intPrimeInterest = @idInterest or
   intSecondInterest = @idInterest
GO

CREATE PROCEDURE sp_SearchByLastName

/* Declare the parameters to be passed in */
@name varchar

AS

/* Retrieve registrations where the last name
   contains the data passed in. */
```

```
select * from guestregister
where chrLastName like '%' + @name + '%'
GO

CREATE PROCEDURE sp_UpdateAuthor

/* Pass in the fields to be updated
   in the profile */
@chrFirstName varchar(255),
@chrLastName varchar(255),
@chrCompany varchar(255),
@chrEmail varchar(255),
@chrURL varchar(255),
@txtAuthorBio text,
@chrUserName varchar(255),
@chrPassword varchar(255),
@idAuthor integer

AS

/* Update the author data */
update author set
    chrFirstName = @chrFirstName,
    chrLastName = @chrLastName,
    chrCompany = @chrCompany,
    chrEmail = @chrEmail,
    chrURL = @chrUrl,
    txtAuthorBio = @txtAuthorBio,
    chrUserName = @chrUserName,
    chrPassword = @chrPassword
 where idAuthor = @idAuthor
GO

CREATE PROCEDURE sp_UpdateBook

/* Pass in the book data to be update */
@chrTitle varchar(255),
@chrISBN varchar(255),
@intPrimeInterest integer,
@intSecondInterest integer,
@chrImageLink varchar(255),
@txtDescription text,
@idPublisher integer,
@txtTOC text,
@idBook integer

AS

/* Update the book data for the specified
   book. */
update book set
```

```
        chrTitle=@chrTitle, chrISBN=@chrISBN,
        intPrimeInterest=@intPrimeInterest,
        intSecondInterest=@intSecondInterest,
        chrImageLink=@chrImageLink,
        txtDescription=@txtDescription,
        idPublisher=@idPublisher,
        txtTOC=@txtTOC
  where idBook = @idBook
GO

CREATE PROCEDURE sp_UpdateLink

/* Pass in the link data to be updated */
@idLink integer,
@chrDescription varchar(255),
@chrURL varchar(255)

AS

/* Update the LinkTrack entry */
update LinkTrack set
    chrDescription = @chrDescription,
    chrURL = @chrURL
  where idLink = @idLink
GO

CREATE PROCEDURE sp_UpdateMessage

/* Pass in the ID of the message,
   the subject of the message,
   the owner of the message, and
   the text of the message */
@idMessage int,
@chrSubject varchar(255),
@chrOwner varchar(255),
@txtMessage text

AS

/* Update the message data for the specified
   message */
update Message set chrSubject = @chrSubject,
        chrOwner = @chrOwner,
        txtMessage = @txtMessage
    where idMessage = @idMessage
GO

CREATE PROCEDURE sp_UpdatePoll

/* Pass in the ID of the poll and the title */
@idPoll integer,
```

```
@chrTitle varchar(255)

AS

/* Update the poll title for the specified poll */
update polls set chrTitle = @chrTitle
where idPoll = @idPoll
GO

CREATE PROCEDURE sp_UpdateRespCount

/* Pass in the ID of the response */
@idResponse integer

AS

/* Begin the transaction so we ensure that
   updates are not overwriting each other */
begin transaction

/* Declare a variable to get the current count */
declare @intRespCount integer

/* Get the current count and store it in the variable */
select @IntRespCount = intRespCount from Responses
 where idResponse = @idResponse

/* Increment the count by one */
select @intRespCount = @intRespCount + 1

/* Update the count */
update Responses set intRespCount = @intRespCount
 where idResponse = @idResponse

commit transaction
GO

CREATE PROCEDURE sp_UpdateResponse

/* Pass in the ID of the response and the text
   of the question */
@idResponse integer,
@chrResponse varchar(255)

AS

/* Update the question */
update responses set chrResponse = @chrResponse,
        dtCreated = getdate()
where idResponse = @idResponse
GO
```

```
CREATE PROCEDURE sp_UpdateSectionName

/* Pass in the ID of the section and the
   name of the section */
@idSection int,
@chrName varchar(255)

AS

/* Update the name of the section for the
   specified section ID */
update section set chrName =
    @chrName where idSection = @idSection
GO

CREATE PROCEDURE sp_UpdateThread

/* Pass in the ID of the thread,
   the name of the thread and
   the owner */
@idThread int,
@chrName varchar(255),
@chrOwner varchar(255)

AS

/* Update the thread name and owner for the
   specified thread */
update thread set chrName = @chrName,
       chrOwner = @chrOwner
where idThread = @idThread
GO
```

Net Resources

This appendix provides a listing of third-party net resource options for adding community functionality to your Web site.

Site	URL	Description
Delphi.com	www.delphi.com	Provides robust, free message boards that can be partially branded.
My Computer	www.mycomputer.com	Provides a number of tools, including a guest register, forums, and polls. There is an option for free versions of these tools as well as paid private branding without the site provider's ads.
Zoomerang	www.zoomerang.com	Provides a robust poll and survey engine.
EZBoard	www.ezboard.com	Provides free message board solution. Partial private branding can be done.
Critical Path	www.criticalpath.com	Provides high-end, private, branded message boards.

INDEX

Note to the Reader: Throughout this index **boldfaced** page numbers indicate primary discussions of a topic. *Italicized* page numbers indicate illustrations.

B

C

E

F

M

N

O

object tags, 471
ODBC DSNs, 59
Office, 41
operating systems in backups, 59
Option Explicit declaration, 70, 72, 471
or clauses in queries, 249
ordering search results, **251–252**, 258, *258*
outsource turnkey solutions, **12–13**
owners, thread, **386–389**

P

page/section-related tracking, 26
page setup in ProcessGuestRegister.asp, **97–98**
passwords, 468
  in AddAuthor.asp, **144–146**
  for author bio data, 142
  for author login, 131, 138, 148, 183–184, *184*
  for content, 130
  e-mail for, 188
  in guest registration, 22
  in server management, 60
  testing, 185
  in UpdateAuthor.asp, **156–157**
  in UpdateAuthorData.asp, **159–160**
peak loading consideration, 61
percentages, poll, **453**
performance
  database connections for, 470
  in Visual Basic 6, 38
performance-enhanced objects in ASP, 35
personalization. *See also* searches
  in community directory interface, 192, *192*
  cookies for, 214–215, **220**
  for Default.asp, **196–197**
  in guest registration, 22
  in polls/surveys, 20
  retrieving, **278**
  testing, **259–261**, *259–261*

updating links for, **273–275**
  user interface for, **219–254**
Personalization Server, 40
Personalize.asp page, **219–220**
  for author and publisher selections, **222–226**
  forms for, **221–222**
  reading cookies in, **220**
poll responses, 20
  counts of, 424–425
    displaying, **450–451**
    retrieving, **449–450**
    updating, 424–425, **448–449**, **452–453**
  deleting, 426, **439–441**
  displaying, **435–437**
  inserting, 424, **437–438**
  names of, **438–439**
  options for, **442–443**, **446–448**
  percentages, **453**
  retrieving, 423, **434–435**
  testing, 457–461, *457–461*
  updating, 425–426
Poll1.asp page
  for displaying options, **446–448**
  linking to, 446
Poll2.asp page
  for displaying percentages, **453**
  for displaying questions, **451–452**
  linking to, 446
  for poll display table, **454**
  for submit button, **454–455**
  for updating poll response counts, **452–453**
PollList.asp page
  for displaying poll date, **429–430**
  header information in, **426–427**
  links in, **428–429**
  links to, 433
  for retrieving polls, **427–428**
  testing, 455, *455*
polls and surveys, **19–21**
  database for
    stored procedures, **421–426**
    tables, **420–421**
  dates of, **429–430**
  deleting, 422–423, **432–433**, 456, *457*

Q

R

S

T

U

V

W

X

Z

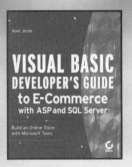
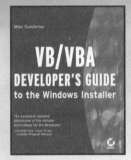
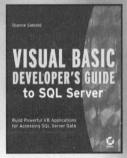
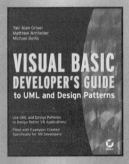

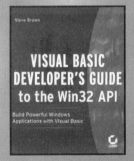